In the early decades of the nineteenth century, Buenos Aires underwent rapid economic growth, dwarfed only by the even greater prosperity that occurred there at the end of the century. Previous studies have focused on the economy as a whole or on a particular sector of production, and most have disregarded how resources were intentionally organized to enable growth. This book focuses on the estancia, the economic organization that led the growth process. The internal structure, production conditions, and economic impact of the estancia are the central issues that Amaral considers. Economic growth and increased freedom were not inevitable on the pampas but rather were the consequences of human actions, both deliberate and unintentional, in the search for an elusive profit. Why freedom, not privilege, prevailed is the key question underlying this study.

THE RISE OF CAPITALISM ON THE PAMPAS

CAMBRIDGE LATIN AMERICAN STUDIES

GENERAL EDITOR
SIMON COLLIER

ADVISORY COMMITTEE
MALCOLM DEAS, STUART SCHWARTZ, ARTURO VALENZUELA

83

THE RISE OF CAPITALISM ON THE PAMPAS

THE RISE OF CAPITALISM
ON THE PAMPAS

THE ESTANCIAS OF BUENOS AIRES,
1785–1870

SAMUEL AMARAL
Northern Illinois University

330.982
A48N

PUBLISHED BY THE PRESS SYNDICATE OF THE UNIVERSITY OF CAMBRIDGE
The Pitt Building, Trumpington Street, Cambridge CB2 1RP, United Kingdom

CAMBRIDGE UNIVERSITY PRESS
The Edinburgh Building, Cambridge CB2 2RU, United Kingdom
40 West 20th Street, New York, NY 10011-4211, USA
10 Stamford Road, Oakleigh, Melbourne 3166, Australia

Cat © Samuel Amaral 1998

The publisher wishes to acknowledge a generous grant from Northern Illinois
University to aid publication of this book.

First published 1998

Printed in the United States of America

Typeset in 11/12 Garamond 3

Library of Congress Cataloging-in-Publication Data
Amaral, Samuel.
     The rise of capitalism on the pampas: the estancias of Buenos
Aires, 1785–1870 / Samuel Amaral.
         p.   cm. – (Cambridge Latin American studies; 83)
     Includes bibliographical references and index.
     ISBN 0–521–57248–7 (hb)
     1. Haciendas – Argentina – Buenos Aires (Province) – History – 19th
century.   I. Title.   II. Series.
HD1471.A72B842   1997
330.982′1204–dc21
                                                        96–53311
                                                          CIP

A catalog record for this book is available from the British Library.

ISBN 0-521-57248-7 hardback

To María Elena,
thirty-six years ago
at the Alliance Française

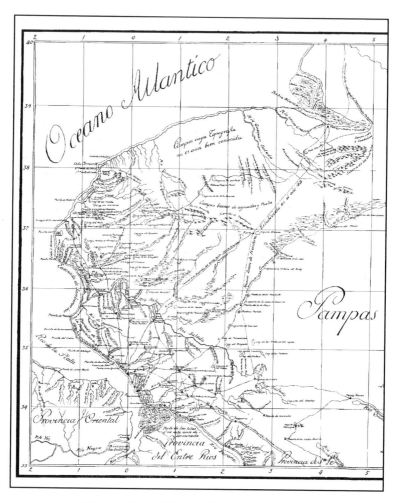

Map 1.1 Buenos Aires, 1828. *Source*: Grau (1949).

Contents

List of maps, figures, and tables

Maps

Figures

Tables

Weights and measures

1 vara = 0.866 meter (m)
1 cuadra = 150 varas
1 league = 6,000 varas
1 square cuadra = 16,874 m^2 = 1.6874 hectares
1 square league = 1,600 square cuadras = 2,699.84 hectares
1 hectare (ha) = 2.47 acres
1 ounce = 28.7 g
1 pound = 16 ounces = 0.459 kg
1 arroba = 25 pounds (lbs) = 11.485 kg
1 quintal = 4 arrobas
1 ton = 20 quintals
1 cwt = 112 lbs
1 pesada = 35 lbs (dry hides) or 60 lbs (salted hides)
1 fanega = 137.27 liters

Sources: Senillosa (1835), Balbín (1881)

Preface

In the first decades of the nineteenth century, Buenos Aires underwent a process of rapid economic growth, overshadowed only by an even greater prosperity at the end of that century. That early process of growth has been studied from the perspective of the economy in general or of a particular sector of production. These explanations, however, disregard how resources were organized to make growth possible. Prosperity was not a necessary consequence of either providential or natural design, but the result of human action in a particular institutional context.

This book focuses upon the economic organization that led that process of growth – the estancia. Its internal structure, the combination of factors of production on it, and their economic results are the central issues considered here. The time frame is delimited by the beginning of the expansion in the late eighteenth century on one end, and the introduction of new technology (railroads, wire fencing, banking) around 1870 on the other.

The book is divided into four parts, studying the internal workings and structure of estancias, the conditions of production restricting estancia operations, the human action required by estancia operations, and the results of estancia operations. The introduction reviews the literature on estancias and early capitalism in Buenos Aires, and the conclusion summarizes the main points covered.

Capital investment, income and expenditure, profit, and the use of labor are key aspects toward understanding the internal workings of estancias as firms. Those operations on a late-eighteenth-century estancia are studied in Chapter 2. Source limitations do not allow for an extension of that study to other periods. In order to account for the evolution of estancias, therefore, a general study of their capital structure in 1820 and 1850 is carried out in Chapter 3. As aggregate information conceals many details of the capital structure, a closer look at some cases is taken in Chapter 4.

Estancia operations were restricted by material, environmental, and institutional conditions of production that changed in the long run but that were fairly stable during the lifetime of individual producers. Cattle reproduction rates and livestock density are the material conditions considered in Chapter 5. The spread of thistles on the pampas and how they affected the environment and consequently cattle raising are the subject of Chapter 6. And institutional conditions resulting from habits and customs at a stage when changing patterns of production turned them into an obstacle for a clear definition of property rights are dealt with in Chapter 7.

Cattle did not breed themselves on the pampas. Part III is a study of the human action required in cattle ranching from the perspective of the estancia. Two problems related to labor demand – labor scarcity and labor instability – are studied in Chapter 8. As with any type of economic organization, estancias required human action to coordinate and organize the use of resources. Management and entrepreneurship are studied in Chapter 9 by means of a description of the actual tasks and problems confronted by rural entrepreneurs.

The economic results of the combination of natural and human factors on the estancias are considered in Part IV. From a microeconomic standpoint, the estancia operations resulted in profit. Estimates of profit are analyzed in Chapter 10 to reveal the factors accounting for the development of estancias as a type of economic organization. From a macroeconomic perspective, the aggregate result of estancia operations was trade, the development of overseas markets for its products. The export of livestock by-products required overseas prices and marketing conditions attractive enough for merchants and producers. Chapter 11 deals with local and overseas prices and marketing conditions, and Chapter 12 studies the share of Buenos Aires products in its main overseas markets and the share of Buenos Aires's main customers for each of its main products.

This analysis of estancias as an economic organization aims at stressing the fact that economic growth and increasing freedom were not an inevitable fate for the inhabitants of the Buenos Aires pampas. That outcome was, instead, the consequence of human action, both deliberate and unintentional, while searching for an elusive profit, which depended upon the natural conditions of the pampas as much as on hard work and shrewd entrepreneurship. Why freedom rather than privilege prevailed is the key question underlying this study.

Acknowledgments

The completion of this project was possible due to the contributions of many people and institutions. For supporting my research I am grateful to the Argentine Scientific and Technological Research Council, the British Council, the Fulbright Program, and the Social Science Research Council. For providing a friendly and stimulating environment over the last fifteen years, my thanks to the Instituto Torcuato Di Tella; to its fellows and staff; to its directors, Roberto Cortés Conde, Alberto Petrecolla, and Adolfo Canitrot; and to the directors of its Centro de Investigaciones Sociales, Natalio Botana and Juan Carlos Torre.

Papers related to this book were presented at the Universidad de Córdoba, University of Chicago, Universidad Carlos III de Madrid, the Instituto Torcuato Di Tella, and the Institute of Latin American Studies (London). I am grateful to the participants in those seminars for their comments. My thanks to my students at the University of La Plata (1986–1988) and the University of Mar del Plata (1992) for their patience and contributions, to Marcela García and Guillermo Quinteros for their assistance in collecting evidence used in Chapters 3, 4, and 5, and to Joe Bonomo for his editing of the final version of my manuscript. For their cooperation with my research, I thank the staffs of the Archivo General de la Nación, Archivo Histórico del Banco de la Provincia de Buenos Aires, Archivo Histórico de la Provincia de Buenos Aires, Biblioteca Forestal, Biblioteca de la Sociedad Rural Argentina, and Biblioteca Tornquist, in Argentina, as well as those of the British Library, London, and Green Library, Stanford University. For a lasting collaboration with my work, I am especially grateful to the librarians of the Biblioteca del Instituto Torcuato Di Tella and Founders Memorial Library, Northern Illinois University.

At Northern Illinois University, I am particularly indebted to the Center for Latino and Latin American Studies and to its director, Michael Gonzales, for research grants that allowed me to go back to British and Argentine archives and libraries, and for a leave of absence during which I wrote key sections of this book. The Department of History, the Graduate School, and the College of Liberal Arts and Sciences have to be thanked for contributing to support my research. Karen M. Blaser, of the College of Liberal Arts and Sciences Manuscript Services, deserves my recognition for her readiness to provide so many printouts, as well as Rich Vaupel and Lenny Walther, of the Laboratory for Cartography and Spatial Analysis, for their help with the graphs and maps. I gratefully acknowledge the contributions of Dean Frederick Kitterle and Dean Jerrold Zar in support of the publication of this book.

Chapter 2 reproduces with a few changes an article published in the *Journal of Latin American Studies*, and a previous version of Chapter 6 was published in *Anales de la Sociedad Rural Argentina*. I thank the editors of these journals for allowing me to use my articles here, and Alan Biggins, for his crucial help with the first of them. My thanks to the editors of the *American Economic Review* for authorizing me to quote from R. H. Coase's Nobel Prize lecture.

Many friends helped me in different ways to carry out this project. For useful information, discussions, suggestions, and other contributions, I thank Fernando Barba, Marcelo Borges, Severo Cáceres Cano, Carlos Cansanello, Guillermo Colombo, Raúl García Heras, Adela Harispuru, María Elena Infesta, Jorge Jeria, Gilda Madrid, Carlos Malamud, Antonio Manna, Gerardo Martí, Zacarías Moutoukias, Carlos Newland, Juan Carlos Nicolau, Leandro Prados de la Escosura, Andrés Regalsky, Eduardo Saguier, and Marta Valencia. For my time in London I am grateful to Colin Lewis and John Lynch; for that at Stanford, to Frederick Bowser, Stephen Haber, John J. Johnson, and John Wirth. I am indebted to John Coatsworth, Lyman Johnson, Erick Langer, Susan Socolow, and Mark Szuchman for their help and advice; to John J. TePaske, for his suggestions; to Jeremy Adelman, for his helpful comments; and to Roberto Cortés Conde, Ezequiel Gallo, and Tulio Halperín Donghi, for their generous support. No person or institution, however, is responsible for my views.

THE RISE OF CAPITALISM ON THE PAMPAS

1

Introduction

The golden age of Argentine growth, from 1880 to 1930, has attracted the attention of countless scholars. Whether the intention is to explain what went wrong later or just to understand what was right then, there is no dearth of interpretations on how agricultural exports led a process of growth that put Argentina among the richest countries on earth by the end of that period.

Whatever the reasons for Argentina's failure to keep that pace after 1930, there is no question about that period of growth, expansion, and development (if this now outdated word means anything at all). It cannot be questioned either that the reasons behind it were a steady overseas demand for agricultural goods, improvements in transportation (railroads and shipping), technological change (ranging from the introduction of wire fencing and windmills to meat-packing plants), an increasing supply of labor (the massive inflow of migrants from southern Europe), and the incorporation of new lands into production. These are the factors usually mentioned, but institutional stability was a key element for it as well. A stable political system, a government with an increasing ability to enforce the law, and a clear set of rules were, in the long run (there were short-term setbacks), decisive for that expansion.

It has always been clear that institutional change was responsible for prosperity. For Mitre, the impressive growth that had taken place from 1810 to the 1870s was possible due to the removal of the colonial restraints in 1810. The amazing expansion of that period, however, became a sort of dark age for many scholars due to the brighter reflections of later affluence. It was a dark age as well because the pattern of landholding emerging at that time was blamed for the twentieth-century troubles. According to this view, large rural properties were good enough to enrich their owners but were socially and economically inefficient – socially inefficient because landless immigrants were forced into tenancy, economically inefficient because output was kept below capacity. Reform-minded scholars – whether conservative, liberal, or Marxist – held that view without noticing that blaming latifundia for those troubles meant the implicit acceptance of their previous efficiency during the upswing.[1] Roberto Cortés Conde and Ezequiel Gallo, however, have dispelled those views by emphasizing the efficiency and economic origin of that pattern of landholding on the pampas.[2]

For early-day Marxist historians, those large rural properties were the manifestation of a pre-capitalist mode of production.[3] Latter-day Marxist scholars have to some extent dismissed that view. Although there are still die-hards for whom the evidence of an increasing partition of landholdings in the long run is not enough to stop them talking about the monopoly of land, there are moderates who fully accept that, in spite of the differences between the industrialized countries and the pampas, a peculiar kind of capitalism developed on the latter.[4]

Scholars who did not feel attached to the early Marxist orthodoxy, less worried by the identification of that stage of capitalism, were ready to accept that that was capitalism. Since for them history was not leading to the proletarian dictatorship, they did not feel any pressure either to look for proletarians or to characterize the mode of production. The problem remained, nonetheless, how to explain the emergence of that capitalism, and how to account for the period preceding that golden age.

Tulio Halperín Donghi has emphasized the accuracy of Mitre's interpretation, using better information and more sophisticated analytical tools.[5] There was a process of growth before 1880 that can be explained both in economic and institutional terms. In economic terms, it was due to the local reaction to foreign stimuli. Overseas demand for agricultural products was met by the rural producers of the pampas by adjusting their production to shifting conditions. In institutional terms, it was due to a fledgling institutional development that, instead of working in favor of privilege and regulations, tended to guarantee the free operation of market forces. Far from its connotations as a stage of economic development (whether in the Marxist or the Rostow version), capitalism, understood as the prevalence of market forces, was therefore prevailing on the pampas in the early nineteenth century, when the colonial mercantilism vanished.[6] Recent scholarship has therefore pushed backward in time the usefulness of

1 "Conservative," "liberal," and "Marxist" are, obviously, hard to define. These concepts refer mainly to the preferences of the authors themselves, without questioning what type of conservative, liberal, or Marxist each of them is. Some crudeness in the utilization of these categories remains inevitable.
2 Cortés Conde (1979), Gallo (1983).
3 Oddone (1956). The first edition of this book is from 1930. For a recent manifestation of this old-fashioned interpretation, see Wedovoy (1994).
4 For review articles of the neo-Marxist literature, see Míguez (1986) and Sabato (1993).
5 Halperín Donghi (1963) and (1989).
6 "Capitalism" is used in this sense by Mises (1963), 258. For "mercantilism," a system in which non-market forces prevail in the allocation of resources, see Ekelund and Tollison (1981).

that concept to describe the organization of the economy on the pampas. From a neo-Marxist perspective, Hilda Sabato used it while studying the economic and social organization of wool production from the 1840s to the 1880s, and from the vantage point of the staple theory, Jonathan Brown has examined that first period of livestock export-led growth, from 1810 to the 1860s.[7] There was capitalism, therefore, because at some early stage after 1810, resources were allocated mainly by market forces.[8]

In a capitalist framework, however, resources should be coordinated and organized for production. Some type of economic organization should emerge for that purpose. Factors are not automatically allocated in the most efficient way. That may happen in the realm of theory, but in the real world there are real people who perform that task – consumers by manifesting their preferences but also producers who supply goods for the satisfaction of demand. While doing so they create economic organizations, firms, that to some extent substitute for the market when allocating resources within them to produce goods.[9] Scholars, whether following a Marxist or a neo-classical lead, tend to ignore, as R. H. Coase pointed out in his Nobel lecture, the role of management and entrepreneurship and, consequently, how goods are produced by firms. Both Marxists and neo-classicals assume a world of zero transaction costs, implying a perfect enforcement of contracts and perfect access to information, while dismissing "what happens in between the purchase of the factors of production and the sale of the goods that are produced."[10] In the real world, far from abstract models, the enforcement of contracts and access to information are costly propositions. Entrepreneurs should coordinate resources in a context of uncertainty and make a profit out of their efforts. None of the general explanations of any process of growth, either before or after 1880, account for that basic organization without which words and figures melt into the air. It is as if profit or the supposed differential rent were just there, waiting in limbo to be homogeneously distributed among whoever entered into rural production. No effort is required in those models to obtain what real people know is hard to get – a positive difference from income and expenditure, equal to or higher than the opportunity cost of the factors

7 Sabato (1989), Brown (1979).
8 The emergence of capitalism in Buenos Aires has been credited to the changes introduced by the 1810 revolution by many historians. But the emphasis has been on a more disciplined organization of labor rather than on the mechanisms for allocating resources. It is in this sense that Halperín Donghi refers to the rationalization of productive activities on the estancia, while discussing Juan Alvarez's and José Ingenieros's interpretations. See Halperín Donghi (1963), 83–86, 97ff.
9 Williamson's "economic organization" and Coase's "firm" are employed interchangeably here. See Coase (1937) and Williamson (1975).
10 Coase (1992), 714.

used for production. So many opportunities are missed that it is hard to believe that comparative advantages can bring about anything by themselves. They are just a precondition, but no automatic revenues are derived from them. Production should be organized by entrepreneurs in a way that a profit is made taking advantage of those conditions, considering the restrictions imposed by a pre-existing institutional framework.

In the nineteenth-century pampas, the economic organization within which resources were coordinated by real managers and entrepreneurs was the estancia. Estancias, those firms, and estancieros, the entrepreneurs, have not been ignored by scholars. But that does not mean that the allocation of resources within the estancia has been explained either. Technological primitivism or the absence of full-fledged proletarians cannot conceal the fact that the estancia was the basic economic organization in the capitalist conditions prevailing on the pampas in the first half of the nineteenth century. Although Brown and Sabato have studied the estancia, their main interest lay in explaining the process of growth in general or the evolution of a sector of production, rather than the internal workings of the basic economic organization, the conditions of production under which it operated, and the result of its operations in micro- rather than macroeconomic terms.[11]

Estancias did not appear on the pampas in 1810. They were there since the early days of Spanish settlement, when land was distributed to secure beef supply to an isolated town. The evolution of estancias in what was thought to be the dark colonial age has been the subject of recent scholarly attention. It is possible to see now that there were no major, dramatic changes at any stage in the internal allocation of resources within estancias and that the basic tasks remained unchanged perhaps until the mid-nineteenth century. But the absence of sudden change did not mean stagnation, since the scale of operations grew steadily from the late eighteenth century, bringing about expansion both for the estancia and for the estancieros' landholdings and cattle-raising operations. This process in turn did change the internal organization of estancias, the conditions of production, and the microeconomic result of their operations, but at a slow pace. All of that was indeed possible, as remarked earlier, because of a growing overseas demand for the pampas' livestock by-products and decreasing governmental interference, paralleled by an increasing but also slowly evolving institutional stability (understood as the rules of the game for production rather than for politics, which certainly overlapped but which were not necessarily identical).

11 Brown studied the formation of the Anchorena cattle business, and Sabato the organization, operations, and economic rationality of sheep-breeding estancias in what are the best chapters of their respective books. See Brown (1979), 174–200; Sabato (1989), 134–168.

Estancias: What was written about them

In the late nineteenth and early twentieth centuries, estancias began to be recognized as a dynamic type of economic organization that was changing the pattern of production on the pampas. In 1875 José María Jurado published a series of articles setting the tone for later studies. In a brief introduction, he traced the origin of cattle on the pampas and the emergence of estancias as cattle-raising establishments. Then he described those estancias and the tasks that cattle ranching required. The second and third parts focused upon horse and sheep breeding, and the fourth and fifth were devoted to the setup and management of estancias.[12]

In the mid-1850s other producers had written on those issues, but for a different reason and describing a different reality.[13] The reason was an inquiry on rural production launched by the head of the Buenos Aires Statistical Department. The reality, Jurado noted, had changed from the mid-1850s to the mid-1870s: from cattle raising on open fields to sheep breeding on fields that were increasingly enclosed. The reality was more mixed, since a small proportion of the province had been enclosed and cattle raising was still an important activity on those open fields. "The cow," remarked Jurado, "will be as it has been the case so far the vanguard of civilization in the occupation of the wild pampa."[14] Quite an unexpected role for a head of cattle, but the metaphor was not that inaccurate. Jurado's description is not different from others, but the vehicle was: a technical publication of the rural producers' organization. He was not describing estancias for outsiders but rather was underscoring – for the producers themselves – the changes that estancias had undergone in recent decades and, to some extent, pointing the direction of further change.

A few years later, Jurado, Ricardo Newton, Felipe Senillosa, and other rural experts published a series of articles devoted to several model estancias.[15] Their extension, capital structure, livestock composition, and in one case its income, expenditure, and profit were described. The intention was, perhaps, to present a few well-established estancias to serve as a model for all rural producers. Less technical, but nonetheless another manifestation of this type of literature, was Estanislao S. Zeballos's account of his visit to rural establishments in the sheep-breeding region.[16] A

---

12 Jurado (1875). The fifth article was "to be continued," but no continuation was found in that publication.
13 REBA (1855). See this text, Chapters 4 and 10.
14 Jurado (1875), 9(6):187.
15 Jurado, Newton, and Jurado (1878); Senillosa, Newton, and Jurado (1878); Jurado and Márquez (1879); Jurado, Almeida, and Jurado (1879); and Jurado (1879).
16 Zeballos (1888). The introduction of *A través de las cabañas* announced that it would be followed by two volumes, devoted to cattle ranching and horse breeding, entitled *A través de los rodeos* and

companion volume on estancias in the cattle-ranching region was promised but never published.

The practice of describing estancias by stressing the changes taking place in rural production on the pampas continued in two different directions: on the one hand, a series of congratulatory publications; on the other, a more analytical approach, which considered the factors accounting for those changes. A manifestation of the former type were A. R. Fernández's descriptions, included in several issues of his *Prontuario informativo*, published between 1902 and 1907. Fernández aimed to stress the changes introduced in the countryside by progressive estancieros, who were raising cattle and breeding sheep according to updated methods and investing in impressive buildings and other improvements. Fernández's tone and intention can be grasped from his description of the estancia "El Retiro," in Chascomús, owned by Narciso Vivot's estate. Vivot had "founded" that estancia in 1866, turning that "barren land, close to the endless plain of that pampa still suffering the constant attacks of the Indians" into what it then was: an establishment with trees, buildings, agriculture, fine breeds. Even more laudatory were F. Scardin's descriptions. He focused upon nine estancias (compared to scores described by Fernández), aiming at displaying before his readers "the wonders carried out by the hacendados" whose estancias were described.[17]

The articles written as a complement to the 1908 National Agricultural Census manifested the second type of contributions, more analytical than congratulatory. Godofredo Daireaux, author of several technical publications, contributed a chapter on "the Argentine estancia," and Heriberto Gibson, a rural producer, contributed one on the evolution of livestock.[18] Even though the tone of these contributions was more technical, their aim was also to stress the changes undergone by rural production in the Buenos Aires countryside during the last three decades. The modernization of rural establishments, characterized by the expansion of agriculture, wire fencing, trees, sheds, fine pastures, and livestock breeding, had started in the late 1870s.

The technical literature was also flourishing in the last decades of the nineteenth century. From the late 1870s to the early 1900s, Miguel A. Lima, José Hernández, Carlos Lemée, and Godofredo Daireaux published several editions of their handbooks for estancieros: *The Practical Estanciero*; *Instruction of the Estanciero*; *The Argentine Estanciero*; *Cattle-raising on the*

A *través de los circos*. The second volume of the same series, published in 1883, described the wheat farm region in Santa Fe.

17 Fernández (1902–1907); Scardin (1908).

18 Daireaux (1909), Gibson (1909).

Pampa.[19] These handbooks, rather than being full-fledged technical text-books, were a collection of practical recommendations covered at best by an unsophisticated technical coating.

Estancias and their owners have never ceased to foster the imagination of the public – to the point that the Argentine version of "Monopoly" is called "Estanciero" – but the literature has changed direction in recent decades. Books describing estancias, praising the achievements of their owners, continued to be published, although the imposition of a personal income tax and the economic crisis of the 1930s conspired, perhaps, against showing off riches that were withering at the same time. A book on the great Argentine estancias, published by Carlos Néstor Maciel in 1939, was the last of that series of congratulatory publications.[20] It described 62 estancias (a few of them in provinces other than Buenos Aires) following Scardin's path: Probably estancieros were still willing to share information on their holdings and lifestyle with curious readers.

The crisis of cattle ranching in Argentina after World War II turned estancias from an archetype of economic success into a murky business. The emergence of an increasingly accepted populist discourse (and even worse, policies) meant that landowners were hardly praised any longer. The nostalgia of better times, however, still captured the minds of writers and the public, so authors such as Yuyú Guzmán, Carlos Antonio Moncaut, Pedro V. Capdevila, and Virginia Carreño have catered to that constituency emotionally attached to things rural and the gilded past.[21] The glorious past remained alive in impressive buildings, which have attracted scholars interested in the history of architecture, such as Jorge O. Gazaneo and Mabel Scarone, and the archeology of rural production, such as Carlos Moreno.[22] A combination of this artistic approach and nostalgia has produced a book on 24 estancias (12 in Buenos Aires, 12 in the rest of the country), lavishly illustrated with Xavier Verstraeten's photographs, accompanied by a non-technical, congenial history of each estancia written by María Sáenz Quesada, the author of a popular book on estancieros. The same approach has been adopted by Juan Pablo Queiroz and Tomás de Elía in a book on 22 estancias (half of them in Buenos Aires). Both books

---

19 Lima (1876), Hernández (1882), Lemée (1887), Daireaux (1887). The fourth edition of Daireaux's book changed its title to *Cattle Raising on the Modern Estancia*. See Daireaux (1908).

20 Maciel (1939).

21 Guzmán (1976), (1983), and (1985); Carreño (1994); Moncaut (1977) and (1978); Capdevila (1978). A combination of family and rural nostalgia can be found in Líbera Gill (1995). Newton (1970) seems to be a late offspring of the previous congratulatory type issued at a time when nostalgia prevailed.

22 Gazaneo and Scarone (1965), Gazaneo (1969), Moreno (1991). See also the study of rural houses carried out by López Osornio (1944).

describe the same type of estancia, and, in most cases, even the same estancias.[23]

The study of colonial estancias has been recently approached by Carlos Mayo and Juan Carlos Garavaglia in a similar way to that undertaken in Chapters 3 and 4, at least from a formal standpoint. They, however, have not organized their studies around the central economic role of estancias.[24] Mayo, more concerned about social than economic issues, frequently fails to understand the latter, substituting picturesque anecdotes for economic analysis. His studies, nevertheless, have helped us to understand, as already suggested by Halperín Donghi and Cushner, that estancias belonging to religious institutions were not necessarily managed according to unsound economic principles. Mayo has shown as well that the late colonial estancias were quite far from the latifundia that other scholars still believe in against all evidence because they suit their theories, and he has also shown that late colonial estancieros were, as stressed by contemporary observers, far from wealthy and powerful.[25] Garavaglia, in turn, has published quite recently several studies of late colonial estancias, which are a remarkable departure from his inconsequential search for Chayanovian peasants (whose existence explains little from an economic perspective).[26] He shows that, in spite of the absence of any drastic innovation, the structure and organization of estancias was actually changing in the late eighteenth and early nineteenth centuries.

For later periods the academic literature on the Buenos Aires estancias is far from abundant. Perhaps the only addition is Eduardo Míguez's book on the British land companies in late-nineteenth-century Argentina, which includes two chapters on estancias. Three of the estancias he studies were located in Buenos Aires: the Espartillar Estancia Company, owned by John Fair; La Germania Estancia Company; and William Walker's landholdings. To the latter corresponds the most detailed account, especially for the late 1890s and early 1900s, which deals with the formation of the estancia and its operations rather than with the economic outcome of those operations.[27] Although not dealing with any particular estancia, it should be noted that Jorge F. Sabato put together an analytical model of estancieros' economic activities, revealing a strategy aimed at the diversification of

---

23 Sáenz Quesada and Verstraeten (1992), Sáenz Quesada (1980), Queiroz and de Elía (1995). For a bit more of rural history (but not estancia history) and less lavish illustrations, see Molinari (1987).

24 For a review of the literature on the Buenos Aires colonial estancias and their comparison to similar rural establishments elsewhere in Spanish America, see Fradkin (1993b). See also Garavaglia and Gelman (1995).

25 Mayo (1991a), (1991b), (1995), and Mayo and Fernández (1993). See also Halperín Donghi (1975) and Cushner (1983). For a staunch fidelity to the colonial latifundia, see Azcuy Ameghino (1995).

26 Garavaglia (1993), (1994), (1995a), and (1995c).

27 Míguez (1985), 45–48, 51–55, and 59–95.

investment in different economic sectors.[28] The novelty of his model is better highlighted when contrasted with the Marxist orthodoxy, which depicted estancieros pitted against industrialists, than when set in the context of more traditional accounts free from those artificial conflicts necessitated by a class-struggle interpretation. Sabato's effort is worthwhile, however, since his depiction of an efficient and aggressive "dominant class" effectively undermines, for those who share his tenets, the image of backwardness and inefficiency popularized by some outdated books still read by the general public in Argentina.[29] Sabato cannot do without a "dominant class," but at least his is an efficient one.

Beyond descriptions of a literary or academic fashion, the economic organization of estancias remains to be explained. But before undertaking the analysis of their operations and capital structure, the conditions of production on them, the human action required by them, and the result of estancia activity, a definition of estancias is in order.

Estancias: What they were

Throughout Spanish America, Félix de Azara remarked around 1800, estancias were rural properties "where different types of goods are cultivated." The Buenos Aires Rural Code, passed in 1865, defined them as "establishments devoted only or mainly to livestock raising, either cattle, horses, or sheep," a definition already given by Francisco Millau in 1772. At the end of the eighteenth century, quintas, vegetable gardens, were located up to 1 league from the city; chacras, cereal growing tracts, up to 6 to 8 leagues; and estancias, up to 30 to 40 leagues. Two centuries of Spanish settlement had barely secured an area extending at most 25 leagues from northeast to southwest, from the Paraná River and Río de la Plata to the Salado River, and 60 leagues from northwest to southeast, from the Pago de los Arroyos to Magdalena.[30]

Cattle spread over the pampas with the first Spanish settlement in the region. Hunting expeditions, known as vaquerías, met the ever-erratic demand for export hides during the seventeenth century, but wild herds were depleted by the early decades of the eighteenth century, as revealed by

---

28 Sabato (1988).
29 Notably Giberti (1970) and Oddone (1956).
30 For the location of quintas, chacras, and estancias, see Millau (1947), 38–39; and Borrero (1911), 4. For the area covered by estancias, see Cipriano Orden Betoño's (Pedro Antonio Cerviño) estimate in *Semanario de Agricultura, Industria y Comercio*, 29 December 1802, 117, quoted by Fernández López (1976), 103; Azara (1910), 84; and Aguirre (1947), 17:333. For a recent study of the soils of the Pampa region and their uses, see Moscatelli (1991); Gómez et al. (1991); Cascardo et al. (1991). For a brief geological and geographical description of the pampas, see Scobie (1964), 15–22. For a more extensive description, see Aparicio and Difrieri (1958).

the absence of new hunting licenses after 1720, and by the first surprise attacks a few years later of pampa Indians looking for domestic cattle.[31] The intensification of foreign demand for hides in the second half of the eighteenth century led in the first place to the spread of vaquerías over Entre Ríos and the Banda Oriental and later to the proliferation of estancias on the Buenos Aires pampas. Due to a decline in the number of cattle head around Buenos Aires, Cosme Bueno pointed out by 1770 that "there are estancias, and [land] owners raising cattle."[32] That shift from simple hunting to cattle raising was a modest but nonetheless remarkable departure for a place that had provided Adam Smith with the example of a primitive economy.[33]

The spread of estancias over the plains started as early as the 1760s and was not legally completed until the 1880s. Along that period the estancia emerged as a distinct type of economic organization, different from other rural enterprises rooted in the colonial past.[34] In the nineteenth century, many travelers crossed the pampas, leaving vivid descriptions of the landscape and the human activities there. Like all cross-cultural observers, those travelers described what was new to them in a way that local people could not do. But because of the same reason, travelers were also burdened by their own individual experiences. Some of them were learned men, scientists such as Félix de Azara and Charles Darwin. They did not accept reality at face value; rather, they looked for explanations. Other foreign observers were businessmen, merchants, and engineers who, although not uneducated, were more prone to be taken in by their first impressions. Their approaches are not exactly scientific, but they also tried to give rational accounts of their experiences on the pampas. Francis Bond Head, William MacCann, and John Miers are some of those in this category. Yet other travelers such as Jean Baptiste Douville, Arsène Isabelle, C. B. Mansfield, and Edmond Temple, tended to believe whatever was told to them and did not make a great effort to neutralize their own prejudices.[35]

---

31 For hide exports in the seventeenth century, see Coni (1979) and Moutoukias (1988). For the Araucanian Indians' malocas, see León Solís (1987). For the end of the "precious mineral of hides" and the beginning of Indian attacks against estancias, see Azara (1910), 79; and Azara (1801), 2:354. My thanks to Osvaldo Pérez for calling my attention to Azara's latter book.

32 See Bueno (1763–1778). On this writer, see Macpheeters (1955).

33 Smith took his information from Ulloa. See Ulloa (1748), 3:243–244; Adam Smith (1984), 1:164, 205, 247. The use made by Smith of Ulloa's information on the Buenos Aires economy has been fully discussed by Newland and Waissbein (1984), and Fernández López (1976). On Ulloa, see also Whitaker (1935) and (1966).

34 For the literature on haciendas, see Florescano (1975), and the review articles by Mörner (1973) and Van Young (1983).

35 For Temple, for instance, the inhabitants of the pampas, when compared to the peasantry of England or France, were "little better than a species of carnivorous baboon." But they, however, were not at the bottom of his human scale, since he never saw amongst them "that abject, that

There are two other types of testimonies: those of people who lived in the region for long periods such as John Brabazon, Juan Fugl, Woodbine Parish, and the Robertson brothers; and those who in the second half of the nineteenth century wrote their accounts, such as Jean Antoine Victor Martin de Moussy and Louis Guilaine, with the purpose of encouraging European migration into Argentina.[36]

Martin de Moussy, a Frenchman who produced a thorough description of Argentina in the 1850s, defined estancias simply as "the establishments where a certain number of head of livestock were raised." The word estancia, he pointed out, referred to the land, buildings, and staff – to the firm as a whole rather than to any of its parts. There were three conditions, he went on, for an establishment to be "fruitful": good quality grasses, abundant water on that tract or in the neighborhood, and an extension of land large enough to accommodate and feed the herds. The latter was the key condition, he remarked. Like Francisco Millau and William Miller before him, Martin de Moussy found estancias usually facing a stream of water, serving as boundary between properties. A naked plain, covered only by grass, was considered the best place to set up an estancia. Forests (a literary license, unless he was referring to thistleries) were not useful, because cattle, looking there for protection in summer, tended to become wild.[37]

Estancias were on the pampas, a "flat open country . . . a vast sea of grass and thistles, without roads or enclosures, and without a habitation, except at long intervals."[38] General William Miller, who visited the pampas in 1817, found that "people living within half a dozen miles consider themselves as next door neighbors."[39] On those treeless plains, only the sight of an ombú, not a tree but looking very much like one, was an indication of human habitation. Vastness, flatness, desolation, distances, and primitivism were the traits stressed by nineteenth-century observers. The foreigners' impressions were shared by some natives, like W. H. Hudson, who left a remarkable account of his childhood in the Buenos Aires countryside, where his parents owned an estancia, "The 25 ombús."[40]

The area covered by estancias steadily grew during the nineteenth century. General Miller reported that the area under control extended up to 97 miles southeast of Buenos Aires, and settlers were already establishing estancias 200 or 300 miles away from the city in that direction. But 15

degrading misery, which is so general among the peasantry of Erin go bragh!" See Temple (1833) 1:60–61.
36 Brabazon (1981); Fugl (1959); Parish (1852); Martín de Moussy (1860–1864); Guilaine (1889).
37 Martin de Moussy (1860–1864), 2:110–111.
38 Stewart (1856), 325.
39 Miller (1829), 1:143–155.
40 Hudson (1918).

years later Darwin, crossing the plains from south to north, found the "first estancia with cattle and white women" 7 leagues south of the Salado River, some 100 miles from Buenos Aires. In 1820, however, a British resident reported the existence of settlers up to 200 miles south of the city, and grazing farms beyond that.[41] This disagreement over distances is not too serious. The expansion of estancias was uneven, both in geographical and temporal terms. It took place first to the southeast, toward the mouth of the Salado River, and much later to the west and southwest. But there were some backward movements due to Indian unrest, most notably that of the mid-1850s caused by the discontinuation of Rosas's appeasement policy.

As there are good accounts of the process of territorial expansion, it is not reviewed here again.[42] Land is considered only as a component of the estancia. To account for the formation and location of estancias, the process of territorial expansion should not be disregarded. But from the perspective of estancias, to account for their structure, operations, and results as a business concern, the pace and peculiarities of the process of territorial expansion are not entirely relevant.[43]

Estancias appeared on the pampas in the late sixteenth century due to land grants made to the early inhabitants of Buenos Aires. The area incorporated into production remained stagnant for two centuries, but as a consequence of the weak demand for estancia products and the risks involved in expanding to the south, a market emerged for land already under control.[44] After 1820, when the rapid expansion took place, there remained a clear difference between fairly secure land on the northern section of the old pampa and the riskier and more distant territories that were incorporated as a consequence of that process. There was plenty of land on the pampas, but while more distant tracts could be obtained in emphyteusis, those tracts closer to Buenos Aires had already been in private hands for many decades (more than twenty in some cases), so they could only be obtained by purchase. The existence of vacant public land in distant regions perhaps affected the market for secure private land, but that

---

41 Miller (1829), 1:151, 155; Darwin (1839), 111; and "Second letter from Buenos Aires," *Monthly Magazine*, 1 April 1821, 352:228. On emphyteusis, see Infesta (1993).

42 For an analytical approach, see Halperín Donghi (1963), (1969); Cortés Conde (1968), (1979); and Sabato (1989). For a geographical history of the expansion, see Randle and Gurevitz (1971). For a more traditional descriptive approach, see Gaignard (1989). The quantitative study of the process of territorial expansion started with the methodologically flawed attempts made by Oddone (1956) and Carretero (1970) and (1972), but Infesta (1986), (1991), (1993); Infesta and Valencia (1987); and Banzato and Quinteros (1992) have revised previous findings using an appropriate methodology.

43 Territorial expansion is observed from a different perspective in Chapter 3, when analyzing the regional differences capital structure of estancias.

44 See Saguier (1993), 69–71.

market was real. Even a secondary market emerged, where the right to hold
a tract in emphyteusis was onerously transferred.[45]

From the perspective of estancia and estancieros, therefore, the existence
of vacant land was not relevant for determining the economic outcome of
estancia operations. Land grants made before the 1820s and land grants
and sales made after 1836 have been considered as a privilege awarded to
a few. Although those few were in fact many, such grants played a central
role in some views stressing the inefficiency of estancias in the long run.
These views have been dismissed, but the access to that and other privileges should be considered to support the opposite view – that estancias
were the manifestation of early capitalism on the pampas.

Estancias: Early capitalism on the pampas

Land grants could be a key factor for estancia formation, but they did not
imply a necessarily successful outcome for their operations. A successful
outcome could have been due to a rational organization and an efficient
allocation of resources within estancias, or to a persistent privilege favoring
estancieros, manifested in regulation and protection granted by the state.
As is shown in this section, the former rather than the latter was the case
in early- and mid-nineteenth-century Buenos Aires.

In his classic study on regulation, George J. Stigler singled out four
benefits that the state can provide to an industry: a direct subsidy of
money, control over the entry of new rivals (and its variant, a protective
tariff), restrictions on substitutes, and price fixing.[46] Comparing these
benefits to those derived from cattle raising in late-eighteenth- and early-
nineteenth-century Buenos Aires, it becomes clear why no regulation was
sought then by the cattle industry or by any person related to it.

Direct subsidies of money were out of the question. The crown was
interested in collecting taxes to support the Spanish and Spanish American
bureaucracies, including the armies at a time of frequent wars. Producers
and consumers were taxed and, in Buenos Aires at least, there are no cases
of direct subsidies to any of them. Rather, new sources of income were
actively sought. For the cattle industry as a whole, to look for a direct
subsidy was also out of the question. There was a gremio de hacendados
(cattleowners' guild), but it was far less powerful than the merchants'
organization. Moreover, the hacendados' main complaints were against
regulations preventing them from taking full advantage of the hide trade.

---

45 The direct beneficiaries obtained title deeds for 37.5% of the land granted in emphyteusis between
1823 and 1840, but 63.5% of the claims were transferred between one and four times before a title
deed was obtained. See Infesta (1993), 104.
46 Stigler (1971), 4–7.

Neither hacendados nor merchants were in a position that enabled them to seek cash subsidies. It can be argued that tax evasion was tantamount to a cash subsidy if other economic sectors were paying their taxes. Although it has been proved that estancieros were very reluctant to pay the direct tax (contribución directa), it remains to be seen whether that was a tolerated evasion – Rosas's complaints point in the contrary direction.[47]

Controlling the entry of new rivals was an impossible task. As new economic opportunities presented themselves, people started moving into the countryside, settling tracts of land beyond the defensive line. As a result of two centuries of stagnation, there was plenty of vacant public land close to Buenos Aires. That land was occupied by the old estancieros after 1750, but there was more land toward the Salado River and much more beyond it. This area was then and for a long time under the formal control only of the Buenos Aires authorities, since their ability to enforce the law there was quite poor. At the beginning of the process of territorial expansion, efforts made to eliminate new entries were unsuccessful. Later, in the 1820s and 1830s, land was granted on a temporary and permanent basis to those who applied for a tract or as reward for military exploits. Access to new land depended then upon political favor, as well as upon exclusion. So political rivals were excluded or even dispossessed of their landholdings, but there was no permanent regulation restricting new entries. Moreover, there was a market for previously settled land.[48]

To put it in other words, there was no effective regulation against new entries. It has been recently argued that the easiness of life on the pampas was the main factor behind the scarcity and instability of labor. The abundant legislation against vagrancy has been interpreted as the result of the landowners' efforts to control labor. But it has also been argued that the same body of legislation aimed at preventing free workers from turning into independent producers. In this sense the anti-vagrancy legislation may be seen as fulfilling one of Stigler's benefits from regulation. It should be noted, however, that the very abundance of that legislation casts doubts regarding the ability of the government to enforce it. One of the reasons for that inability was the expense required by techniques of population con-

---

47 For the income and expenditure of the Buenos Aires treasury in the late colonial and early national periods see Halperín Donghi (1982), and Amaral (1984) and (1988). For the gremio de hacendados, see Fradkin (1987); for the Consulado, see Tjarks (1962); for the Buenos Aires merchants in the late colonial period, see Socolow (1978a). Mayo (1991a) has emphasized the differences between the Buenos Aires ranchers and those of other Spanish American regions in late colonial times. He is concerned, however, with the ranchers' power vis-à-vis the "lower classes," rather than vis-à-vis the rulers. For a study of the estancieros' local power, see Marquiegui (1990). For the Buenos Aires direct tax, see Estévez (1960).

48 For the legal aspects of territorial expansion, see Cárcano (1972); for access to land in the 1820s-1850s, see Infesta (1991) and (1993), and Infesta and Valencia (1987).

trol, but another reason was the lukewarm interest of the landowners in its enforcement. They tolerated informal settlers (agregados) on their land because there was an implicit mutual-protection agreement between them. So, on the one hand, landowners may have been interested in restricting access to production, but on the other, they were fostering potential competitors.

No protective tariff was ever needed by the cattle industry. On the contrary, cattle producers were very much interested in removing protection. They wanted their hides and other cattle by-products to flow freely to the overseas markets demanding them. In late colonial times and after independence as well, cattleowners were the solid rock supporting the expansion of liberalism. Civil liberties were hard to establish after the May 1810 Revolution, but full-fledged free trade was soon the law of the land. Attacks on free trade during the Rosas period were unsuccessful. Rosas in fact granted protection to his main constituents, the Buenos Aires landowners, not from outside competitors but from other provinces' governors who were asking him to set up protective barriers for their non-competitive, primitive manufactures. So no protective barriers were either asked for by cattleowners for their products or set up by the rulers.[49]

Restriction on substitutes does not apply to the Buenos Aires case, since hides and other cattle by-products produced by the estancieros were for export. Those products had a very limited local demand. Beef was the only cattle by-product meeting the local demand. But the increase of hide exports meant also the slaughtering of more head than was required for local consumption. Foreigners were shocked when learning that passersby killed cattle in the countryside just for their tongue or other delicacies, leaving the rest to predators. Although wheat production did not keep pace with population growth so that flour had to be imported from Brazil or the United States, there is no record of beef imports.[50]

Price fixing was always opposed by cattleowners. The price of beef had been traditionally regulated to favor urban consumers. Wheat price regulation kept agriculture in a critical situation and contributed to its decline.[51] The cattle industry was spared from a similar fate by the sudden rise of the demand for hides. As in late colonial Buenos Aires cattleowners

---

49 For the hacendados' complaints against regulation, see Fradkin (1987); for the 1809 debate on free trade, see Molinari (1939); for the 1830s debate on the same issue, see Burgin (1946), 218–237. On the effectiveness of Rosas's protectionist legislation, see also Burgin (1946), 237–248; Espalla (1967); and Cáceres Cano (1987).

50 As discussed earlier, travelers' accounts cannot be taken at face value. Their accounts of slaughtering for tongue-eating purposes, however, are believable. Stray cattle, the passersby's victims, did not have a price higher than that of their hides, and most probably their hides were less valuable than that of rodeo cattle.

51 Throughout this book agriculture refers to crop farming only, not to livestock production.

were less powerful than merchants, the former had to struggle against the latter's attempts at controlling the hide trade. But the progressive demise of the colonial regulatory framework after May 1810 let the hacendados' and merchants' interests blend. The shift of powerful merchants, such as the Anchorenas, from trade to cattle ranching is an appropriate symbol of that process. Beef price regulations did not fade away easily, but in post-independence Buenos Aires, they were not enough to deter the growth of cattle production.[52]

This review of Stigler's arguments on the benefits that producers can expect from state regulation shows that no benefits derived from it for the Buenos Aires cattleowners. This exercise may look futile since it has always been known that the Buenos Aires hacendados were (until the 1930s) steady supporters of free trade. But it is one thing to know that, and quite another to explain the advantages that they were expecting from it and the disadvantages that could have derived from rent seeking.

Economic actors downplay their rent-seeking activity when its cost is higher than the expected return. Three situations are likely to produce such a result: (1) an increase in the number of rent seekers; (2) a decrease in the power of the rent givers; and (3) an increase in the cost of enforcing the rules. These three situations may be reduced to the last one, since the first two also meant an increase in the cost of enforcement. It is then, therefore, when market arises as the main resource allocation device. And, according to the most usual definitions, the prevalence of market mechanisms means capitalism.

In late-eighteenth- and early-nineteenth-century Buenos Aires, there was an increase in the number of rent seekers, and the rent giver – the government – could not distribute rents from the most sought resource: land. Or even worse than that: The distribution of land did not mean much. Land was but a fraction of the total investment required to set up an estancia and turn it into a profitable concern. And although land was unavoidable, livestock was the most important factor. As remarked by Pedro de Angelis, the Italian intellectual who lived for three decades in Buenos Aires, a monopoly on livestock was impossible in the pampas.[53] Land grants were sought, but no automatic rent derived from grants. Law enforcement was not secured in the countryside, so high risks were confronted when settling there. Juan Francisco de Aguirre remarked that most estancieros lived on their landholdings, closer to their head of cattle than

---

52 For the opposition to price fixing and the conflict over the hide trade, see Fradkin (1987); on the Anchorena family, see Brown (1978). The first writer to point out the symbolism of the Anchorena case was Vicuña Mackenna. Cf. Vicuña Mackenna (1936), 118.

53 de Angelis (1834), 173.

to bureaucrats.[54] Therefore, as rent seeking was returning so little, competition prevailed. On the estancias of Buenos Aires, resources were allocated according to the signs posted by the markets, not according to privileges conceded by any authority. Transactions conducted within or outside the firm, the estancia, were guided by market prices. That was the rise of capitalism on the Argentine pampas.

Estancias: A type of economic organization

Estancias have always been part of the pampas' landscape and culture, so it has not been thought necessary to explain their rise, features, and rationality. But estancias were an economic organization where resources were used in a particular way for a particular purpose. The questions are, therefore, why were there estancias at all; what was the combination of factors characterizing them as such; what were the conditions of production restricting estancia operations; and what were the results of estancia operations.

Sources do not allow historians to answer all the questions they can imagine about a particular person, institution, process, or period. What follows is an attempt to answer in a direct or indirect way as many of those questions as possible. This attempt begins with an examination of the organization of production on a late-eighteenth-century Buenos Aires estancia and the evolution of capital structure of estancias in the first half of the nineteenth century.

54 Juan Francisco de Aguirre, "Diario . . . ," AGN, Biblioteca Nacional, leg. 17, 1:242.

PART I

Estancias

2

The organization of production

Many travelers and observers, from Millau in the 1770s to Martin de Moussy in the 1850s, described the organization of production on the Buenos Aires estancias.[1] The operations required for cattle raising, since cattle was their main business, were roundups, aquerenciamiento, branding, sorting, dehorning, and gelding.[2] All that is known. But the economic result of those and other operations on one particular estancia for a number of years is much harder to uncover.

Sources for a precise analysis of the estancia operations are not plentiful, and those that have survived usually relate to the rural properties of religious institutions that came under state control following the expulsion of the Jesuits in 1767 or the 1822 ecclesiastical reform.[3] The organization of production on those estancias, however, was not necessarily the same as that of the more numerous non-ecclesiastical rural establishments. Other sources are necessary to study those non-ecclesiastical, privately owned estancias. Probate records are the best source of information on them. When a landowner died, inventories were taken, so the land, barns and sheds, farming tools, livestock, and slaves were described and evaluated.[4] In cases where the heirs disputed the division of the estate – particularly when children were involved, there being legal provisions protecting their interests – it is possible to find income and expenditure accounts covering the period of litigation. Clemente López Osornio's was one of such cases.

This chapter studies the Clemente López Osornio estancia from 1785 to 1796, for which both income and expenditure accounts as well as inventories are available. Those accounts and inventories made possible an analysis of what was on that estancia, what it was selling and buying, what was the

---

1 Millau (1947), 38–42; Martin de Moussy (1860–1864), 2:110–119.
2 For the meaning of Spanish words, see the Glossary.
3 Halperín Donghi (1975); Cushner (1983); Mayo (1991b), 107–149; Salvatore and Brown (1987); de la Fuente (1988); Gelman (1989a); and Mayo (1994).
4 For more on probate records, see Appendix B.

profit made out of those operations, and how forced and free labor were used to carry out the normal operations on that estancia.

The late-eighteenth-century estancia has been described as geared toward overseas markets, producing cattle but also other export goods, and doing so by an increasing use of slaves due to the difficulty of hiring permanent free workers. The López Osornio estancia does not completely fit into that picture. It is difficult to determine whether that was typical or not, since accounts for other non-ecclesiastical estancias are still to be found. Maybe it was not typical in that sense, but there is no reason to think either that it was completely atypical. Maybe the difficulty lies in deciding what were the typical characteristics of estancia production in the late eighteenth century. While that question waits for a proper answer, the inner workings of the López Osornio estancia reveal a pattern that could not have been too peculiar – cattle were produced for a sound profit in a context of uncertainty. This may sound like a simple proposition, but it was not. The positive economic result of the López Osornio estancia in that period was due to factors that are evident from the analysis of its accounts, as cattle reproduction, and factors that are implicit, as the adequate conditions of production and the proper managerial and entrepreneurial skills.

After Clemente López Osornio was murdered by Indians on the Salado River in December 1783, a protracted lawsuit took place.[5] By his first wife, Martina Arroyo, López Osornio had had two children: Andrés Ramón, killed alongside his father, and Catalina Felipa. When his wife died, he married María Manuela Rubio, by whom he had three children: Agustina Teresa (subsequently the wife of León Ortiz de Rozas and the mother of Juan Manuel de Rosas), José Silverio, and Petrona Josefa. It was thanks to litigation between Catalina Felipa – by then married and the mother of two daughters – and her stepmother, continued after their deaths by Pedro Nolasco Arroyo, Martina's brother, that accounts for 11 years have survived to the present day. They shed light upon the organization of production on one estancia on the Buenos Aires old pampa at the end of the eighteenth century. The first section of this chapter studies López Osornio's landholdings and what was on the land; the second, income; the third, profit; and the fourth, the use of free and forced labor.

Capital

Rural capital in late-eighteenth- and early-nineteenth-century Buenos Aires was formed mainly by land and livestock. The conventional division

---

5 All the following data have been taken from (unless otherwise stated) the records of Clemente López Osornio's estate, in AGN, Tribunales, Sucesiones, 6726, 6727, and 6728. Throughout the book the word *estate* is used to refer to "the assets and liabilities left by a person at death."

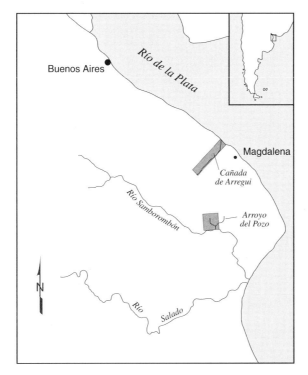

Map 2.1 Location of Clemente López Osornio's estancia (Cañada de Arregui) and invernada (Arroyo del Pozo).

between fixed and working capital does not apply in this case, since cattle were managed in a way that skipped depreciation by selling older head while retaining younger. Capital formation, dealt with later, in the section devoted to profit, was equivalent in the short run to the increase of the cattle stock, while only in the long run could it mean land valorization or the expansion of improvements.[6] This section studies the capital of the estancia belonging to Clemente López Osornio according to four different inventories.

The López Osornio estancia was located in the Cañada de Arregui, in the Magdalena district (Map 2.1). It consisted of a *suerte principal* (main piece of land) 9,000 varas long by 3,100 varas wide, and an adjoining strip 428.5 varas wide by the same length. A *bañado* (marshland) 3,500 varas wide by 6,000 varas long lay between the river and the suerte principal, and behind it there was a further plot known as the *cabezadas*, 6,000 varas wide by an

6 For recent studies on capital productivity in agriculture, see Campbell and Overton (1991). For studies on land productivity, see Van der Wee and Van Cauwenberghe (1978).

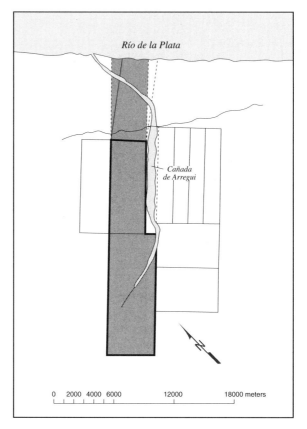

Map 2.2 Clemente López Osornio's estancia, Cañada de Arregui, Magdalena,
1824. *Source*: MOP, Magdalena, duplicado de mensuras antiguas, N°17.

undetermined length (Map 2.2). Converting varas to hectares gives us an
area of 2,382 hectares for the suerte principal plus the contiguous piece of
land, 1,575 hectares for the bañado, and about 5,400 hectares for the
cabezadas. The last figure is based upon a length of 2 leagues suggested by
measurements taken in 1824. The total area of the estancia was therefore
9,357 hectares.[7]

Two tracts of vacant public land were claimed by López Osornio in
1775, one at the Rincón de la Reducción (afterward Rincón de López) on
the Salado River, the other by the Arroyo del Pozo on the Samborombón
River. López Osornio had apparently taken possession of these lands in
1761 and 1769, respectively, but, since he could not obtain deeds to them,
his estate consisted solely of the Cañada de Arregui estancia. His estancia

7 For varas, leagues, and hectares, see the Weights and Measures list in the front matter.

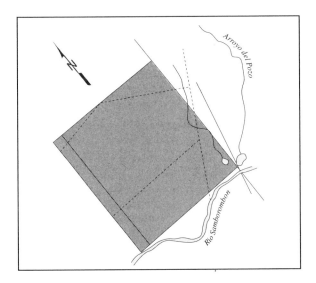

Map 2.3 Clemente López Osornio's invernada, Arroyo del Pozo, 1814. *Source*: See
this chapter, n. 8.

appears in a land census taken in 1789 as being 3,540 varas wide by 9,000
long, equivalent to 2,329 hectares. Neither the bañado nor the cabezadas
was mentioned, but fields for wintering cattle were. These, the *invernada*,
located at the Arroyo del Pozo and forming part of the lands claimed by
López Osornio in 1775, were sold by the government to José Silverio,
Clemente's son, on 25 June 1811. According to a survey of 1778, its area
was 9,989 hectares, but a second survey in 1814 registered 8,527 hectares
(Map 2.3).[8] The total surface area under exploitation (estancia plus
invernada) amounted to 17,883 hectares. Given the lack of fences around
the estancia, however, it should be stressed that this figure did not represent the exact area actually occupied by López Osornio's livestock.

The land maintained the same value through each of the four inventories, which were taken in 1786, 1787, 1792, and 1795 (Table 2.1). The
suerte principal and the adjacent piece of land were valued at 2 reales per
vara, the bañado at 1 real, and the cabezadas at $1\frac{1}{4}$ reales. As the values
were based upon the width alone, assuming a uniform length of 9,000
varas (the usual length of *suertes de estancia*), they would have been 1.5 reales
for the bañado, 2 reales for the suerte principal, and 0.94 real for the

8 Clemente López Osornio's claim to the lands at Rincón de la Reducción and Arroyo del Pozo, in
  AHP, Escribanía Mayor de Gobierno, legajo 11, No. 384. The same file contains Agustina Teresa
  López Osornio's legal claim to the land at Rincón de la Reducción. The 1789 register of estancias
  is in AGN, IX-9-7-7. The survey of the Arroyo del Pozo tract is in MOP, Magdalena, Survey
  Duplicate (mensuras antiguas) No. 14.

Table 2.1. *López Osornio's estancia: Inventories, 1786–1795*
(in pesos of 8 reales)

	1786	1787	1792	1795
Land	2,257	2,257	2,257	2,257
Improvements	1,918	1,697	1,876	1,876
Tools	393	257	281	287
Cattle	2,640	2,170	3,389	5,882
Sheep	167	167	181	250
Horses and mules	641	534	467	447
Slaves	1,250	1,350	1,100	900
Total[a]	9,268	8,432	9,552	11,900

[a] The 1786 inventory wrongly records a total of 9,467 pesos 6 reales. Totals for the other years are those recorded in each year's inventories. Figures have been rounded to the nearest peso, so the adding of the columns is not exactly the same as the total for each year.
Source: AGN, Tribunales, Sucesiones, leg. 6726, 6727, and 6728, Clemente López Osornio.

cabezadas, the values differing according to the quality of grass and access to water. The value of the suerte principal and the cabezadas was 2,150 pesos in 1786, but they had been purchased by López Osornio in 1752 from a certain Martín de Gamboa for 850 pesos. This 153% increase implied an annual rate of growth of 2.8%. Although prices had certainly fluctuated between 1752 and 1786, this does not necessarily mean that the rate of inflation in Buenos Aires was as high. The Price Revolution in sixteenth-century Spain averaged an annual rate of inflation of 1.35%, and a general price index estimated for Santiago de Chile (a closer comparison in time and space) increased at an annual rate of 0.6% between 1754–1758 and 1784–1788. That increase in land prices should not be attributed therefore to inflation, since such a rate could have hardly passed unobserved. As individual prices do not always behave according to the general index, the increase in land values between 1752 and 1786 should not be attributed to inflation but to the growing demand for cattle products.[9]

The total value of the lands (excluding the invernada) stood at 2,257 pesos in each of the four inventories, but as a percentage of capital, it fell

9 The purchase of the Cañada de Arregui estancia by López Osornio, in AGN, Escribanías, Registro 2, 1752, 425v. The sixteenth-century inflation rate for Spain has been estimated from Hamilton's composite price index in Hamilton (1934), 403. The price index for Santiago de Chile is in Ramón and Larraín (1982), 328. My thanks to Armando de Ramón for giving me a copy of their impressive book.

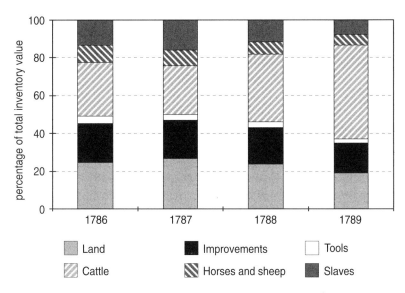

Figure 2.1. López Osornio's estancia: Capital structure, 1786–1795.
Source: Table 2.1.

from 26.8% in 1787 to 19% in 1795 (Figure 2.1).[10] The relatively low and declining figure for land as a proportion of the Cañada de Arregui estancia's total inventory value makes it certain that there was increasing investment in other items. The value of improvements (*mejoras*, that is, ranchos, quintas, corrals, ditches, and fences) varied between 20.7% of total investments in 1786 and 15.8% in 1795. Tools accounted for 4.2% in 1786 and 2.4% in 1795; sheep for 1.8% and 2.1%; and horses and mules for 6.9% and 3.8%. These items varied in value from one inventory to the next according to differences in quantity rather than in prices. Slaves were an exception since their value was affected by health – a sick slave's recovery explains the rise in their share of total capital from 13.5% to 16% between the 1786 and 1787 inventories. In 1795 three slaves (there had been five in 1786–1787) accounted for 7.6% of capital.

As the proportional value of all these items fell between the first and last inventories, one item at least should have increased. That item was cattle. Its proportional share rose from 28.5% in 1786 to 49.4% in 1795. It increased by 122.8% between the first and last inventories and by 171.1% between the second and last. Cattle capitalization therefore explains the

---

10 For the ratio of land value to total estancia value, see Chapter 3; for profit estimates, see Chapter 10.

24.8% rise in total inventory values from 9,267 pesos in 1786 to 11,900 pesos in 1795, this despite stagnant or falling real figures for all other items. The increase in the value of cattle was due to their steadily growing numbers, since prices remained firm at about 1 peso 2$\frac{1}{4}$ reales for the average inventory value, and 3 pesos for those sold for urban meat consumption.

Sheep, horses, and a few head of mules did not account all together for more than 8.7% of capital at any one time, and farming tools accounted for no more than 4.2%. These figures prove that production was based not on mules, sheep, or agriculture but almost entirely on cattle. López Osornio's estancia, however, did not reflect the traditional image of cattle production for the period, supposedly geared toward the production of hides for export.

Income

Quantitative data on estancia production are not abundant. Félix de Azara explained why cattle production was preferred to agriculture in Buenos Aires. Although he disregards the question of capital investment (the land, cattle, improvements, and equipment necessary for ranching), he tells us that the chief advantage of cattle production, employing the same amount of labor as other types of production (he failed to consider their cost), was its higher productivity per worker.[11] Azara's analysis is partial but far from misleading. Cattle raising was the most profitable activity carried out on the pampas.

Proof in a different case is provided by the Fontezuela estancia (some 200 miles north of Buenos Aires), studied by Tulio Halperín Donghi. Its records supply data on income and expenditure from 1753 to 1809, but the composition of the former is known for just one year, 1771, when 46.2% of income came from the sale of mules, 16.2% from hides, 16.2% from fat and tallow, 5.2% from bricks and tiles, and 16.2% from the sale of other miscellaneous items.[12] It should be noted that these figures predate the Upper Peruvian revolts of the 1780s, which disrupted the mule trade, and also predate the 1778 free-trade regulations, which according to hide export figures undoubtedly encouraged cattle production.[13]

Instead of mules for Upper Peru or hides for export, the López Osornio estancia was producing beef-cattle for the urban market. The sale of live cattle was the main source of income during the period for which data are available (August 1785–December 1795), accounting for 71.7% of total

---

11 Azara (1943), 7–8. For more on Azara's estimate of labor productivity, see Chapter 8.
12 Halperín Donghi (1975), 459–460.
13 For hide export figures, see Table C.1.

Table 2.2. *López Osornio's estancia: Income, 1785–1795*
(in pesos of 8 reales)

	1785	1786	1787	1788	1789	1790	1791	1792	1793	1794	1795	Total
Cattle	795	1,025	894	77	537	318	745	483	795	674	800	7,144
Atahona	84	30	97	44	176	143	67	216	146	124	72	1,200
Hides	73	113	81	163	54	–	–	183	14	19	30	731
Sheep	112	20	5	–	–	–	29	26	10	–	–	202
Horses	108	26	65	2	–	–	19	14	24	24	48	331
Grease*a*	18	–	25	46	–	–	–	–	–	–	–	90
Hen	–	–	19	–	–	–	–	–	–	–	–	19
Wheat	74	–	–	–	–	–	–	–	–	–	–	74
Slaves	–	–	166	–	–	–	–	–	–	–	–	166
Total	1,265	1,213	1,353	332	767	461	861	922	989	842	951	9,957

a Grease and tallow.
Note: Figures have been rounded to the nearest peso.
Source: See Table 2.1.

income, ranging from 23.2% in 1788 to 86.6% in 1791 (Table 2.2).[14] The only year in which the sales of other items exceeded cattle was 1788. Apart from cattle, only the *atahona* (mule- or horse-driven mill), which accounted for 12.1% of total income, generated income every year. Sales of hides represented 7.3% of total income, and those of sheep, mules, horses, fat and tallow, chickens, and wheat, 7.2%. The remaining 1.7% came from the sale of a slave.

The estancia went through three income and expenditure cycles: 1785–1787, 1788–1790, and 1791–1795 (Figure 2.2). During the first cycle, cattle had to be sold off in order to meet the extraordinary expenses required to put the estancia – which had been abandoned after its owner's death – back in production. Consequently, 1,954 head of cattle were sold for 2,713 pesos 6 reales, at an average price of 1 peso 3 reales per head. During the second cycle, 307 cattle were sold at 3 pesos each for a total of 932 pesos. Finally, during the third cycle, the sale of 1,125 cattle raised 3,498 pesos 2 reales, averaging 3 pesos 1 real per head. The fluctuation in

---

14 Throughout this chapter, including the tables, 1785 refers to accounts from August 1785 to April 1786; 1786, from January 1786 to January 1787; and 1787, from February to December 1787. The accounts submitted by the estancia's foreman to the legal executor of López Osornio's estate are not sufficiently detailed for finer distinctions to be made. There is no overlapping in the accounts between January and April 1786 because the foreman's own accounts were not altered. The accounts for August 1785–April 1786 have been used here as if representing a full year because of their similarity to later years and because of the drastic changes in the estancia's operations brought about by the death of the landowner. For an exception to this rule, see n. 30.

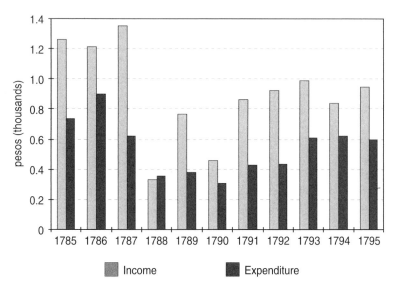

Figure 2.2. López Osornio's estancia: Income and expenditure, 1785–1795.
Sources: Tables 2.2 and 2.5.

average prices was due solely to the quality of the cattle sold in each cycle, since prices remained constant for each type of animal: 2 pesos for cows and from 3 pesos to 3 pesos 4 reales for beef-cattle. The average value per head of animal in all four inventories was around 1 peso $2\frac{1}{4}$ reales, with slight variations of no more than $\frac{1}{2}$ real. This shows that, after the first cycle, when the average price per head sold was almost identical to the average inventory value, only beef-cattle for urban consumption were sold (Table 2.3).

There was a net increase in cattle stock of 111% between 1786 and 1795, but this figure conceals the 25% fall of 1787. Taking 1787 as the base year, the net increase in cattle stock stood at 181% by 1795. The annual rate of growth was, therefore, 8.7% in the first case and 13.8% in the second. The rate of cattle extraction (number of cattle sold as a percentage of the year's stock) was 9.8% for the entire 1786–1795 period, but the averages varied in each cycle: 30.7% in the first (excluding 1785), 5% in the second, and 7% in the third (Table 2.4). The gross rate of growth of cattle stock (number of head of cattle sold in 1 year plus the difference between that year's stock and the previous year's, taken as a percentage of the previous year's stock) was 12.8% for the whole period. (Considering cattle sales from 1787 to 1795 plus cattle stock in 1795 divided by cattle stock in 1786, the annual rate of growth is 12.7%). There were also large differences between cycles: −8.4% for 1787 (the only year

Table 2.3. *López Osornio's estancia: Cattle sales, 1785–1795*
(in pesos of 8 reales)

	3 pesos and more per head			Less than 3 pesos per head			Total			
	N	V	X_s	N	V	X_s	N	V	X_s	X_i
1785	118	354	3.00	618	441	0.69	736	795	1.09	–
1786	147	441	3.00	710	583	0.81	857	1,024	1.19	1.22
1787	153	510	3.34	208	384	1.84	361	894	2.47	1.34
1788	22	77	3.50	–	–	–	22	77	3.50	–
1789	179	537	3.00	–	–	–	179	537	3.00	–
1790	106	318	3.00	–	–	–	106	318	3.00	–
1791	190	621	3.25	45	123	2.75	235	745	3.19	–
1792	131	450	3.44	13	33	2.53	144	483	3.34	1.28
1793	265	795	3.00	–	–	–	265	795	3.00	–
1794	208	644	3.09	15	30	2.00	223	674	3.00	–
1795	244	781	3.22	14	19	1.34	258	800	3.09	1.28
Total	1,763	5,529	3.13	1,623	1,614	1.00	3,386	7,144	2.09	1.28

Note: N = number of head; V = total value; X_s = average sale price per head; X_i = average inventory price per head. Figures in columns N and V have been rounded to the nearest peso.
Source: See Table 2.1.

Table 2.4. *López Osornio's estancia:*
Cattle stock and rate of extraction, 1785–1795

	Cattle stock	Head sold	Extraction rate (%)	Growth rate (%)
1785	–	736	–	–
1786	2,173	857	39.4	–
1787	1,630	361	22.1	–8.4
1788	1,796[a]	22	1.2	11.5
1789	1,978[a]	179	9.0	20.1
1790	2,180[a]	106	4.9	15.6
1791	2,402[a]	235	9.8	10.2
1792	2,646	144	5.4	16.2
1793	3,177[a]	265	8.3	30.1
1794	3,815[a]	223	5.8	27.1
1795	4,581	258	5.6	26.8
Mean			9.8	12.8

Notes: Cattle stock: number of cattle head according to inventory; [a] estimated according to the rate of growth between two inventories. Head sold: number of cattle head sold according to the estancia accounts. Extraction rate: number of head sold as percentage that year's stock. Growth rate: head sold in 1 year plus the difference between that year's stock and the previous year's stock.
Source: See Table 2.1.

in the first cycle for which it can be estimated), and averages of 15.7% and 22.1% in the second and third cycles. Considering the two inventories of the third cycle (1792 and 1795), therefore adding cattle sales from 1793 to 1795 to cattle stock in 1795 and dividing the result by cattle stock in 1792, the annual gross rate of growth is 26.3%. This rate is representative of three normal years, but normal years were not that frequent. In further estimates the 22.1% rate is preferred because it includes the 1791 drought, a regular occurrence affecting production.[15]

The 1786 inventory registered a further herd of 1,200 head of cattle, but their value was not mentioned. At the average inventory value of 1 peso $2\frac{1}{4}$ reales, their total value would have been 1,537 pesos 2 reales. Between October 1785 and November 1786, 714 pesos were spent on rounding up herds pasturing in Tuyú and Ajó. Altogether, 770 head of cattle were rounded up; their value, according to the average inventory price, would have amounted to 986 pesos 3 reales. There were no unpriced cattle mentioned in later inventories.

The number of sheep increased from 1,340 to 2,000 head between the 1786 and 1795 inventories. By adding the difference (660) to the number of sheep sold over the same period (721), a total of 1,381 is reached, representing a 103% gross stock increase and implying a yearly growth rate of 8.2%. As this is lower than the expected growth rate for sheep, the 889 animals sold in 1785 should be deducted from the 1786 inventory stock figure (it has already been observed that the 1785 accounts in fact ran to April 1786) to obtain the true rate. There is thus a stock difference of 1,559 sheep between 1785 and 1795; this, added to the number sold in 1786–1795, results in a total of 2,280 sheep. Taking as a basis the number of sheep recorded by the 1786 inventory and subtracting the number sold in 1785 (1,340 − 899 = 441), there is a 417% increase, equivalent to an annual growth rate of 20%. If the same calculation is carried out for 1792–1795, and the 210 head sold in 1792 are subtracted from that year's stock figure (1,450 head), a stock of 1,240 sheep is left for 1792. Thus the 2,000 head of sheep in 1795 plus the 210 sold in 1792 and the 81 sold in 1793 yield a total of 2,291 sheep, representing a total annual increase of 84.8% and an annual rate of growth of 22.7% for the 3-year period.[16] It should be

15 For a graphic representation of the recurrence of droughts, floods, excessive rain, fires, and locusts from 1770 to 1820, see García Belsunce (1988), 342.

16 The natural increase in sheep at the end of the nineteenth century was 25%, according to Mulhall and Mulhall (1892), quoted by Cortés Conde (1979), 59. Therefore, rates of growth around 20% for the 1790s (22.7% in this case) do not seem too low. But if the 8.2% rate is accepted, such a modest growth in sheep stocks has to be accounted for. It must be assumed then that some sheep were killed to feed the foreman, peons, and slaves. Bernardo Gutiérrez and Félix García's advice to kill steer rather than sheep to feed the staff implies that the practice was not unknown in the 1850s. See REBA (1855), 2:44.

noted that neither the sale of wool nor the payment in wool or sheepskins for goods or services is recorded in López Osornio's estancia accounts. The wool may have been worked on the estancia by the slaves' and peons' womenfolk, and sheepskins may have been used for manufacturing riding equipment, garments, and other articles, but the accounts simply fail to hint at such possibilities. It could also be that wool was not sheared because of its low quality (resulting in a non-profitable market price) and that the over-supply of sheepskins pushed down prices to such an extent that the expense of transporting them to town could not be justified.

The López Osornio estancia was not geared toward commercial agricultural production. Only once, in 1785, the sale of wheat was recorded. The inventories carried out in 1787, 1792, and 1795 provide no data on the farming tools used on the estancia because these were not itemized separately. Even the more detailed 1786 inventory mentions only a small quantity of sickles. Since no wheat was bought as food for the slaves and peons, there might have been some agricultural production for home consumption. There is, however, no evidence to support this. The atahona obtained its income from the milling of grain produced outside the estancia. On average, 174.5 fanegas of grain a year were milled during the period 1785–1795. According to Azara's estimates, one person consumed 2.36 fanegas of wheat a year, so 174.5 fanegas would have fed 74 persons.[17] This suggests that the atahona was milling grain for the immediate neighbors' own consumption.

López Osornio's estancia therefore produced mainly beef-cattle for the city market. The difference between these beef-cattle and the ordinary herds is shown by the price of 3 pesos per head fetched by the former at market as against the average inventory value of 1 peso $2\frac{1}{4}$ reales per head. Not all animals, then, were considered suitable for catering to the urban population and, indeed, a certain type of cattle seems to have been selected, if not bred, for this purpose. This is evidence of the rationality behind the ranching methods used and further proof is provided by the increasing cattle growth rate and the decreasing cattle extraction rate (Table 2.4).

Although it is not certain that all estancias around Buenos Aires were producing beef-cattle for the city, the fact that this particular estancia did so and used the methods it did hardly tallies with the descriptions left to us by Azara, Gillespie, Vidal, and other foreign travelers who considered local ranching methods far too slack.[18] Local methods would indeed seem

17 Azara (1943), 7–8. According to the foreman's accounts, 5 reales were charged as the cost of grinding each fanega. This figure has been used to estimate the amount of wheat ground on the estancia.
18 See, for example, Azara (1969), 286ff.; Gillespie (1921), 118, 130; and Vidal (1923), 201, quoted by Levene (1962), 2:307. Slatta has drawn attention to the ethnocentric nature of foreign observers' accounts of rural labor in Buenos Aires. See Slatta (1983), 24–26.

slack to Europeans used to other farming practices, but the accounts for
López Osornio's estancia nevertheless reveal that the establishment was run
neither haphazardly nor irresponsibly but on sound economic grounds and
in response to market demand and profit margins.

Profit

A proper estimate of profit can only be carried out when information
on capital investment is known. The rarity of such information has
led to some estimates of the rate of profit as the percentage of total
expenditure represented by the difference between income and expenditure.[19] Such calculation, however, does not take into account originally
invested capital and capital growth (non-cashed profit). Since profit is
the difference between income and expenditure, the rate of profit, understood as the net return over capital, can only be estimated if capital is
known.

The total profit made by López Osornio's estancia is estimated here from
the figures for net cashed profit (the difference between income and expenditure) and non-cashed profit (the difference between the inventory values
of two consecutive years). For net cashed profit, the aforementioned income
data are used together with the expenditure data shown in Table 2.5. For
non-cashed profit, existing inventory values will be used to estimate figures
for the intervening years (Table 2.6). Once the figures for cashed profit are
known, the annual return on investment, defined as its percentage over the
previous year's inventory value, can be estimated. Figures for non-cashed
profit allow us to estimate the inventory variation, likewise its percentage
over the previous year's inventory value. The sum of cashed and non-cashed
profit gives us the total profit, which in turn is used to calculate the annual
rate of profit, the sum expressed as a percentage over investment, that is,
the previous year's inventory value. In analyzing these accounts, constant
prices have been assumed, since seasonal or short-term price fluctuations
should not be necessarily taken as evidence of inflation. Inventory cattle
prices remained unchanged during this period, and there is no evidence for
any major change in relative prices.[20]

The three income and expenditure cycles define cycles pertaining to the

---

19 Halperín Donghi (1975), 454; Brown (1978), 176; and Gelman (1992b), 501, have used that
    method.
20 A lively debate on the behavior of prices in late colonial Buenos Aires has taken place lately, but
    the arguments (concerned with methodology rather than substance) miss an obvious factor: the
    meaning, from an economic standpoint, of any price behavior and that behavior in particular. See
    Romano (1992) and Johnson (1990) and (1992).

Table 2.5. *López Osornio's estancia: Expenditure, 1785–1795*
(in pesos of 8 reales)

	1785	1786	1787	1788	1789	1790	1791	1792	1793	1794	1795	Total
Peons[a]	135	286	191	120	131	109	152	166	254	297	324	2,166
Foremen	91	168	203	150	146	144	144	165	192	192	192	1,788
Workers[b]	370	344	–	–	–	–	8	–	–	–	–	722
Slaves												
Stipend	–	–	24	31	25	24	26	21	16	18	23	209
Clothing	54	–	23	5	40	–	25	7	37	–	1	192
Food	38	20	31	36	25	6	11	6	4	9	19	203
Tools	14	18	56	7	4	–	1	4	–	15	12	131
Upkeep	5	25	24	5	8	23	61	33	22	5	24	238
Legal[c]	20	40	70	–	–	–	–	34	12	12	–	188
Taxes	–	–	–	–	–	–	–	–	68	72	–	140
Other	8	–	–	4	2	–	1	–	7	–	–	23
Total	735	901	622	359	382	307	429	437	613	620	595	6,001

[a] Peons' wages.
[b] Wages paid to other temporary workers.
[c] Legal expenses.
Note: Figures have been rounded to the nearest peso.
Source: See Table 2.1.

Table 2.6. *López Osornio's estancia:*
Inventory variation, return on investment, and rate of profit, 1785–1795

	K pesos	i_n pesos	V %	i_c pesos	R %	i pesos	b %
1785	9,268[a]	–	–	529	5.7	529	5.7
1786	9,268	–	–	312	3.4	312	3.4
1787	8,432[b]	–836	–9.0	730	7.9	–100	–1.1
1788	8,645[b]	213	2.5	–27	–0.3	186	2.2
1789	8,863[b]	218	2.5	386	4.4	604	7.0
1790	9,087[b]	224	2.5	154	1.7	378	4.3
1791	9,317[b]	230	2.5	432	4.8	662	7.3
1792	9,552	235	2.5	485	5.2	720	7.7
1793	10,278[b]	726	7.6	376	3.9	1,102	11.5
1794	11,059[b]	781	7.6	221	2.2	1,002	9.7
1795	11,900	841	7.6	356	3.2	1,197	10.8

Notes: K = capital according to inventory ([a] the following year's value has been used;
[b] estimated according to the cumulative rate of growth between inventories); i_n = non-cashed
profit; V = inventory variation; i_c = cashed profit; R = return on investment; i = total profit
(i_n+i_c); b = rate of profit. See Appendix A for definitions.
Sources: See Table 2.1; data: Tables 2.2, and 2.5.

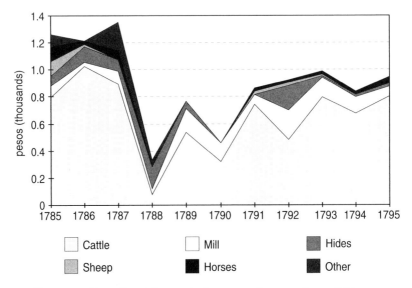

Figure 2.3. López Osornio's estancia: Income, 1785–1795. *Source*: Table 2.2.

overall management of the estancia: 1785–1787, when both income and expenditure were high; 1788–1790, when income and expenditure figures were as low as one-third those of the previous cycle; and 1791–1795, when income and expenditure were roughly equal to the average for the two previous cycles (Figure 2.3). Apart from the natural conditions that may have contributed to producing them, these cycles mainly reflected the instability caused by the legal disputes over López Osornio's estate. For a time there were conflicts between his widow and daughter by his first marriage, and the estancia was neglected to such an extent that, when they finally agreed to farm it again, large incidental expenses had accumulated, making a partial liquidation of capital necessary (achieved through cattle over-selling). As a consequence, this first cycle was followed by a 3-year retention cycle aimed at restoring its productive capacity. Normal operation was resumed after 1791, when the effects of the legal dispute were no longer apparent, even though it had still not been resolved in the courts.

The chief item of expenditure in the estancia was labor, which accounted for 81.4% of expenditure during the period 1785–1795 (Table 2.5 and Figure 2.4). The percentage breakdown was as follows: peons, 36.1% of the total; the foreman, 29.8%; men contracted for specific jobs (peons for five cattle roundups in 1785 and 1786, and a skinner in 1791), 12%; and slaves (who were given a weekly allowance of 1 real for soap and tobacco), 3.5%.

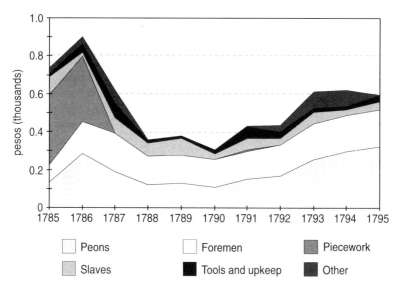

Figure 2.4. López Osornio's estancia: Expenditure, 1785–1795. *Source*: Table 2.5.

During the normal-operation cycle (1791–1795), labor also accounted for 81.4% of total expenditure, but this time the percentage composition is slightly different: peons, 44.3%; the foreman, 32.9%; men employed for specific jobs, 0.3%; and slaves, 3.9%. Not counting the foreman (assuming that he was not needed while the owner was still alive) or the casual laborers (assuming that their services would not have been required under normal circumstances), the peons' wages would have amounted to 61.2% of total expenditure over the whole period and 65% during the normal-operation cycle.

The purchase of clothes for the slaves (and only for them) and food (mainly salt and yerba mate, presumably for everybody at the estancia) represented 6.6% of total expenditure for the whole 1785–1795 period. The purchase of farming tools and money spent on the maintenance of equipment (particularly the atahona) represented 6.1%, and other expenses (legal fees, taxes, valuations, slaves' medical care and burial fees, transportation of goods), 5.8%. The only tax paid was the tithe, in 1793 and 1794: The payments were made separately in each year, not including arrears, and represented 11.1% and 11.6% of total expenditure for those years.

The return on investment ranged from a low of −0.3% in 1788 to a high of 7.9% in 1787, with 3.3% as the annual rate for the whole period. The inventory variation fluctuated from −9% in 1787 to 7.6% between 1793 and 1795, 2.3% being the annual rate for the period (Tables 2.6 and 2.7).

Table 2.7. *López Osornio's estancia:*
Rate of profit, 1785–1795

	R %	V %	b %
1785–1787	5.4	-2.9	2.6
1788–1790	1.9	2.5	4.4
1791–1795	3.6	5.0	8.7
1785–1795	3.3	2.3	5.0

Note: R = return on investment; V = inventory
variation; b = rate of profit. See Appendix A for
definitions.
Source: Table 2.6.

The annual rate of profit was 2.6% in the first cycle, 4.4% in the second, and 8.7% in the third.[21] The annual rate for the whole period was 5%. In normal-operation years, the annual rate of profit must have been the same as during the third cycle. This is a better rate than for the entire 11-year period since it excludes the liquidation and recapitalization cycles, which were a consequence of legal disputes, not economic factors. The excess 2.7%, arrived at by comparing the normal annual rate of profit for the estancia (8.7%) with the 6% usual interest rate, yielded a 45% premium that, although certainly a reward for the risks involved in rural activities and the entrepreneurial skills demanded by them, also serves to explain the expansion of the rural sector at the end of the eighteenth century.

Labor

On the López Osornio estancia, both free and forced labor were employed. Peons and slaves carried out the tasks demanded by cattle raising and the other rural activities performed on that estancia. Why both types of labor were used in rural production has been the subject of debate from Juan Agustín García onward.[22] To explain that here, the employment and payment of free labor is considered first, and then peons' and slaves' productivity and daily profit are compared.

21 At a constant price of 1 real per head, the highest and lowest estimates of annual sheep consumption on the estancia (see n. 16) would have represented an annual average expenditure of 59 pesos $6\frac{1}{4}$ reales and 15 pesos $2\frac{1}{2}$ reales, respectively. These expenditures, added to the total expenditure for normal-operation years (1791–1795), would have brought the profit rate down from 8.7% to 8.2% or 8.5%.

22 García (1966), 179–180; Halperín Donghi (1975), 457–459; and Mayo (1984), 614–615. See this text, Chapter 11.

The estancia's free labor force consisted of peons and a foreman. The foreman was in charge of running the estancia and generally supervising routine ranching duties. The peons were men hired to carry out these duties. Some of them were paid for a particular piece of work; others were paid on a time-work basis. For the sake of clarity, the word *peon* will be reserved for the latter, the former being referred to simply as workers or laborers. Craftsmen engaged in repair work have not been categorized here as free labor because the sums paid to them are taken to be maintenance costs.

The foreman, engaged on a long-term contract, was accountable to the estancia's legal executor. From August 1785 to December 1795, three successive foremen were put in charge of the estancia for different periods and on different salaries. The first foreman worked for 19 months and 16 days on a salary of 14 pesos a month, then for 27 months and 7 days for a monthly salary of 12 pesos 4 reales. The salary was paid in two lump sums at the end of each period: 273 pesos and $2\frac{1}{2}$ reales, and 341 pesos. An advance of 51 pesos 4 reales was made to him 3 months before the end of the second period, but he did not pay it back, and it was not mentioned when he was given the second payment, which implies that it must have been added to his total salary. His average monthly salary was therefore 14 pesos $3\frac{1}{4}$ reales. The second foreman worked for 3 years, 1 month, and 11 days and was paid 12 pesos a month. He received 432 pesos for the 3 years and 16 pesos 3 reales for the 1 month and 11 days. The third foreman worked for 3 years and 6 months for a monthly salary of 16 pesos, receiving 672 pesos in one payment at the end of his term. The accounts submitted by the legal executor did not record any partial payment made to the foremen.

Some temporary workers were hired for specific jobs and paid according to the nature of their work rather than for the time worked. Those laborers who took part in the cattle roundups in Tuyú and Ajó in 1785 and 1786 were paid 7 pesos in the first and second roundup, 8 pesos in the third, only 4 pesos in the fourth (the roundup was a failure, and two of the laborers and the baqueano agreed not to be paid at all), and between 8 and 10 pesos in the fifth. The variations in payment were probably due to the season, the amount of time spent on the job, and the laborers' differing abilities. Additional laborers were employed to work with their own horses at the cattle's wintering station (invernada) and were paid 4 to 6 reales per day. In 1791 a skinner was paid 2 reales per bullhide and $1\frac{1}{2}$ reales per cowhide; these figures may have included payment for the time he took to reach the spot where the dead animals were lying and to return with the hides. In 1796 fourteen laborers "who walked to the Salado River with wintering cattle" were paid 2 pesos each for the job. Since all such cases were not typical and we have no precise information on either the length of employment or wages paid, they have been taken into account only partially in our analysis of the employment of temporary free labor on the estancia, which is concerned mainly with the peons.

For normal-season ranch work, temporary unskilled workers were hired and paid on a time-work basis; as stated previously, they (and only they) are referred to here as peons. From August 1785 to June 1796, a total of 100 peons were hired for 160 terms of work of varying duration. Sixty-nine peons were employed only once and 31 two or more times. The first group worked for 4,732 days, and the second group for 7,044 days, with averages of 68.6 and 227.2 days, respectively. The total average is 117.8 days for each peon. During the 3,975-day period under consideration, 11,778 man-days were worked, equivalent to three peons working non-stop. Why did the estancia employ 100 peons for 160 terms of work instead of three peons a day over the 11 years? The answer is to be found in the foremen's accounts.

From February 1787 to January 1792, these accounts recorded not only the number of days each peon had worked but also the dates. Therefore, the number of man-days worked during each one of those 60 months can be estimated. In 1,826 calendar days, 3,186 man-days were worked by an average of 1.7 peons a day (Table 2.8).[23] The hiring of peons did not follow a regular pattern throughout the 5 years. Forty-five peons did 63 terms of work, the average for each term was 50.6 days, and each peon worked an average of 70.8 days. For 31 of the 60 months (51.7% of the time), an average of one peon or fewer was hired, and 418 man-days (13.1%) were worked. At the other extreme, three or more peons were hired over 18 months (30% of the time), and 2,049 man-days (64.2% of the total) were worked. Their labor was not evenly distributed within each year: On the one hand, an average of one peon or fewer was hired for 4 months in 1787, 8 months in 1788, 7 months in 1789, 4 months in 1790, and 7 months in 1791; on the other hand, three or more peons were hired for 7 months in 1787, 4 months in 1788 and 1789, 1 month in 1790, and 2 months in 1791. The differences in the demand for peons over the years are explained by the fact that the data correspond to the three production cycles: 1 year in the liquidation cycle (1787), 3 years in the retention cycle (1788–1790), and 1 year in the normal-operation cycle (1791), whereas differences in each year's demand can only be attributed to seasonal factors (Figure 2.5).

23 Peons working for monthly wages of 2 and 3 pesos have been excluded from Table 2.8. In that category are Josef el Muchacho, who worked 429 days uninterrupted for 3 pesos a month, and three peons working at the wintering station for 30, 120, and 214 days, respectively, at 2 pesos each per month. The reason for their exclusion, and why it was possible to hire peons long-term for 3 pesos a month, is explained later when considering the present value of slaves (see n. 38).

Table 2.8. *López Osornio's estancia: Man-days worked,*
February 1787 to January 1792

	J	F	M	A	M	J	J	A	S	O	N	D	Total
1787	nd	3	26	5	30	137	130	89	97	142	127	77	863
1788	36	2	0	15	31	0	0	17	129	134	151	86	601
1789	6	0	0	40	99	140	139	93	61	34	7	42	661
1790	4	69	62	73	100	72	71	0	0	0	65	63	579
1791	5	0	18	60	59	30	20	28	77	102	59	19	477
1792	0	nd	nd	nd	nd	nd	nd	nd	nd	nd	nd	nd	0
Total	51	74	106	193	319	379	360	227	364	412	409	287	3,181
Mean	10	15	21	39	64	76	72	45	73	82	82	57	636

nd = no data.
Note: Salaries of 2 and 3 pesos have been excluded. Between January and May 1790, one peon
is known to have worked 5 days, but they have not been taken into account here because it was
not possible to ascribe them to any one month. This explains the difference between the total of
man-days worked by peons as shown in this table and the total obtained by adding the days
worked for a wage of 4 pesos or more during the same period (Table 2.10).
Source: See Table 2.1.

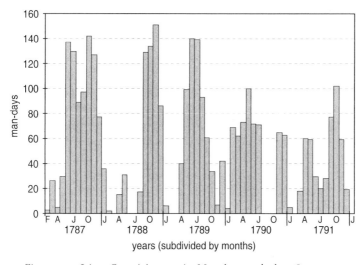

Figure 2.5. López Osornio's estancia: Man-days worked, 1787–1792.

The answer to the question raised earlier is therefore simple: Three
peons did not work all the year round because there were seasonal variations in the demand for labor inherent in the nature of rural work – 2
months spent rounding up and branding cattle at the beginning of fall, 2

months spent sowing between the end of fall and the beginning of winter, another 2 months herding and branding in the spring, 2 months harvesting at the end of spring and beginning of summer, and periods in between when no urgent work needed to be done.[24] Natural factors underlay these strong seasonal fluctuations in the cattle-breeding year: To reduce the risk of infection, branding and gelding were not carried out in the summer, when flies were abundant; and roundups were only possible (or cheaper) when thistles fell in the fall and before they grew again in the spring.[25] Labor instability was therefore due not to the lack of industriousness on the part of the rural labor force or to the existence of a subsistence sector but, as in all pre-industrial rural economies, to seasonal demand.[26]

When a job for which a peon had been hired was completed, his employment was at an end. Peons themselves could not pick and choose between working or not working; they were at the mercy of seasons. Evidence for this is found in the same estancia accounts. If one peon should quit his job and leave work unfinished, another had to be taken on to finish it. In that case, the second peon ought to have started his term of work soon after the previous peon left. But in only two cases between February 1787 and January 1792 could such a changeover have taken place – Mariano Renegado's and Felipe Santiago González's terms of work in August 1787 and Antonio Suárez's and Juan Pedro Ximénez's terms in August 1790 are close enough to assume that the second was hired to finish a job abandoned by the first. These two cases involve four peons and four separate terms of work, representing 8.9% of peons hired and 6.3% of their work terms. In the remaining cases, terms of work overlap or are so far apart as to discount direct substitution of one peon by another. Further proof that the peons were in no hurry to leave their jobs is the fact that in only two cases out of a total of 160 work terms was money stopped from peons' wages for the days they did not go to work: Pedro Céspedes, who worked from 3 October 1787 to 10 January 1788, was paid for 90 days instead of 100, and Francisco Rosales, who worked from 8 November 1790 to 12 January 1791, was paid for 45 days instead of 66. So when there was work to be found, the peons worked.[27]

---

24 Grigera (1819).
25 On the consequences of thistles for cattle raising, see Chapter 6.
26 For a more detailed discussion of "labor instability," see Chapter 8. On labor in pre-industrial economies, see Thomas (1964), 50–62; and Thompson (1967), 59–67. On the concept of time, see Le Goff (1977), 66–79. Unlike García, Juan Alvarez did mention the seasonality of labor demand. His remark is true for the whole sector but not for each particular estancia, where demand was not continuous throughout the peak season. See Alvarez (1984), 70.
27 Only one peon fled from the Riblos estancia between 1727 and 1729, and the rest were dismissed. See Mayo and Fernández (1991).

Peons came back to work for a salary when there was demand for their labor, although not always to the same estancia. It has been pointed out already that 69 peons served for only one term of work on the estancia. Some of them were migrants and after working on the López Osornio estancia might have left the area. Joseph el Cordovés, Francisco el Santiagueño, Joseph el Santiagueño, Pedro Santiagueño, and Francisco Cordovés were, obviously, from Córdoba and Santiago del Estero; Miguel el Paraguay was from Paraguay; and Joseph de Adentro, Sevastián el Indio, and Mariano Renegado were probably pampa Indians.[28]

The 31 peons who worked more than once on the estancia accounted for 91 of the 160 terms of work. Seven peons accounted for 21% of those terms. Ramón Montes de Oca and Juan León Gallo worked six terms; one Salvador, for five (but if he was Salvador Lencinas, also for six); Fernando Aguilar, Francisco Rosales, one Isidoro, and Pedro Santiagueño, for four. Some peons were from established families of the region. Apart from Ramón Montes de Oca, Domingo and Lorenzo Montes de Oca worked for one term each. Francisco and Cipriano Luna worked for two terms each, and Gervasio for one term. There were among those peons also three Ruiz, two Aguilar, two Cabral, two Céspedes, two Coria, two Frías, two Farías, and two Pochy (or Bochi). In one case, one peon, Pedro Alcántara, worked both at the beginning and the end of the period, in 1786 and 1796. When there was demand, peons were ready to work. As there were many estancias in the region and no special ties between employers and peons, estancias hired whoever was available, and peons worked for whoever demanded their work. As demand was seasonal, when one estancia was demanding temporary labor, the others were also doing so. Given those conditions it is remarkable to find some peons coming back to the same estancia.

An analysis of the productivity and daily profit of free labor explains the behavior of labor demand. To estimate the productivity, the expenditure on free labor, and the value of cattle sold in each cycle will be considered. Expenditure on free labor during the first cycle totaled 1,326 pesos, 360 pesos during the second, and 1,201 during the third (Table 2.5). Income from the sale of cattle was 2,713 pesos 6 reales during the first cycle, 932 pesos during the second, and 3,498 pesos 2 reales during the third (Table 2.3). Assuming that income for cattle sold was the exclusive product of free labor, its productivity (income divided by expenditure) was 2.05 pesos during the first cycle, 2.59 pesos during the second, and 2.91 pesos during the third.

---

28 Migration from the Interior provinces to Buenos Aires was not a new development. On the Riblos estancia in the late 1720s, at least 15 out of 25 peons hired in a 3-year period were from other provinces. See Mayo and Fernández (1991).

The number of man-days worked during each cycle allows us to estimate the daily profit of free labor. During the first cycle, 6,076 man-days were worked, 2,205 during the second, and 5,830 during the third – a total of 14,111 man-days for the whole period, with monthly averages of 209.5, 61.2, and 97.2 man-days. The cost of each man-day worked (wages divided by man-days) was 0.22, 0.16, and 0.21 peso for each cycle and 0.20 peso for the whole period. The income per man-day worked (income divided by man-days) was 0.45, 0.42, and 0.60 peso for each cycle and 0.51 peso for the whole period. So the daily profit of free labor (income per man-day less expenditure per man-day) was 0.23 pesos in the first cycle, 0.26 pesos in the second, 0.39 pesos in the third, and 0.31 peso for the whole period.

Finally, the profit per head of cattle can be estimated, considering the number of head of cattle sold – 1,954, 307, and 1,125 head in the first, second, and third cycles. The income per head of cattle (income divided by the number of cattle sold) was 1.39, 3.04, and 3.11 pesos respectively, averaging 2.11 pesos for the whole period. The cost per head (expenditure on wages divided by the number of cattle sold) was 0.68 pesos in the first cycle, 1.17 pesos in the second, 1.07 pesos in the third, and 0.85 pesos for the whole period. In this way, profit per head went from 0.71 pesos in the first cycle, to 1.86 pesos in the second, and 2.04 pesos in the third, while it was 1.26 pesos for the whole period (Table 2.9).[29]

The productivity of free labor grew then 4% from the first to the third cycle, its daily profit grew 7%, and profit per cattle head sold grew 18%. These estimates would show a noticeable increase if non-cashed profit (unsold cattle) were taken into account – all except the cost per man-day, which would not be affected. A comparison of the different consequences arising from the use of free labor between the first and third cycles shows that the average monthly income from cattle sales fell by 37.7% (from 93.6 pesos to 58.3 pesos a month); the average number of man-days worked per month fell by 53.6% (from 209.5 days to 97.2 days a month); the average number of cattle sold per month fell by 72.3% (from 67.4 head to 18.7 head); and the average monthly expenditure on free labor fell by 56.2%

29 Data for these and the following estimates have been taken from Tables 2.3 (cattle), 2.5 (expenditure), and 2.10 (peons). In order to estimate the total number of man-days worked by laborers other than peons in 1785 and 1786, the amounts paid to them were divided by the average amount paid to a peon per day in each year. Consequently, if 135 pesos were paid in 1785 for 600 man-days (Table 2.5), 370 pesos would have been paid for 1,644 days, and if 286 pesos were paid in 1786 for 1,196 man-days, 344 pesos would have been paid for 1,439 days. By adding these figures to the 11,028 man-days worked by peons from August 1785 to December 1795 (Table 2.10), we should have a total of 14,111 man-days worked by all free laborers during this period. The skinner hired in 1791 is excluded from this estimate because he was paid for his job, not for his time of service.

Table 2.9. *López Osornio's estancia:*
Daily profit and productivity from free labor, 1785–1795

	Cattle head sold		Man-days worked		*P*	*G*	*D*
	head	pesos	days	pesos			
	a	b	c	d	b/d	b–d/a	b–d/c
1785–1787	1,954	2,714	6,076	1,326	2.05	0.71	0.23
1788–1790	307	932	2,205	360	2.59	1.86	0.26
1791–1795	1,125	3,498	5,830	1,201	2.91	2.04	0.39
1785–1795	3,386	7,144	14,111	2,887	2.47	1.26	0.30

Note: *P* = productivity; *G* = profit per cattle head sold; *D* = daily profit.
Sources: Tables 2.3 (cattle sold), 2.5 (free workers' wages), and 2.10 (man-days worked).

(from 45.7 pesos to 20 pesos).[30] These figures reveal that much more income, in relation to wages paid to free laborers and the number of man-days worked by them, was being generated during the third cycle than during the first, and that this income came precisely from the sale of a comparatively small number of cattle. The same figures fully account for the revival of the estancia after the owner's death – or, rather, after the liquidation cycle which financed that revival. They also make plain that any contraction or expansion of production had to be matched by a similar contraction or expansion of demand for free labor, although there was no mechanical relationship involved here since management played an important role in the rational use of and demand for free labor and its economic outcome. The analysis of the peons' different wage levels points in the same direction.

Peons' wages fluctuated between 2 pesos and 7 pesos a month (Table 2.10). Peons hired at 7 pesos a month worked 23.8% of the total days worked; peons at 6 pesos a month, 61.4%; those at 5 pesos a month, 6%; those at 4 pesos a month (including some who worked for 4 pesos 4 reales), 1.1%; those at 3 pesos a month, 4.6%; and those at 2 pesos a month, 3.1%. Although the percentage of days worked by peons at 5 pesos a month or less remained steady during the three cycles (11.1%, 19.2%, and 16.7% respectively), there were marked variations among the 6- and 7-peso workers. During the first cycle, peons hired at 7 pesos a month worked 75.7% of total days worked, but during the last two cycles this percentage fell to 4.8% and 7.5%. By contrast, 6-peso wages rose from 13.2% during

30 To estimate monthly averages in this paragraph, the first cycle has been taken into account not for 3 full years (see n. 14) but for the actual 29 months that ran from August 1785 to December 1787. In this way, a distorting element in the pattern of free labor hiring has been avoided.

Table 2.10. *López Osornio's estancia: Man-days worked by peons*
according to monthly wages, August 1785 to June 1796

| | Man-days worked by peons earning | | | | | | | | |
	7 pesos	6 pesos	5 pesos	4 pesos	3 pesos	2 pesos	Man-days	Months	Mean[a]
1785–1786[b]	450	150	–	–	–	–	600	9	66.7
1786–1787[c]	1,069	127	–	–	–	–	1,196	9	132.9
1787[d]	746	117	–	–	–	334	1,197	11	108.8
1788	64	472	–	65	–	31	632	12	52.7
1789	41	620	–	–	–	–	661	12	55.1
1790	–	584	–	–	328	–	912	12	76.0
1791	–	297	180	–	122	–	599	12	49.9
1792	435	216	60	–	–	–	711	12	59.2
1793	–	1,178	75	45	–	–	1,298	12	108.2
1794	–	1,230	240	15	90	–	1,575	12	131.2
1795	–	1,497	150	–	–	–	1,647	12	137.2
1796[e]	–	750	–	–	–	–	750	6	125.0
Total	2,805	7,238	705	125	540	365	11,778	131	89.9
Percentage	23.8	61.4	6.0	1.1	4.6	3.1	100		

[a] Average number of man-days per month worked by all peons in each period.
[b] August 1785–April 1786.
[c] May 1786–January 1787.
[d] February–December 1787
[e] January–June 1796
Source: See Table 2.1.

the first cycle to 76% and 75.8% during the second and third cycles. A closer look at wages in the 2- to 5-peso range reveals that 2-peso wages accounted for 11.1% of total days worked during the first cycle; 3-peso wages, for 14.9% during the second; and 5 peso-wages, for 12.1% during the third (Figure 2.6).

The higher 7-peso wages paid to peons in the first cycle were intended to attract labor at a time when there was a pressing need to put the estancia back in production. This forced the management to hire peons regardless of the pressures of agricultural demand. Two peons were paid 6 pesos for their work in November and 7 pesos during December, "since it was harvest time." The 7-peso wages paid in 1792 were probably due to out-of-season hirings made necessary by the previous year's drought.[31] Lower wages of 4 and 5 pesos were probably paid because of a seasonal oversupply of labor or else were paid for specific out-of-season work. Wages of only 2 pesos were paid for wintering cattle, and the 3-peso wage went to a certain

31 Ardissone (1937), 170–175.

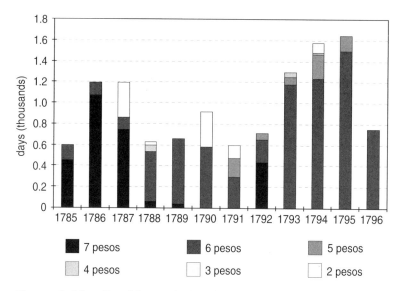

Figure 2.6. López Osornio's estancia: Man-days worked according to wages paid to peons, 1785–1796. *Source*: Table 2.10.

Josef el Muchacho, who worked continuously on the estancia for a whole year, the longest period worked by any one peon.

There is no evidence that López Osornio's estancia paid its wages in anything other than hard cash. Since peons were probably provided with meals, it could be said that they received part of their wages in kind. However, we have discovered no cases of payment in clothes or any other goods.[32] Clothing was bought only for the slaves, the estancia accounts even mentioning the names of the slaves to whom clothes were given. Sheepskins and wool may have been used to pay for services and goods, but as the accounts did not record such payments in kind, this can be only a matter of speculation.

Debts – between a peon and the landowner or vice versa – were not adopted as a compulsory method of retaining free labor. The estancia accounts show two cases of wages having been paid in advance (a third advance payment was made to one of the foremen) and only one case of delayed payment of wages. In May 1787 Mariano Ortega and Jerónimo

32 Peons working on the Riblos estancia in the 1720s were paid partially in kind. The proportion of cash payments was greater there than on a Jesuit estancia in Córdoba in later decades. See Mayo and Fernández (1991).

Leguisamo were paid advances of 6 and 7 pesos each for the following
month, and on 5 October 1792, Ramón Montes de Oca was paid 12 pesos,
which the estancia owed him for breaking in horses and for "some other
jobs."[33]

Peons on the López Osornio estancia were hired seasonally and sometimes for piece work. They were not bound to the estancia by debts, and
their salaries were paid in cash. As the estancia activities were regularized,
peons tended to be hired for lower salaries, a sign that demand tended to
adjust to supply conditions when possible. Due to climatic or other reasons, adjustment was sometimes not possible, therefore higher salaries
were paid. Peons did not abandon their jobs. Rather, they were terminated
by the employer's decision. Few peons came back to work on the estancia
year after year, but as there were many estancias in the region demanding
free temporary labor at the same time, that fact is hardly surprising.
Although pertaining to the realm of management rather than to that of
labor, during the third cycle, a higher income was obtained from labor.
Peons remained on the estancia for short spans. Only on a few occasions
were some hired for longer-than-season periods. But slaves were on the
estancia year-round.

Why were slaves on the estancia on a permanent basis and peons not
employed during the seasonal troughs of low labor demand? Why did
slaves not completely take the place of peons at periods of high seasonal
demand? The various advantages of employing free or forced labor are
understood if we compare their present value, productivity, and daily
profit.

There were five slaves on López Osornio's estancia in 1786; one of them
was sold in 1787, and another died in 1793. Three slaves were listed in the
1795 inventory, although a fourth (who usually worked as a shoemaker in
town) was also employed on the estancia. The inventory value of a normal,
healthy slave was 300 pesos, and he could be expected to give service for at
least 20 years, perhaps more.[34] Each slave cost the owner 14 pesos a year for
living expenses: 4 pesos 6 reales for clothing, 2 pesos 3 reales for food, 3
reales for health care, and 6 pesos 4 reales for the weekly allowance given

---

33 On the coercion of free labor, see Bauer (1979), 53–58; and Knight (1986). On reversed debt
peonage, see, for example, Brading (1978), 112; and Van Young (1981), 249. Another study of
peons' salaries on the Buenos Aires estancias for an earlier period confirms that debts were not used
to retain labor. See Mayo and Fernández (1991).

34 The average age of 16 slaves included in José Januario Fernández's estate was 42.5 years.
Twelve of these slaves were adult men, with an average age of 48.7 years. Assuming that they
were bought at the age of 15 years, this would mean an average service of 33.7 years per slave.
Four slaves were over 60 years old and still had inventory values of between 50 and 110 pesos
(AGN, Tribunales, Sucesiones, 5873). From this evidence, 20 years' average service does not seem
too long.

to each slave "for soap and tobacco."[35] In order to estimate a slave's present value, we should add to his cost, or inventory value, a sum which, invested at 6% annual interest, would pay for his living expenses over 20 years.[36] This sum amounted to 170 pesos 2 reales; thus the slave's present value was 470 pesos 2 reales. Comparing this with a peon's present value helps us to understand why both types of labor were used on the estancia.

To calculate a peon's present value, his annual average wage should be estimated. Since demand for cattle-ranching labor and demand for agricultural labor were to a certain degree complementary, with overlapping at harvest time (the end of spring and beginning of summer) and at crop-planting time (the end of fall and the beginning of winter), a peon's annual average wage can be estimated at 50 pesos – 2 months at a rate of 7 pesos (when the two types of work overlapped), 6 months at 6 pesos (2 months working on the land and 4 with cattle), and 4 months without wages when there was no demand for labor from either sector. In this case a peon's present value would have been equivalent to 608 pesos (the total needed to pay wages of 50 pesos over the same 20 years) plus 54 pesos 6 reales for food (at 4 pesos 4 reales per year) during the same period.[37] The peon's present value was therefore 662 pesos 6 reales.

A comparison of both present values shows that by the tenth year, a peon's present value exceeded a slave's (425.19 pesos for the former, 409.22 pesos for the latter), while the figures for the ninth year are 360.49 and 400.93 pesos, respectively. Over a 20-year period, a slave's present value amounted to 71% of a peon's. Given that 10 or more years of service were expected from a slave, it was therefore more convenient for the landowner to employ forced labor for permanent jobs. Employing free labor in the long run would have been viable only if a peon's present value had been lower than a slave's. This would have been possible if a peon had been on a yearly wage of 38 pesos 5 reales or, after deducting 4 pesos 4 reales for food, 34 pesos 1 real. As a result, the last figure could have been used in two ways: (1) to hire a peon on a monthly wage of 6 pesos for 5

35 The annual average expense on each slave's food has been calculated by dividing total expenditure on food (Table 2.5) by the number of years, and this figure divided by the average number of people on the estancia (1 foreman, 3.7 slaves, and 3 peons). Likewise, the average annual expenditure on a slave's clothes has been calculated by dividing total expenditures on this item by the number of years and then by the annual average number of slaves (3.7). The same method has been used to calculate expenditure on health care (from a total of 15 pesos 2 reales, included in "Others" in Table 2.5). The annual expenditure on a slave's allowance for "soap and tobacco" is based on weekly expenses of 1 real per slave, the actual amount given to each one starting in 1787.
36 To estimate the present value, a fixed rate equivalent to the usual interest rate (6%) has been substituted for the income expected from a slave or a peon in order to reduce uncertainty, because interest rates were much more stable than future incomes. It has also been assumed that that rate was the opportunity cost of capital invested in a slave. See Appendix A.
37 A peon's food expenses have been estimated in the same way as a slave's. See n. 35.

months 21 days; (2) to hire a peon on a monthly wage of 2 pesos 7 reales for a whole year's work. Three peons were hired for periods exceeding the normal seasonal demand (they represented 3% of all peons employed at the estancia and 6% of all days worked), and these, by coincidence, were paid wages of 2 and 3 pesos a month.[38] Comparing peons' and slaves' present values partly conceals the risks of free and forced labor as investments. Although both types of labor were substitutive, they were not wholly so. When a slave fell ill or died, further expenditure was necessary to get someone to cover for him, whereas when a peon fell ill or died, a replacement could be found without paying more than his wages. Even though we took the risk factor into account when choosing a 20-year average amortization period, this average would have seemed negligible to a landowner deciding whether or not to buy a new slave, particularly if he owned only a few slaves: The new slave could die prematurely, and so could other new slaves bought as replacements. This dilemma could be avoided by adjusting a slave's amortization period so as to eliminate that risk, but the estimate of present values does not seem an appropriate method to apply to the 1780s, not so much for the lengthy calculations required as for the particular concept of capital involved in it. We shall therefore use a different method of calculation, probably less accurate but also less anachronistic, proceeding as follows: If the slave owner faced with the option of employing either free or forced labor chose not to buy a slave, he could invest the 300 pesos instead and earn 18 pesos at 6% annual interest. At the same time, he saved 14 pesos on the slave's living expenses. The resulting total of 32 pesos was enough to pay a peon's wages (at 6 pesos a month) and food (at 3 reales a month) for 5 months. But then, of course, the slave owner could not have afforded to hire him for the remaining 7 months of the year. Even assuming that labor costs were nil for 4 months of the year, there would still have been no funds left to take on peons during the other 3 months. But as long as there were some permanent jobs to be seen to on the estancia (running the atahona, repairing and maintaining equipment, looking after sheep), it was in the owner's interest to buy slaves to do those jobs.

The foregoing calculations have sought to justify the use of slaves on the estancia, but the presence of peons has yet to be explained. To do this we need to compare the productivity of slaves and peons and the daily profit derived from each during the normal-operation period (1791–1795). In order to estimate productivity (income divided by expenditure), peons are awarded 3,498 pesos 2 reales for the value of cattle sold, and slaves 1,067 pesos for the other income (atahona, hides, horses, and sheep). This alloca-

---

38 These peons on 2- and 3-peso monthly wages have been excluded from Table 2.8 and Figure 2.2 because their present value was similar to a slave's. See n. 23.

tion of income may not fully account for the income actually produced by peons and slaves, since there were peons performing tasks not directly related to cattle raising, and slaves performing tasks directly related to it. It has been assumed that income produced in these ways cancels each other. A better specification of this assumption may, naturally, vary the outcome of the estimates that follow.

As peons cost the owner 1,214 pesos (their wages) and slaves 448 pesos 4 reales (200 pesos 7 reales for living expenses and 247 pesos 4 reales for amortization), their average productivity during the normal cycle was 2.88 pesos for peons and 2.34 pesos for slaves, compared with average total productivity of 2.75 pesos (Tables 2.11, 2.12, and 2.13).[39] Since peons' and slaves' labor was quasi-substitutive, their productivity levels should logically tend to cancel each other out. The fact that slaves' and peons' productivity levels are similar but not equal to total productivity reveals a certain inelasticity in the substitution arising from the cost involved in getting rid of a slave when his productivity began to fall with respect to the peons', and in buying other slaves when the peons' own productivity fell.

The daily profit (income less expenditure divided by time worked) derived from a peon's and a slave's labor was 0.39 and 0.10 peso, respectively, as against an average total daily profit of 0.24 peso. Peons' and slaves' productivity and daily profit figures show wide fluctuations from one year to the next during the normal cycle (Tables 2.11 and 2.12). Nevertheless, there was a less significant dispersion of each year's combined (peons' plus slaves') daily profit and productivity figures with respect to the average (Table 2.13). Daily profit figures highlight the very different uses to which free and forced labor were put – the first seasonal, the second permanent – but the slight dispersion on either side of the average total daily profit and productivity marks shows that the two types of labor were more complementary than substitutive.[40]

In order to compare the peons' and slaves' productivity and daily profit, these estimates have ignored (as warned in Table 2.11) non-cashed income,

---

39 The figure for amortization was obtained by multiplying the number of slaves on the estancia in 1791–1795 by 1/20 of the value of each slave for each year (see Table 2.12).

40 This chapter reproduces with only minor changes an article published in 1987 [see Amaral (1987a)], which has already attracted some criticism. Mayo [(1995), 136–137] dismisses my estimate of labor productivity and daily profit on two grounds. First, he questions my method because its complexity, he argues, could not have been understood by illiterate estancieros. This candid view implies that historians should stick to methods used at the time they study. If accepted, it would mean the rejection of all modern historians' writings, including his. Second, he argues that my estimate does not take into account that peons' and slaves' jobs overlapped. But because of that very reason, my estimate assumed an equal distribution of non-cashed income between peons and slaves. Mayo's criticism is unfortunately fruitless, since he fails to offer any analytical alternative to my estimate.

Table 2.11. *López Osornio's estancia:*
Productivity and daily profit from peons, 1791–1795

	T_p	I_p	E_p	R_p	D_p	P_p
1792	711	483	168	315	0.44	2.88
1793	1,298	795	256	539	0.42	3.11
1794	1,575	674	301	373	0.24	2.24
1795	1,647	800	334	466	0.28	2.40
Total	5,830	3,498	1,214	2,284	0.39	2.88

Notes: T_p = days worked by peons; I_p = income (cattle sales); E_p = expenditure: peons' wages (Table 2.5), plus peons' food expenses (A_p) estimated as

$$A_p = \frac{A\ T_p}{T}$$

where A = total food expenses, and T = total days worked by peons and slaves ($T_p + T_s$); R_p = profit generated by peons ($I_p - E_p$); D_p = daily profit from peons (R_p/T_p); P_p = productivity of peons (I_p/E_p).
Non-cashed profit has not been taken into account in either this table or Tables 2.12 and 2.13, assuming it was homogeneously distributed among peons and slaves.
Source: See Table 2.1.

Table 2.12. *López Osornio's estancia:*
Productivity and daily profit from slaves, 1791–1795

	T_s	I_s	E_s	R_s	D_s	P_s
1791	1,460	116	113	3	0.002	1.03
1792	1,464	439	87	352	0.24	5.05
1793	1,185	194	104	90	0.08	1.87
1794	1,095	167	67	100	0.09	2.49
1795	1,095	150	77	73	0.07	1.95
Total	6,299	1,067	448	618	0.10	2.38

Note: T_s = days worked by slaves; I_s = income (other than cattle sales); E_s = expenditure: allowances for soap and tobacco, plus clothing, plus amortization equivalent to one-twentieth of the average value of slaves estimated at 275 pesos for 1791 and 1792, and 300 pesos for the other years), plus slaves' food expenses (A_s) estimated as

$$A_s = \frac{A\ T_s}{T}$$

where A = total food expenses, and T = total days worked by peons and slaves ($T_p + T_s$); R_s = profit generated by slaves ($I_s - E_s$); D_s = daily profit from slaves (R_s/t_s); P_s = productivity of slaves (I_s/E_s).
Source: See Table 2.1.

Table 2.13. *López Osornio's estancia:*
Productivity and daily profit from peons and slaves, 1791–1795

	T	I	E	R	D	P
1791	2,059	861	268	593	0.29	3.21
1792	2,175	922	255	667	0.31	3.62
1793	2,483	989	360	629	0.25	2.75
1794	2,670	842	368	474	0.18	2.29
1795	2,742	951	411	540	0.20	2.31
Total	12,129	4,565	1,662	2,903	0.24	2.75

Note: T = total days worked by peons and slaves (T_p+T_s); I = total income (I_p+I_s); E = total expenditure (E_p+E_s); R = profit generated by peons and slaves $(I-E)$; D = daily profit generated by peons and slaves (R/T); P = productivity of peons and slaves (I/E).
Sources: Tables 2.11 and 2.12.

assuming it was equally distributed between peons and slaves. If non-cashed income (from Table 2.6) is distributed according to the number of days worked by peons and slaves (Tables 2.11 and 2.12) and then added to the income figures, the peons' daily profit for the 1791–1795 period would rise from 0.39 peso to 0.65 peso, and the slaves' from 0.10 peso to 0.31 peso. The peons's productivity, in turn, rises from 2.88 pesos to 4.11 pesos, and the slaves' from 2.38 pesos to 5.38 pesos. These figures, however, suffer from a distortion introduced by considering a peon's day work equivalent to a slave's. That was not always the case, since temporarily unfit peons were dismissed, while slaves were retained. In spite of this, it remains clear that the advantage of using slaves for permanent jobs was their higher long-term productivity, whereas the advantage of employing peons was their higher daily profit.

Conclusion

Production geared toward overseas markets, limited production for home consumption and, as a result of its specialization in market produce, the inability to respond to changing circumstances (drought, flood, the death of the owner) except by cutting down production are, according to Halperín Donghi, the three characteristic features of the Buenos Aires estancia in the late colonial period.[41] The López Osornio estancia partially proves the first point, given that it produced live cattle for the urban

41 Halperín Donghi (1975), 462–463.

market rather than hides or mules for export. With respect to the second characteristic, production for the estancia's own consumption was restricted to foodstuffs (all except salt, yerba mate, and peppers), whereas the other requirements (clothing, wood, and metal goods) were supplied from the market. Regarding the third feature, the options to overcome climatic, political, legal, or economic difficulties were to reduce or expand cattle sales. Money borrowing was restricted by a primitively organized credit market, where only religious institutions could provide a limited amount of long-term loans, and a few merchants could provide even smaller amounts of short-term funds. Therefore, the financial requirements of estancia production were met by cutting down on cattle stocks and, consequently, by employing more free labor. The López Osornio estancia did not resort to any outside source for credit to meet legal expenses and restore the conditions of production; it raised the extra funds by selling off low-quality head, incurring at the same time higher labor expenses.

The coexistence of forced and free labor and the instability of the latter were due to the advantages of investing in slaves to meet labor requirements during seasonal periods of low demand, while using peons to meet additional requirements during periods of high demand. The supply of free labor was steady, but demand was dictated by the seasons.

Profit, cattle-extraction, and capitalization rates on the López Osornio estancia underscore its rationality as a business concern. During the normal-operation years, the estancia made an annual profit higher than the annual interest rate usually paid on loans, and the cattle-extraction rate was kept well below the cattle-reproduction rate. Cattle were raised on open fields using very primitive methods, but the sound economic result of that activity belies the image of slack production methods depicted by foreign travelers and local observers. The result was not a necessary outcome of the workings of nature, but due to skillful entrepreneurship. Cecilio Sánchez de Velasco, the executor of the López Osornio estate, was the entrepreneur obtaining those results.

The actual operations of an estancia have been studied in this chapter. Income and expenditure accounts have been analyzed to understand the evolution of that enterprise, what goods it was producing, and how it was producing them. No similar accounts have been found for later periods. Consequently, the evolution of estancias as a type of economic organization during the first half of the nineteenth century, studied in Chapters 3 and 4, is based on a different source – estancia inventories.

3

Capital structure

Haciendas in northern Mexico, the Orinoco llanos, and central Chile, fazendas in the Brazilian sertão, and British and Dutch farms, all were rural establishments devoted to cattle raising. Their purpose was similar, but the ways of achieving it were not. The production of any good requires a particular use of capital, which may be combined in varied ways for different types of rural establishments. The estancias of Buenos Aires raised cattle on open, endless plains to provide beef for urban consumers, and hides, tallow, and jerked beef for export. Land, cattle, other livestock, improvements, and tools were required by all estancias but not to the same extent. Estancias used those items in a particular way, and such use evolved over time.

The evolution of the capital structure of the estancias of Buenos Aires can be traced by studying probate inventories. They were carried out after someone's death in order to determine how much the estate was worth before splitting it among the heirs. Probate inventories have been used by other scholars for different purposes since a few decades ago. Alice Hanson Jones used them for her massive studies of personal wealth in late colonial America, and European scholars mainly for the study of the material culture.[1] Other scholars, however, moved along a similar path: Jan de Vries studied farm operations in the Low Countries in the sixteenth and seventeenth centuries; and David Brading studied the capital structure of the late colonial Mexican haciendas.[2] This literature has inspired several recent studies of the Buenos Aires estancias. Mayo studied the estancieros' wealth in the late colonial period; Mayo and Fernández described "the anatomy" of the Buenos Aires estancias in the same period; and Garavaglia focused

---

1 Jones (1969), (1977), and (1980). For Europe, Van der Woude and Schuurman (1980); and Baulant, Schuurman, and Servais (1988). Seventeen papers were published in the first volume and 23 in the second, but only one of those 40 papers [Duplessis (1988)] deals with patterns of investment. Jones (1982) mentions many possible scholarly uses for probate inventories, but the study of the capital structure of rural establishments was not listed among them.
2 De Vries (1974), Brading (1975).

upon the estancias of four districts also in the late colonial period.[3] Sabato
used probate inventories in her study of the sheep-breeding estancias
during the period 1850–1880, as did Adelman, in his comparative study
of frontier development in Canadian prairies and the Argentine pampas in
the late nineteenth century.[4]

Probate inventories have advantages and limitations as a source of
information. All items belonging to a deceased person should be recorded
right after his or her death, but it is not possible to ascertain how precise
was such a record. Peter H. Lindert warned about the methodological
problems of probate sampling: the dispersion of evidence and the extra-
legal distribution of wealth.[5] The former is not relevant to Buenos Aires in
the first half of the nineteenth century, since there was no other court in the
province. The latter, the decedent's nakedness, as Lindert calls the extra-
legal distribution of wealth, cannot be neutralized. The underreport of
debts and personal belongings does not apply because they have not been
taken into account as part of the capital structure of estancias, but cattle are
movable. One or more heirs could have removed cattle from the estancia
before the inventory was recorded, not necessarily to steal from the estate
but to meet legal expenses. Land is another missing item to which Lindert
alerts us. Land was not always registered in Britain and America because
of fixed rules for the inheritance of real estate, according to common
law. Legal traditions were different in Argentina, where land could be
underrecorded because in those years of territorial expansion, title deeds
claimed by estancia owners might be still pending when the inventory
was recorded.[6] Probate inventories, however, in spite of their shortcom-
ings, are a unique source for the study of personal wealth, material culture,
and the capital structure of rural establishments.

The evolution of the capital structure of the Buenos Aires estancias is
studied here using two samples of probate inventories: one for 1818–1822,
and another for 1848–1851.[7] The first section of this chapter studies the
capital structure of the Buenos Aires estancias around 1820; the second
section does the same for 1850; and the third section compares the

---

3 Mayo (1991a); Mayo and Fernández (1993); and Garavaglia (1993).
4 Sabato (1989), 130–182; Adelman (1994), 276–284.
5 Lindert (1981).
6 Clemente López Osornio held only one tract in property, located in Magdalena. Two other tracts, as
   pointed out in Chapter 2, were claimed and used by him, but title deeds for them were obtained by
   his daughter and son many years after his death.
7 In this chapter, as in Chapters 2 and 4, capital has not been divided into fixed and working capital.
   It has already been pointed out that there are two main reasons for doing so. First, tools and
   equipment (part of the working capital) do not account for a significant share of total capital. And
   second, the way cattle were managed allows us to consider them fixed. For methodological problems
   concerning the analysis of probate inventories, see Appendix B.

estancias of 1820 to those of 1850 in order to underscore the changes affecting their capital structure. The analysis of the evolution of the capital structure of the estancias along that period offers a different approach to the interpretation of the process of territorial expansion and production growth.[8]

Capital structure, 1820

In 1820 and 1850, there were inventories that recorded the land and others that did not. Those cases in which land was recorded are called here *estancias on owned land,* since land was expressly mentioned as part of the estate. Those cases in which land was not recorded are called *estancias on non-owned land.* Why land was not recorded in these cases is a matter of speculation. Title deeds were probably pending, as mentioned earlier, or they might never have been applied for. Whatever the case, there were improvements, livestock, and even slaves on those estancias, and there was an inventory recorded in order to split the estate. Estancias on owned land and estancias on non-owned land were different, so their characteristics are described separately.

The average value of estancias on owned land in 1820 is 9,231 pesos. Cattle account for 66% of that figure; land, 11%; improvements, 7%; tools, 2%; other goods, 1%; horses, 3%; sheep, 4%; slaves, 5%; and other items, 1% (Table 3.1, Figure 3.1). The average value of estancias and the proportion corresponding to each category vary from region to region. The average value for estancias located in the South is 19,579 pesos; for the North, 10,803 pesos; for the Center, 4,535 pesos; and for the Frontier, 3,425 pesos.[9] Land accounts for 10% of total value in the North, 11% in the Center, 13% in the South, and 7% on the Frontier. Improvements account for 12% in the Center, 19% on the Frontier, 4% in the North, and

---

8 Two recent studies of the capital structure of Buenos Aires estancias in the late colonial period do not account for change. Mayo and Fernández (1993) study a sample of 66 inventories from all districts from 1750 to 1810, without differentiating either periods or regions. Garavaglia (1993) studies 281 inventories of four districts (Arrecifes, Luján, Areco, and Magdalena) from the 1750s to 1815, paying attention only to changes in the composition of livestock by regions. As the process of expansion of cattle production accelerated in the last decades of the eighteenth century, the 1750 estancias were probably different from those of 1810. There might have been differences regarding ownership, because land claims apparently increased during that period, and regarding size, because new claims were larger than the old estancias. Although valuable, these contributions miss the changes introduced by that process into the economic organization of estancias. For changes in land ownership and estancia size, see Banzato and Quinteros (1992), and Azcuy Ameghino (1994), though the latter only indirectly addresses these issues. For changes related to markets for livestock by-products and their prices, see Garavaglia (1994) and (1995a). For changes on three estancias, see Garavaglia (1995c).

9 Regions are defined in Appendix B.

Table 3.1. *Capital structure of 33 estancias on owned land, 1818–1822*

	North (11)		Center (14)		South (6)		Frontier (2)		Total (33)	
	X	%	*X*	%	*X*	%	*X*	%	*X*	%
Land	1,072	9.9	499	11.0	2,505	12.8	177	7.4	1,035	11.2
Improv.	419	3.9	540	11.9	1,306	6.7	455	18.9	634	6.9
Tools	157	1.5	199	4.4	208	1.1	195	8.1	187	2.0
Cattle	7,853	72.7	2,221	49.0	13,727	70.1	1,197	49.8	6,129	66.4
Horses	207	1.9	191	4.2	512	2.6	44	1.8	246	2.7
Sheep	315	2.9	412	9.1	645	3.3	32	1.3	399	4.3
Slaves	679	6.3	356	7.9	413	2.1	225	9.4	466	5.0
Other	19	0.2	68	1.5	71	0.4	80	3.3	136	1.5
Total	10,803	100.0	4,535	100.0	19,579	100.0	2,403	100.0	9,231	100.0

Notes: improv. = improvements; *X* = average in pesos of 8 reales.
Source: Table B.1.

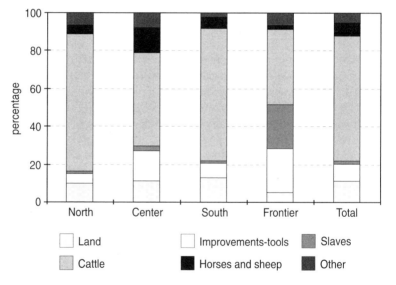

Figure 3.1. Capital structure: Estancias on owned land, 1820.

7% in the South. Tools include both working tools (such as carts, shovels, hoes, sifters, etc.) and all other types of instruments and utensils (buckets, cutlery, pans, pots, etc.) related to production. They account for 8% on the Frontier, 1% in the North and South, and 4% in the Center. Cattle value ranges from 49% on the Center and 50% on the Frontier to 70% in the South and 73% in the North. Sheep account for 1% on the Frontier, 3%

in the North and South, and 9% in the Center. Horses account for 2% in the North, 3% in the South and the Frontier, and 4% in the Center. Slaves account for 2% of total value in the South, 5% on the Frontier, 6% in the North, and 8% in the Center. There were, however, more slaves on estancias located in the North, but they represented a lower percentage of total value. And there was only one-third of that number of slaves on the Frontier, but they represented a similar proportion of total value.

Estancias located in the South were worth almost twice that of those in the North, four times more than in the Center, and about six times more than on the Frontier. They held larger herds of cattle and more horses and sheep, and improvements were more valuable than those of other regions. There were fewer slaves than in the North, but tools and other goods were similar to those of other regions.

The average size of an estancia was 3,278 hectares (Table 3.2, Figure 3.2). That average varies for the different regions: 1,372 hectares for the Center; 2,616 hectares for the North; 7,448 hectares for the South; and 7,763 hectares for the Frontier. The average investment per hectare in land (land price), livestock, and other items can be estimated using those figures and the average value for land, livestock, and other categories. The average value of land per hectare (total land value divided by total size of all estancias) is 0.32 pesos for all regions, 0.41 pesos for the North, 0.36 pesos for the Center, 0.34 pesos for the South, and 0.02 pesos for the Frontier. The average investment in livestock per hectare (total value of livestock divided by the total size of all estancias) is 2.07 pesos for all regions; 3.20 pesos for the North; 2.06 pesos for the Center; 2.00 pesos for the South; and 0.16 pesos for the Frontier. The average investment per hectare in other items (total value of improvements, tools, slaves, and other goods divided by the size of all estancias) is 0.43 pesos for all regions; 0.52 pesos for the North; 0.88 pesos for the Center; 0.29 pesos for the South; and 0.12 pesos for the Frontier.

These figures underscore the differences between the older regions and the Frontier, but they also reveal some differences among those regions. There was a higher investment per hectare in the North than in the Center and South. The average investment in land is similar for those three regions, but the difference is accounted for by a higher investment in livestock per hectare. There is therefore a sequence of territorial stabilization uncovered by these figures, going from the North, with a higher investment in livestock per hectare, to the Center, with a higher investment in improvements per hectare, to the South; much further behind according to the level of investment was the Frontier.

The average value for estancias on non-owned land is 2,775 pesos (Table 3.3, Figure 3.3). The highest regional average value is that of the South (3,761 pesos), but differences with the other regions are less marked

Table 3.2. *Investment per hectare: 33 estancias on owned land,*
1818–1822

Average	North	Center	South	Frontier	Total
Size (hectares)	2,616	1,372	7,448	7,763	3,278
Land value (pesos)	0.41	0.36	0.34	0.02	0.32
Livestock value (pesos)	3.20	2.06	2.00	0.16	2.07
Other items (pesos)	0.52	0.88	0.29	0.12	0.43
Total (pesos)	4.14	3.31	2.63	0.31	2.82

Note: Other items = improvements, tools, slaves, and other goods.
Sources: Tables 3.1 and B.1.

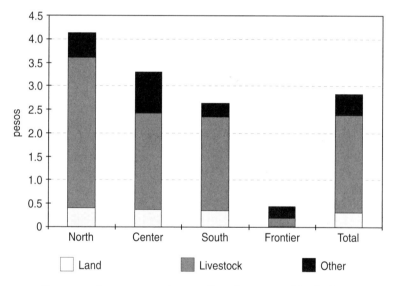

Figure 3.2. Investment per hectare: Estancias on owned land, 1820.

(except for the Frontier) than in the case of estancias on owned land. The average value for estancias in the South is 36% above the total average; in the North, 10% below; in the Center, 1% below; on the Frontier, only 51% of the average total value.

Improvements account for 6% of the average total value, tools for 4%, other goods for 2%, agricultural goods for 1%, and slaves for 6%. The main category is again cattle, accounting for 68% of total value. As horses account for 5% and sheep for 8%, all livestock account for 81% of the

Table 3.3. *Capital structure of 33 estancias on non-owned land, 1818–1822*

	North (9)		Center (14)		South (7)		Frontier (3)		Total (33)	
	X	%	*X*	%	*X*	%	*X*	%	*X*	%
Improv.	191	7.6	112	4.1	316	8.4	55	3.9	172	6.2
Tools	117	4.7	121	4.4	92	2.4	72	5.1	109	3.9
Cattle	1,611	64.0	1,871	68.3	2,541	67.6	1,194	84.6	1,881	67.8
Horses	240	9.5	111	4.0	159	4.2	49	3.5	151	5.4
Sheep	171	6.8	235	8.6	382	10.2	32	2.3	230	8.3
Slaves	128	5.1	179	6.5	226	6.0	0	0.0	159	5.7
Other	57	2.3	112	4.1	46	1.2	9	0.6	74	2.6
Total	2,516	100.0	2,741	100.0	3,761	100.0	1,411	100.0	2,775	100.0

Notes: improv. = improvements; *X* = average in pesos of 8 reales.
Source: Table B.2.

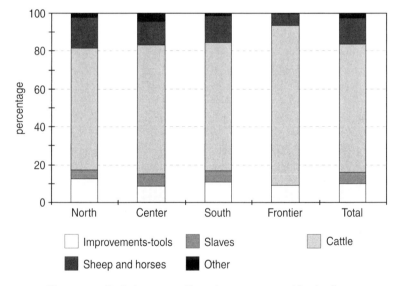

Figure 3.3. Capital structure: Estancias on non-owned land, 1820.

average total value. Regional variations are again less marked than for estancias on owned land. The most salient regional differences are those for improvements, which account for 8% in the North and South, and 4% in the Center and on the Frontier. There are no slaves on the Frontier estancias, and the figures for the other regions are quite similar (5% and 6%) but do not represent in any case more than the usual price of an adult slave. Agricultural goods account for 1% or less in all regions, and other goods are also 1% or less in all regions except the Center, where they account for 3% of the average value for that region. The Frontier differs from the other regions with a low figure for sheep, 2%, whereas it was 7% to 10% in the other regions.

Figures for the Center are similar to those of the North and South, but that similarity conceals a subregion different from the rest of the Center and from all other regions. Three out of 14 estancias located in the Center were in the outskirts of Buenos Aires (OBA), in San Isidro, Morón, and Las Conchas, less than 20 miles west or northwest of the city.[10] Those three estancias differ from the other estancias in the same region mainly regarding cattle, sheep, slaves, and other goods. Cattle account for 23% on those estancias, but for 78% in the region; sheep for 31% and 4%; slaves for 12% and 6%; and other goods for 15% and 1%. Whereas other estancias on non-owned land located in the Center, further away from the city, were similar to estancias on non-owned land in the North and South, the OBA estancias held less cattle, more sheep, and more slaves.[11]

A comparison of the capital structure of estancias on owned and non-owned land shows that some categories have similar figures as proportion of average total value, which is the case with improvements, agricultural goods, and slaves. The proportion of cattle, horses, and sheep over average total value is slightly higher for the latter, but all livestock account for 9 percentage points more. That difference disappears if estancias on non-owned land are given an equal proportion for land to that of the estancias on owned land. The proportion for all livestock is then similar in both cases. There is a higher proportion of cattle and a lower proportion of horses and sheep in the latter case, but cattle remain as the main item, with a value eight to twelve times higher than sheep and horses.

The average for all 66 estancias, on owned and non-owned land, shows that land accounts for 9% of the average total value, improvements for 7%, tools for 3%, other goods for 1%, cattle for 67%, horses for 3%, sheep for 5%, agricultural goods for 1%, and slaves for 5%. For this estimate the total area of the 33 estancias on owned land was divided by the total number of estancias. If land is estimated for all estancias at 11% of total value, the proportion for the other categories do not fall more than 0.2 percentage points, except for cattle, which falls 1.9 percentage points.

When all 66 estancias are distributed according to region, the average value for those in the South is still the highest at 11,062 pesos, followed by

---

10 Table B.2, numbers 25, 26, and 30.
11 There were other goods as well, but the difference in this case is due to a number of bricks on one of the estancias. It cannot be determined whether they were made on it or had been bought for a building.

the North at 7,074 pesos, the Center at 3,638 pesos, and the Frontier at 2,217 pesos. Land ranges from 3% of total value on the Frontier to 11% in the South, while it accounts for 8% in the North and 7% in the Center. Cattle range from 56% and 57% in the Center and on the Frontier to 70% in the South and 71% in the North. The highest averages for improvements, tools, and agricultural goods are those of the Frontier, but the reason (a chacra on one estancia there) has already been pointed out. The Center has the next highest average for improvements and the highest averages for sheep and slaves.

Although some regional differences emerge from this analysis, the overwhelming presence of cattle dims all other items of the capital structure. There was cereal agriculture in all regions, as well as sheep breeding and horse and mule rearing. Although no pattern is discernible regarding horses and mules, agriculture and sheep tended to be more common in the Center, where estancias were also smaller than those of the North and much smaller than those of the South. The Frontier was still on the Salado River. Estancias in that region were much larger than those in other regions (with the exception of the South) and also, as shown by a capital structure where land and cattle accounted for a much lower average than those of other regions, their settlement was still recent and precarious.

The study of the capital structure of the Buenos Aires estancias around 1820 carried out in this section has shown the existence of different types of estancias, with a different capital structure according to region and size. Although cattle ranching was their main concern, head were raised with more or less slaves, on a larger or smaller tract of land, with ownership rights already defined by a title deed or still unclear, and in combination with sheep and horses and, to a lesser extent, with some agriculture, dairy, and carting. Cattle head were of different age and used for different purposes, and they were spread over the different regions according to different stocking rates. The value of estancias was directly related to the number of cattle head, by far the most important item of the capital structure of all estancias, regardless of their size, value, or location. The location of those estancias was still the old pampa, a territory occupied before the 1780s, or between that decade and the 1810s. There were a few estancias on the Salado River but none beyond it. Dolores, located 30 miles south of the Salado, was founded in 1817 and surely had some estancias around it. But the fact that they are absent from this sample is a proof of the still precarious occupation of such territory.

That landscape changed during the next thirty years. New land beyond the Salado River was put into production, from Ajó, Tuyú, and Pila to Azul and Lobería. That expansion was also accompanied by changes in the capital structure of the Buenos Aires estancias. Cattle did not relinquish their hegemonic role on the pampas, but sheep started to compete for land in some regions. And in all regions, as the next section shows, a new combination of factors was apparent.

Capital structure, 1850

From 1820 to 1850, Buenos Aires underwent many changes: Population grew, exports increased, and territorial control expanded. These changes were in fact the expression of one major development affecting the Buenos Aires economy. The overseas markets for its agricultural goods, which had emerged at the end of the eighteenth century but mainly after the severance of colonial ties, were more bullish than ever. Buenos Aires benefited in many ways from such opportunity that allowed her few goods to reach distant markets, bringing back home a prosperity that even protracted civil wars and arbitrary rule failed to ruin.

In those 30 years, the Buenos Aires population grew from 55,000 to 90,000 inhabitants in the city, and from 60,000 to 180,000 inhabitants in the countryside. Hide exports, still the main item of a somewhat more diversified basket, doubled or tripled, and tallow, jerked beef, and wool were growing at an even faster pace. Flocks had been refined and multiplied, displacing cattle to the south. Finally, the area producing goods exported through the Buenos Aires port more than doubled. The Salado River, still the southern boundary in 1820, had been crossed. Herds of cattle rather than armies (there were military campaigns in the 1820s and 1830s) led that process of territorial expansion.

These changes affected the combination of factors in rural production. This section studies the capital structure of the Buenos Aires estancias around 1850. It provides information about the transformation undergone by estancias, the economic organization spearheading that process. The lack of information on slaves reveals one of the most important changes of the capital structure of estancias in 1850. Almost 40 years after the Free Birth law, slavery had faded away. The master–servant relationship was perhaps alive, but slaves were no longer part of the capital structure of estancias.

Other changes become evident only after a more careful study than that revealing the absence of slaves. Production was undertaken on some tracts of land, with some improvements, some tools, some beasts, and some labor. But, again, the particular combination of those factors (other than labor) emerging from the analysis of inventories yields a particular picture of those estancias. Although referred to for brevity's sake as 1850, the period covered by the 63 inventories included in this sample goes from 1848 to 1851.[12] This section examines the capital structure of those estancias

---

12 See Appendix B, Tables B.3 and B.4.

according to region, value categories, and livestock holdings, as was done in the previous section.

Out of 63 estancias included in the 1850 sample, land was recorded in 41 cases, while in 22 cases it was not. The reasons for this persistence of estancias on non-owned land may have been the same as those present in 1820, but there might have been some new motives at play. The process of expansion had not finished yet, so in many cases the absence of land could have been due to the fact that procedures to secure rights were still underway. It might have also been due to the fact that some estancieros probably were in fact illegal occupants of public or private land.[13]

The capital structure of the 41 estancias on owned land shows a remarkable change when compared with 1820. Land accounts now for 51% of the average total value, and improvements went up to 15% (Table 3.4, Figure 3.4). Cattle, consequently, went down, accounting for only 24% of average total value. The proportion of tools, other goods, and agricultural goods over the average total value remained low; paradoxically, the proportion of sheep was also lower.

When the different regions are considered, some variations emerge without altering the overall pattern. The proportion of land over the average total value is higher in the Center (47%) and in the South (48%) than in the North (39%), but much higher in the New South (64%). Those percentages stress the fact that there was a strong demand for the land of the New South and that in older regions establishments were better developed, with a higher proportion of improvements and a lower stocking rate (i.e., less hectares were required per head).

The availability of water was still a determining factor for land prices. References can be found in some cases to the lack or the presence of permanent watering stations (*aguadas*), although the lack of nearby tracts with and without them does not allow for a precise comparison.[14] The bottomless bucket had been introduced in the mid-1820s, and although there is no special mention of any one on those 63 inventories, there are frequent references to dump-holes or cisterns (*pozos de balde*), which might have been used for bottomless buckets.

Other elements apart from water, such as the distance to Buenos Aires and the quality of the land, also played a role in determining land price. The latter, if there is no explicit mention, as in two cases referring to

---

13 The main criterion in deciding the inclusion in the sample of a small estancia on non-owned land was the right to brand cattle with its own brand, evidenced by the record of an iron brand and its *acción*, the permit to use it legally.

14 AGN, Sucesiones, 5706, Juan Fernández Márquez, Navarro, 1851; and 5939, Juan José Gutiérrez, Luján, 1850.

Table 3.4. *Capital structure of 41 estancias on owned land, 1848–1851*

	North (10)		Center (14)		South (8)		New South (9)		Total (41)	
	X	%	*X*	%	*X*	%	*X*	%	*X*	%
Land	45,399	39.2	46,827	47.1	40,094	48.2	123,200	63.5	61,930	51.2
Improv.	17,868	15.4	17,029	17.1	21,435	25.8	15,977	8.2	17,862	14.8
Tools	3,666	3.2	1,936	1.9	1,315	1.6	1,459	0.8	2,132	1.8
Cattle	34,737	30.0	25,370	25.5	12,653	15.2	41,399	21.4	28,692	23.7
Horses	9,617	8.3	4,733	4.8	3,973	4.8	5,756	3.0	6,000	5.0
Sheep	2,347	2.0	3,003	3.0	2,603	3.1	3,627	1.9	2,902	2.4
Other	2,124	1.8	587	0.6	1,092	1.3	2,459	1.2	1,472	1.2
Total	115,758	100.0	99,485	100.0	83,164	100.0	193,877	100.0	120,990	100.0

Notes: improv. = improvements; X = average in pesos of 8 reales.
Source: Table B.3.

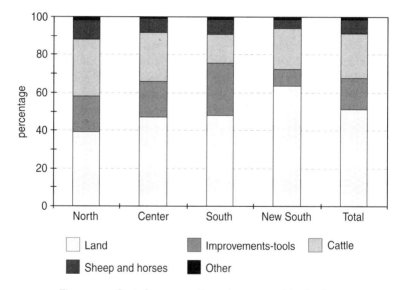

Figure 3.4. Capital structure: Estancias on owned land, 1850.

bañados, is more difficult to assess.[15] But the former presents less difficulty. A tract in Mar Chiquita in 1851 was valued at 35,000 pesos per league, equivalent to 13 pesos per hectare. The same year, in Luján, another tract

15 AGN, Sucesiones, 6513, Eulalio López de Osorio, Ensenada, 1850; and 6517, José Benito Ramos, Magdalena, 1850.

was valued at 25 pesos per vara (usually one front vara by a length of 9,000 varas), equivalent to 37 pesos per hectare. The same quality for both tracts are assumed when comparing them, but there is no way to determine how good those tracts were apart from the fact that they had a different land price. A few years before that, in 1848, a tract in Morón, much closer to Buenos Aires, had been valued at 45 pesos per vara, equivalent to 66.7 pesos per hectare. Against that argument, based upon the distance and arguing in favor of differences due to land quality, is the fact that in the same year, a tract in Cañuelas, as close to Buenos Aires as Morón, was valued at 16 pesos per vara, equivalent to 23.7 pesos per hectare.[16]

Characteristically, land measures were more carefully recorded in the 1850 inventories than in those of 1820. Measured either in varas, square leagues, cuadras, or suertes, land was properly recorded in all but three cases. There are 11 cases in which a lump sum is mentioned for a tract of land, instead of the unitary value per vara or league. For 1820, there was complete information in 13 cases (all but one in varas), and front varas were recorded in 22 cases (there were 2 cases with 2 tracts of land, 1 with complete measures and the other with front varas only). In 28 out of 33 cases (not considering as separate cases those estancias with two tracts of land), the value per unit of measure was given, and in 5 cases a lump sum for a tract of land was mentioned. The more careful record of land measures must have been related to the higher proportion of total value of land in 1850; both facts were manifestations of the process of land valorization that was taking place.

The proportion of improvements over the average total value varied from 8% for the New South, to 15% and 17% for the North and Center, to 26% for the South. But when the average values are considered, the range goes from 17,000 to 18,000 pesos for the Center and North to 21,000 pesos for the South, for estancias of comparable size, and 16,000 pesos for estancias in the New South, seven times larger on average. The proportion of tools rises to 3% in the North, a figure that is double those of the other regions. More tools could mean more agriculture and more carting, mainly the latter since carts were among the most expensive items included in that category.

The proportion of sheep is similar for all regions: 2% for the North and the New South, and 3% for the Center and South, but their average value goes from 2,300 pesos in the North to 3,600 pesos in the New South. The proportion of horses was much higher in the North (8%) than in the other regions, as was the average value of horses (about 10,000 pesos). These proportions and figures show that sheep and horses were everywhere,

16 AGN, Sucesiones, 8169, Francisco Suárez, Mar Chiquita, 1851; 7209, Pedro Navarro, Luján, 1851; 6806, Fructosa Morales, Morón, 1848; 6806, Leandro Muñoz, Cañuelas, 1848.

although as proportion of total value, both together did not account for more than 10% in any case and were usually one-third of the total value of cattle.

No discernible pattern emerges from the consideration of the proportion or average value of other goods and agricultural goods in the different regions other than the fact that they were the lowest categories of the capital structure. The low proportion of agricultural goods does not mean that agriculture was not practiced (it does not mean the opposite either), since only by chance may grain (for sowing or for sale) have been recorded in those inventories. Other rural activities, such as pig or fowl breeding, left few traces in the inventories. They were minor components of the capital structure (although maybe not from the point of view of estancia consumption).

The average value for the 41 estancias on owned land was 121,000 pesos, but when regions are considered, that value goes from 83,000 pesos for the South to 194,000 pesos for the New South, with the Center and the North (99,000 and 116,000 pesos) closer to the former than to the latter. The average area of the estancias of the North, Center, and South was similar, so those figures also mean a higher average investment per hectare in the North (43 pesos), and a much lower average for the New South (12 pesos), with the Center (42 pesos) and the South (37 pesos) in the same range than the North (Table 3.5, Figure 3.5). The highest land value is found in the Center (20 pesos), the region closer to the city of Buenos Aires, and the lowest land value is found in the New South (7 pesos), with the North and South within the same range (17 and 18 pesos), closer to the Center than to the New South. The average value of land per hectare (price of land) for all estancias was 11 pesos.

The highest value of livestock per hectare is found in the North (17 pesos), with lower figures for the Center (14 pesos) and the South (9 pesos), and a much lower one for the New South (only 3 pesos). The average value of livestock per hectare for all estancias was 7 pesos. Other items include improvements, tools, other goods, and agricultural goods, but mainly the first two. The average value on other items per hectare also stresses the differences between the older regions (8 to 11 pesos) and the New South (1 peso). The average value of other items per hectare was 4 pesos. Production was therefore more intensive in the older regions than in the New South, which had, however, higher average values for land, cattle, and sheep than any other region. This is explained by the different average area of estancias in the different regions. In the older regions, the average area fluctuated between 2,260 hectares for the South and 2,718 hectares for the North, but that of the New South was six times larger (16,596 hectares).

Table 3.5. *Investment per hectare: 41 estancias on owned land, 1848–1851*

Average	North	Center	South	New South	Total
Size (hectares)	2,718	2,379	2,260	16,596	5,559
Land value (pesos)	16.70	19.68	17.74	7.42	11.14
Livestock value (pesos)	17.18	13.92	8.51	3.06	6.76
Other items (pesos)	8.70	8.22	10.55	1.20	3.86
Total (pesos)	42.59	41.82	36.80	11.68	21.76

Note: Other items = improvements, tools, other goods.
Sources: Tables 3.4 and B.3.

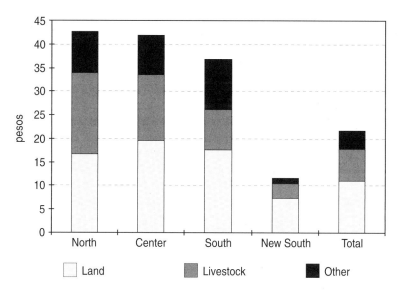

Figure 3.5. Investment per hectare: Estancias on owned land, 1850.

The capital structure of estancias on non-owned land presents more striking regional variations (Table 3.6, Figure 3.6). Although improvements account for 48% in the South and 21% in the North, they only account for 12% in the Center and 6% in the New South. In spite of the lack of a clear right to a tract of land, those estancias in the South and to some extent in the North were well developed in terms of buildings, corrals, fences, ditches, and other improvements. So the lack of a title deed in those regions might have been due to reasons that differed from those for

Estancias

Table 3.6. *Capital structure of 22 estancias on non-owned land, 1848–1851*

	North (4)		Center (7)		South (6)		New South (5)		Total (22)	
	X	%	*X*	%	*X*	%	*X*	%	*X*	%
Improv.	3,890	21.1	3,390	11.9	21,521	47.8	1,213	5.6	7,857	26.7
Tools	503	2.7	1,228	4.3	1,227	2.8	375	1.7	902	3.1
Cattle	5,989	32.5	10,751	37.8	11,548	26.0	17,433	80.9	11,634	39.5
Horses	3,223	17.5	3,036	10.7	1,558	3.5	1,540	7.1	2,323	7.9
Sheep	4,500	24.4	9,415	33.1	5,369	12.1	670	3.1	5,431	18.5
Other	325	1.8	603	2.1	3,474	7.9	329	1.5	1,274	4.4
Total	18,429	100.0	28,423	100.0	44,427	100.0	21,560	100.0	29,420	100.0

Notes: improv. = improvements; *X* = average in pesos of 8 reales.
Source: Table B.4.

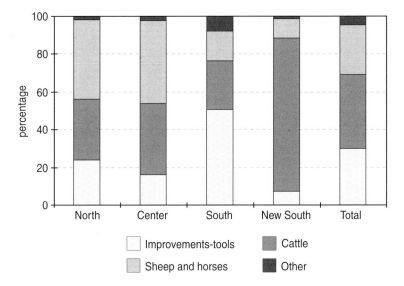

Figure 3.6. Capital structure: Estancias on non-owned land, 1850.

the more precarious establishments of the Center and New South. What those reasons were, however, is more difficult to guess. Those estancias might have been longstanding settlements on public lands, affected neither by the 1820s emphyteusis laws and regulations nor by the 1836 public land sale law. Procedures (and the result of those procedures) were expensive, and many de facto occupants of the land might not have been too attracted by the prospect of a clear right to what was already in their hands, especially if that process implied (as it did) a cash outflow.

Tools account for a low 2% in the New South and a high 4% in the Center, so those estancias on non-owned land do not seem to have been devoted mainly to agriculture. It should be noted that the practice of agriculture required a higher investment in oxen than in tools, but those estancias did not have a larger proportion of oxen than estancias on owned land. The average value of oxen stock is 920 pesos for estancias on owned land and 517 pesos for estancias on non-owned land.

The main regional difference in the capital structure of estancias on non-owned land is found in the proportion of cattle and sheep over total value. While the former accounts for 26% in the South, 33% in the North, and 38% in the Center, it accounts for 81% in the New South. And sheep, which account for only 3% in the New South and 12% in the South, reach 24% in the North and 33% in the Center. In absolute terms the average value of sheep in the Center is 75% higher than in the South, double that in the North, and 14 times more than in the New South. It should be noted also that in the North, again, horses account for a higher proportion of total value (17%) than in the other regions. Since the average value of horses in the North is higher, but not that much higher, than the average values for the other regions, part of that difference is explained by more horses, but another part by a lower average value for other categories (improvements in the North, for instance, are half the proportion reached in the South but only 21% of its average value).

Estancias on owned and non-owned land located in the outskirts of Buenos Aires (OBA) shared in general the same features of the other estancias in the Center, but there were a few differences. Compared to the other estancias in the Center, estancias on owned land in the OBA had a higher proportion for improvements and a lower proportion for land, and estancias on non-owned land in the OBA had less improvements, less cattle, more horses, and more sheep. Unlike in 1820, the main differences are found between estancias on owned and non-owned land in the Center rather than between estancias in the OBA and the rest of the Center. A further differentiation among estancias of the Center, between those on the old Frontier (Navarro and Lobos) and those in the near west (Luján and Pilar), shows both regions sharing a common pattern, only slightly different than that of the OBA, where tools account for 3 percentage points more and sheep for 3 percentage points less. The main difference among those subregions is found in the average value of estancias, and consequently in the average value of the different items of their capital structure. Estancias on owned land in the near west were worth on average 125,000 pesos, whereas those in the OBA were worth 95,000 pesos and those in the old Frontier, 80,000 pesos. So, according to their average value, estancias in the near west are closer to those in the North, and estancias on the old Frontier are closer to those in the South.

The average value for estancias on owned land was 121,000 pesos, four times higher than the 29,000-peso average value for estancias on non-owned land. When the averages for the different categories are compared, however, the average value of sheep in the latter is almost double than in the former, being the other way around for all the other categories. So, on estancias on non-owned land, sheep accounted for a larger proportion of total value, which is still the case when a proportional amount for land is added to those estancias on non-owned land. Cattle and improvements, nevertheless, were above the average for sheep on those estancias. When all estancias are considered together, the capital structure is similar whether actual value of land is divided by the total number of estancias or a proportional amount for land is added to estancias on non-owned land. In both cases the most important item of investment is land, accounting for around half of total value. Cattle come in second place with about a quarter of total value, and improvements come in third with about 15% of total value. Sheep account for only about 4% of total value. Land value, consequently, had risen and the estancias of Buenos Aires, on owned or non-owned land, were still mainly devoted to cattle raising. This statement is possible only when dealing with averages, since individual cases reveal a more varied landscape when compared to that of 1820, as is apparent in the next chapter.

When all estancias are considered together, regional differences still remain. The average values for estancias in the North, Center, and South are within the same range, at or slightly below the average total, but estancias in the New South are more than 50% above that level. The value of land still accounts for 60% of total value in the New South, but from 34% to 41% in the other regions, so the average value of land for estancias in the New South is 2 to 3 times larger than that for other regions. Improvements reach their highest proportion in the South (34%) and their lowest in the New South (8%), with the North and Center in between (16% and 17%). The average value for the South is 97% to 150% higher than those for other regions.

The proportion of cattle over total value for all regions is within the 18%–30% range, but the average value of cattle on estancias in the New South (33,000 pesos) is 2.7 times higher than that of estancias in the South (12,000 pesos), and still higher than that of the Center (20,000 pesos) and the North (27,000 pesos), where the highest proportion over total value is found (30%).

The highest average for sheep is found in the Center (5,000 pesos), but as proportion of total value for that region, it accounts for 7%. Averages and percentages are lower for the other regions, where they are in the 3,000–4,000 pesos range and are from 2% to 6% of total value. The highest average for horses is found in the North (8,000 pesos), accounting for 9% of total value for that region. The other regions are in the 3,000–4,000 pesos range, accounting for 3% to 6% of total value.

Land is the most important category of the capital structure in all regions. Cattle is the second most important category in all regions but the South, where improvements displace it to third place. Horses are in a distant fourth place in the North and New South, but in the Center and South, sheep have displaced them (in the latter case by the slightest margin).

Capital structure, 1820–1850: A comparison

The estancias of Buenos Aires around 1850, in all regions, were mainly devoted to cattle production. Sheep raising had increased since 1820, but it had not overtaken cattle raising in any region. The steady demand for livestock by-products had resulted in an expansion of the productive area as well as in the valorization of land. The most relevant differences emerging from a comparison of the 1820 and 1850 estancias are the increased proportion of land value over total value and the increased value of land in the marginal areas (the Frontier in 1820 and the New South in 1850). In order to fully explore the consequences of these and other changes, this section compares the capital structure of those estancias in both nominal and real terms.

In 1820 land accounted for 11% of the total value of an average estancia on owned land, whereas that proportion rose to 51% in 1850. Improvements rose from 7% to 15%, and horses rose from 3% to 5%. There are stagnating or declining figures for the other categories: from 66% to 24% in cattle, and from 4% to 2% in sheep. Estancias on non-owned land also show drastic variations. Improvements accounted for 6% in 1829 but rose to 27% in 1850; horses rose from 5% to 8%; and sheep rose from 8% to 19%. The most remarkable decline is for cattle – from 66% to 39%. When an equivalent proportion of land is added to estancias on non-owned land, the proportion of improvements over total value rises from 6% to 13%, and that of sheep from 7% to 9%, whereas the proportion of cattle falls from 60% to 19%

When all estancias (on owned and non-owned land) are considered together, the proportion of land shows an increase from 9% to 45% of the total value of an average estancia between 1820 and 1850. Improvements rose from 7% to 16%, and horses rose from 3% to 5%, whereas cattle declined from 67% to 26%, and sheep declined from 5% to 4%. No significant changes regarding those figures are evident when a proportional amount for land is added to estancias on non-owned land. It should be noted, however, that the average size of estancias had increased from 3,278 hectares in 1820 to 5,559 in 1850.

A comparison of estancias on owned land in the different regions shows that in the older regions (North, Center, and South), the proportion of land rose 30 to 36 percentage points (Tables 3.1 and 3.4). The proportion of improvements rose 11 percentage points in the North, 5 in the Center, and 19 in the South. The proportion of cattle fell 43 percentage points in the North, 23 in the Center, and 55 in the South. The rise in the proportion of sheep was not so amazing in percentage points or in absolute terms, but it was remarkable in relative terms. In the North sheep rose from 0.2% to 3% of total value, in the Center from 1.5% to 3%, and in the South from 0.4% to 3.1%.

In 1820 and 1850 land accounted in the North for a lower proportion of total value than in the Center and South. The highest proportion of improvements was found in the Center in 1820 but in the South in 1850. The highest proportion of horses was also in the Center in 1820 but in the North in 1850. In 1820 the North and South had a similar proportion of cattle (over 70% of total value), which was higher than that of the Center (49%). In 1850 the highest proportion of cattle was in the North (30%) and the lowest in the South (15%), with the Center in between (25%).

The average value of an estancia on owned land rose 13 times from 1820 to 1850. Comparing the average value of an estancia in each region, the North increased 11 times; the Center, 22 times; the South, 4 times. Although the Frontier and the New South are not comparable, since they were two different regions, the value in those marginal regions rose 57 times in the same period.

A comparison of estancias on non-owned land within each region shows that an average estancia in the North was worth seven times more in 1850 than in 1820, in nominal terms (Tables 3.3 and 3.6). Estancias in the Center were 10 times higher, those in the South 12 times higher, and those in the New South 15 times higher than those on the Frontier. The 1850 total was 11 times higher than that of 1820.

In 1820, on estancias on non-owned land in the North, Center, and South, cattle accounted for 64% to 68% of total value. That proportion fell in 1850 to a range from 33% for the North to 38% for the Center. Only in the marginal regions did cattle account for a similar proportion: 85% for the Frontier in 1820, and 81% for the New South in 1850. Improvements accounted from 4% (Center) to 8% (North and South) in 1820 but from 12% (Center) to 48% (South) in 1850. Sheep rose from a range of 7% (North) to 10% (South) in 1820 to a range of 12% (South) to 33% (Center) in 1850.

When considering all estancias together, the average value for those in the North in 1850 was 12 times higher than in 1820; for those in the Center, 21 times higher; for those in the South, 6 times higher;

for those in the New South, 60 times higher than those on the Frontier; and on average their total nominal value was 15 times higher than in 1820.

Land in the North rose from 8% of total value in 1820 to 37% in 1850, from 7% to 41% in the Center, from 11% to 34% in the South, and from 3% on the Frontier in 1820 to 60% in the New South in 1850. Improvements rose in the older regions from a range of 5%–9% in 1820 to a range of 16%–32% in 1850. The only other remarkable difference is the fall in the proportion of cattle from 71% in 1820 to 30% in 1850 for the North, from 56% to 27% for the Center, from 70% to 18% for the South, from 57% for the Frontier in 1820 to 25% for the New South in 1850, and from 67% to 26% for all estancias in all regions.

The investment per hectare in the different regions shows similar land values for the older regions both in 1820 and in 1850. Discrepancies emerge when considering livestock and other items. In 1820 the average investment in livestock per hectare in the North was 60% higher than in the South and 55% higher than in the Center, and investment in other items was 203% higher in the Center than in the South and 69% higher than in the North (Tables 3.2 and 3.5). Total investment per hectare was 57% higher in the North than in the South and 25% higher than in the Center. Total investment on the Frontier was only 13% that of the North. In 1850 the North still had the largest average total investment per hectare, but the Center and South were much closer. The average for the North was 19% higher than in the South and 11% higher than in the Center. Average investment per hectare in the New South was 25% that of the North.

The comparison of the average investment per hectare within the same region shows that total investment in the North in 1850 was in nominal terms 12 times higher than in 1820, but land value per hectare was 47 times higher. Total investment per hectare in the Center in 1850 was 13 times higher than in 1820, but land value was 58 times higher, and in the South total investment was 16 times higher, while land value was 59 times higher. Comparing the two marginal regions, total value per hectare in the 1850 New South was 23 times higher than on the 1820 Frontier, and land value was 263 times higher. On average for all regions, in 1850 total investment per hectare was 8 times higher and land value 37 times higher than in 1820.

All these estimates have been based upon the nominal value of estancias in 1820 and 1850. Since the intermediate years saw the first round of paper money inflation in Buenos Aires, the 1820 and 1850 figures should be compared again according to a common standard of value.

In order to compare values for 1820 with those for 1850, price variations should be taken into account. A comparison of money values, however, is hindered by the introduction of paper money in 1826. Paper money was subject to greater and much faster inflationary alterations than specie, the only legal tender until April 1826.[17] Therefore, a comparison is only possible by turning paper money values into constant values. This can be done in two ways: first, by using the average value of a head of cattle in those two sets of inventories; and second, by using the average price of the silver peso.[18] The former tells us how many head were necessary to purchase a unit of land or other goods. An average head of cattle remained unchanged between 1820 and 1850, since no improvements were evident in cattle breeding. The latter, specie, gives us all values in terms of what still was considered the ultimate means of payment, since outside payments for overseas imports as well as for imports from the Interior provinces were only made in specie (or quasi-perfect substitutes such as libranzas and bills of exchange).[19]

The average value of a head of cattle for 1818–1822 was 4.1 pesos (values are given in pesos of 8 reales but using decimals instead of reales). The average value of a head of cattle for 1848–1851 is 19.8 pesos. In nominal terms, the average value of a head of cattle rose 5.1 times from 1818–1822 to 1848–1851.

Turning monetary values into real values, the average estancia rose from 2,266 head of cattle in 1820 to 6,111 head in 1850 (Table 3.7, Figure 3.7). As the average estancia grew from 3,278 hectares to 5,559 hectares, a total value of 3,604 head of cattle is obtained by converting the values for the latter to the size of the former. Therefore, an average 1850 estancia of the same size as the average 1820 estancia was worth 59% more than the latter. The different items of the capital structure, however, did not evolve homogeneously. Land value increased 632%; improvements, 241%; tools, 36%; other goods, 40%; and horses, 198%. Conversely, cattle decreased 43%; sheep, 10%; agricultural products, 35%; and slaves, obviously, 100%. On estancias on non-owned land, improvements increased 782%; agricultural products, 780%; sheep, 349%; and the overall value of those estancias, 104%.

These variations point to a change in the relative value of cattle vis-à-vis the other items of the capital structure. That variation is partially due to the lower number of head on the average estancia in 1850. The evolution of the capital structure of estancias in the different regions explains this decline in the number of head.

As the average size of estancias varied according to region, investment

---

17 For the different characteristics of monetary and fiduciary inflation, see Amaral (1989).

18 For a methodological discussion of these estimates, see Appendix B.

19 Paper money was declared the only legal tender in May 1826, but in September 1827, the free election of the means of payment was re-established. For government payments, only paper money was used. See Amaral (1989).

Table 3.7. *Capital structure of estancias in head of cattle, 1820 and 1850*

| | Estancias on owned land | | | | Estancias on non-owned land | | |
	1820 A	1850 B	1850 C	Increase D	1820 E	1850 F	Increase G
Land	252	3,128	1,845	632	–	–	–
Improvements	155	902	532	243	45	397	782
Tools	46	108	64	39	29	46	59
Cattle	1,495	1,449	854	-43	495	588	19
Horses	60	303	179	198	40	117	193
Sheep	97	147	87	-10	61	274	349
Slaves	114	–	–	-100	42	–	-100
Other	33	74	43	30	19	64	237
Total	2,266	6,111	3,604	59	730	1,486	104

Notes:
A Average value in head of cattle for an average-size estancia on owned land in 1820 (3,278 ha).
B Average value in head of cattle for an average-size estancia on owned land in 1850 (5,559 ha).
C Average value in head of cattle for an 1820 average-size estancia on owned land in 1850 (3,278 ha).
D Increase from 1820 to 1850 for a 3,278-hectare estancia (percentage).
E Average value in head of cattle for an average estancia on non-owned land in 1820.
F Average value in head of cattle for an average estancia on non-owned land in 1850.
G Difference between E and F (percentage).
Average value of a head of cattle: 1820 = 4.1 pesos; 1850 = 19.8 pesos.
Sources: Tables 3.1 and 3.5.

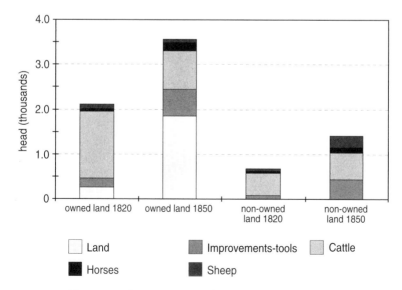

Figure 3.7. Capital structure of estancias, 1820 and 1850.

per hectare serves for comparison. In all cases, in terms of head of cattle, there is a marked increase in the value of land. In the North it jumped from 0.10 to 0.84 head of cattle between 1820 and 1850, a 740% increase (Table 3.8, Figure 3.8). In the other regions, however, it was even more remarkable: 1,000% in the Center; 1,025% in the South; and 7,582% from the 1820 Frontier to the 1850 New South. On average, considering all regions together, land value increased 600% from 1820 to 1850. Total value per hectare increased 113% in the North, 160% in the Center, 191% in the South, and 436% from the Frontier to the New South.

Livestock value per hectare had an uneven behavior. It increased 14% in the North, 40% in the Center, and 275% from the Frontier to the New South, but it declined 10% in the South and 32% for all estancias. Cattle value per hectare grew 38% in the Center and 160% on the Frontier–New South, but it declined 10% in the North, 38% in the South, and 43% for all regions (Table 3.9, Figure 3.9). Cattle as proportion of all livestock fell in the North from 94% to 74%; in the Center, from 78% to 71%; in the South, from 92% to 65%; on the Frontier–New South, from 100% to 87%; and from 92% to 76% for all regions. The counterpart of this decline of the proportion of cattle is an increase in the proportion of horses and sheep.

The average value of sheep per hectare remained unchanged at 0.03 head of cattle. The regions, however, followed a different pattern. In the Center it declined from 0.07 head to 0.06 head; but it grew in the North from 0.03 head to 0.04 head; in the South, from 0.02 head to 0.06 head; and in the Frontier–New South, from almost nothing to 0.01 head.

The average value of horses per hectare grew for all regions from 0.02 head in 1820 to 0.05 head in 1850: in the North, from 0.02 head to 0.18 head; in the Center, from 0.03 head to 0.10 head; in the South, from 0.02 head to 0.09 head; and in the Frontier–New South, from almost nothing to 0.02 head.

A different way of turning nominal paper peso values into real values is deflating the former by the average value of the silver peso.[20] As the use of a different deflator cannot reveal a different set of internal relations among the categories of the capital structure, the figures resulting from using both deflators are compared to emphasize changes in relative prices.

The average value of an estancia in 1820 was 2,250 head of cattle and 9,292 silver pesos; in 1850 it was 5,927 head of cattle and 6,792 silver

20 The value of silver vis-à-vis other goods may have changed due to other factors (not just due to its relation to paper money), such as the long-term trends operating on a worldwide scale. But in the short run (a 30-year period is not too long when considering the price of silver), because of the constant use of paper money in daily transactions, silver value may have been seen as constant.

Table 3.8. *Investment per hectare in head of cattle, 1820 and 1850*

	North 1820	North 1850	G	Center 1820	Center 1850	G	South 1820	South 1850	G
Land	0.10	0.84	740	0.09	0.99	1,000	0.08	0.90	1,025
Livestock	0.78	0.87	12	0.50	0.70	40	0.49	0.43	-12
Other items	0.13	0.44	238	0.21	0.42	100	0.07	0.53	657
Total	1.01	2.15	113	0.81	2.11	160	0.64	1.86	191

	Frontier NS 1820	Frontier NS 1850	G	All regions 1820	All regions 1850	G
Land	0.00	0.37	7,582	0.08	0.56	600
Livestock	0.04	0.15	275	0.50	0.34	-32
Other items	0.03	0.06	100	0.10	0.19	90
Total	0.08	0.59	638	0.69	1.10	59

Notes: NS = New South; G = growth from 1820 to 1850 (percentage).
Sources: Tables 3.2 and 3.5.

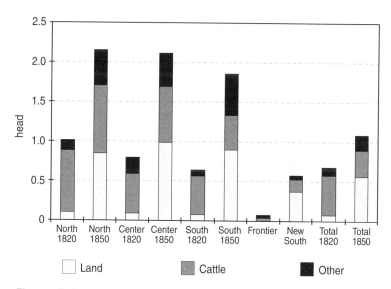

Figure 3.8. Investment per hectare: Estancias on owned land, 1820 and 1850.

Table 3.9. *Investment in livestock per hectare in head of cattle, 1820 and 1850*

	North 1820	North 1850	Center 1820	Center 1850	South 1820	South 1850	Frontier NS 1820	Frontier NS 1850	All regions 1820	All regions 1850
Cattle	0.73	0.66	0.39	0.54	0.45	0.28	0.04	0.13	0.46	0.26
Horses	0.02	0.18	0.03	0.10	0.02	0.09	0.00	0.02	0.02	0.05
Sheep	0.03	0.04	0.07	0.06	0.02	0.06	0.00	0.01	0.03	0.03
Livestock	0.78	0.89	0.50	0.70	0.48	0.43	0.04	0.15	0.50	0.34

Notes: NS = New South. Due to rounding, the livestock total for each year may differ from the addition of the values corresponding to the different types of livestock.
The value of cattle per hectare for each region and for all regions in head of cattle (C) have been estimated as

$$C = \frac{X_c}{VZ}$$

where X_c = the average value of cattle per estancia for each region or on average for all regions (Tables 3.1 and 3.4); Z = the average size of estancias for each region or on average for all regions (Tables 3.2 and 3.5); V = the average value of a head of cattle (see Appendix B). The average value of horses (H) and sheep (S) have been estimated in the same way, substituting X_h and X_s for X_c, where X_h is the average value of horses per estancia for each region or the average for all regions (Tables 3.1 and 3.5); and X_s, the same for sheep.
Sources: Tables 3.1, 3.2, 3.4, and 3.5.

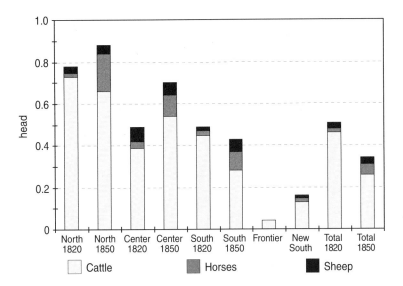

Figure 3.9. Investment in livestock per hectare, 1820 and 1850.

pesos.[21] Consequently, there is a 163% increase in head of cattle, but a 27% decline in silver pesos. As the average 1850 estancia was 62% larger than the average 1820 estancia, the average value of an estancia for each region and for all regions have been converted into the average value of a head of cattle and a silver peso per hectare. While in head of cattle the increase from 1820 to 1850 ranges from 97% for the North to 436% for the Frontier–New South, in silver pesos there is a decline ranging from −19% in the South to −42% in the North, but the Frontier–New South grew by 50%. For all estancias the average value per hectare increased 55% in head of cattle but declined 57% in silver pesos (Table 3.10, Figure 3.10).

The main reason for this decline in silver pesos is the dramatic fall in the average price of a head of cattle in silver pesos. From an average value of 4.1 pesos (silver pesos) in 1820, it fell to 1.06 silver pesos (equivalent to the average value of 19.8 paper pesos) in 1850, a 74% loss. That fall was a manifestation of the abundance of cattle (and land to raise them), but it was also related to the evolution of international prices for cattle by-products.

The comparison of the value of 1820 and 1850 estancias is affected by the deflators. Those deemed more appropriate have been used here: the average value of a head of cattle and the average value of the silver peso. But the fluctuations of cattle values and silver peso prices were neither homogeneous nor necessarily similar to those of other prices. Taking the average value for 1850 as the 100 base, the price of the silver peso was 144 in 1848, 124 in 1849, and 119 in 1851, and the average value of a head of cattle was 98 in 1848, 103 in 1849, and 87 in 1851. That uneven behavior was not paralleled by the evolution of the average price of oxhides, which was 90 in 1848, 93 in 1849, and 126 in 1851.[22] The difference between cattle values and hide prices is due to the fact that they are different products and that the sources are inventories for cattle values and newspapers for hide prices. While the former are based on appraisals of an existing herd, the latter are the average of market transactions. So hide prices (as the price of a silver peso) may be affected by short-run scarcities or gluts, while cattle values tended to be affected by market factors in the long run and by natural factors in the short run. As with any comparison of values over a long period, all the figures produced here should be interpreted as indicative of trends rather than of actual, precise differences between the 1820 and 1850 estancias.

21 The total value of each estancia on owned land (estancias on non-owned land are excluded) has been deflated using the average value of a head of cattle and the average value of the silver peso corresponding to the year of the inventory, both for the 1820 and the 1850 samples (Table 3.10).

22 Ox hide prices have been taken from Broide (1951), 152.

Table 3.10. *Real value of estancias on owned land, 1820 and 1850*
(head and pesos per hectare)

| | 1820 | | 1850 | | Increase (%) | |
| | head | pesos | head | pesos | head | pesos |
	A	B	C	D	E	F
North	1.01	4.13	2.21	2.34	119	−43
Center	0.81	3.31	2.11	2.24	162	−32
South	0.64	2.63	1.86	1.98	190	−25
Frontier–New South	0.08	0.31	0.59	0.63	681	102
All regions	0.69	2.82	1.10	1.17	60	−59

Notes:
A and C: the average value per hectare in head of cattle (E_c) has been estimated as

$$E_c = \frac{X}{V_c Z}$$

where X_e = the average value of an estancia (Tables 3.1 and 3.5); V_c = the average value of a head of cattle (4.1 pesos for 1820; 19.8 pesos for 1850); and Z = the average size of estancias (Tables 3.2 and 3.5).

B and D: the average value per hectare in silver pesos (E_s) has been estimated as

$$E_s = \frac{X}{V_s Z}$$

where V_s is the average annual value of a peso fuerte = 18.63 pesos moneda corriente for 1848–1851 [Own estimate. Daily quotations from Espiñeira (1864), following Broide's (1951) method to estimate the average for each year].

E is the difference between A and C as percentage of C; and F is the difference between B and D as percentage of D.

Sources: Tables 3.1, 3.2, 3.4, and 3.5.

As there was an evolution in livestock values from 1820 to 1850, there also was a physical evolution. The average number of livestock units (LU) on the average estancia on owned land was 2,187 LU in 1820 and 1,964 LU in 1850, a 10% decline. As the average estancia was larger in 1850 (5,559 hectares) than in 1820 (3,274 hectares), considering average estancias of equal size, the number of head drops to 1,157 in 1850, a 47% decline. Those figures are affected, however, by the different characteristics of the marginal regions, the Frontier in 1820 and the New South in 1850. Removing those marginal regions, considering the other regions only, the average estancia in 1820 had 2,989 hectares and 2,304 LU, and the average 1850 estancia had 2,455 hectares and 1,635 LU. An 1850 estancia of equivalent size to the 1820 average estancia would have had 1,991 LU, a 14% decline (see Tables B.1b and B.3b; for LU, see Table 3.11).

The composition of LU on estancias on owned land within each region shows that the proportion of cattle dropped in the North, South, and the

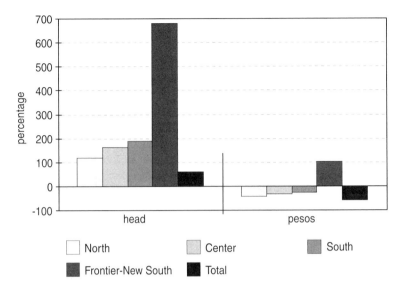

Figure 3.10. Real value of investment per hectare: Differences between 1820 and 1850.

marginal regions, while it grew in the Center. Conversely, from 1820 to 1850, there is a decline in the proportion of horses and sheep in the Center. From the viewpoint of livestock composition, estancias in the older regions in 1850 are more similar than in 1820, with a slightly higher proportion of cattle in the Center, horses in the North, and sheep in the Center and South. Considering all regions cattle accounted for 79% of all LU in 1820 and for 73% in 1850, horses for 15% and 21%, and sheep for 6% in both cases. There is no clear explanation for that growth in the proportion of horses, but it should be stressed that the proportion of sheep remained unchanged and that cattle still accounted for about 75% of all LU.

Considering all estancias (on owned and non-owned land), the proportion of cattle drops from 75% in 1820 to 71% in 1850, that of horses grows from 17% to 21%, and that of sheep from 7% to 8%. These figures show that estancias on non-owned land had a larger proportion of horses in 1820 and that the proportion of sheep was larger on them than on estancias on owned land. These figures, however, do not change the overall picture.

The composition of livestock has been estimated here for the average estancia in each region. Estancias, however, were of different average size in each region and in each period. A better indicator, therefore, is the average number of LU per hectare (Table 3.11, Figure 3.11). The number of cattle per hectare declined in the North and South from 1820 to 1850 by 37%

Table 3.11. *Livestock units per hectare, 1820 and 1850*

	North 1820	North 1850	Center 1820	Center 1850	South 1820	South 1850	Frontier 1820	NS 1850	All regions 1820	All regions 1850
Cattle	0.81	0.51	0.46	0.48	0.50	0.32	0.04	0.15	0.51	0.26
Horses	0.14	0.21	0.24	0.14	0.08	0.12	0.00	0.03	0.11	0.07
Sheep	0.04	0.04	0.11	0.06	0.03	0.05	0.00	0.00	0.04	0.02
Livestock units	0.99	0.77	0.81	0.68	0.61	0.49	0.05	0.19	0.67	0.35

Notes: NS = New South. Due to rounding, the livestock units total for each year may differ from the addition of the values corresponding to the different types of livestock. Livestock unit (LU): 1 head of cattle = 0.8 horse = 8 sheep (see Buenos Aires 1883, lviii). *Sources*: Inventories, 1818–1822 and 1848–1851 (see Appendix B).

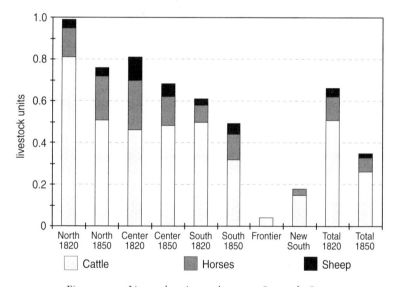

Figure 3.11. Livestock units per hectare, 1820 and 1850.

and 36%, while there was an increase of 4% in the Center and 275% in the Frontier–New South. When all regions are considered, there is a 49% decline, but only a 22% decline when excluding the Frontier–New South. The number of horses per hectare grew 50% in the North and South and 896% in the marginal regions (but figures are extremely low in this case), and it dropped 42% in the Center. Considering all regions there is a 36% drop, but when excluding the Frontier–New South, there is a 23% increase. The number of sheep per hectare remained unchanged in the North, grew 67% in the South, dropped 45% in the Center, and grew 359% in the Frontier–New South (but, again, the figures are too low to be meaningful.) For all regions there was a drop of 50%, but when excluding the Frontier–New South, the number of sheep per hectare did not vary. Considering all LU per hectare, there was a decline of 22% in the North, 16% in the Center, and 20% in the South, while there was a growth of 280% in the Frontier–New South. When all regions are considered, there is a decline of 48% in the number of LU per hectare, but when excluding the Frontier–New South, there is only a 13% decline.

Considering the process that Buenos Aires was undergoing in those decades, these figures look paradoxical: The incorporation of new lands into production and growing exports resulted in a less intensive use of the land. The explanation of this paradox is found in an increasing delimitation of property rights. In other words, livestock occupied more than the actual extension of the estancia in 1820, while in 1850 there were less vacant lands to spread over, so the number of LU was related in a more direct way to the actual size of the estancia. Complaints about the overcrowding of estancias close to the city and demands of legal action to prevent it in the mid-1850s are evidence of a more intensive use of the land, in spite of these figures.[23]

Conclusion

The 1820 and 1850 estancias have been compared in this Chapter according to regions, value categories, and livestock holdings. Land value rose as a proportion of total value, and that rise was more remarkable in the older regions. Cattle value as proportion of total value fell in all regions due to the rise of land value rather than to the expansion of sheep. Wool exports were growing in 1850, but sheep value as a proportion of total value was still quite modest. Land was in 1850 the main item of the capital structure instead of cattle. Only the marginal regions retained a similar pattern in both samples. As a consequence of land valorization, the average value of an estancia rose in all regions both in nominal and real terms. But the average value of estancias on non-owned land also moved in the same direction.

In order to make possible a comparison of 1820 and 1850 values, the head of cattle has been taken as the common standard of value for both periods. That showed an amazing increase in the real value of an estancia of the same size. But when a different deflator is used – the average value of the silver peso – there is a decline in the average value of investment per hectare in the older regions, although it grew in the New South. This

---

23 See ACR, passim. Livestock overcrowding as a threat to other landowners' property rights is discussed in Chapter 7.

decline was due to the decline of the average value of a head of cattle in silver pesos, resulting from the local abundance and falling international prices for cattle by-products.

Livestock distribution figures hint at changes in the use of the land in the different regions. Land was more intensively used in the New South than on the Frontier, but not to the same extent as in the older regions, where the number of livestock units per hectare remained almost unchanged in spite of changes in the composition of livestock.

4

Model and reality

In 1856, answering to an inquiry on the conditions of production, Bernardo Gutiérrez and Félix García, rural producers from Mercedes, described the procedure to set up an estancia.[1] Oddly enough, the purchase of a piece of land is not mentioned. Either Gutiérrez and García were taking land for granted, or that was not a necessary step. Actual possession was perhaps more urgent than legal ownership, and probably the best way to secure it. Once on the land, a water well was dug, for water was indispensable for building improvements. Three ranchos were then built: one for the owner, one for the peons, and a kitchen. The owner's rancho would be 6 varas long; the peons' and the kitchen, 7 varas long each. Paja (a coarse grass) was used for roofing, and hardwood poles were required for their structure. Nails were used for the doors, and hides for the poles. Three peons would work 45 days to build those ranchos.

A corral for cattle, made of ñandubay poles placed vertically forming a wooden wall (palo a pique), should follow. For 1,500 head of cattle, a corral should be 150 varas on each side, requiring 1,100 poles. Two ditches, zanja and contrazanja, were dug around it. One peon would build the corral and ditches in 12 days.

Finally, a watering place for the livestock (jagüel) was required: a well, 5 or 6 varas long and 2 varas wide. The jagüel would be used when neighboring streams or lagoons, if any, dried up. A small dam kept the water surging from the well while it was not demanded by livestock. The dam should be 1 vara wide, 50 varas long, and one half-vara deep.

No other improvements were necessary to get started, but from that basic model, the estancia would grow as required by the expansion of operations. The concept of evolution present in that estimate was at the basis of the actual practice of estancieros. Livestock would reproduce itself, so more corrals and watering places would be needed for them, and more

---

1 REBA (1855), 2:39. This testimony is studied from a different perspective by Infesta de Guerci (1983).

ranchos to accommodate a larger number of peons. Later, puestos to round
up new herds and, eventually, more land would be added.

In 1831 Pedro Trapani, a well-known estanciero, had estimated for the
British minister, Woodbine Parish, the amount of money required to set
up an estancia. Trapani did include the price of land, but Parish had
specifically requested it.[2] Trapani, rather than describing the aforementioned procedure, listed the different capital items and the corresponding
amounts required by them. His estimate shares the sense of evolution with
the Gutiérrez–García model, but it starts at a higher investment level.
Trapani's estimate, 58,410 pesos, was probably the amount a British
minister should invest to enter into the rural business rather than what was
required by a native of the pampas.

The Buenos Aires economy was growing in the first half of the nineteenth century, and the firms providing the foundations for growth were
also expanding. In order to illustrate that evolutive process from 1820 to
1850, some individual estancias are now described. This selection has been
made to show the passage from the Gutiérrez–García model to more
complex types of organization of production. Sophistication should not be
exaggerated, but it should not be underestimated either. The point is not
how typical these estancias were but that they did exist at all.

The 1820 estancias

The Gutiérrez–García model holds true for 1820. Felipe Santiago Burgos's
estancia, located on the Cañada de la Cruz, was a case adjusted to that
model (Table 4.1).[3] It was 500 varas wide and 9,000 varas long, equivalent
to 337.5 hectares. As in the model, there were three ranchos there, one of
them 6 varas long, with brick and adobe walls, and a paja roof. There was
a water well and an oven for baking bread. Unlike the model, there were
a few trees: five fig trees, seven poplars, and just one ombú (useless as fuel
or for building purposes but appreciated for its shadow). Apart from seven
ñandubay poles, corrals and fences were made of lower-quality woodsticks,
estimated by cartfuls.

Two sickles, 2 plows, and 13 oxen were the evidence that agriculture
was practiced there. There were 157 head of cattle, 39 heifers, 20 calves, 10
entire horses, 1 redomón, 8 colts, 72 mares, 25 foals, 94 sheep, and 18
lambs. Cattle accounted for 58% of the total inventory value; horses, 6%;
sheep, 3%; land, 11%; improvements, 8%; tools, 14%; other goods, less
than 1%; and agricultural products, 1%. There were no slaves on that
estancia.

---

2 Pedro Trapani's estimate in PRO, Foreign Office 354/8, Woodbine Parish Papers, 66v–67.
   Trapani's estimate was first studied by Barba (1967).
3 AGN, Tribunales, Sucesiones 3920, Felipe Santiago Burgos, 1820. See Table B.1, number 2.

Table 4.1. *Capital structure of selected estancias, 1820*

	Burgos pesos	%	Echevarría pesos	%	Caxaraville pesos	%	Gómez pesos	%
Land	188	11.0	4,862	9.6	8,750	12.1	5,330	7.8
Improv.	129	7.6	40,722	80.4	4,320	6.0	1,048	1.5
Tools	238	14.0	890	1.8	391	0.5	186	0.3
Cattle	980	57.5	258	0.5	53,903	74.8	57,791	84.8
Horses	94	5.5	382	0.8	1,665	2.3	725	1.1
Sheep	52	3.1	413	0.8	1,755	2.4	403	0.6
Slaves	-	0.0	3,125	6.2	340	0.5	2,675	3.9
Other	24	1.4	-	0.0	967	1.3	11	0.0
Total	1,704	100	50,652	100	72,090	100	68,169	100

Notes: improv. = improvements; pesos = pesos of 8 reales; % = percentage over total value.
Sources: AGN, Tribunales, Sucesiones 3920, 5590, 4843, and 5910.

In the 1820s estancia buildings were mainly ranchos, but on a few occasions, houses are mentioned in the inventories. A rancho was a one-room building, whereas houses had a living room and one or more bedrooms. Adobe walls and straw roofs were used in both ranchos and houses, but brick walls and tile roofs were for houses only. Kitchens were usually a separate building to which a structure of wooden poles with straw roof but no walls (ramada) was added.

Corrals were usually of ñandubay poles but seldom included as many as the Gutiérrez–García model specified. The typical number of ñandubay poles invested in corrals was from 300 to 500, but occasionally there were more than 1,000. Instead of ñandubay or as a complement, softwood poles were used – mainly peachwood, poplar, and other palos blancos (white sticks). Ditches ranging from 1.5 to 8.5 cuadras were a regular feature, but not all estancias had them. Fences are mentioned in 12 cases. Unidentified wood was used for fencing, but occasionally ñandubay and tala poles were used. In a few cases, live *tuna* (agave) fences of about 1,000 varas were found.

Trees were one of the main improvements on those estancias. More than ombúes there were peach trees on the pampas, often forming groves of more than 1,000 trees. There were also fig, quince, apple, and orange trees, and even vines. A few talas, espinillos, algarrobos, willows, and poplars are also mentioned. No other type of tree was in greater number than peach trees, which were the main supply of firewood as Paucke found in the 1770s, Darwin in the 1830s, and Bishop in the 1850s.[4]

4 For the use of peachwood as fuel, see Paucke (1942), 125; Darwin (1839), 53; Bishop (1869), 82; MacCann (1969), 19; Douville (1984), 124.

José Mateo de Echevarría's estancia in San Vicente was devoted almost exclusively to fuel-wood production (Table 4.1).[5] That estancia was on a tract of land 9,724 varas wide and 8,000 varas long, equivalent to 5,834 hectares. There were 1,100 sheep, 31 oxen, 5 milch cows, 3 steers, 4 yearlings, 22 horses, 14 mares, 16 colts and fillies, and 156 mules. Buildings included a house, a chapel, the slaves' quarters, and corrals and fences made out of brick. The most valuable item in that inventory was a grove with 221,250 peach trees for fuel wood and 2,139 fruit trees. That grove was protected by a ditch 7,140 varas long. The grove accounted for 58% of the total inventory value; land, 10%; tools, 2%; other improvements (excluding the trees), 22%; livestock, 2%; and 15 slaves, 6% (Table 4.1).

The main business of that estancia was the supply of fuel wood to the city. How profitable that activity was cannot be determined just with the inventory information, but in spite of the productive potential of the 5,834-hectare estancia, only 1.7% of its extension, just 57.5 cuadras, equivalent to 97 hectares, was occupied by the grove.

That fuel-wood-producing estancia was not an isolated case. The inventory of Manuel Torres's estancia, in Quilmes, included a grove with 14,394 peach trees and a few other trees. Around the quinta there was a 21-cuadra ditch and agave fence. The quinta, including trees and the ditch, accounted for 24% of the total inventory value. There was a plot where wheat had been sowed, five plows, and some other agricultural tools. There were six ranchos and a house with living room, one bedroom, and kitchen. Improvements included 15 ombúes, two corrals, and several pieces of timber. All improvements accounted for 51% of the total inventory value; slaves, 16%; cattle, 5%; horses, 1%; 4,017 sheep and 306 lambs, 19%; tools, 8%; and land was not recorded. To a lesser extent and on a smaller scale than Echevarría's, the main business of the Torres estancia was also peachwood production, combined with sheep breeding.[6]

An example of a large 1820s estancia was Andrés Caxaraville's in Magdalena, devoted mainly to cattle raising (Table 4.1).[7] Land, 31,500 hectares, accounted for 12% of the total inventory value; improvements, 6%; tools and slaves, less than 1% each; cattle, 75%; horses and sheep, 2% each; and the other items, 1.3%.

Improvements included six ranchos. The largest was 11 varas long and 4.5 varas wide, with two rooms. Another rancho of similar size served as the peons' kitchen. The wooden structure of the former was of palm and willow; that of the second, of ñandubay and palm poles and tacuara canes.

5 AGN, Tribunales, Sucesiones 5590, José Mateo de Echevarría, 1817.
6 For that reason, this estancia has not been included in the sample. Cf. AGN, Tribunales, Sucesiones 8458, Manuel Torres, 1818.
7 AGN, Tribunales, Sucesiones 4843, Andrés Caxaraville, 1820. See Table B.1, number 5.

The smallest rancho was 7 varas wide and 4 varas long. Building materials were the same, but peachwood was also used. There was also a well with a brick wall and an adobe oven to bake bread. The quinta contained 6,191 peach trees and several quince and fig trees, espinillos, poplars, and one walnut tree. Peach trees alone accounted for more than one-third of the total value of improvements. There were also two ombúes, but they were not listed as part of the quinta.

Other important improvements were a 6-cuadra tala fence, and 1,400 ñandubay poles invested in corrals and palenques. A fence around the quinta and a smaller corral for the sheep were made of peachwood poles. Two sides of the quinta were protected by an almost 3-cuadra-long ditch. There was also one puesto, consisting of only one rancho, with a well, a corral, and a few tools. The size of this rancho was similar to those of the main población, but building materials were just peachwood and canes.

There were 6,874 breeding cows, 26 oxen, 3 milch cows, 1,856 year-lings, and 2,365 calves on the estancia, plus 1,969 breeding cows, 7 milch cows, 1,147 yearlings, and 310 calves on the puesto. The presence of oxen reveals the practice of agriculture, since no carts are mentioned in the inventory. The small number of milch cows shows they were supplying milk mainly for estancia consumption rather than for the market.

Cattle head were grouped in three different rodeos on the estancia, two on the puesto, and some head were referred to as "grazing" cattle. The largest rodeo was formed of 3,168 breeding cows, 877 yearlings, and 900 calves. Yearlings and calves represent 28% each of the number of breeding cows in that rodeo, and taking into account all the head of cattle on the estancia and puesto, the number of yearlings and calves were 34% and 30% of the number of breeding cows. These figures are very close to the usual rate of reproduction, estimated at 30%.

Although cattle raising was the main business of this estancia, there were also horses and sheep. Horses were grouped in ten herds, according to hair color, but there were also 200 breeding mares, 96 mules, 2 male asses, and 294 female asses. These figures indicate that horses and mules were produced for the market. The same was probably true for sheep, since there were 3,000 of them on the estancia.

Another large estancia was María R. Gómez's, located in San Pedro.[8] Land, 17,499 hectares, accounted for 8% of the total inventory value; improvements, 2%; slaves, 4%; and cattle, 85% (Table 4.1). The main building was described as a house, with a living room and one bedroom, but its wooden structure was of palm, and it had a paja roof and adobe walls. Woodwork, however, was more expensive than usual: pine doors and

8 AGN, Tribunales, Sucesiones 5910, María R. Gómez, 1821. See Table B.1, number 9.

a cedar window. Fences and corrals contained 1,400 ñandubay poles and 300 ñandubay stakes, apart from 11 cartfuls of willow and peach wood. The estancia also included a well, an earthen oven, and one ombú. There was also one puesto, formed by one rancho and one corral.

A typical 1820 estancia, therefore, included from one to three ranchos, one corral, the quinta, and fences and ditches protecting the dwellings and grove. The ranchos did not exceed 11 varas long and 5 varas wide, and they were usually made of adobe walls, a wooden structure, and paja roof. Ñandubay poles were the best and most expensive building material for the wooden structures and for corrals. Willow, palm, and peach poles were also used for the same purposes. Most estancias had a well and an oven to bake bread. A quinta with fruit trees was also common, and the peach tree was the most usual tree there. A few ombúes gave shade, and tala and agave were sometimes used as live fences.

Estancias on non-owned land were somewhat different from estancias on owned land regarding the quality of buildings and other improvements. In 14 out of 33 estancias on owned land, the main building was referred to as a house rather than as a rancho, whereas among the 33 estancias on non-owned land, only 4 buildings were described as houses. Four houses had tile roofs among the former, but none among the latter. This seems to be a more important difference, since many of those described as houses had, as ranchos, raw adobe walls. The better quality of buildings on estancias on owned land is an indication of their more established nature. The quantity of buildings, however, was not that different. Twenty-five estancias on owned land and 23 estancias on non-owned land had two or three buildings. Five estancias on owned land and four estancias on non-owned land had more than three buildings, but only two of the former had less than two buildings, as did six of the latter.

Forty-five percent of estancias on owned land had ovens, 61% wells, 55% quintas, and 85% corrals. Eighteen percent of estancias on non-owned land had ovens, 15% wells, 33% quintas, and 70% corrals. Tools indicated the practice of some additional activities, such as agriculture and transportation. There were plows on 61% of the estancias on owned land, and carts on 85% of them, while there were plows on 45% of the estancias on non-owned land, and carts on 55% of them.

These figures complement the Gutiérrez–García model. Ranchos, wells, ovens, corrals, and groves were the most significant improvements. No activity could be carried out without dwellings and corrals, but carts and plows show that transportation and agriculture were vital activities. Wheat and firewood were produced on many estancias to meet their own needs, and probably for the market as well. Other activities were less frequent: There were atahonas on three estancias and, in spite of the widespread presence of sheep, there was a loom on only one estancia.

The 1850 estancias

The 1850 estancias often differ from the Gutiérrez–García model: They evolved from humbler beginnings than those of the model and had bigger and more elaborate buildings, but corrals, wells, fences, and ditches were usually less developed.

Houses account for 34% of all buildings on estancias on owned land and 18% on estancias on non-owned land; 44% of the former and 36% of the latter had two buildings or more. Ranchos were usually bigger than in the 1820s. The largest rancho was 20 varas long and 5 varas wide, and most ranchos were more than 10 varas long. The 6- and 7-vara-long ranchos mentioned in Gutiérrez and García's model were more frequent in 1820 than in 1850. Building materials had not changed: Adobe walls, with occasional use of brick, paja roofs, with tiles in a few cases, and ñandubay poles were still preferred for the wooden structure.

Other improvements depart from the model in a different way. There were corrals in 93% of those estancias, but they were usually smaller and weaker structures than that of the model. According to the model, 1,100 ñandubay poles were necessary for corrals, and ditches should be cut to protect them. Although many estancias had far more livestock than the model, only 20% of those with land had corrals with more than 1,000 ñandubay poles. Other softer, less durable woods were used instead, such as peach, poplar, and willow.

Ditches around corrals are mentioned also in 20% of the estancias. One ditch was longer than in the model, but most were usually shorter than the 600 varas required by a corral measuring 150 varas on each side. Another 22% of the estancias on owned land had ditches protecting the quinta or the población. Only two estancias on non-owned land (9%) had ditches, but they were 2,000 varas and 5,000 varas long, the longest among the 1850 inventories.

Other improvements also departed from the model. There were wells on 49% of the estancias on owned land and on 23% of the estancias on non-owned land. Lacking a well, water was probably obtained from other sources, such as a nearby stream or lagoon. The proportion of wells in the 1850s estancias was similar to that of the 1820s, but that of ovens was much lower. It declined from 45% to 15% of the estancias on owned land, and from 18% to 14% of estancias on non-owned land. The reasons for this variation may have been a decline of bread consumption, the spread of commercial bakeries, or a decline of domestic agriculture. In any case, plows also declined between 1820 and 1850 from 65% to 20% of the estancias on owned land, and from 45% to 27% of the estancias on non-owned land.

Another complementary activity, transportation, does not follow exactly the same pattern. The proportion of carts rose from 55% to 61% of estancias on owned land between 1820 and 1850 but fell from 70% to 41% of estancias on non-owned land. Quintas also fell from 63% of estancias on owned land in 1820 to 51% in 1850, and from 33% of estancias on non-owned land to 23% of estancias on non-owned land. Peach trees still prevailed, but in a few cases, poplars were also grown for building purposes. In the 1850s, as much as in the 1820s, there were several thousand peach trees for every ombú.[9]

Other improvements not included in the Gutiérrez–García model were less frequent. The 1850 sample includes five atahonas, one oven for bricks, another one for lime, and two dovecotes. Tools were similar to those of the 1820s except for two machines: one for thrashing wheat, the other for maize.

In 1850 there were new types of estancias not found in 1820. One of them was a small concern devoted mainly to sheep breeding (identified by the right to brand livestock), probably evolving from a puesto on someone else's land or from de facto occupation of a tract of public land. Another type of estancia, larger and less established than those of the older regions, was located beyond the Salado River.

An example of that type of estancia was Domingo Lastra's (Table 4.2).[10] Land accounted for 30% of the total inventory value; cattle, for 68%; and 1 rancho, a few tala stakes, 116 mares, 3 stallion-asses (burros hechores), 10 horses, and 4 branding irons accounted for the remaining 2%. Five thousand head of cattle roamed over 15 square leagues, equivalent to 40,500 hectares. Adding the horses to their number, the stocking rate was 7.8 hectares per livestock unit (h/LU). The low density and precarious improvements underscore the primitive stage of development of Lastra's estancia, which is consistent with its location in Lobería, close to the frontier.

Even larger than Lastra's holdings were those of Francisco Suárez, but his estancias, in Mar Chiquita and Pila, far away from the frontier, were better established (Table 4.2).[11] Land, 16,200 hectares, accounted for 81% of the total inventory value of the Mar Chiquita estancia. Improvements accounted for 11%, including a house (4%) and 1,122 ñandubay poles (5%). Cattle, 550 head, accounted for another 4%. This estancia had two puestos, with one rancho in each of them, but no cattle around. The Pila estancia was formed by two estancias (but recorded as a unit). Land, 30,825 hectares, accounted for 83% of the total inventory value; improvements, 7%; and livestock, 6%. Six hundred head of cattle, 613 mares and 38

9 For a description of ombú and its uses, see Hudson (1918), 4–5.
10 AGN, Tribunales, Sucesiones 6512, Domingo Lastra, 1848. See Table B.3, number 19.
11 AGN, Tribunales, Sucesiones 8169, Francisco Suárez, 1851. See Table B.3, numbers 35 and 36.

Table 4.2. *Capital structure of selected estancias,*
south of the Salado River, 1850

	Lastra		Suárez (Mar Chiquita)		Suárez (Pila)	
	pesos	%	pesos	%	pesos	%
Land	45,000	30.4	210,000	80.8	340,500	83.5
Improvements	800	0.5	29,469	11.3	28,670	7.0
Tools	120	0.1	2,327	0.9	1,992	0.5
Cattle	100,000	67.6	13,930	5.4	10,800	2.6
Horses	1,910	1.3	3,585	1.4	9,761	2.4
Sheep	–	0.0	–	0.0	1,955	0.5
Other	–	0.0	300	0.1	14,160	3.5
Total	147,830	100	259,787	100	407,838	100

	Tobal (Chascomús)		Tobal (Pila)		Miller	
	pesos	%	pesos	%	pesos	%
Land	114,100	52.5	140,000	52.8	299,400	32.5
Improvements	55,160	25.4	27,895	10.5	47,528	5.2
Tools	4,648	2.1	2,971	1.1	6,325	0.7
Cattle	18,406	8.5	55,708	21.0	460,180	49.9
Horses	6,336	2.9	12,276	4.6	44,429	4.8
Sheep	15,993	7.4	24,444	9.2	63,318	6.9
Other	2,676	1.2	1,683	0.6	520	0.1
Total	217,319	100	264,977	100	921,920	100

Notes: pesos = pesos moneda corriente (paper money); % = percentage over total value.
Sources: AGN, Tribunales, Sucesiones 6512, 6811, 8169, and 8463.

horses, and 786 sheep made a total of 1,512 LU. The stocking rate was therefore 20.4 h/LU. Both Suárez's estancias were understocked when compared to the 5.3 h/LU average for the New South (Table 5.7) and to the 7.8 h/LU rate of the less developed Lastra estancia. The only explanation for this understocking is that cattle were sold before the completion of the inventory.

Celestina Tobal's estancias were in a similar stage of development but were not understocked.[12] She owned 7,335 hectares in Chascomús and 16,200 hectares in Pila (Table 4.2). Land accounted for 53% of total value in both cases; improvements, 25% and 11%; and livestock, 19% and 35%. The Chascomús estancia held 997 head of cattle, 266 horses, and 1,150 sheep, making a total of 1,473 LU. Consequently, the stocking rate on that estancia was 5.0 h/LU. If that was a sign of development, a better sign were the buildings: a brick house, with two rooms and azotea roof; two brick

12 AGN, Tribunales, Sucesiones 8463, Celestina Tobal, 1850. See Table B.3, numbers 38 and 39.

ranchos, one with ramada, the other with two rooms; and two adobe ranchos, a shed for coaches, and a dovecote. The quinta, protected by a 1,450-vara ditch and a 675-vara cane fence, was formed by 205 willows, 209 poplars, 1,180 paraísos, several fruit trees (apricot, fig, apple, quince) and 7,389 peach trees. The jagüel, more elaborate than in the Gutiérrez–García model, included 28 ñandubay poles, 95 peach stakes, and some other wood. A piece of canvas listed with the jagüel was probably used as a botomless bucket.

Another sign of development were the three puestos. Puesto del Divisadero had two ranchos, one ñandubay corral, one water well, but no livestock other than 17 pigs. Puesto del Salado had no improvements, but just 1,245 sheep. And puesto del Inglés had two ranchos, one corral for sheep, and 1,735 sheep.

The Pila estancia was in a similar stage of development, but the buildings, five ranchos, were less elaborate, since the owner's main residence was on the other estancia. There were three corrals for cattle, horses, and sheep. The first two were made of ñandubay; for the latter "branches" were used. Jagüel, patio, palenque, potrero, and quinta were also part of that estancia. The quinta, protected by a 990-vara ditch, contained about 1,800 peach trees and 188 poplars, among other trees. There were two puestos – puesto de la Vigilancia and puesto del Mojón – the former with rancho, corral, potrero, palenque, and jagüel; the latter with rancho, corral, and quinta. The estancia and puestos held 1,040 head of cattle, 544 horses, and 3,497 sheep, making a total of 2,157 LU. The stocking rate was therefore 7.5 h/LU. Two out of three flocks of sheep were "mestizas finas," fine mixed breeds, fathered by four male Merino animals.

Juan Miller's estancia in Saladillo is the best example of a fully developed estancia in the 1850s (Table 4.2).[13] The estancia was formed by 2.25 square leagues owned by Miller and 10.47 square leagues held in emphyteusis, equivalent to 34,344 hectares. Land held in property was valued at 40,000 pesos per league, but that held in emphyteusis only half that amount. Land value, estimated in that way, accounted for 32% of total value, but estimating it at the value of land held in property, its proportion over total value rises to 45%. There were 2,711 horses on the estancia, 11,001 sheep, and 8,017 head of cattle; apart from those roundup head, another 9,600 were scattered over five neighboring estancias, and 3,000 to 4,000 stray head were up to 12 leagues around. Considering roundup cattle only, there were 12,781 LU, but 25,881 LU if stray head are added up. The stocking rate in the first case was 2.7 h/LU, and in the second case 1.3 h/LU.[14] The latter

---

13 AGN, Tribunales, Sucesiones 6811, Juan Miller, 1852. Due to price fluctuations in 1852, that year's inventories were not included in the 1850 sample.

14 The reason to include stray cattle in the estimate of density rate can be that a similar number of cattle belonging to neighboring estancias could have been on Miller's.

figure is the same as the average for the North, and the former is not too distant from that for the South (2.0 h/LU), and just below the 2.8 h/LU average for all regions (Table 5.7).

The main house, 20 varas long and 15 varas wide, had "mud" walls. There was a rancho used as a kitchen, another 25-vara rancho for the peons, with its own kitchen, a 25-vara shed, and two 5.5-vara rooms. The quinta, protected by a ditch, held 270 paraísos, 224 poplars, 150 weeping willows, 34 quince trees, and 175 peach trees. There was a plot sown with alfalfa, also protected by a ditch, and corrals and potreros. The better-established puestos had ranchos, corrals, potreros, and jagüel, but other puestos had just a rancho and a potrero.

Improvements accounted for 5% of the total inventory value; cattle, 50%; horses, 5%; and sheep, 7%. The herds and flocks of the main estancia accounted for 95% of cattle and 45% of horses but only 17% of sheep. The remaining cattle and horses were on six puestos, but 83% of the sheep were held by four medianeros (sharecroppers), who had their own puestos within the estancia. They were all foreigners: Byrne, Green, Murray, and Cornieul. Half of their flock was theirs, and half belonged to the estancia. Their situation was precarious, as shown by the fact that all the sharecroppers' improvements were equivalent to a mere 1.4% of the value of all improvements on the estancia.[15]

Miller's estancia was an exceptional case. Most of the estancias included in the sample were not at such a stage of development. But with Suárez's and Tobal's estancias, Miller's also underscores the trend: the ownership of several tracts and the establishment of puestos. It is the emphasis along those lines rather than their novelty that stems from the 1850 inventories. As seen in Chapter 2, López Osornio held several tracts but owned just one of them, and no puestos were mentioned on the Cañada de Arregui main tract. The 1820 sample includes one case of multiple landholdings, but again, only one was held in property. A different case is that of Juan Pedro Aguirre and Marcelo Ignes, studied in Chapter 9, who bought two different tracts of land in the mid-1820s. There are only two estancias with puestos in the 1820 sample, with only one puesto in each case. The 1850 sample includes nine estancias with puestos, five of them with two puestos. This is the result of the expansion to the south of the Salado River and the larger estancias prevailing there.

The 1850 estancias described so far were all south of the Salado River. Their different stages of development show that even within that region there were variations, related mainly to their location. There was a sequence of development going from Miller's estancia in Saladillo, to Tobal's estancia in Pila, to Suárez's estancia in Mar Chiquita, and Lastra's estancia

15 For an account of an Irish immigrant's life and economic evolution as sharecropper, see Brabazon (1981). See also Korol and Sabato (1981).

Table 4.3. *Capital structure of selected estancias,*
north of the Salado River, 1850

| | Figueroa | | Larredia | | de la Aguila | |
	pesos	%	pesos	%	pesos	%
Land	105,140	30.3	30,000	49.8	1,250	6.6
Improvements	61,732	17.8	25,635	42.6	1,502	7.9
Tools	19,275	5.5	200	0.3	322	1.7
Cattle	121,700	35.0	1,255	2.0	6,796	35.6
Horses	31,585	9.1	1,515	2.5	1,430	7.5
Sheep	6,562	1.9	1,107	1.8	5,778	30.3
Other	1,500	0.4	500	0.8	2,000	10.5
Total	347,495	100	60,212	100	19,078	100

Notes: pesos = pesos moneda corriente (paper money); % = percentage over total value.
Sources: AGN, Tribunales, Sucesiones 3507, 5706, and 6514.

in Lobería. Estancias located to the north of the Salado River were smaller
but better established.

Marcelina Figueroa's estancia on the Arrecifes River is an example of a
developed establishment of the North (Table 4.3).[16] Land, 3,547 hectares,
accounted for 30% of the estancia's total value; improvements, 18%; tools,
6%; cattle, 35%; horses, 9%; and sheep, 2%. There were 4,068 head of
cattle, 1,660 horses, and 1,875 sheep, making a total of 6,377 LU. The
stocking rate was 0.6 h/LU. This rate can be seen as a sign of overdevelop-
ment. Lack of fences and increasing herds were posing problems for
estancieros in the older regions in the mid-1850s, as evidenced by the
already referred to demands of restricting the number of head according to
the size of each tract.[17]

Figueroa also owned two houses in the city and a plot in the village of
San Antonio de Areco. Two stagecoaches served for commuting between
the estancia, the village, and the city. These stagecoaches, included in the
tools category, account for its higher proportion over total value than the
average for the North. The proportion of horses and sheep over total value
was average or slightly below average, while that of cattle was above
average. Because the proportion of land over total value was well below the
average for the region, Figueroa's case looks like a good example of an
efficient combination of capital items on an estancia in 1850. To make a
profit out of that combination would have required an efficient use of labor,
techniques, and managerial skills, but that was a good starting point.

16 AGN, Tribunales, Sucesiones 5706, Marcelina Figueroa, 1850. See Table B.3, number 16.
17 See ACR, 19, 22, 24, 37–38, 40, 45–46, 50, 52, 56, 57–58, 66–67, 74.

Ana María Larredia's estancia in Magdalena is a case pointing in a different direction (Table 4.3).[18] A state of paralysis, rather than an inefficient combination of capital items, is the dominant picture emerging from its inventory. On a tract of land 3,000 varas wide and 9,000 varas long (referred to, however, as a square league), there was an elaborate brick house with a living room and two bedrooms, azotea, and a tile roof; a 14-vara shed; a 12-vara kitchen and ramada; and a solidly built corral, with 413 ñandubay poles and 176 ñandubay stakes. Land accounted for 50% of the total inventory value; improvements, 43%; and livestock, a mere 6%. There were on this estancia only 81 head of cattle, 74 horses, and 369 sheep, making a total of 220 LU on 2,025 hectares, equivalent to 9.2 h/LU. Medical, legal, and other non-productive expenses following the owners' death probably prompted the heirs to sell most of the cattle, which interrupted the normal cycle of production.

Finally, a different kind of estancia should be exposed. Juan de la Aguila's estancia, located on Cañada de la Cruz, was a typical case of the smaller estancia found in the older regions, where sheep breeding would soon expand (Table 4.3).[19] The estancia was on a small plot, 125 varas wide and 9,000 varas long, equivalent to 84.4 hectares. On that thin tract (or rather, somewhere around it), there were 227 head of cattle, 92 horses, and 672 sheep, for a total of 426 LU. The stocking rate is an extremely high 0.20 h/LU, underscoring the overstocking problem that Alsina inquired about in 1856. Land accounted for 7% of the total inventory value; improvements, 8%; cattle, 36%; horses, 7%; and sheep, 30%. The configuration of the plot was a remnant from the past, but production was pointing in a different direction.

Conclusion

The practice of both cattle raising and sheep breeding on de la Aguila's estancia, the medianeros on Miller's estancia in Saladillo, and the capital structure of the 1850 estancias define the stage of evolution of sheep breeding on the pampas. Wool exports were expanding but not necessarily the flocks on the estancias, nor was a new type of estancia yet apparent. As a comparison of the 1820s and the 1850s flocks reveals, refinement accounts for increasing exports. A new type of organization, the emergence of medianeros, also accounts for such increases.

From 1820 to 1850, there were considerable changes affecting livestock production on the pampas. Those changes were only partially related to the goods produced and the technology used to produce them. Rather,

18 AGN, Tribunales, Sucesiones 6514, Ana María Larredia, 1848. See Table B.3, number 18.
19 AGN, Tribunales, Sucesiones 3507, Juan de la Aguila. See Table B.3, number 2.

relative price variations affected the combination of the different factors. Land values increased several times in real terms, while cattle values went down.

The productive landscape around 1850 looks, therefore, consistently negative: increased land value, decreasing cattle value, technical stagnation. It was, however, a period of an astonishing productive and territorial expansion. The explanation for such a contradiction is, by default, that higher land prices and lower cattle prices did not prevent estancieros from making sound profit out of their businesses. Only such an elusive element as profit (considered in Chapter 10) can explain a positive outcome from apparently negative factors.

Production was, therefore, carried out in a more efficient way and, barring technical changes (only the bottomless bucket can be noted), the only factor explaining such increasing efficiency is management. Managerial efficiency must have been responsible for decreasing production costs, in such a way that declining agricultural prices and the increasing valorization of land could be offset. That was not achieved by a more intensive use of land, since the number of livestock units per hectare decreased from 1820 to 1850. The higher investment per hectare in terms of head of cattle probably reflects better the change in the relative price of cattle vis-à-vis other goods. Whether that managerial efficiency was achieved at the expense of labor is an open question. For that to be possible, labor should not be scarce but plentiful. Circumstantial evidence and conventional wisdom do not support such a view.

A more efficient use of resources also meant diversification of production. Cattle by-products included hides, fat and tallow, horns, and hoofs, as well as beef, both fresh for an expanding urban consumption and salted for export. Horse by-products included hair, hides, and colt oil (aceite de potro). Sheep by-products were wool and sheepskins. Although the range of products may look limited, diversification is a crucial factor in explaining the estancieros' ability to counter adverse conditions.

This chapter has been devoted to the qualitative description of estancias. After contrasting models and realities, a key factor emerges. Estancias, although not failure-proof concerns, coped with business fluctuations by means of their adjusting mechanisms: Cattle could be sold or retained (if the tract was not already exceeding its carrying capacity, quite an improbable development on that unfenced countryside). But the balance was delicate, and it was the province of management to preserve it.

The Gutiérrez–García model should be understood as such, as a model. Real estancias were different from it. The basic idea underlying that estimate, however, is valid. From a starting point, which may or may not have been that of Gutiérrez and García, the estancia would grow. As shown by the different elements of the capital structure of the real estancias studied in Chapter 3, the starting point was much humbler than that of the model. In both 1820 and 1850, there were smaller corrals, fewer ditches and fences, and fewer wells and jagüels. There were, however, especially in 1850, better buildings, and in both cases many quintas, which were not part of the model. And in both the 1820s and the 1850s, there were many carts, serving for transportation of goods to and from the estancia, a factor also disregarded by the model.

Two generalizations derive from a comparison of the 1820s' and the 1850s' estancias. On the one hand, mainly north of the Salado River, an increasing relationship between urban centers and the countryside was underway. Houses in Buenos Aires or in neighboring villages, the presence of stagecoaches, and on the negative side, some extremely poor buildings on the estancia, are indications of that relationship. On the other hand, there was the emergence of a different kind of precariousness. Estancias on non-owned land in the 1820s looked in many cases like estancias on owned land. The title was missing, but settlement and development had taken place long ago. Estancias on non-owned land in the 1850s were less developed, less established – probably a consequence of the amazing territorial expansion that had taken place in the 30 years under review. While the old pampa grew at a slow pace from the 1780s to the 1820s, a faster pace after 1820 made room for many new enterprises that had to start from scratch.

If one factor is underscored after analyzing the Gutiérrez–García model and the 1820s' and 1850s' estancias, it should be growth. As business concerns, estancias grew out of their own resources. The López Osornio case (see Chapter 2) has shown the crucial role of cattle capitalization. The comparison of the 1820s' and 1850s' estancias point in the same direction. Given the right conditions, profit rates could be high (see Chapter 10), but much of the profit was reinvested on the estancia, either as larger herds or better buildings, corrals, ditches, fences, and means of transportation.

A comparison of the averages for different items of the capital structure has shown in Chapter 3 that the proportion of land value over total value was much higher in the 1850s. The analysis of individual cases undertaken in Chapter 4 has revealed a more complex landscape of estancias in different stages of development, with a different combination of their capital structures. Such differences push the analysis into a different direction, where natural factors and human action should be taken into account. These chapters have studied from different perspectives the capital structure of estancias according to inventories recorded at different stages of estancia development. They have served to depict a still life of estancias in 1820 and another one in 1850. These two pictures have been contrasted to account for the evolution of estancias between them. These pictures have also been compared with estancia models to account for the discrepancies between the image and the reality of estancias. But only static pictures of the capital structure have emerged from those inventories. They say nothing either of the conditions under which production was carried out or about the human effort involved in production.

PART II

Conditions of production

5

Cattle

Agrarian production is undertaken all over the world within restrictions determined by nature, technology, and institutions. Climate, soil, fauna, vegetation, water, and other natural conditions are key factors in understanding how production is carried out, but they are not discussed here. Rather, their consequences on production are discussed, along with those of human activity. Although the isolation of natural factors from human action is not always possible, their degrees of interplay vary. Conditions of production should not be thought of as given. They are constantly changing, at a different pace. Those material, environmental, and institutional conditions of production in the pampas in the first half of the nineteenth century are considered in this and the next two chapters.

Natural and to some extent man-made conditions resulted in specific cattle reproduction rates and stocking rates (or density). From stocking rates and total number of head, the actual area occupied by livestock is estimated. Rather than describing natural or human factors affecting rural production, this chapter focuses upon the outcome of those factors over production. In spite of differences in matter and method, these chapters deal with conditions resulting from the interaction between man and nature. Nature is in the forefront when considering material conditions, but human action was still present behind reproduction and stocking rates, since those apparently all-natural conditions did not determine production on their own. Man is in the forefront when considering institutions, but those habits and customs developed in a particular natural setting as an answer to conditions that human action itself was modifying. And a balance between man and nature is found when considering those natural elements directly changed by human action but, in turn, directly affecting it.

This chapter examines first the rate of cattle reproduction on the Buenos Aires pampas in the first half of the nineteenth century. Estimates of travelers and experts are compared to information supplied by primary sources, and the natural factors affecting those rates are considered. Then, similar sources are used to estimate the stocking rates or density, defined as the number of hectares required by a head of cattle on the pampas. And, finally, combining cattle reproduction and stocking rates with information supplied by other sources, the evolution of the cattle-raising area is estimated for 1800, 1820, and 1850.

Reproduction

The pampas cattle were of an unrefined type. Breeding would be a development taking place in the late nineteenth century, when the prospect of gaining overseas markets other than those demanding jerked beef began to materialize. So, the head of cattle wandering over the pampas were just the product of natural selection. What was good for their survival in those agreeable conditions, however, was not necessarily as good for human consumption. Drawings and paintings from the first half of the nineteenth century depict a skinny, bony, horny animal, whose value in fat and meat was far from that of the refined animal of the last years of the century.

There is no lack of contemporary estimates on the rate of cattle reproduction. In 1780, Pedro Dies de Chabes, representative of the Buenos Aires cattleowners, estimated it at one-third of the stock, while around 1800 Alvear and Lastarria gave figures of one-quarter to one-third for the Banda Oriental (Table 5.1). On the López Osornio estancia in Magdalena, the rate of reproduction was on average 12.8% between 1786 and 1795, but for 1791–1795 (the period defined as normal), it was 22.1% (Table 2.4). Poinsett gives for Buenos Aires in 1811 an annual rate of reproduction of 25%, and Robertson says that even by selling or killing 25% of the stock every year, it would grow. Trapani's estimate implies a 29.4% growth rate for cattle. In 1847 MacCann reported rates of reproduction of 34%, 35%, and even 40% for cattle. On the primitive estancia (around 1850), according to Daireaux, from a 1,000-head rodeo, usually composed in the fall of 300 young bulls and steers, 250 male and female yearlings, and 450 cows 2 years old and above (there are 50 head missing to make 1,000, but he does not mention them), a 20% to 40% calving could be expected, depending on how rainy the previous spring had been. Finally, around 1900, Miatello reported a rate of reproduction of 25% to 35% for cattle.[1] Consequently, a rate of reproduction of 25% was probably normal in the first half of the nineteenth century, while calving (counting calves who would not survive) might have been as high as 30% to 40%.

Information on horse and sheep reproduction rates is less plentiful. According to Trapani's estimate, they were 28.7% for the former and

1 DHA, 4:22; Lastarria (1914), 238; Alvear (1900), 316; Robertson (1838), 1:55; Poinsett to Sumter, Buenos Aires, 15 June 1811, in Poinsett (1984a), 198; Barba (1967), 66–67; MacCann (1969), 207; Daireaux (1908), 400; Miatello (1901), 97.

Table 5.1. *Livestock reproduction in Buenos Aires, 1783–1850*
(percentage)

Source	Year	Cattle	Horses	Sheep
Dies de Chabes	1780	33	–	–
López Osornio	1791–1795	22.1	–	12.4
Robertson	1810	25	–	–
Poinsett	1811	25	–	–
Trapani	1831	29.4	28.7	49.1
MacCann	1847	34–40	33	33.7
Daireaux	1850	20–40	–	–

Sources: See this chapter, note 1.

49.1% for the latter. According to MacCann, it was 33% per year for horses and from 21% to 41% for sheep, with an average of 33.7% for the five cases he studies. Hutchinson says, based upon information obtained in Entre Ríos in 1861, that 5,000 sheep and 260 rams would produce 21,500 lambs in 5 years, requiring therefore a 38.5% annual rate. He also mentions an exceptional case, that of Mr. Braham, a breeder from San Pedro, who had obtained in 1 year 900 lambs out of 1,900 sheep, with a reproduction rate of 47.4%. Again, at the turn of the century, Miatello mentioned rates of reproduction of 30% to 40% for sheep and 25% to 40% for horses.[2]

Apart from the quality of the animals themselves, the rate of reproduction depended upon the quality of the fields and the care given to livestock. Stray or cimarrón cattle had an estimated reproduction rate of about half that of roundup cattle, which was a consequence, among other factors, of attacks on the offspring by wild dogs, which proliferated over the pampas. It was not a mean threat. A reference to the "extraordinary number of dogs which eat young calves and other young beasts" is already found in Acarete du Biscay's account of his visit to Buenos Aires in the 1660s. In the first half of the eighteenth century, they were mentioned in Isaac Morris's and Cardiel's accounts of their travels across the Buenos Aires plains. A British observer remarked in 1752 that there were more dogs on the pampas than anywhere else in the world; in 1772, Millau found dog herds all over the countryside, ravaging cattle even more than tigers, and Juan Francisco de Aguirre made a similar remark in the early 1780s. In 1783 the number of wild dogs threatened the regular supply of beef to Buenos Aires. That was probably an exceptional case, but wild dogs could always be severely harmful for individual establishments: A 1788 report complains about the

2 Barba (1967), 66–67; MacCann (1969), 31, 60, 200–202; Hutchinson (1945), 305–308; Miatello (1901), 97.

loss of two-thirds of the annual calving to dogs. Special expeditions were sent to the countryside to kill wild dogs. Sergeant Major Felipe Antonio Martínez, of the Areco militia, on 16 November 1790 reported to have killed 2,437 dogs.[3]

References to wild dogs at the beginning of the nineteenth century are not different from those of previous decades. In 1810 Poinsett found that cattle remnants scattered over the fields were devoured by troops of dogs wandering along the plains as wolves did in the north. Rosas, in his 1819 *Instrucciones a los mayordomos de estancias*, directed his overseers to kill, while rounding up cattle, as many wild dogs and other *bichos* (lions, tigers, skunks) as they could without disregarding their main task. And around 1820, a British traveler reported that "herds of wild dogs" were "dangerous to one who travels alone" in the countryside.[4]

As time went by, however, wild dogs vanished. Beaumont reported in 1826 that dogs were less numerous than in the past, and Darwin, who crossed the pampas in 1833, and MacCann, who did so in 1847, do not mention them. The threat, nevertheless, was not completely gone. In 1856, in Chascomús, Brabazon got rid of the dogs harassing his flocks by killing mares and poisoning their flesh with arsenic. And even in 1869, in a trip to Balcarce, Armaignac heard a story of dogs devouring a human being just a few years earlier.[5]

As harmful as wild dogs were stray mares. In 1748 Cardiel found "an extraordinary number of droves everywhere." They not only competed with cattle for grass but destroyed with their hoofs the common feeding source. Overstocking the fields could have a similar effect, as remarked by Alvear in 1783 and Daireaux in 1900.[6]

Droughts, locusts, floods, and diseases could also deprive cattle of their natural food and provoke their sudden death, affecting reproduction rates. "The season continues yet unfavorably dry and . . . we shall lose a good

3 Brito Stífano (1953), 349; Morris's and Cardiel's accounts in Vignati (1956), 31, 123; Acarete du Biscay (1672), 7; González Garaño (1940b), 523; Millau (1947), 51; Aguirre (1947), 235–236; Alvear (1900), 316; Representación del Fiel Ejecutor, 2 May 1783, AGN, IX–19–3–2; AGN, IX–12–9–9, Solicitudes civiles, 1788, quoted by Montoya (1984), 50. On the *bando* ordering the elimination of wild dogs and its implementation in Areco, see AGN, IX–14–4–1, quoted by Melli (1974), 49. On wild dogs, see Cabrera (1932) and Gallardo (1963).

4 Poinsett (1984b), 105; another reference in a letter from Poinsett to Sumter, Buenos Aires, 15 June 1811, ibid., 198; Rosas (1942), 36, 56; and "Notes written during a late Residence at Buenos Ayres, by an English Gentleman, formerly of Bene't College, Cambridge," *Monthly Magazine*, 1 August 1821, 356:33.

5 Beaumont (1957), 64; Darwin (1839); MacCann (1969); Brabazon (1981), 140–142; Armaignac (1962), 18.

6 Cardiel (1956), 131; Clemente López Osornio to the Cabildo, 6 April 1780, in AGN, Archivo del Cabildo, IX-19-3-2, f. 414, quoted by Montoya (1984), 68; Alvear (1900), 318; Daireaux (1908), 394–395.

many calves, this years' calving, from the poorness and weakness of the mothers," reported James Hodgson from Buenos Aires to his partner in Liverpool, on 20 July 1831, referring to their estancia in Monsalvo, south of the Salado River. Those natural disasters did not necessarily affect the whole countryside at the same time. When drought struck, the lowlands of Magdalena provided a refuge for cattle from other districts. But excessive rains frequently caused floods, as happened to the Salado River in September 1833 when Darwin crossed it on his way to Buenos Aires. A year later, in October 1834, subsequent storms left the area from Chascomús to Tuyú under water for several months. And John Brabazon's tracts in Chascomús were also flooded between July and September 1856.

What was catastrophic for producers could be beneficial in the short run for consumers. The coincidence of drought and locusts in 1772 caused an oversupply of the best beef at inferior prices when cattle from distant and fertile lands were compulsorily sent to the market. But that was a temporary advantage, since that period of stock depletion must have been followed by another of stock recovery, with rising prices and worsening quality. Disasters did not necessarily strike one by one: In 1791 drought and the so-called "grain disease" (enfermedad del grano) coincided, and in 1832 a long drought was followed by floods.[7]

The locust, a frequent disaster, was not eradicated until DDT was introduced in the 1950s. Temple, who met a manga (swarm) in Córdoba in January 1826, describes its effect as "the melancholy of winter in the middle of the summer." Scrivener, who met a swarm in Santiago del Estero the same year, describes it as "a dense fog rising from the horizon," passing over his head for more than hour. Darwin, on 25 March 1835, just before arriving in Luján de Cuyo, Mendoza, was overpassed by a locust swarm so dense that the sky could not be seen. Locusts had devastating effects on agriculture as well as on cattle raising, since grasses were also affected. Cattle sales had to be anticipated because of the risk posed by "the inevitable plague of the locust" on Juan Pedro Aguirre and Marcelo Ignes's estancia at Arroyo del Tala in October 1824. Sometimes grasses were destroyed in large areas, as mentioned by John Miers, who found them covering 200 miles between Cañada de Lucas and El Cerrillo, along the road from Santa Fe to Córdoba, in the early 1820s. Darwin described the vain efforts of the inhabitants of the countryside to draw the swarm

7 James Hodgson to Joseph Green, Buenos Aires, 20 July 1831, in JRM, James Hodgson letters, 1831–1846, 9; DHA, 7–8, 116–119; José de la Rosa to Francisco de Paula Sanz, Buenos Aires, 20 February 1788, in AGN, IX–30–4–1, f. 66; Darwin (1839), 136, 155–157; Miller (1829), 1:145, 154–155; Brabazon (1981), 45–46, 139; and George Gibson to Robert Gibson, letters from October 1834 to February 1835, in NLS, Gibson Papers. On the "grain disease," see D'Orbigny (1835), 1:165, 546. On the pattern of rain in Buenos Aires, see Ardissone (1937).

away: Smoke, shouts, and branches sweeping the air were not enough to persuade them to shift their destructive path.[8]

Droughts, floods, locusts, and wild dogs were some of the factors affecting the rate of reproduction or, rather, the rate of survival of calves. Proper care could reduce losses but at some expense. In 1856 losses were still estimated at 15% to 20% for stray cattle, 5% for domesticated cattle, 3% for horses, and 15% in winter and 5% in summer for sheep.[9]

Density

Cattle roamed over the open pampas undisturbed by any artificial obstacle. Estancias were delimited, at best, by some landmarks (mojones), placed by surveyors when measurements were carried out. But those mojones, seldom respected by men, certainly did not prevent cattle from walking past the estancia boundaries. The absence of physical obstacles did not mean, however, that there was no relationship between the number of head and the extension of landholdings. By the mid-nineteenth century, estancieros were aware of the number of head a particular tract could hold, and the persistence of old overstocking customs created problems. This does not mean that the relationship between the number of head and the extension of a tract was previously ignored, as contemporary estimates show.[10] Because livestock density is a basic indication of land productivity, changes in density stress the evolution of estancia efficiency as much as, in combination with output figures, the process of territorial expansion. In order to prove this, two sources are used: density estimates

---

8 Temple (1833), 1:79; Miers (1826), 1:204; Beaumont (1957), 73; Darwin (1839), 402–403; Scrivener (1937), 56; Marcelo Ignes to Juan Pedro Aguirre, El Tala, 22 October 1824, in ABP, 031-5-3-10.

9 REBA (1855), 2:34.

10 Stocking rate or density (both are used here as equivalent) is the number of hectares needed for each head of cattle or equivalent. The number of head per hectare is usually preferred, but it would have led us to use too many decimals. The estimate of hectares per livestock unit is also pertinent for a time when land rather than cattle was the dependent variable. In recent decades, the ratio for the whole Pampa region is about 1 head of cattle per hectare [Fienup, Brannon, and Fender (1969), 72; and Peretti and Gómez (1991), 274]. Throughout this book, a livestock unit is 1 head of cattle, or 0.8 horse, or 8 sheep, according to the estimate of the 1881 Buenos Aires census [Buenos Aires (1883), lviii]. That equivalence has been preferred to another given by Gregorio J. de Quirno in 1863, while answering Alsina's second inquiry, who estimated that 1 square league could hold 4,000 head of cattle, or 1,000 mares, or 24,000 sheep. For him, therefore, one head of cattle was equivalent to 1/4 horse or 6 sheep [ACR, 215]. For eighteenth- and nineteenth-century Germany, Slicher van Bath gives an equivalence of 1 cow = 2/3 horse = 10 sheep [Slicher van Bath (1963), 294]. Recent estimates have been made in Argentina using the equivalence of 1 head of cattle = 1 horse = 5 sheep [Fienup et al. (1969), 72]. Even more recent technical studies use an equivalence of 1 head of cattle = 6.3 sheep. See Eduardo Vaquer y Ariel J. García, "Reconversión ganadera: Cría de ovinos," *La Nación*, 26 de noviembre de 1994, section 4, 1.

made by contemporaries, and figures obtained from returns and probate inventories.

Before considering these estimates, it is convenient to bear in mind, for comparative purposes, figures of livestock density in Europe. This can serve to explain both the astonishment of foreign observers in the early decades of the nineteenth century and the considerable increase in land productivity in Buenos Aires during that century. Slicher van Bath mentions that in the early nineteenth century from 7 to 12 hectares were required in Germany to feed one draught animal. Perhaps this figure is so high due to the use to which the animal was subject. Plain cattle demanded less land. In Britain around 1800, one cow required 0.94 hectares if fodder crops were given, or 1.88 hectares of pastureland if not.[11]

Going back then to the density estimates for Buenos Aires, Azara mentions in his 1801 *Memoria* a proportion of 2,000 head of cattle per square league. A square league was equivalent to 2,700 hectares, so the density was 1.35 h/LU (Table 5.2). In the same writing, however, he estimated a total cattle stock of 48 million head for an area of 42,000 square leagues. The stocking rate was, consequently, 2.36 h/LU. In his *Histoire naturelle des quadrupèdes*, the same Azara estimated that a 15,000-by 5,000-vara estancia, equivalent to 5,625 hectares, could hold 4,000 head of cattle – a stocking rate of 1.41 h/LU. His estimates for individual estancias showed a greater density than in the region as a whole.[12]

John P. Robertson estimated in 1810 that an estancia of 80 to 100 square miles could hold from 12,000 to 15,000 head of cattle, roughly 13,500 head on 23,040 hectares, equivalent to 1.71 h/LU. In 1815 in a proposal for moving the frontier to the south, Francisco Xavier Viana estimated a density of 12,000 head of undifferentiated livestock for 43,200 hectares. If those livestock were all cattle, the density was 3.6 h/LU for the new region.[13]

An advertisement placed in a Buenos Aires newspaper in November 1826 offered an estancia for sale, located 25 miles to the southwest of the city, with 5,000 head of cattle, 200 horses, and 1,500 sheep on 10,125 hectares. The density was in that case 1.86 h/LU. Five years later Pedro Trapani estimated 1,500 head of cattle, 150 horses, and 500 sheep for a 4,050-hectare estancia on the Salado River, equivalent to a density of 2.31 h/LU.

L. B. Mackinnon, who sailed up the Paraná River in 1846 with the Anglo-French fleet, says that 9 square miles (2,330 hectares), probably in Buenos Aires or Santa Fe, could hold 1,000 head of cattle and 500 horses,

11 Slicher van Bath (1963), 294, 296–297.
12 Azara (1943), 11; Azara (1801), 2:367.
13 Robertson (1838) 1:54; "Proyecto de Francisco Xavier Viana," in Azara (1910), 85ff.

Conditions of production

Table 5.2. *Livestock density in Buenos Aires, 1793–1887*
(estimates)

E	Place	Year	Land	Cattle	Horses	Sheep	LU	h/LU
1	BA	1801	2,700	2,000	–	–	2,000	1.3
2	BA	1801	5,625	4,000	–	–	4,000	1.4
3	S	1815	43,200	–	–	–	12,000	3.6
4	SW	1826	10,125	5,000	200	1,500	5,437	1.9
5	BA	1831	4,050	1,500	150	500	1,750	2.3
6	RC	1833	8,100	10,000	–	–	10,000	0.8
7	S	1847	2,700	1,000	–	–	1,000	2.7
8	N	1847	2,700	2,500	450	4,500	3,625	0.7
9	BA	1847	2,700	–	–	13,000	1,625	1.7
10	BA	1847	2,700	–	–	50,000	6,250	0.4
11	T	1847	48,600	25,000	2,500	5,000	28,750	1.7
12	RS	1847	54,000	40,000	–	–	40,000	1.3
13	BA	1848	2,700	3,000	–	–	3,000	0.9
14	BA	1855	2,700	6,000	–	–	6,000	0.4
15	V	1855	2,700	1,500	200	2,000	2,000	1.3
16	M	1855	2,700	2,500	700	1,500	3,562	0.8
17	BA	1860	2,700	–	–	19,000	2,375	1.1
18	BA	1887	3.4[a]	4	–	–	4	0.8
19	BA	1887	3.4	3.4	–	–	3.4	1.0
20	S	1888	32,400	22,000	–	60,000	29,500	1.1

[a] Alfalfa meadows
Notes:
Estimates (E): 1–2, Azara; 3, Viana; 4, *La Gaceta Mercantil*; 5, Trapani; 6, Rosas;
7–12, MacCann; 13, Arnold; 14, Vicuña Mackenna; 15–16, *Registro Estadístico de
Buenos Aires*; 17, Hinde; 18–19, Senillosa-Frers; 20, Daireaux.
Places: BA, Buenos Aires; S, south of Buenos Aires; SW, 25 leagues southwest of
Buenos Aires; N, north of Buenos Aires; T, Tapalquén; RS, Río Salado; V, Vecino; M,
Mercedes.
Land: in hectares.
Livestock unit (LU): 1 head of cattle = 8 sheep or goats = 0.8 horse, mule, or
donkey = 1 pig.
h/LU: hectares per livestock unit.
Sources: See this chapter, notes 12–14.

equivalent to a density of 1.43 h/LU. A few years later, William MacCann
reported that the lands of then-southern Buenos Aires could put up with
1,000 head of cattle per square league, while those of northern Buenos
Aires, of a better quality, 2,000 to 3,000 head of cattle, 400 to 500 horses,
and 4,000 to 5,000 sheep on the same area. The stocking rates were
therefore 2.70 h/LU for the south and 0.74 h/LU on average for the north.
Without locating the land, he also said that a square league was good to
feed from 12,000 to 14,000 sheep, without storing food for them or
removing them during bad seasons; a good-quality land in the same region

could feed up to 50,000 sheep. The density was, consequently, 1.66 h/LU on average in the first case and 0.43 h/LU in the second. The same author mentions some specific estancias. Dr. Dick's "Los tres bonetes," located a 3-day horse-ride away from Tapalqué, had around 25,000 head of cattle, 2,000 to 3,000 horses, and "a good number of sheep" on 48,600 hectares, equivalent to 1.73 h/LU without considering sheep. Anchorena's "Camerón" (actually "Camarones"), located close to the Salado River, had 40,000 head of cattle on 54,000 hectares, equivalent to a stocking rate of 1.35 h/LU. Also in the late 1840s, another foreign observer, Samuel Greene Arnold, reported 3,000 head of cattle per square league, equivalent to 0.9 h/LU. Chilean writer Benjamín Vicuña Mackenna, who stopped in Buenos Aires in 1855, mentioned twice that number of cattle for the same area, equivalent therefore to a density of 0.45 h/LU. Reports submitted by cattleowners at the request of the head of the Buenos Aires Statistical Department in the mid-1850s mentioned 1,500 head of cattle, 200 horses, and 2,000 sheep per square league in the Vecino district, 200 km south of Buenos Aires, beyond the Salado River, and 2,500 head of cattle, 700 horses, and 1,500 sheep for the same area in Mercedes, 90 km west of Buenos Aires, north of that river. The stocking rates were 1.35 h/LU for the Vecino estancia and 0.76 h/LU for the Mercedes estancia. At about the same time, Federico Hinde, a breeder, estimated between 18,000 and 20,000 sheep for each league of good land, equivalent to a density of 1.14 h/LU. Finally, in the late 1880s, stocking rates, according to Senillosa and Frers, were around 1 h/LU for ordinary fields and 0.84 h/LU for alfalfa meadows. And Daireaux recorded a density of 1.1 h/LU for enclosed tracts 100 leagues from Buenos Aires (the distance to Tres Arroyos, although no particular region was mentioned).[14]

In 1856 Valentín Alsina's inquiry yielded twenty estimates of livestock density for different regions of the province (Table 5.3).[15] Those estimates range from 0.36 h/LU, reported by Faustino Alcina, from Baradero, for a tract of 338 hectares holding 7,500 sheep, to 1.35 h/LU reported by Valentín Fernández Blanco, from Morón, for a tract of 4,050 hectares holding 24,000 sheep. The mean for the twenty estimates is 0.74 h/LU, but regional differences are evident: The mean for the North (San Nicolás and Baradero) is 0.58 h/LU; for the Center (Matanza, Cañuelas, Morón), 0.71 h/LU; for the West (Mercedes, Chivilcoy), 0.79 h/LU; and for the

14 *La Gaceta Mercantil*, 16 November 1826; Trapani's estimate in Barba (1967), 66–67; Rosas's estimate in Saldías (1958), 3:38; Darwin (1839), 170; Mackinnon (1957), 153–154; MacCann (1969), 63, 108, 194, 207; Arnold (1951), 186; Vicuña Mackenna (1936), 120; REBA (1855), 2:33, 41, quoted by Infesta de Guerci (1983); Hinchliff (1955), 231; Federico Hinde's estimate in Hutchinson (1945), 310; Senillosa and Frers (1887), 22; Daireaux (1888), 2:213–216.
15 For more on the Alsina inquiry, see Chapter 7.

Table 5.3. *Livestock density in Buenos Aires, 1856*

Producer	Region	Hectares	Cattle	Horses	Sheep	LU	h/LU
L. Lagos	Matanza	2,700	–	–	–	6,000	0.45
J. Linch	Baradero	2,025	3,000	–	–	3,000	0.68
J. Linch	Baradero	2,700	–	–	–	6,000	0.45
J. Hannah	Ranchos	2,700	–	–	18,500	2,313	1.17
B. Gutiérrez	Mercedes	180	200	100	750	419	0.43
M. Villarino	Chivilcoy	2,025	1,500	200	2,000	2,000	1.01
M. López	Chivilcoy	2,025	2,000	100	2,000	2,375	0.85
P. Linch	Not mentioned	2,025	2,000	600	600	2,825	0.72
F. Alcina	Baradero	2,025	3,000	–	3,000	3,375	0.60
F. Alcina	Baradero	338	–	–	7,500	938	0.36
N. Villegas	Chivilcoy	2,025	2,000	600	6,000	3,500	0.58
M. Benítez	Chivilcoy	1,350	1,250	–	–	1,250	1.08
M. Benítez	Chivilcoy	169	–	–	2,250	281	0.60
V. Casalins	Ranchos	2,700	500	500	9,000	2,250	1.20
F. Halbach	Cañuelas	2,700	–	–	25,000	3,125	0.86
J. Benítez	S. Nicolás	2,700	4,000	–	–	4,000	0.68
I. Correas	Not mentioned	2,700	3,000	–	–	3,000	0.90
I. Correas	Not mentioned	2,700	–	–	18,000	2,250	1.20
V. F. Blanco	Morón	4,050	6,000	–	8,000	7,000	0.58
V. F. Blanco	Morón	4,050	–	–	24,000	3,000	1.35
Mean		2,194				2,945	0.74

Note: for LU and h/LU, see Table 5.2.
Source: ACR, passim.

South (Ranchos), 1.18 h/LU. The most balanced observation was Bernardo Gutiérrez's: The number of head of livestock that a particular tract could feed, he remarked, depended upon the quality of land – not just on the soil, it may be added, but also on how long livestock had been grazing on a tract. Decades of grazing were required for a tract to be "done," that is, for hard grasses to turn into soft grasses. Regional differences are the evidence of how that land improvement process was carried out in the Buenos Aires countryside.[16]

Azara, Trapani, Senillosa and Frers, Daireaux, and the estancieros who reported to Alsina in 1856, all had first-hand experience of rural production. Their estimates, although some optimism could never be ruled out, were better founded than those of travelers, most of them only occasionally acquainted with the pampas and sometimes even without a proper knowledge of the language. Among those travelers too candid to be believed

16 ACR, 14–15, 19, 22, 25–26, 37, 40, 43, 45–46, 48, 50, 52, 56, 58, 65, 67, 74–75. On the transformation of the quality of grasses due to livestock action, see Daireaux (1908), 18–19, and Schmieder (1927a, 1927b).

Table 5.4. *Livestock density in five Buenos Aires districts, 1789*

Region[a]	Hectares	Cattle N	Horses N	Sheep N	LU	Density h/c	h/LU
Areco	35,751	30,275	7,554	15,430	41,646	1.18	0.86
Cañada de Escobar	11,845	4,094	–	–	–	2.89	–
Río de las Conchas	20,872	2,260	–	–	–	9.23	–
Pilar	31,445	12,930	–	–	–	2.43	–
Magdalena	123,641	27,040	7,210	–	36,052	4.57	3.43
Total	223,544	76,599				2.92	2.05[b]

[a] Only rural establishments with complete data have been considered.
[b] Areco and Magdalena only.
Note: N = number of head; h/c = hectares/cattle head. For LU and h/LU, see Table 5.2.
Source: AGN, IX–9–7–7, Padrón de Estancias, 1789.

ranks Alexander Gillespie, a British officer captured in 1806, who mentions an estancia with 60,000 head of cattle and horses on 10,752 hectares. If true, the density would have been a fantastic 0.18 h/LU. Other observers may have been the victims of typographical errors. The American agent Joel R. Poinsett assured to have seen a million head of cattle, 500 to 600 horses, and a similar number of sheep on a square league. If we assume a typing error and the number of head of cattle is turned from 1 million into 1,000 head, then the density is a reasonable 1.54 h/LU.[17]

Observers and travelers estimated livestock density according to their knowledge of rural matters. Their estimates were valuable then and still today but are no substitute for actual cases found in primary sources. One of these sources is the 1789 estancias return.[18] It recorded information about the extension of the estancias and the number of cattle on them for five of the rural districts: Areco, Cañada de Escobar, Río de las Conchas, Pilar, and Magdalena (Table 5.4). Cattle density fluctuated from 1.2 hectares per head in Areco to 9.2 hectares per head in Río de las Conchas, with an average of 2.9 hectares per head. As the number of horses is known only for Areco and Magdalena and the number of sheep only for Areco, the number of hectares per livestock unit can be estimated for them: 0.86 h/LU for Areco and 3.43 h/LU for Magdalena.

A detailed examination of the Magdalena district shows stocking rates ranging from 1.1 h/LU for the region between Arroyo del Gato and Cañada de Arregui to 11.1 h/LU for Samborombón (Table 5.5). These rates, how-

17 Gillespie (1986), 114; Gallardo (1984), 119.
18 AGN, IX–9–7–7. That return has been studied by Azcuy Ameghino and Martínez Dougnac (1989). A different equivalence for the livestock unit is used by these authors, but they do not give any reason for choosing it.

Table 5.5. *Livestock density in Magdalena, 1789*

Region[a]	Hectares	Cattle N	Horses N	LU	Density h/c	h/LU
Arroyo del Gato	44,195	6,600	2,130	9,262	6.7	4.8
A. del Gato–Cañada de Arregui	9,290	6,530	1,490	8,392	1.4	1.1
South of Cañada de Arregui	7,020	2,160	760	3,110	3.2	2.3
Cabezadas	15,886	7,750	2,630	11,037	2.0	1.4
Samborombón	47,250	4,000	200	4,250	11.8	11.1
Total	123,641	27,040	7,210	36,052	4.6	3.4

[a] Only rural establishments with complete data have been considered. The 1789 census recorded 67 establishments in Magdalena, 6 in Chascomús, and 5 in Samborombón.
Note: N = number of head; h/c = hectares/cattle head. For LU and h/LU, see Table 5.2.
Source: AGN, IX–9–7–7, Padrón de Estancias, 1789.

ever, cannot be accepted at face value, as shown by the case of the López Osornio estancia. According to the 1789 return, its extension was 3,450 varas wide and 9,000 varas long, equivalent to 2,329 hectares. The 1786 inventory, however, recorded an extension equivalent to 9,356.5 hectares, including bañado, suerte principal, and cabezadas; adding to this 8,526.8 hectares of the non-contiguous invernada, results in a total area of 17,883.3 hectares. The number of livestock was also underestimated in that return: only 800 head of cattle and 200 horses, equivalent to 1,050 livestock units. The number of livestock for 1789 estimated according to the inventories is, however, 1,978 head of cattle, 817 horses, and 1,383 sheep, making 3,172 livestock units. Consequently, the actual extension held by López Osornio was 7.7 times larger than that of the 1789 return, and the number of livestock units was 3 times higher. The 1789 estancia return underrecorded both land and livestock but in different proportions, therefore density was affected. The stocking rate for the López Osornio estancia according to that return was 2.22 h/LU, while according to the inventories it was 2.95 h/LU not including the invernada, and 5.64 h/LU including it. A further point should be stressed – those rates were not static. The stocking rate for all López Osornio's landholdings improved according to inventories from 4.9 h/LU in 1792 to 3.0 h/LU in 1795.

This is the main problem affecting all estimates, both those based upon the more or less informed guesses of travelers and experts, and those stemming from static sources: They fail to account for the evolution of the relationship between cattle and land on a single estancia. In a more general sense, however, the accumulation of information for different estancias and regions can give an idea of the regional evolution of cattle ranching. Bearing this in mind, other estancia inventories can be compared to the observers' estimates and the 1789 estancia return (Table 5.6). On the

Table 5.6. *Livestock density in Buenos Aires, 1788–1850*

Owner	Place	Year	Hectares	Cattle	Horses	Sheep	LU	h/LU
L. Osornio[a]	Magdalena	1789	2,329	800	200	–	1,050	2.2
L. Osornio	Magdalena	1789	17,883	1,978[b]	817[c]	1,383[c]	3,172	5.6
L. Osornio	Magdalena	1792	17,883	2,646	676	1,450	3,672	4.9
L. Osornio	Magdalena	1795	17,883	4,581	900	2,000	5,956	3.0
Lastra	Monsalvo	1822	24,300	4,448	140[c]	4,623		5.3
Segismundo	Chascomús	1825	47,250	11,122	2,486	521	14,295	3.3
Segismundo	Macedo	1825	48,600	863	145	–	1,044	46.6
Aguirre	A. del Medio	1827	3,560	2,273	120	550	2,492	1.4
Several	Azul	1839	602,436	111,527	10,512	43,450	130,098	4.6

[a] Figures from the 1789 estancia return.
[b] Estimate from Table 2.4.
[c] Estimate.
Note: for LU and h/LU, see Table 5.2.
Sources: See this chapter, note 19.

estancia bought in 1822 by Lastra, Green, and Hodgson in Kakel, in the Monsalvo district, there were 4,448 head of cattle and 7 droves of horses and mares on 9 square leagues, with a density of about 5.4 h/LU. In Chascomús, in 1825, on Juan Bautista Segismundo's estancia, located between the Samborombón and Salado rivers, there were 11,122 head of cattle, 2,486 horses, and 521 sheep on 47,250 hectares, with a density of 3.3 h/LU. Both estancias were in a region of recent settlement but were fairly well established, according to their stocking rates. Estancias recently established on land still very much on the frontier were a different case. An estancia in the Macedo district also belonging to Segismundo held 863 head of cattle and 145 horses on 48,600 hectares, with a stocking rate of 46.4 h/LU. On estancias recently established in regions already incorporated into production, land was used more intensively from the beginning. That was the case of Aguirre and Ignes's estancia on Arroyo del Medio, which in 1827 held 2,492 LU (2,273 head of cattle, 120 horses, and about 550 sheep) on 3,559 hectares, with a density of 1.43 h/LU. A frontier region where settlement had been supported by the government by means of land distributions had in the late 1830s stocking rates similar to those found close to the Salado River a decade earlier. In 1839, 82 estancias in Azul held 138,152 LU on 650,670 hectares, with a density of 4.71 h/LU.[19]

19 JRM, Hodgson and Robinson Papers, Green and Hodgson Ranch Account, 1822–1825; AGN, Tribunales, Sucesiones 8146, Juan Bautista Segismundo; AGN, VII–1–5–2, f. 1291; ABP, Juan Pedro Aguirre archive, 031–5–2–10, 031–5–3–2, 031–5–3–3, 031–5–3–6, and 031–5–3–15; and "Censo de propietarios y ganaderos de la frontera del Arroyo Azul . . ." (1930).

Table 5.7. *Livestock density in Buenos Aires, 1820 and 1850*

	1820 Hectares A	1820 LU B	1820 Density C	1850 Hectares D	1850 LU F	1850 Density G
North	28,771	28,606	1.01	27,177	20,829	1.30
Center	19,204	15,491	1.24	33,301	22,569	1.48
South	44,685	27,312	1.64	18,080	8,925	2.03
Frontier–New South	15,525	723	21.47	149,366	28,230	5.29
Total	108,185	72,166	1.50	227,924	80,556	2.83

Notes:
A Total area of 33 estancias on owned land, in hectares.
B Total number of livestock units on 33 estancias on owned land.
C Livestock density: hectares per livestock unit (A/B).
D Total area of 41 estancias on owned land, in hectares.
F Total number of livestock units on 41 estancias on owned land.
G Livestock density: hectares per livestock unit (A/B).
Sources: Tables B.1 and B.3.

A different picture of the regional evolution of ranching emerges from the 1820 and 1850 inventories studied in Chapter 3. Livestock density varies from region to region in the 1820 inventories. For the North it was 1.01 h/LU; for the Center, 1.24 h/LU; for the South, 1.64 h/LU; and for the Frontier, 21.47 h/LU (Table 5.7). When individual estancias are considered, the highest stocking rates are found in the North and Center, the oldest cattle-raising areas. Livestock density was also different for each region in the 1850 inventories. For the North it was 1.30 h/LU; for the Center, 1.48 h/LU; for the South, 2.03 h/LU; and for the New South, 5.29 h/LU. When individual cases are considered, the highest stocking rates are found again in the North, and the lowest stocking rates are found mainly in the New South. In 1820, the average density was 1.50 h/LU for all regions and 1.30 h/LU for the older regions, and in 1850, 2.83 h/LU and 1.50 h/LU.

These figures can be interpreted in two complementary ways. On the one hand, there is a decline in the livestock density due to the more extensive ranching carried out south of the Salado River, and due to a dramatic reduction of the extension of public land in the older regions. Estancias located north of the Salado River were using in the 1820s more land than was actually owned, since cattle could stray into public land. The implementation of emphyteusis in the 1820s and the land sales of the late 1830s meant that cattle could only stray on privately held land. Therefore, the 1850 stocking rates are closer to the actual receptivity of those land-holdings. On the other hand, the decline of stocking rates was slight, underscoring the stabilization of production in the older regions and, given the massive transfer of public land into private hands, an increasing efficiency in land use.

Livestock density is usually related to land quality (assuming a constant demand of land for each type of livestock and no changes in those types), but in nineteenth-century Buenos Aires, it was related to the stage of development that each estancia and region had reached. An overview of the different observers' estimates show an evolution from 2.3 h/LU to 1.3 h/LU for land in the Salado River area, and to 0.8 h/LU in the older regions. Information from primary sources confirms the same trend, but the contrast between the lands north and south of the Salado River is more marked. On the whole, the process of evolution can be defined as the transition from stocking rates of about 3 h/LU in the 1790s to just above 1 h/LU in the 1820s for the older regions, and from 20 h/LU or more in the 1820s to about 5 h/LU in the 1850s for the recently settled regions.

The 1881 provincial census ratified these trends. A reelaboration of its data by Roberto Cortés Conde shows that the average density was 0.8 h/LU for the older region (partidos settled before 1833), 1.2 h/LU for a transition zone (partidos invaded by Indians after 1855, totally or partially settled in 1876), and 2.7 h/LU for the new lands (territory totally or partially settled in 1880).[20] Taking into account only land devoted to grazing according to the 1881 census (excluding dubious cases), stocking rates in the North (partidos located north of the Salado River) fluctuate from 0.44 to 0.89 h/LU in the north and west of the city of Buenos Aires (North and Center in Chapter 3), and 1.14 for those to the east and south of the city (South in Chapter 3). South of the Salado River, stocking rates fluctuated from 1.3 h/LU for coastal partidos to 4.65 h/LU for inland partidos closer to the frontier. Information from individual estancias also confirms this trend toward a more intensive use of land, especially in the older regions. In the late 1870s, density was estimated at 0.94 h/LU for "El Rosario," in Las Flores; and the actual figures for "Los Manantiales" and "El Espartillar," in Chascomús, and "Tatay," in Carmen de Areco, were 0.74, 0.87, and 0.82 h/LU, respectively.[21]

Stocking rates are ultimately related to the size of cattle and the quality of land, but for nineteenth-century Buenos Aires, they are also the evidence of different stages of estancia evolution. Consequently, livestock density was related to the pattern and time of settlement and to the human effort devoted to cattle raising. The figures examined in this section point, in a general way, to a pattern of evolution that goes from North to South, and then to the New South, showing a trend of increasing land productivity in

20 Buenos Aires (1883), lviii, 347; and Cortés Conde (1968), 25.
21 Jurado, Newton, and Jurado (1878), 500; Jurado and Márquez (1879), 4; Jurado, Almeida, and Jurado (1879), 135; and Jurado (1879), 466.

that direction. That increase could be due to the transformation of grasses over time due to cattle ranching: The lands of the New South were less productive than those of the North because cattle were still carrying out a transformation in the former that was over in the latter.

Area

Reproduction and stocking rates set the ultimate limits for cattle expansion over the pampas, but in the early nineteenth century, there were plenty of vacant lands being incorporated into production. The question is, therefore, what was the pace of cattle-ranching expansion? If the annual cattle production is known, the area covered by cattle ranching can be estimated using reproduction and stocking rates. Due to the lack of production figures, tithe returns and export figures are used here to estimate the area actually incorporated into cattle ranching for three different periods: 1800, 1820, and 1850.

For 1800 the departing point is the tithe return. The first step is to estimate the total cattle stock. To do that the amount paid for the livestock tithe (diezmo de quatropea) is divided by the value of a head of cattle. In that way, the number of head collected as that year's tithe is revealed. The total annual reproduction is found by multiplying that figure by ten. By dividing the total annual reproduction figure by a reproduction rate, we find the total number of head necessary to produce the tithed head.[22] There are two caveats: (1) evasion is not taken into account; and (2) the diezmo de quatropea included all livestock, not just cattle. As for the first, no information has been found to make possible an estimate of evasion; as for the second, there is no information to determine the composition of the livestock tithe. Consequently, it is assumed that the tithed livestock was all cattle.

To estimate the area occupied by cattle, the figure of total stock should be multiplied by the stocking rate (the number of hectares per head). For the first estimate, the average value of tithe between 1776 and 1803 is used; for the second, the highest value of that period, corresponding to 1796 (Table 5.8). For the first estimate, a 22% reproduction rate, a 3.4 h/ LU stocking rate and an average value per head of 5 reales are used. The reproduction rate is that of the López Osornio estancia; the average value per head is that of yearlings and stray cattle on the same estancia (see Chapter 2); and the density is that of Magdalena in 1789 (see Table 5.5).

---

22 A similar method is used in the "Estadística del apoderado general de hacendados, de cinco partidos de Buenos Aires, a fin de regular el abasto", 3 October 1780, in DHA, 4:22. In that case, the price was omitted because the number of tithed cattle was known. Tithe figures have been taken from Amaral and Ghio (1990), 630.

Table 5.8. *Cattle-raising area in Buenos Aires, 1800–1850*

		T	P	O	R	S	D	Q
I.	1776–1803	6,524	0.625	104,384	22	474,473	3.4	1,613,207
II.	1796	11,792	0.625	188,672	22	857,600	3.4	2,915,840

		X_t	BA	X_{ba}	R		D	Q
III.	1820	506,670	75	380,003	22		1.5	2,590,926
IV.	1850	2,495,278	54.4	1,357,645	22		2.8	17,464,252

Note for I and II:

$$\text{Cattle area } Q = \frac{10\,T\,D}{P\,R} = \frac{S}{D}$$

where T = livestock tithe, diezmo de quatropea (pesos); P = price per cattle head (pesos); O = number of head produced ($10\ T/P$); R = cattle reproduction rate (percentage); S = total cattle stock (O/R); D = cattle density (hectares per head); Q = total cattle-raising area (hectares).

Note for III and IV:

$$\text{Cattle area } Q = \frac{X_{ba}\,D}{R}$$

where $X_{ba} = X_t\,(BA/100)$, being X_t = total hide exports, and BA = percentage of total hide exports corresponding to Buenos Aires; R, D, and Q, same as for I and II.
Sources: T, Amaral and Ghio (1990), 630; P and R, see Chapter 2; D, Tables 5.5 and 5.7; X_t and BA, see this chapter, notes 26 and 27.

The average value of livestock tithe for 1776–1803 is 6,524 pesos. At an average value of 5 reales, that figure is equivalent to 10,438 tithed head. The annual reproduction would have been 104,384, which at a reproduction rate of 22% would have meant a total stock of 474,473 head. At the 3.4 h/LU stocking rate, the total area covered by those head would have been 1,613,207 hectares. The highest amount collected for livestock tithes is 11,792 pesos, which at an average value per head of 5 reales would have been equivalent to 18,867 head of cattle. Total reproduction for that year would have been 188,672 head, which at a 22% reproduction rate would have required a total stock of 857,600 head. The area occupied by those head at the same stocking rate would have been 2,915,840 hectares. The cattle-ranching area was estimated by Cerviño at the beginning of the nineteenth century as 19 leagues wide and 60 to 70 leagues long.[23] If an average length of 65 leagues is accepted, that area would have been

23 Cipriano Orden Betoño's [Pedro Antonio Cerviño] estimate in *Semanario de Agricultura, Industria y Comercio*, 29 December 1802, 117.

3,334,500 hectares. The first estimate is 48% of that figure; the second one, 87%.

For an estimate of the cattle-ranching area around 1820, the figures of hide exports can be used. The annual average for 1818–1822 is 506,670 hides. In order to estimate from that figure the total cattle stock, the reproduction rate found on the López Osornio estancia, 22%, can be used. In that case the total cattle stock would have been 2,303,045 head. This figure is reached under the assumption that extraction and reproduction rates were the same. That may be the case at present, but not necessarily in the 1820s. At present, cattle rather than land is the dependent variable, so cattle stock should be adjusted according to the availability of land. Cattle capitalization is possible for individual establishments after periods of productive decline, but for the whole area, there are restrictions imposed by the overall availability of land (unless technical improvements can be introduced due to a favorable cost–price relationship). In recent years (1980–1987) the average rate of extraction has been 24.3% as a result of an average stock of 53.9 million head and an average slaughtering of 13.1 million head.[24] The rate of extraction on the López Osornio estancia was 9.8% for 1786–1795 (Table 2.4). While there are reasons to accept a reproduction rate of 22%, since most of the contemporary estimates are not too far from it, the same cannot be said for the extraction rate. That was the extraction rate on the López Osornio estancia, but there are no other figures to compare it with. The only piece of information in this direction is due to Pedro de Angelis who in 1834, while estimating tax evasion, assumed an extraction rate of 20%.[25] So, taking the 22% reproduction rate, not too distant after all from de Angelis's extraction rate, the average export figure for 1818–1822 would have required 3,454,568 hectares at a density of 1.5 h/LU.

Since a portion of the hides exported from Buenos Aires came from other regions, not all those hectares were in Buenos Aires. In the 1830s about 25% of the hides were coming from the Interior provinces: According to Parish about 855,000 hides were exported in 1829 and about 824,000 in 1837, while the average introduction into Buenos Aires from the Interior between 1831 and 1835 was about 210,000 hides per year.[26] Taking away 25% as the contribution from the Interior, the area for Buenos Aires would have been 2,590,926 hectares. This figure is only 57% of the 4.5 million hectares estimated for the Buenos Aires productive region around 1820,

24 Naciones Unidas (1988).

25 de Angelis (1834), 171.

26 Parish (1958), 511; Rosal (1992), 63. From 1810 to 1821, introduction of hides from the Litoral accounted on average for 17.4% of exports. See Humphreys (1940), 59–60, for exports figures, and Wentzel (1988), 207, for introduction of hides into Buenos Aires.

but stocking rates were not homogeneous all over the pampas. A rate of 3 h/LU, instead of 1.5 h/LU, would cut down that gap.

A similar approach can be attempted for 1850. According to figures given by Maxwell, the average export from Buenos Aires for 1849–1852 was 2,495,278 hides (adding up dry and salted hides). Introduction from the Litoral and Banda Oriental in 1850–1851 reached 759,939 hides.[27] Hides coming from those regions accounted for 66.8% of all hides introduced in 1831–1835. So, if that proportion was still true for 1850, total introduction would have been 1,137,633 hides. Taking away this figure from average hide exports, 1,357,645 hides remain for Buenos Aires.[28] At the same rate of reproduction used for 1820, 22%, a total cattle stock of 6,171,114 would have been required for that export. At an average density of 2.83 h/LU (Table 5.7), the total area would have been 17,464,252 hectares. Since this figure exceeds by 48% the 11.8 million hectares supposedly settled around 1850, either the reproduction and stocking rates are too low, or the introduction of hides from the Interior was a much higher proportion of total exports than in the 1830s.

Using the same reproduction and stocking rates but different export and introduction figures, the area shrinks but still looks oversized. The average annual export figure for 1856–1858 was 1,534,147 hides; the average annual figure for the introduction from the Interior was 324,936 hides, equivalent to 21.1% of total exports. Taking away the latter figure from the former, a total export of 1,209,211 hides per year is left for Buenos Aires. That number of hides (at the same reproduction rate) required a stock of 5,471,543 head, which would have required (at the same stocking rate) 15,484,467 hectares.

Another estimate can be made for 1850 from the figures of jerked-beef exports. The average for 1849–1852 was 476,761 quintals. According to Rosas 1.22 quintals of jerked beef could be obtained from a head of cattle, so 390,788 head were necessary for that average. A figure for urban and rural consumption should be added to that in order to estimate annual reproduction. The population of Buenos Aires was around 400,000 inhabitants, who at an average 1.6 head per capita would have consumed 640,000 head of cattle.[29] Around 1,030,000 head of cattle were necessary

27 Maxwell (1863); Parish (1958), 512, 518.
28 Hides produced in Buenos Aires accounted for 73.9% of total hide exports in 1849 and 64.1% in 1850. See Schmit and Rosal (1995), 593.
29 Jerked-beef export figures are from Maxwell (1863); population figures from Parish (1958), 602. For Rosas's yield estimate and the 1792 average consumption, see this text, Chapter 6. De Angelis (1834), 87, estimated in the early 1830s a total consumption (rural and urban) of 584,000 head. Assuming a 2% annual growth rate (in fact, total population grew at an annual rate of 1.5% between 1836 and 1855, but it is known that the figures for the latter year are not complete [Table 8.6]), total consumption in 1850 was about 800,000 head.

then for salting and consumption. A total cattle stock of 4,660,634 head was necessary for that annual reproduction, at the same reproduction rate already used, and 13,189,593 hectares would have been needed for that stock at the average 1850 density of 2.83 h/LU.

From these estimates it is more interesting to retain magnitudes rather than exact figures. From a cattle stock of 500,000 head covering an area of 1.6 million hectares in the last decades of the eighteenth century, there was a growth around 1820 to 2.3 million head on 3.4 million hectares, and around 1850 from 4.7 to 6.2 million head on 13.2 to 17.6 million hectares. These figures may not be accurate, but they have been estimated from reasonable figures for exports and reproduction and stocking rates, and they serve to underscore the process of expansion of cattle production on the pampas.

Another look at that process of expansion can be taken by observing the evolution of the introduction into Buenos Aires of cattle head for consumption and salting. Information on cattle introduction started to be published in *La Gaceta Mercantil* in mid-1832. The first complete year is 1833, and figures for that year can be compared with those for the last complete year, 1851, since that newspaper was discontinued after Rosas's ousting. In 1833, 17.6% of the head introduced into Buenos Aires came from the North. (For a definition of the regions, see Appendix B.) The Center accounted for 17.3%, the South for 46.2%, and the New South for 16.6%; in 2.3% of the cases, the place was not recorded. All the head from the New South (the region beyond the Salado River) came from Dolores. The total number of head introduced in the Buenos Aires tabladas (offices in charge of registering cattle introduced for urban consumption) was 183,416, of which 84,815 were from the South. A closer look at the South reveals that 52.7% of the head introduced into Buenos Aires from that region came from Chascomús, with a further 20.2% from Monte and Ranchos, regions located far from the city, close to the frontier. San Vicente, Quilmes, and Ensenada – districts that were close to Buenos Aires – contributed 13.5%, and 13.6% was contributed by Magdalena, a district ranging from the neighborhood of the city to the frontier. Most of the cattle introduced into Buenos Aires (53.5%) came therefore from the newly developed areas of the older pampa, between the Salado River and the Río de la Plata (Chascomús, Ranchos, Monte, Magdalena), and the New South (Dolores).[30]

In 1851 that landscape had changed in two main directions. On the one hand, there was a fourfold increase in the number of head introduced into Buenos Aires; on the other, most of those head were coming from districts beyond the Salado River. The South contributed 11.7%, but the number

---

30 *La Gaceta Mercantil*, 1833, passim. For a definition of regions see Appendix B.

of head was almost the same as in 1833: 88,043 head in 1851 vis-à-vis 84,815 in 1833. This shows that the South had already reached its limit in 1833. The Center and the North accounted in 1851 for a lower proportion of the total number of head introduced into Buenos Aires (9.3% and 19.8%), but the number of head sent by those regions in that year were double and four times the figures for 1833. Introduction from the New South grew from the 30,000 head sent from Dolores in 1833 to 444,000 head. Of this number, 31% came from Lobería, 15% from Chapaleofú, and 24% from Azul, while 14 other districts contributed 30%. A regional distribution of those head coming from beyond the Salado River shows that the first district that had been settled, from Dolores to Ajó and Tuyú, contributed 15% of the total number of head sent from the New South. The central district (Azul and Chapaleofú, mainly) contributed 43% of that number. The southern district (mainly Lobería) contributed 36%. And the far south (Bahía Blanca) and the southwest (Bragado, Junín) contributed 1% and 5%.[31]

If the New South produced 444,000 head per year, at the same rate of reproduction used previously, a cattle stock of 2,009,050 head results. Since in 1850 the density was 5.29 h/LU (Table 5.7), that number of head would have required 10,627,875 hectares. Adding this figure to the 3,500,000 hectares north of the Salado River, the cattle-raising area rises to 14,100,000 hectares. If the number of head sent by each of the three regions located to the north of the Salado River is taken as the total production of those regions for 1851, those head would have required (at the same reproduction rate) a cattle stock of 674,000 head in the North, 317,000 head in the Center, and 398,000 head in the South. According to the density estimated for those regions in 1850 (Table B.8), the area required for that stock would have been 876,000 hectares in the North, 469,000 hectares in the Center, and 808,000 hectares in the South. Adding up the area of the four regions, the total cattle-raising area in Buenos Aires was 12,800,000 hectares. This figure is based on cattle introduced alive into the Buenos Aires markets, and the hides of cattle killed in the countryside (for consumption or by natural causes) would increase it.

Whatever the precise figure for the total cattle-raising area, if any can actually be estimated, the fact remains that from 1833 to 1851, there was an extraordinary expansion to the south, beyond the Salado River. Lands that had not even been settled in 1833 were sending the bulk of the number of cattle head introduced into Buenos Aires less than two decades later, and most of those head were from districts still on the frontier. The number of cattle introduced into Buenos Aires increased four times, and the cattle-raising area increased about three times.

31 *La Gaceta Mercantil*, 1851, passim.

Conclusion

Cattle reproduction rates and density changed at a slow pace, and the effects of change could only be perceived in the long run. Cattle roamed free over the pampas but reproduced themselves according to certain rates. Each head of cattle required a certain number of hectares, and cattle production extended over a determined area. Reproduction rates could not be easily modified by human action, but better care of the herds could mean an improvement in the rate of survival. The regularity of roundups and the expansion of corrals operated in that direction, but only the introduction of wire fencing in the last decades of the nineteenth century would mark a more radical change.

Livestock density was variable since the quality of land was far from homogeneous. The overstocking of the fields on the older pampa shows also a different pattern of land occupation. The 1856 estimates reveal a higher density than in the first decades of the nineteenth century, but a comparison of the stocking rates stemming from the 1820 and 1850 inventories makes clear that there was also a temporal factor determining livestock density in the different regions.

The area covered by cattle ranching had an amazing growth from the late eighteenth to the mid-nineteenth centuries. It jumped from between 1.5 and 3 million hectares occupied in 1800 to between 13 and 18 million hectares in 1850. These latter figures may be too high, but taking the highest estimate for 1800 and the lowest for 1850, a fourfold growth of the cattle-ranching area occurred.

This study of the material conditions of production on the pampas in the late eighteenth and early nineteenth centuries shows that the process of land occupation and territorial expansion was restricted by factors (livestock reproduction rates and density) that remained constant in the short run. It was only due to hard work that the environmental conditions of the pampas could be controlled. But the very expansion of livestock over the pampas changed those conditions.

6

Environment

In January 1852, when the Grand Army was advancing toward Buenos Aires to put an end to Rosas's protracted tyranny, he tried to stop it by burning the dense thistleries covering the countryside.[1] The fires were put out by rain, and the battle of Caseros resulted in his ousting from power. The use of the environment for military purposes is as old as war itself and is a manifestation of the influence of man on the environment. Rural production also affects and is affected by the environment, but changes – unlike those introduced by Caseros – are only perceptible in the long run. This chapter deals with the environmental conditions of production, that is, how an environmental factor determined the pattern of rural production in nineteenth-century Buenos Aires.

Environmental changes are triggered by natural phenomena (climate variations, volcanic eruptions, earthquakes, droughts, floods) but also by the action of men and beasts. Men and beasts, in return, are affected by the transformations of the environment that their actions cause. War, conquest, trade, and migrations have been fundamental factors in the dispersion of plants and animals. The potato, a native of the American continent, which transformed eating patterns and habits in Europe, is one of the best-known cases. The repeated failure of its harvest in Ireland in the 1840s provoked a famine but seems to have been a crucial element in that country's eighteenth-century population revolution. The expansion of phylloxera in Europe in the 1870s is another example of the consequences of human action on production. Carried by Californian vines, the parasite almost completely destroyed the European vineyards. The Andean tuber and the Californian vine caused sensible alterations in eating habits and production but no visible ecological change.[2]

---

1 The word "thistleries," large concentration of thistles, seems to have been used for the first time, according to later writers, by W. P. Robertson. See L.D[illon]., (1867), 61.
2 The relationship between man and environment has been studied since Marsh (1874). On the introduction of the potato into the Old World, see Salaman (1949) and Crosby (1972), 165–207. On "the potato theory of population," see Matossian (1989), 88–104. On the consequences of phylloxera on European vineyards, see Loubère (1978).

Intentionally or not, human beings have helped the diffusion or caused the extermination of vegetal species. Beginning in the Middle Ages, deforestation brought about remarkable changes in the European landscape, as today's deforestation of the Amazon will probably generate. Other, less dramatic cases also have affected production and the relationship between man and environment. The expansion of the Russian thistle over the U.S. wheat region at the end of the nineteenth century is an example; another is that of halogeton over the western U.S. sheep-breeding region in the 1940s.[3]

By 1800 Félix de Azara observed in the Buenos Aires countryside that as soon as a hut was built, plants appeared that before were only found several leagues away, and as soon as a road was opened, the same plants appeared along its sides. Those plants served for Azara as testimonies of the human influence over nature. Animals, he remarked, caused the same effect. He had seen estancias covered in a few years by thistles due to the action of livestock. These alterations provoked by livestock influenced in turn, he remarked, human activities.[4] In that way Azara summarized – partially, at least, since that was not the end of the story, as he himself knew – a cycle of environmental changes that affected the pattern of rural production on the pampas.

Unintentional human action caused both the appearance and disappearance of thistleries on the Buenos Aires pampas. Thistles have not completely vanished, but they do not cover those plains as depicted by late-eighteenth and early-nineteenth-century travelers and observers. During their heyday, thistles played a key role in the evolution of rural tasks, determining the seasonal pattern of cattle production and labor demand. Focusing upon the types of thistles and their biological cycle, their habitat and uses, and the way they affected cattle-raising activities, this chapter stresses the role of environmental conditions of production. Thistleries spread and declined due to human and animal action on the environment, but they were in turn one of the major environmental constraints for cattle ranching on the nineteenth-century pampas. In order to understand that process and its implications, the types and cycle of thistles are considered, as well as the habitat of thistles, its uses, and the pattern of rural activities and how thistles disrupted it.

Thistles

Types and cycle

On the treeless plains of Buenos Aires, the only forests, as called by many travelers, were of thistles. The thistles of the Buenos Aires pampas were

3 Anderson (1956), Clark (1956), Dewey (1894), and Young (1988).
4 Azara (1801), 2:338–339.

Cynara cardunculus, or cardo de Castilla, and *Silybum marianum*, or cardo asnal. Thistles were intruders on those plains. Native to southern Europe and northern Africa, they reached the shores of the Río de la Plata apparently in the second half of the eighteenth century. Favorable environmental conditions, a mild climate, and weaker native plants facilitated their expansion. Observers mentioned two or three types of thistles. Charles Darwin, who visited the pampas while traveling around the world, refers to *Cynara cardunculus* as cardoon, differentiating it from the great thistle, which scientific designation does not mention, described by F. B. Head. The former was as high as a horse; the second, higher than the head of a horserider. In *Far Away and Long Ago*, William Henry Hudson mentions two types: the cardoon thistle, or wild artichoke, of a bluish or grey-greenish color, and the giant thistle, cardo asnal for the natives and *Carduus marianum* for botanists, with white and green leaves. William MacCann, who crossed over the pampas in the late 1840s, refers to three types of thistles but neither describes them nor gives their botanical names. According to him, those thistles indicated different types of soil, but he did not elaborate on that relationship either.[5]

In the early twentieth century, cardo asnal – maybe Darwin's great thistle – was the most common type of thistle on the pampas. But its hegemony was threatened by *Carduus macrocephalus*, another European intruder – maybe MacCann's third variety. Cardo asnal is an annual or biannual plant, 2 or 3 meters high. Its leaves are 40 to 70 cm long and have a lanceolate-oblong shape, with a serrated-thorny edge and a marbled upper surface. Its flowers are violaceous, in apical small heads, protected by thorns. Its fruits are numerous, with oleaginous albumen and a crown of simple white hairs (pappus, known in Buenos Aires as panaderos, bakers) spread by the wind. Its nourishing value for livestock is quite good, especially in winter, when the leaves are growing and fodder is scarce. The cardo de Castilla or cardón is frequently perennial; in the late summer, from the base of its stalks appear the sprouts that blossom the following spring. This type of thistle develops as a thorny, grayish bush, reaching a 2-meter height. Its leaves are big, with a central, pulpy stem, terminal thorns, and the inferior face densely covered by a smooth nap. Its bluish-violaceous flowers bloom at the top of the stalks, protected by thorny leaves, and they carry numerous fruits crowned by a plumy pappus. In winter, while vegetating, it can also serve as fodder for cattle, but it is less nourishing than cardo asnal.[6]

5 Bunbury (1855), 188–189; Schmieder (1927b), 310; Scarlett (1957), 50; Darwin (1839), 138, 143, 172; Head (1986), 22; Hudson (1918), 64, 71; Burmeister (1943), 1:39, 136–137; Miers (1826), 1:238–239, 2:344; Hinchliff (1955), 243; MacCann (1969), 218.
6 This is a summary of a technical description of *Cynara cardunculus* and *Silybum marianum*. See Universidad de Buenos Aires (1923). My thanks to the late Eduardo Ciafardo for giving me a copy

The best description of the biological cycle of thistles found among travelers' accounts is Francis Bond Head's. Thistles sprouted in March. In winter the leaves were "large and luxuriant," but only at ground level. In spring there was an extraordinary change: "The whole region becomes a luxuriant wood of enormous thistles, which have suddenly shot up to a height of ten or eleven feet, and are all in full bloom." Summer brought about another rapid change: "The thistles suddenly lose their sap and verdure, their heads drop, the leaves shrink and fade, the stems become black and dead." They remained standing up until February or March if spared by the frequent fires of the summer and the violent pampero winds, which flattened them to ground level, where they rotted and faded away.[7]

Several testimonies recorded these seasonal differences, confirming the cycle described by Head. Travelers of the early spring saw thistles growing (Darwin), and those of the late spring and summer saw thistles fully grown (Scrivener) or dry, ready for harvesting as fuel (Robertson). Travelers of the fall and winter (Miers, Hibbert, Gillespie) failed to mention them, as did those who crossed the pampas in times of drought (Gillespie). On 29 August 1852 a foreigner traveling to a chacra 15 miles away from Buenos Aires saw in some places large quantities of thistles, "at this season [late winter] only a few inches high, having no stalks, but only a clump of leaves spreading over the ground." Hudson says that their green period began in April and ended in November, but the Mulhalls point to Christmas as the limit to their life. Sergeant Major Martínez's attempt to eliminate wild dogs were hampered, as he acknowledged in his report, by large thistleries covering the fields in November 1790. Charles Brand went over the pampas at the end of July to find it entirely covered by thistles. He did not mention their height, however, which could not have been beyond ground level then.[8]

The height reached by thistles when fully grown depended on the type. Darwin's cardoon, the same that Miers saw in Chile, was 4 or 5 feet high. Hinchliff says that while riding a horse he was forced to protect his face with his hands. For him the smaller type was 3 to 4 feet high, the bigger one 6 to 8 feet. Beaumont states 6 to 8 feet; MacCann, up to 8 feet; W. P.

of this publication. For other technical studies, see Cabrera (1963), Parodi (1926) and (1930), and Hauman (1925).

7 Arnold (1951), 17; Latham (1868), 196; Head (1986), 22; Marcelo Ignes to Juan Pedro Aguirre, San Nicolás, 29 August 1826, in ABP, 031–5–3–14; Beaumont (1957), 227; Caldcleugh (1943), 109; D'Orbigny (1835), 1:592–593; Hudson (1918), 64, 68, 70–71; Mulhall and Mulhall (1869), 1(C):5.

8 Darwin (1839), 138; Scrivener (1937), 24–25; Temple (1833), 1:59; Robertson (1838), 2:185; Caldcleugh (1943), 108; Miers (1826), vol. 1; Hibbert (1824); Gillespie (1986), 110; Hudson (1918), 67–68; Mulhall and Mulhall (1869), 1(C):5; Mansfield (1856), 162; Melli (1974), 49; Brand (1828), 37.

Robertson, 8 feet; and Temple and Scrivener, 8 to 10 feet. Head refers to a maximum height of 10 to 11 feet, the same given by the Mulhalls almost 50 years later. In the mid-1850s Bishop saw "extensive forests of gigantic thistles, which grow to such a height that men, passing through them on horseback, are hidden by the lofty stems." Hudson does not mention the height of the cardoon, but he mentions 6 to 10 feet for cardo asnal.[9]

The thistle forests were tall for the level terrain of the pampas, but they were also seasonal. Thistles were not native to those plains; they spread over them because of human and livestock action. The area covered by thistleries, consequently, was linked to the expansion of cattle ranching.

Habitat

Thistles are closely linked to human activity. Around houses or wherever men were, Azara remarks, mallow, nettle, and thistle could be seen, in spite of their absence within 30 leagues all-around. Human and livestock presence, he concludes, provoked changes in the vegetal realm, destroying native plants and making room for new ones. Three decades later, during his trip to Cruz de Guerra, Parchappe did not find any thistle south of the Salado River except around the lakes, due to human settlement, especially Indian. Thistles are one of the plants that in this country go with men, he remarked. A few years later, after crossing the Salado River, changes in the outlook of the fields amazed Darwin. To the north it was covered by thistles, while to the south of the river, none was to be seen. He explained this by the different nature of the soil but later accepted the local explanation attributing it to cattle grazing and manuring. He guessed, then, that the spread of cattle would facilitate the expansion of the thistle region.[10]

Thistles did not grow in an isolated way but rather in vast, dense groupings. Roads across the pampas unfolded between two walls of thorny stalks, which blocked any sight beyond them. These walls were an impassable barrier for people but not for cattle, which used to go into thistleries. Estancias were located in the neighborhood of dampened depressions for two reasons: access to water, and absence of thistles.[11]

9 Beaumont (1957), 56, 230, 234; Darwin (1839), 172; Latham (1868), 184, 189; Miers (1826), 2:344; Hinchliff (1955), 243, 248; MacCann (1969), 218; Robertson (1838), 1:228; Temple (1833), 1:59; Scrivener (1937), 25; Head (1986), 22; Mulhall (1869), 1(C):5; Bishop (1869), 39; Hudson (1918), 64.
10 Azara (1969), 80; D'Orbigny (1835), 1:566; Darwin (1839), 138–139, 143; Schmieder (1927b), 310.
11 Head (1986), 22; Hinchliff (1955), 248; Temple (1833), 1:59; Robertson (1838), 2:186; Darwin (1839), 172.

Thistleries began just outside the city, sparsely first, but after 5 to 7 leagues, when low and muddy terrain had been left behind, the whole plain was uninterruptedly covered, so roads were just paths across them. Thistleries spread over to the west for 180 miles, according to Head, although there were "extraordinary seasonal variations." There were also variations from year to year. Hudson recalls those "thistle years" when the whole pampas seemed to be covered by them. In 1821 Caldcleugh found them along the road to Córdoba up to the postas of Arroyo del Medio and Arroyo del Sauce, 54 and 74 leagues northwest of the city, where they gradually faded away. In 1799 an anonymous traveler describing the road from Mendoza to Buenos Aires found the first thistleries in Arrecifes and increasingly from chacras de Ayala, 31 leagues away from Buenos Aires, onward. In 1825 Scrivener found their boundary near Fontezuela, and Temple found it by the Saladillo River. In 1848 Arnold saw them vanishing between Salto and Pergamino, but Sarmiento, who went over that region with Urquiza's Grand Army in January 1852, mentions a 7-hour march among thistles. Caldcleugh, coming back to Buenos Aires in late June 1821, found them in San Pedro. In 1811 Robertson pointed to the Arroyo del Medio, but he also remarked that by the time he left the country in the late 1820s, thistles had spread beyond that stream. Beaumont, who traveled over northern Buenos Aires in 1826, recorded their vanishing for 1 or 2 miles near San Andrés de Giles, but the countryside was densely covered up to Arrecifes. Back to Buenos Aires along the coast, he found a new interruption near San Pedro. The whole road between San Pedro and Baradero was covered by thistles, but none were seen after Baradero because Beaumont was traveling over low and muddy lands. The southern boundary of thistleries was around Guardia del Monte, according to Darwin, and at the Salado River, according to D'Orbigny. Two decades later, in January 1853, MacRae, who was coming from the west, found thistleries 12 miles before arriving in Rosario. This was their northern boundary. Although typical of the Buenos Aires pampas, thistles were also found in neighboring regions. Dámaso Larrañaga, the priest so closely associated with Artigas, rode along thistleries for 5 hours after leaving Montevideo on his way to Paysandú in May 1815. Beaumont saw them in November 1826 near Arroyo de la China, in Entre Ríos, when his ship was stopped by local authorities. Years later Hinchliff found them near Gualeguay, also in Entre Ríos.[12]

12 Brand (1828), 37; Scarlett (1957), 50; Robertson (1838), 2:185; Beaumont (1957), 55, 221, 226, 227–233; MacCann (1969), 216; Hudson (1918), 67–68, 71–72; Caldcleugh (1943), 107–108, 114, 222; Head (1986), 22; González Garaño (1940a), 541; Scrivener (1937), 29; Temple (1833), 1:59; Arnold (1951), 187; Sarmiento (1958), 182; Robertson (1838), 2:185; Hinchliff (1955), 248; Darwin (1839), 138; D'Orbigny (1835), 1:566; MacRae (1855), 40; and Larrañaga (1985), 15. My thanks to Ana Frega for sending me information concerning other editions of Larrañaga's diary.

Thistleries, therefore, covered large extensions of the rolling pampas of Buenos Aires and the Banda Oriental. The Salado River was the southern boundary of the thistleries, and the Arroyo del Medio the western boundary. They could have spread beyond those boundaries, but when livestock crossed those rivers, other conditions changed, checking the advance of thistleries. On the old pampa, thistles were a nuisance for cattle-ranching activities, but some uses were found for this abundant resource.

Uses

On the Buenos Aires treeless plains, thistles were one of the main sources of fuel, as Paucke found in the 1770s. At the end of February, when the thistles were already dry, the annual harvest took place. *Leña de cardo*, thistle fuel, was burnt in the bakeries' ovens and used to burn bricks and roof tiles (tejas), both in Buenos Aires and the Banda Oriental.[13] Hudson remembers woodpiles as big as houses, "the wood being nothing but stalks of the cardoon thistle or wild artichoke, which burns like paper, so that immense quantities had to be collected to supply fuel for a large establishment." Soldiers of the forts guarding the frontier and passersby of the pampas at the end of the eighteenth century and the first half of the nineteenth century used it to cook. Francisco Betbezé, in his reconnaissance of the frontier in March 1779, did not find thistles when he reached Laguna del Sebo, so he had to burn horse dung, which was, along with bones and fat from cattle, horses, and sheep, the alternative fuel of the pampas.[14]

Thistles were also burnt for other purposes. In 1823 the Indians set up fires forcing soldiers and beasts of Martín Rodríguez's expedition to remain for three hours inside the Laguna Limpia with water up to their necks. In 1852 Rosas burned the fields around Urquiza's army to deprive its horses of the natural food. According to Sarmiento, success skipped him because "God's finger is visible and the peoples' curse overwhelms the bloody tyrant." Such Homeric intercession manifested itself in the torrents of water poured by the skies to end the fires. The diary of a Brazilian lieutenant also accounts, in a less poetic way, for a "terrible march over fields that had been burnt that very day." The Grand Army was spared, but

---

13 Paucke (1942), 125; Bishop (1869), 52; "Notes written during a late Residence at Buenos Ayres, by an English Gentleman, formerly of Bene't College, Cambridge," *Monthly Magazine*, 1 August 1821, 356:31. "Leña de cardo" was recorded as one of the items sold by José Antonio Otalora's estancia in 1819–1820 (AGN, Sucesiones 7274, No. 6, f. 56). For the Banda Oriental, see Larrañaga (1985), 15.

14 Robertson (1838), 1:187; Poinsett (1984b), 103; Sepp (1971), 1:121; Temple (1833), 1:59–60; Beaumont (1957), 56, 65; Azara (1910), 82; Zizur (1910), 234, 237; Caldcleugh (1943), 112; Scrivener (1937), 25; Cabodi (1952), 68; Miers (1968), 44; Chijachev (1967), 18; Vidal (1923), 193; Mackinnon (1957), 457; MacCann (1969), 107; Brabazon (1981), 70; Hudson (1918), 19.

its horses suffered from lack of grass. Most of the summer fires were, however, accidental. A spark from a cigarette of a careless smoker or a passersby who left a fire burning in his resting place was enough to kindle them. Other fires were intentionally kindled by soldiers of the forts looking for partridges or by farmers (chacareros) seeking to drive away deer and other beasts from their cultivated fields. The threat of fire was always present on hot summer days, so at the first sight of smoke in the distance, people jumped on their horses and rushed to help fight the fire. In February 1821 a fire combined with a pampero to blacken the sky over Buenos Aires in the middle of the day, also filling it with smoke.[15]

Cattle, horses, vizcachas, and other beasts took advantage of thistleries for their shade, for protection against predators, and as fodder. "Thistle fields," remarked Bishop, "serve to the wild animals of the pampas as an undisturbed lair." In Chile, where thistles had been introduced as fodder, between November and March, when the hills were bare of grass, cattle had to live on thistles. They were also used for human consumption (and still are): Mary Graham tells her readers she used to eat them in salads and stews, and passersby calmed their thirst with the sap of their stalks. The abundance of thistles marked the years of fat cows, or rather fat livestock, since horses, sheep, and pigs also ate their seeds or leaves.[16]

The dense and extended leaves of thistles, however, reduced the space for forage plants with more nourishing qualities. In its first stage, thistles were not adequately nourishing and caused diarrhea. Even when seeds fell down, cattle could feed better on other grasses, but thistles hindered their growth. Extirpation was only possible in small stretches of land. This task was done in two steps: in the early spring and at blossoming time. If grasses could be helped in such a way, Wilfrid Latham optimistically remarked, gradually they would spread because their pressure over the thistle's roots would restrict its exuberant growth and density to deprive it finally of favorable reproductive conditions. Thistles, however, had some advantage: Latham recommended them to prevent the spread of prickles, which ruined the quality of wool. He preferred the extinction of both, but

---

15 D'Orbigny (1835), 1:566, 606; Sarmiento (1958), 171, 184; Parish (1958), 268–269; and Justo Maeso's note on the fires previous to the battle of Caseros [Parish (1958), 269]. A description of those fires and their effects was recorded by Frederico Augusto do Amaral Sarmento Menna, "Itinerario da marcha da 1a. Brigada de Infantaria ao mando do Coronel F. F. da P. Pereira Pinto que marchou da Colonia do Sacramento a 14 de dezembro de 1851, para ir fazer parte do Exercito do General Urquiza," in Arquivo Histórico do Rio Grande do Sul, arquivos particulares, lata 42, maço 7. *El Telégrafo Mercantil*, 31 January 1802, 62; Hudson (1918), 69–70; *The British Packet and Argentine News*, 24 December 1831, No. 279.

16 Robertson (1838), 2:186: Burmeister (1943), 1:37; Darwin (1839), 143; Miers (1826), 2:344; Bishop (1869), 39; Graham (n.d.), 306; Scarlett (1957), 50; Hudson (1918), 71–72; Mulhall and Mulhall (1869), 1(C):5.

there was no way to eradicate the former. Mr. Tweedie, the gardener of the Santa Catalina Scottish colony, invented in 1828 a machine that, according to *The British Packet*, in a short time would clear those fields of thistles. It failed, however, and thistles kept on blossoming every spring on the pampas.[17]

Apart from a biological function, thistleries also fulfilled a social one, since they facilitated or hindered different criminal practices. When Darwin inquired about robberies in the countryside, he was baffled by the answer: Thistles had not grown yet. Summer was robbers' season, since thistleries made it easy for them to conceal their activities and to escape. Soon after Darwin's visit to Buenos Aires, abundant rain helped thistles to grow in such a way that robbers were doing better than ever, complained *The British Packet*. Another type of offense was carried out when thistles fell down. Indians looking for livestock began their operations in February, when thistles had been flattened by wind or fire, and continued until April. More than a fear of thorns, as Joseph Andrews guessed, that seasonal preference was due to a rational choice: There was no use in driving livestock at a time when the head could get lost in the thistleries.[18]

Thistles had an annual cycle but also a long-term one. They spread over the pampas at some time in the eighteenth century, following humans and livestock, but human and livestock action also served to check the expansion of thistles. This futher evolution in that chapter of the human interaction with nature took place in the second half of the nineteenth century, when sheep, wire fencing, and agriculture were introduced into the pampas. Until then, for more than a century, thistles imposed severe restrictions on cattle-ranching activities.

Thistles and cattle raising

Wheat was sown by the end of the fall and the beginning of winter and was harvested by the end of the spring and the beginning of summer. Tillage of the land required some labor during May or June and thrashing from November to January.[19] There is no doubt regarding the seasonality of agriculture. Much less evident is the seasonality of cattle raising. It seems like cattle could be rounded up at any time, whenever peons accepted work, and that any time was good for branding and gelding.

17 Latham (1868), 188–189, 195–196; *The British Packet and Argentine News*, 23 August 1828, No. 107, in Lapido and Spota de Lapieza Elli (1976), 193.
18 Darwin (1839), 143; *British Packet and Argentine News*, 15 December 1832, No. 330; Robertson (1838), 2:186; Miers (1826), 1:239; Andrews (1827), 1:25; Hudson (1918), 71.
19 REBA (1855), 2:36; Grigera (1819), 16–30, 43.

Cattle-raising tasks, however, were also determined by the season. Cattle were raised in open fields, with aquerenciamiento as the only method to retain them in a particular area. But the effectiveness of such a method was challenged by droughts, floods, locusts, and fires, which forced the cattle to move from place to place looking for better feeding conditions. It looks like in the early- and mid-nineteenth century estancia, under such conditions, there was neither order nor regularity in the tasks related to cattle raising. The most important of those tasks, rounding and branding, were carried out in late summer or early fall or in late winter and early spring. Seasonality could be better attributed to the regularity of calving rhythms than to any mysterious cultural factor compelling the peons to work at that time and not at the peak of the summer or winter. But such cultural factors did not exist, and biological ones did not necessarily force a seasonality as marked as in agriculture. Another factor operated in favor of such seasonality of cattle-raising tasks: Thistles, born in the fall, fully grown in the spring, and dried along the summer, were one of the major reasons that those tasks followed a seasonal rhythm.

Thistles therefore imposed a marked seasonality on rural tasks. At the end of August 1826, Marcelo Ignes wrote to his partner Juan Pedro Aguirre that in a few days time it would be impossible to round up cattle on their Arroyo del Tala estancia because thistles were already growing. In another letter, written at the end of December 1826, Ignes remarked that vast thistleries were preventing him from rounding up their cattle.[20] Cattle-raising tasks were carried out in late winter and early spring, before the stalks grew, or in late summer or early fall, after thistles flattened. A brief description of cattle-raising tasks shows to what extent thistles could affect them.

Tasks on an estancia were of many sorts. Some were performed on a permanent basis, others only occasionally. The right time to carry out the latter was determined by seasonal, biological, and environmental factors, not by cultural factors (for example, the peons' supposed preference for an independent lifestyle). Calving set a first restriction on cattle-raising tasks. Between August and October, while calving was taking place, roundups could not be carried out without running the risk of hurting the calves.

The work demanded by a newly established estancia was different from work on an established one. On the former, the main task was aquerenciamiento, to get cattle used to a particular place. To do that, frequent roundups were necessary. On the latter, the main tasks were branding and gelding, and the roundups preceding these tasks. Such

---

20 Marcelo Ignes to Juan Pedro Aguirre, San Nicolás, 29 August 1826 and 23 December 1826, in ABP, 031–5–3–14 and 031–5–3–15.

activities were carried out preferentially in March or April, but sometimes branding was postponed for the spring to help calves develop properly. On Aguirre and Ignes's estancias in northern Buenos Aires, there were two brandings, in fall and spring, the former more important than the latter. Gelding was usually carried out before branding. Other sources mention roundups and brandings as early as February and as late as October or November. On the one hand, tasks were carried out according to the weather rather than to the calendar. Frost, rain, and heat affected rural tasks more than the transition from one month to the next. So an early fall or a late spring would have made it possible to work the cattle in February or October.[21] On the other hand, when individual cases are considered, their special circumstances should be considered also. It was possible to carry out out-of-season tasks, but that was more expensive. Cattle could be rounded up in spite of thistles, but that would take more peons, more days, and consequently more money; cattle could be branded and gelded in summer, but infections were more likely, or in winter, but calving rates could be affected.

From the late eighteenth century to the mid-nineteenth century, those tasks did not see any drastic changes. There was no other technical innovation than the bottomless bucket, introduced in the mid-1820s. Cattle were still raised on open fields, since wire fencing, introduced in the mid-1840s, did not spread over the pampas until the last decades of the century. The increase of jerked-beef exports brought about some alterations in cattle-raising patterns.[22] Saladeros operated mainly from November to March, according to MacCann, because cattle were then at their best, and the long and sunny summer days could dry beef better and faster than in winter. The diversification of rural production, consequently, did introduce certain changes in the marked seasonality affecting rural tasks.[23]

The expansion of sheep breeding brought about a different rhythm to rural tasks, further altering the pattern of labor demand. Lambing took place mainly during the fall and to a lesser extent during the spring. Shearing was carried out in October and November. The main difference was that flocks, unlike cattle herds, required daily care. Consequently, there was a stable demand for labor throughout the whole year, with

21 MacCann (1969), 208; Beaumont (1957), 94; Darwin (1839), 170; Lemée (1905), 18; Daireaux (1908), 388–389, 398; Marcelo Ignes to Juan Pedro Aguirre, El Tala, 25 March 1824, in ABP, 031-5-3-9; *ibid.*, El Tala, 11 April 1824, in ABP, 031-5-3-10; *ibid.*, San Nicolás, 18 April 1827(?), and San Pedro, 13 August 1827, in ABP, 031-5-3-16; REBA (1855), 2:34; *Documentos para la Historia del Virreinato . . .* (1912), 2:27; and Scarlett (1957), 52.

22 For jerked-beef exports, see Chapter 12.

23 Montoya (1971), 152; Sbarra (1964), 79ff.; Sbarra (1973), 45–63; MacCann (1969), 52, 154; Vidal (1923), 193.

seasonal peaks at shearing time.[24] Sheep breeding did not eliminate the seasonality of labor demand, but a new pattern emerged. This new pattern was due both to sheep breeding itself and to the way that sheep helped to control the expansion of thistleries.

This declining phase of the long-term cycle of thistles over the pampas did not put an immediate end to thistleries. In the late 1880s, a handbook for estancieros still included recommendations on how to control thistle expansion. Lemée, the author of that handbook, argued that sheep exhausted good grasses but were unable to check the expansion of thistles.[25] They did so, but only in the long run. Consequently, thistleries would remain strong for many decades. Human activities altered the environment, but at a very slow pace.

Conclusion

Azara had seen how human and livestock action contributed to the expansion of thistles at the expense of pajonales (the concentration of coarse, tall grasses). Due to livestock multiplication and the course of time, he remarked, natural grasses would disappear, and if sheep were introduced, the pace of destruction would be faster. That was exactly what happened on the older pampas, north of the Salado River and east of Arroyo del Medio, with the expansion of sheep from the 1840s onward. Maxwell in 1863 and the Mulhalls 6 years later still mentioned huge thistleries. But sheep and later agriculture contributed to their disappearance. The cycle of decline was completed (if Karl Kaerger, the German agricultural attaché in Buenos Aires around 1900, is to be believed) when thistles started to be cultivated as forage in some regions of Buenos Aires at the beginning of the twentieth century. It is tempting to think that the German scientist was a victim of local wit, but at that time thistles were reportedly thought to help fertilize the soil. Saturnino Unzué, a major landowner, bought thistle seeds in Europe for that purpose by the end of the nineteenth century, following perhaps the recommendations of current textbooks on estancia management.[26]

Wild thistles were still seen by Holland around 1910 in the neighborhood of La Plata, but mainly on the roadsides and railroad embankments. The technical literature would be plagued for many years with advice

24 Lemée (1905), 26–27; MacCann (1969), 61–62; Korol and Sabato (1981), 84–86, 104–113; Brabazon (1981).
25 Lemée (1887), 19, 58, 171.
26 Armaignac (1962), 16–17; Azara (1969), 80; Maxwell (1863), 6; Mulhall and Mulhall (1869), 1(C):5; Kaerger (1901), 1:596–597; Luis González Guerrico to the author, Buenos Aires, 13 March 1991; Lima (1885), 32.

about thistle control and some occasional suggestions about its potential industrial use. A sign of resignation, coexistence, or defeat is found in a recent article praising thistles as a "new alternative of production" due to their virtues as a "liver reconstituent."[27] Thistles did not disappear, certainly, but in the late nineteenth century, they were no longer a factor determining the seasonal pattern of rural production. From the late eighteenth century to the 1880s, however, the seasonal emergence of large thistleries was one of the major environmental conditions of production on the Buenos Aires pampas. For rural producers thistleries were a given factor that they were unable to change in the short run. Thistle seasonality could only be countered at great expense; usually, hacendados had to adjust production to its pattern. Cattle ranching on the pampas was an advantageous proposition, but it was carried out within restrictions imposed by material conditions, as seen in Chapter 5, environmental conditions, as seen in this chapter, and institutional conditions, as is seen in the next chapter.

27 Holland (1913), 225–226. For recommendations about the industrial use of thistles, see "La industria del aceite en la Argentina: Perspectivas que ofrece el aprovechamiento industrial de la semilla de cardo," *La Nación*, 22 May 1921, and "El cardo de Castilla: Un químico argentino señaló en 1910 el carácter utilizable del cardo maleza para la extracción industrial de aceite," *La Nación*, 5 June 1921. For recent literature on thistle control, see, for instance, E. González Laguingue, "Con herbicidas pueden combatirse los cardos," *La Chacra*, June 1955, 25(295); Jorge Elías Vélez, "Control del cardo de Castilla," *Dinámica Rural*, September 1972, 5(49); "Cardos y abrepuños en ganadería: Algunos consejos para su control," *Campo Moderno y Chacra*, April 1976, 45(545). For the medicinal use of thistles, see "Una nueva alternativa de producción: Silybum Marianum cardo asnal," *Información Agropecuaria*, 1981, 3(19).

7

Institutions

Institutions, as a web of long-term contracts, usually do not change overnight. Formal contracts, those specified by legislation, could be modified by new legislation; informal contracts, those expressed by habits and customs regulating rural production, could seldom be altered in the short run. The expansion of cattle raising over the pampas in the first half of the nineteenth century brought about rapid change in the conditions of production, and legislation, customs, and habits had to adjust to them. A new definition of property rights over land, labor, cattle, water, and grasses was required.

The redefinition of property rights over land and labor has not failed to attract the attention of scholars. Land was distributed to private individuals at the time of the founding of Buenos Aires, and later by grants made by governors on behalf of the king. Since land was also settled without proper titles, a process of legalization began around 1750. In the late eighteenth and early nineteenth centuries, a complex and slow procedure was followed by settlers who wanted to legally obtain a tract in property. But the massive privatization of public land, started with the emphyteusis system in the early 1820s, peaked with Rosas's land grants and sales of the late 1830s and early 1840s. A new round would take place in the 1870s and 1880s, when the Conquest of the Desert was completed.[1]

Compulsory forms of labor other than slavery did not develop in colonial Buenos Aires. Encomienda and repartimiento were not viable due to the lack of a significant sedentary Indian population. Slavery was mainly domestic, whether in urban or rural areas, similar to traditional Old World slavery rather than to New World plantation slavery. Slaves were intro-

---

1 Avellaneda (1865), Cárcano (1972), and Coni (1927) studied the legal process of private appropriation of public land. Valencia de Placente (1983), Infesta and Valencia (1987), Infesta (1991) and (1993), and Banzato and Quinteros (1992) have studied the actual process of private appropriation. There are some less satisfactory contributions, such as those of Oddone (1956), and Carretero (1970) and (1972). See also Burgin (1946), 96–100, 252–255; and Sabato (1989), 51–78.

duced into rural production as a consequence of the late-eighteenth-century trade expansion, to perform (as argued in Chapter 2) the permanent tasks on estancias. Before and after slaves were introduced, the bulk of labor was supplied by free workers. They worked on estancias for a salary on a seasonal basis. The rapid process of expansion attracted immigrants from the Interior, but perhaps not to the extent required by seasonal peaks of labor demand. Restrictions to the mobility of potential peons and the toleration of precarious settlers were the instruments used by estancieros to get access to seasonal labor. Papeletas de conchabo, proofs of lawful employment, and estantes or agregados, those precarious settlers, were therefore two sides of the same coin. The former was a legal instrument to put pressure on potential peons, the latter, a way out of that pressure. In the first half of the nineteenth century, the workers would remain subject to that moderate coercion, stemming from the seasonal pattern of rural labor demand. The views on coercion differ, but there is no doubt that for rural producers the main question remained how to obtain the right labor at the right time.[2]

The definition of rights over land and labor was therefore a crucial issue in Buenos Aires in the first half of the nineteenth century. But there was more than that. Cattle raising was regulated by habits and customs developed to define the cattleowners' rights to their cattle. Those habits and customs, however, were affected by the expansion of production. Informal arrangements that were useful in the past were challenged or disregarded by producers, so the rules of the game for cattle raising were also asking for a redefinition.[3]

This chapter, consequently, deals with the institutional conditions of production. Material and environmental conditions of production (Chapters 5 and 6) did not change in the short run, although they did change in the long run (stocking rates improved, and thistleries disappeared). The rules of the game in rural production underwent a similar process but were marked in this case by the conscious endeavor of some individuals and formal government action. The first section of the chapter examines the inquiry launched by Valentín Alsina in the mid-1850s to determine what those habits and customs regulating rural production were; the second section studies the rural producers' answers to Alsina's inquiry; and the third section reviews the formalization of the previously informal contracts by the Rural Code in the early 1860s.

2 Coercion is emphasized by Lynch (1981), 104–117; Slatta (1980), 458–460; and Slatta (1983), 30–56, 106–125. It is played down by Sabato (1989), 79–129. An emphasis on market mechanisms for labor recruitment is found in Salvatore (1991), and on peons as "rational agents" in Salvatore (1993).
3 For the role of custom in regard to other aspects of rural life, see Mariluz Urquijo (1972) and Fradkin (1995).

Inquiry

In 1856 Valentín Alsina, minister of Government of Buenos Aires, launched an inquiry about rural uses, habits, and customs. He sent a set of questions to a Comisión de Hacendados, which was to circulate it among landowners. That questionnaire included twenty-two questions, nine related to livestock raising, seven to agriculture, and six to "common matters."[4] The underlying issues were the redefinition of property rights, and the problems of public order and law enforcement in a countryside affected by three decades of expansion. Custom was a source of justice in the countryside since colonial times, but Alsina's method – asking for the hacendados' views in a direct way – was a significant innovation.[5]

Property rights were affected by the subsistence of habits and customs pertaining to a different age, when production was organized in a different way.[6] The older pampa was in the 1850s much more populated (in the sense that the word was used at that time in Buenos Aires, meaning both by cattle and people) than at the beginning of the century, and it had been excessively subdivided. Tracts of land a few varas wide by the usual 9,000-vara length were common.[7] They stemmed from a practice that privileged the access to water over the extension of the landholding itself, since there was plenty of vacant, public land where the growing herds could stray. From around 1820 onward, however, the older pampas had been consistently occupied, and public land had all but disappeared. So activities carried out on those small, unfenced, and unmarked tracts could be harmful to the rights of neighbors if cattle were kept in excess of what was a reasonable receptivity for those holdings. Alsina, therefore, asked about the advantages of restricting the number of livestock on a particular tract of land (having those small tracts in mind); what the composition of livestock on that tract should be; and whether neighbors should compensate the owners of those tracts (if production on them was banned) or should be forced to buy them.

Other externalities had always existed, but Alsina's concern shows that they were reaching a critical stage. In winter and in case of drought, livestock walked to the nearest water irrespective of whose lands were crossed over and who owned the land around the water. Should cattleowners be forced to supply water to their cattle? asked Alsina; should transit over other people's lands be regulated? As agricultural land was also

---

4 ACR, 4–13.
5 On custom as a source of justice, see Storni (1986).
6 Old practices and habits were harmful to sheep farming in the 1860s. See Latham (1868), 133–137.
7 Those extremely small tracts appear in the 1789 estancias return (AGN, IX–9–7–7) and were one of the reasons for Maxwell's complaints more than 70 years later. See Maxwell (1863), 5.

affected by transit problems, Alsina asked whether chacareros should be forced to build fences around their tracts, leaving paths along the sides to facilitate livestock transit.

Rural tasks were regulated by a set of informal rules, "more or less rational and respected." Those rules, however, could be disregarded in a way that could turn harmful for livestock owners. Roundups, sortings, brandings, geldings, and other rural tasks were regulated by custom. But custom itself failed to protect the rights of rural producers against malevolent neighbors, who took advantage of the unintentional "blend" of herds and flocks due to lack of fencing.

That openness of the pampas, where restrictions to movements of livestock and people were non-existent, was also propitious for another set of externalities. People pursuing legal activities were also harmful to land and livestock. Beavers, partridges, and ostriches were hunted for their skins, flesh, and feathers; wild dogs were hunted to protect herds and flocks; tall grasses (juncos, totoras, paja) were sought for building purposes; and fires were kindled to "clean" a tract of land. All those activities were legal but could affect someone else's rights. Beasts and vegetals tended to be seen as free, common goods, but they were some landowners' property; fires could go out of control; persecuting wild dogs damaged the fields.

Another set of questions was related to law enforcement. The first set dealt with externalities, damage caused (to some extent, at least) by unintentional action; the second set examined how to protect life and property from purposeful, harmful action. Too many different brands were used by estancieros, and each one could use as many as he wanted. Although all brands should have been properly registered, the proliferation eventually helped rustlers. Alsina asked about the advantages of restricting brands to one for each estanciero. Rustlers and skinners were helped by the fact that sheep were marked in their ears to avoid harm to wool and sheepskins. But sheepskins, therefore, could not be identified. One solution was to order that all sheepskins sent to the market should include the ears for proper identification of their legal origin. In order to control the circulation of goods, to protect the rights of their legal owners, and to prevent the circulation of illegally obtained goods, guides (guías), livestock markets (tabladas), and the transportation of livestock should be regulated. Alsina wanted to know what the best way was to protect property by making the circulation of stolen livestock and livestock by-products more difficult.

A third set of questions addressed the issues of public order and labor relations. Law enforcement was the problem, since there was no shortage of regulations. The use of knives, the sale of alcoholic beverages, and gambling were all regulated. Mobile pulperías were the main source of public disorder as well as an incentive to stealing. The purpose of those regulations was to protect peons' lives and landowners' properties, but labor relations were marked by a consistent failure to comply with the rules, as underscored by the landowners' answers to Alsina's questionnaire.

The hacendados' views

Alsina received two sets of answers, the first when he started his inquiry in 1856. Forty-seven hacendados answered on cattle-raising matters, 25 of them signing a common statement; 12 hacendados answered on agricultural matters, and 21 hacendados answered on common matters. Alsina left the ministry of Government to become governor of Buenos Aires, and the inquiry was discontinued. At the end of 1862, however, he resumed it when asked to prepare the draft for the Rural Code. He published the same questionnaire in *La Tribuna*, one of Buenos Aires's most important newspapers and got eight new responses. Alsina is not ambiguous when referring to the landowners' indifference to the second round of his inquiry,[8] but the information obtained in 1856 and 1863 served his purposes, as shown by the fact that some suggestions saw their way into his draft, and through it into the Rural Code.

The urgent need to introduce order in the countryside and to enforce the laws protecting property were the principal issues addressed by those answers. But it was easier to agree on a diagnosis than on solutions. An examination of Alsina's questions sheds light on the hacendados' views on what rights should take preference. Not all hacendados answered in a straight way, but three questions were answered by most of them. These questions dealt with the restriction of the number of head on a tract, the compulsory sale of small tracts, and the restriction of the number of brands.

Of those three questions, 54 hacendados answered one or more: the 47 who answered Alsina's questions in 1856 plus 7 out of 8 who answered in 1863. One hacendado ignored all questions to focus upon one single issue – horse stealing. All of those 54 hacendados answered the question on the restriction of the number of head on a tract; 50 answered the question on forced land sales; and 52 the question on the restriction of the number of brands. Thirty-seven hacendados (69%) were against restricting the number of head on small tracts, but 17 (31%) were in favor of doing so (Table 7.1). The main argument supporting the former's views was that too many different types of land made it impossible to regulate the number of head on a tract. Consequently, they preferred to let landowners enjoy the property of their tracts, coping with the potential overstocking according to the provisions of an old (but poorly enforced) decree of 20 November 1823, which made livestock invasions a crime similar to

8 See Alsina (1865), 6–7.

Table 7.1. *Alsina's inquiry: Hacendados' answers on property rights,*
1856–1863

Hacendados	Restriction of number of head		Forced sale of small tracts		Restriction of number of brands	
	N	%	*N*	%	*N*	%
In favor	17	31	6	11	15	28
Against[a]	37	69	44	81	37	69
No answer	0	0	4	7	2	3
Total	54	100	54	100	54	100

[a] Twenty-five hacendados signed a common answer.
Source: ACR, passim.

rustling.[9] Four hacendados (7%) of those opposed to regulating the number of head were, however, in favor of some government action (fines, punishment) to prevent cattle spillover due to overstocking. Those hacendados in favor of restricting the number of head had no doubt about the number of head a tract could hold, and they wanted government action to prevent overstocking. Consequently, although no suggestion was made in that regard, a governmental agency would have to be in charge of counting the head on small tracts, all of them supposed to have the same soil and grasses and therefore the same density, in order to punish those small landowners who overstocked their land. Given the government's inability to enforce other laws in the countryside, this regulation was costly and impracticable.

Four hacendados (7%) out of 54 answering the first question did not answer the question on the compulsory sale of small tracts to neighboring landowners. Forty-four hacendados (81%) were against compulsory sales, but 6 (11%) were in favor. For the former, the right to enjoy what had been inherited (small plots stemmed from splitting larger tracts between heirs) was paramount. For the latter the deliberate overstocking of small plots was a criminal behavior punishable with the loss of the right to enjoy that property. Considering that the 1823 decree was poorly enforced, it is doubtful that this view could have ever been turned into an enforceable law. Apart from a weak institutional development in the countryside, the main impediment was that the compulsory collaboration of neighboring landowners was required, since they would be forced to buy those small tracts. Four hacendados who opposed compulsory sales were in favor of imposing fines to prevent the overstocking of small tracts. Another two of those hacendados were in favor of forcing small landowners to rent out

9 See RO (1821), 125–126; and RO (1823), 180.

their tracts, a measure that also would have required the forced collaboration of neighboring landowners, now as tenants rather than buyers.

The third question, on the restriction of the number of brands, was answered by 52 of the 54 hacendados who had answered the first question. Thirty-seven hacendados (69%) were against restricting the number of brands that one hacendado could hold, but 15 (28%) were in favor of restrictions. The main concern of the former was practical – different brands were used for different herds on one estancia, and for different estancias belonging to the same owner, as Marcelo Ignes did on his three estancias in San Pedro and San Nicolás.[10] The main concern of those favoring restrictions was cattle rustling. Although all brands should be registered with the police, according to a decree of 23 February 1822, the use of many brands, they argued, facilitated robberies.[11] It is not too clear why a single brand would deter them. The Anchorena brand was known all over the countryside, so it was more difficult to drive his cattle or transport his hides illegally. But, as one of those opposing restrictions stressed, other large landowners' brands were less well known, so their use of a single brand did not have a similar effect.[12]

Alsina adopted the view of the majority for the Rural Code in all three cases. The different views on the definition of property rights show the variety of concerns and the difficulties underlying any definition. Property should be protected from externalities, but that protection was costly, both in monetary terms (an issue often disregarded) and in terms of other rights. In the first case, the high cost (a new enforcing agency, constant control) and lack of practicality (impossible to determine the right charge for every single tract) of the minority view were clear. In the second case, its complete impracticality (compulsory land sales and compulsory land buyings) was also clear. In the third case, the minority view was enforceable and to some extent useful, but it ran against entrenched habits that were not entirely unreasonable.

Other questions were answered in a less straightforward way, and the hacendados' views are more difficult to define. Two questions addressed problems as important as those already considered – livestock transit and water supply. Driving cattle across the still unfenced pampas meant crossing other people's lands, consuming their grasses and water. There was no other way for cattle to reach the urban market, so some accommodation was necessary in order to continue that inevitable practice while reducing its externalities. The views on this matter ranged from those who favored

10 Marcelo Ignes to Juan Pedro Aguirre, Tala, 25 February 1826, ABP, 031–5–3–13.
11 RO (1822), 73–74.
12 Máximo de Elía stressed the advantages of a single brand for Nicolás Anchorena but not for other
      cattleowners. See ACR, 32–33.

the construction of roads (whatever that could mean in the open pampas) to the assignment of predetermined places to in-transit herds, from impos- ing fines to charging for grass and water consumption. The latter sugges- tion was Juan Dillon's and was adopted (with a devious wording) by Alsina in his Code. Thirty-five of 54 hacendados gave a clear answer to the question on livestock transit, and 47 answered the question on compulsory water supply. Most of the latter (42 hacendados) were in favor of forcing landowners to supply water to their herds to prevent dispersion in case of drought. Five hacendados were against any compulsion. Matías Ramos Mejía gave the best reason for supporting the former's view – tracts with a natural water supply were ruined by other people's herds, while lands without water recovered as soon as the drought was over.[13] But if that was the case, an artificial waterer would clearly have the same result. Unless water could be cheaply obtained by every landowner, there was a negative incentive to build artificial waterers. The bottomless bucket introduced in the mid-1820s was not good enough (horses and riders were necessary to operate it), so the time was not right until Pellegrini invented the dump bucket in 1853, or even until artesian wells, water pumps, and windmills started to spread over the pampas in the 1870s.[14]

The answers to less pressing issues, such as hunting and epizootics, were even more diffuse. Thirty hacendados responded to the former. Twenty-six of them were in favor of banning it, and 4 were in favor of regulating it. Hunting was already regulated, but enforcement was perhaps poor.[15] Thirty-seven hacendados answered the question on epizootics. For 3 of them, affected livestock should be locked up in corrals and isolated from other herds; for another 4, the authorities (municipalities, justices of the peace) should implement adequate measures. There was one suggestion that a committee of hacendados should be organized eventually to cope with that problem. Twenty-nine hacendados, however, asked for no action. There had never been any epizootic yet, they argued, and due to the dispersion of livestock on the open fields of the pampas, they thought it quite unlikely that any would develop in the near future.

Apart from answering Alsina's questions, many hacendados expressed their concerns on diverse issues. All these comments aimed at a better definition of property rights by increasing government action and re- gulation. Government action was required to build roads between pro- perties, as suggested by Juan Cornell, to establish departmental boundaries, as recommended by Leonardo Brid, and to improve the topographical map of the province, as proposed by Lino Lagos, especially

13 Juan Dillon and Gregorio J. de Quirno expressed exactly the same view. See ACR, 55, 72, 218.
14 Sbarra (1973), 65–77, 114–169.
15 RO (1821), 125–126, decree of 22 November 1821.

the area surrounding Buenos Aires that had not been included in the 1830 *Registro Gráfico*.[16]

The enforcement of already existing regulations was required to stop abuses concerning roundups and brandings. But new regulations were asked for multifarious pet concerns such as restricting the number of dogs on an estancia, demanding a justification from whomever would wear botas de potro (a traditional foot gear made out of the skin of a colt's leg) to stop illegal colt slaughterings, imposing fines to passersby cutting across a flock, ruling out nocturnal drivings and roundups, restricting the number of poblaciones on an estancia, regulating the appropriation of stray cattle, and banning cattle raising or horse breeding on tracts smaller than one suerte de estancia (equivalent to 2,025 hectares). Other regulations were suggested by some hacendados to force their colleagues to hold a certain number of cattle and horses on a tract, to establish the boundaries of their properties, or, in collaboration with the government, compulsorily to move agregados to rural villages.[17]

No restrictions were imposed on the number of dogs on an estancia, and agregados were not relocated to rural villages, but, as already remarked, some hacendados' views were incorporated into the Code. In their quest to define their property rights and counter externalities better, some hacendados suggested new regulations that would be difficult and costly to enforce, and, if enforced, would create new externalities: Juan Dillon denounced the attempt to do away with small properties, and Gregorio J. de Quirno considered it a manifestation of "feudalism."[18] Consequently, the liberty to enjoy property rights fully was upheld by the Code, as requested by a majority of those hacendados who bothered to answer Alsina's questions, and fines, as recommended by others, were turned into the main means to cope with violations of those rights. Such fines would serve to strengthen the law enforcement ability of governmental agents in the countryside. The inquiry itself was an important landmark in the process of institutional consolidation, but even more significant was the passing of the Rural Code.

---

16 The *Registro Gráfico* of 1830 did not register land around Buenos Aires because those tracts had not been surveyed after the establishment of the Topographical Department. See *La Gaceta Mercantil*, 7 September 1832, quoted by Díaz (1959), 190–191. Those blanks were erroneously taken for public land by Sabato (1989), 54–55.

17 These measures were suggested by Bernardo Gutiérrez, Máximo de Elía, Patricio Linch, Mariano Benítez, Venancio Casalins, Ignacio F. Correas, Valentín Fernández Blanco, Leonardo Brid, Gregorio J. de Quirno, Juan Cornell, and Francisco A. Pearson. See ACR, 28–31, 35–37, 44, 52–53, 68, 75, 79, 216, 257, 299.

18 See ACR, 231, 216.

The Rural Code

The Buenos Aires Rural Code was passed on 6 November 1865. For drafting it Alsina used the landowners' views he had collected and laws and decrees on rural matters passed in Buenos Aires since 1821. He also used other sources, such as agricultural books sent to him by Mariano Balcarce, the Argentine minister in France, and Maxwell's statistics. The European publications, Alsina reported, were less useful than expected due to the "profound and radical differences" between the Buenos Aires and European countrysides regarding the methods of rural public administration, types of rural industries, systems of exploitation, and even "the moral conditions of the inhabitants."[19]

The most difficult problem Alsina confronted when drafting the Code was the weak institutional development in the countryside. The main law enforcement agency, the police, was controlled by the national government. That was a temporary situation due to the incomplete organization of the national administration inaugurated in 1862. The Buenos Aires government could rely on the police anyhow, but civilian institutions were inefficient or non-existent. Municipalities were not yet organized in all partidos and, even if they were, due to dissent among their members or their lack of care, the justice of the peace was left in charge of making decisions.[20] In that way a governmental appointee performed judiciary, police, and municipal tasks. That was wrong, but the Rural Code could not change anything in that regard. A full implementation of the Rural Code could hardly be expected under those conditions of undifferentiation of public office.[21]

Of a different nature was the problem for Alsina in adjusting his draft to the existing legislation. Many of the hacendados' suggestions were dismissed due to potential violation of constitutional rights and regulations (Alsina does not give any concrete example). But even more complicated was drafting the Rural Code before the codification of civil, criminal, and procedural laws. Alsina proudly remarked that his code, once passed, would be the only Rural Code on earth. There was none in Spain, Prussia, Belgium, the United States, or even France, "that nation essentially prone to regulation."

The Rural Code comprised 319 articles, divided into a brief introduc-

19 CRBA, v–vi; Maxwell (1863).
20 The justice of the peace presided over the municipality according to the law passed on 10 October 1854. See Díaz (1959), 84.
21 On the confusion of roles of the justice of the peace (police, judiciary, agent of the executive branch under Rosas), see Díaz (1959), 89–91, 136–140; and Brabazon (1981), 54–55.

tion supplying some general definitions (articles 1–5) and five parts: cattle ranching (articles 6–146), agriculture (articles 147–206), other rural matters related both to cattle raising and agriculture (articles 207–284), the rural police (articles 285–309), and local authorities and general issues (articles 310–319). The sections devoted to labor relations (Part III, section 3) and to vagrancy and other crimes (Part IV) have attracted the attention of scholars interested in rural labor. But the larger segments devoted to the specification of rights related to all other aspects of rural activities (Parts I and III) have been largely disregarded. These sections deal with beasts, goods, and services rather than with people, but those beasts, goods, and services were at the core of Buenos Aires's wealth, and their particular use is in no way less important than the supply of labor.

Alsina had inquired about the advantages of restricting the number of livestock on an estancia and setting a limit to the minimum extension of an estancia.[22] The Rural Code left both the extension of an estancia and the number of livestock to each landowner's judgment, but boundaries were to be clearly marked within 5 years. Those who failed to comply with this obligation would pay a fine of 300 pesos per month for each league of land.

No restriction was imposed over the number of brands allowed to each cattleowner. As in the past, brands would be registered with the police, but municipalities should also have their own records. The reason for this double record seems to be the spread of livestock over the countryside. The proliferation of livestock owners made it difficult to keep track of brands and, consequently, of the rightful owners of hides sent to Buenos Aires.[23]

Therefore, regarding those issues that had caught the preferential attention of the landowners who answered Alsina's inquiry, the Rural Code imposed no restrictions on the full use of property rights, but fines were introduced to prevent externalities. That delicate balance between the right to enjoy one's property and the prevention of damages to other people caused by that very right was present throughout the Code.

Intrusion on someone else's land was also subject to a fine. No excuse was valid, neither livestock roundups, nor ostrich hunting, nor casual camping. Poblaciones should be established at a distance from the boundaries, and livestock should be driven away from neighboring tracts. Land-

---

22 These questions were dealt with in Part I. Part I was divided into eighteen sections covering different aspects of cattle-raising activities. Those sections dealt with brands and marks; sortings and sorters; horses; transit with animals; merchants dealing in rural products; brandings; grazing; marks on sheep; livestock mixups; transit permits for rural products (guides); waterers; people transporting rural products; beef suppliers; the judge of corrals (urban cattle markets); the offices controlling the introduction of cattle into the city (tabladas); jerked beef- and tallow-producing establishments (saladeros and graserías); and stray cattle. See CRBA, 4–28.
23 CRBA, 6–7, articles 17–25.

owners who found other people's head on their estancias should report that to the authorities, who should verify their complaints. If the complaint was valid, the stray head should be locked up and the owner fined. If the fine was not paid, those cattle would be auctioned to meet the expenses, and the remainder would be given to the original owner. If cattle had caused some damage to fences, trees, or ditches, that amount should be retained. Auctioned cattle should be immediately slaughtered, to prevent any claim by their owner. The dispersion of cattle due to droughts, fires, floods, or any other disaster, however, was not their owner's fault, nor the damage cattle could unintentionally cause to other people's lands, houses, or quintas. There was therefore a distinction made between the deliberate aquerenciamiento of a herd on someone else's land and the accidental dispersion of cattle. The former would not be tolerated; the latter was impossible to prevent. Consequently, there were provisions to regulate sortings of mixed-up head.

Cattleowners should round up their cattle for sortings whenever asked to, but calving, droughts, or labor shortage were listed among the exceptions to that obligation. Such roundups were to allow cattleowners to sort their head out of other people's herds. Although the intentional invasion of someone else's land was punished, there was no way to prevent the accidental mix-up of neighboring herds. Cattleowners were not forced to maintain those roundup head for more than 6 hours, and they could refuse to carry out roundups in the afternoon. In case of dissent over livestock ownership, the "most immediate authority," perhaps the justice of the peace, would decide.[24] Sortings had been regulated by custom, but the Rural Code introduced a third party into that practice, the local authority.

The role of the local authority was extended by other provisions of the Code beyond the mere enforcement of accepted practices. Brandings should be announced to neighbors at least 6 days in advance, to allow them to take their head away from the herds to be branded. A representative of the justice of the peace would be present when the branding was carried out, but his absence was not a reason for suspending it. Failure in giving notice of the branding was subject to a fine of 1 peso per head, estimated according to the number of head in the herd to be branded. Municipal authorities or the justice of the peace were in charge of collecting fines. On the date of the branding, herds should be ready for 6 hours before the beginning of the operation, to give time for neighbors to take their head away. The representative of the justice of the peace would take note of all cattle and horses marked with unknown brands and try to find their owners, charging them for the expenses. Once the branding had begun, the estanciero could not be asked to carry out any roundup until the operation

24 CRBA, 7–8, articles 26–33.

was over. If someone else's cattle were branded by mistake, they should be counter-branded, but if they were branded on purpose, their rightful owner would be paid double their value, and criminal charges could follow. In case of drought, epidemics, or public disorder, the government could ban brandings.[25] Brandings were a private business, but the regulations of the Rural Code, designed to protect the property right on cattle, introduced an external power into that practice.

Law enforcement was not free. Fines were imposed to finance the protection of property rights. The holders of unfenced tracts could not keep transit away. Herds could stop to rest for 12 hours, and carts for 3 days. The drivers of those herds or carts should stay on the main road, keep the beasts under control, and ask the landowner for a place to camp. In case of dispersion of the herds, they could do whatever was necessary to bring them together again without paying for any expenses to the landowner. But if dispersed animals got mixed with the landowner's herds, a permit for a roundup should be requested. There were fines for those drivers who did not comply with the rules. But more remarkable than the imposition of those fines was their destination: half for the landowner and half for the municipal treasury. The only reason (although none was given) for splitting fines was that to make the offenders pay the involvement of the justice of the peace or the police would be required. Another new element introduced by the articles referring to transit was that the stay on someone else's land could not be impeded, but it was not free. The twisted wording of an article pointed out that "if the landowner, holder, or tenant of a tract refused not to charge any compensation," he would be able to charge 10 pesos per hour for every 100 head of cattle or horses or 50 pesos for every 1,000 sheep.[26] Grass was not a free good on the pampas any longer.

The provision of water on each estancia, a key improvement in preventing livestock dispersion, was also an issue considered by the landowners answering Alsina's inquiry. Despite the views of those who emphasized the drawbacks of waterers, the Code established the obligation for each landowner and tenant to build artificial waterers. A 1,000-peso fine would be charged to those disregarding the rule. If due to lack of access to water on their estancia, livestock invaded someone else's land, the owner of that land could charge 5 pesos per head of cattle or horse to their owner for the supply of grasses and water. Municipal authorities and justices of the peace would appoint committees to inspect artificial waterers and see that their number was according to the number of head on each estancia. Only in case of drought would free access to water be available, irrespective of property

25 CRBA, 11–13, articles 48–55.
26 CRBA, 10–11, articles 40–42.

rights on a water source. The obligation to build waterers fell upon landholders, but the enforcement of that rule fell upon the government. No funds were appropriated for it, but violators were charged for the consumption of grass and water by their livestock on other people's land. After the Code was passed, there was an active search for water-supply devices, such as pumps, artesian wells, and later windmills. Perhaps this rule helped the spread of those devices over the pampas.[27]

The protection of property rights required a detailed specification of those rights. The openness of the pampas did not facilitate such specification, but the regulations of the Rural Code were building upon habits and customs, changing those traditions that were no longer suitable for the protection of rights over land and livestock. Hunting wild animals – ostrich, partridge, fowl, deer, beaver, and armadillo – was a traditional activity in the countryside. For a few decades after 1810, the export of furs and feathers of wild animals reached a significant level. In the 1860s such exports were not relevant, but the supply of wild animals was still plentiful. The Rural Code sought to change the way in which hunting was carried out. Wild animals were no longer common property but rather belonged to the holder of the tract where they were found. Landownership was the main criteria in determining rights over wild animals. They were owned by the landholder on whose land they were found. If they were hurt and fled to a different estancia, they belonged to that estancia holder. More than protecting the actual revenue that landholders could expect from hunting those animals or from granting licenses to other people for doing so, this ruling aimed at keeping poachers far from livestock to prevent their dispersion. The same can be said about dog hunting. There were still wild dogs in the countryside, and they were still disturbing livestock. But they should be eliminated by poisoned meat. Hunting could only be carried out with permission granted by a landholder. Fines for disregarding this rule would be 500 pesos, and those who were unable to pay it would be destined to public works until the salaries earned were equal to the amount of the fine. Public lands would also be free from hunters, unless a proper hunting permit was obtained from the municipal authorities or the justice of the peace.

Environmentally correct avant-la-lettre, Alsina's Rural Code provided for the protection of wild species, following (and going beyond) the provisions of the decree of 22 November 1821.[28] Each municipality would determine blackout periods for each species. Hunting during those periods would be illegal, and fines and punishments would be determined by

27 CRBA, 19, articles 99–102. For the spread of pumps, artesian wells, and windmills, see Sbarra (1973).
28 RO (1821), 125–126.

municipalities. Blackouts were not restricted to public lands: Even land-holders would be punished for out-of-season hunting on their own land. This was perhaps the only regulation introduced by the Rural Code that restricted the full enjoyment of property rights, but it aimed to serve a superior common good – the preservation of wild species.[29]

The gathering of "spontaneous products of the soil" was as much a problem for estancieros as was hunting. Thistles, paja, and other coarse grasses used as fuel, as well as stones and shells, were declared the property of the estancia holder. No such products could be collected without the landholder's permission. The same applied to public land, where a munici-pal permit had to be obtained to collect those products. Fines would be similar to those applicable to hunting. The reason for this rule was the prevention of intrusions rather than the protection of plants or minerals.

The district authorities (municipalities, justices of the peace) were in charge of overseeing that small tracts were not overstocked, that landown-ers did not rent small portions of their tracts to tenants, that landholders helped to control thistleries, and that trees were planted for providing the flocks shade in summer and cover from wind in winter. For all those and similar purposes, no law enforcing instrument was devised other than "advice and persuasion." Local authorities were also left on their own to offer incentives to exterminate insects (mainly locusts) and to deal with droughts and epidemics.[30]

Property rights were redefined in this way by the Rural Code in the mid-1860s. Property was protected from encroachment and from inten-tional and accidental damage. Legal instruments were devised to deal with conflict over livestock and rural goods. Access to pasture and water would no longer be free, and the usual activities performed on estancias, such as roundups, brandings, and sortings, were regulated to prevent landholders from being hurt by other people's actions as well as to prevent their actions from hurting their neighbors.

All this regulatory activity aimed at a better definition of rights, but it relied on a poor law enforcement ability. Municipal authorities were not organized in all districts, and justices of the peace did not control the police. The process of institutional organization of the countryside was, however, underway. The very fact that habits and customs were turned into legislation underscored a trend, slowly evolving since the beginning of the expansion over the pampas. Habits and customs could be self-enforced, but due to the rapid growth of population and territory, an external arbiter was necessary to reorganize the institutional conditions of production. The Rural Code does not account for the process of institutional evolution, but

29 CRBA, 47–48, articles 259–268.
30 CRBA, 59–60, articles 310–312.

it serves as a picture taken at a moment of change. Elements pointing to the past and to the future can be recognized in assessing the direction of institutional evolution.

Conclusion

The expansion of cattle raising over the pampas was affected by institutional conditions defined by laws and regulations, habits and customs. Those conditions revolved around two types of connected problems: on the one hand, the redefinition of property rights to cope with the externalities set in motion by an expanding production; on the other hand, the problem of public order. In both cases there was a delicate balance between the protection of rights, both from externalities and crime, and the cost of enforcing such protection. This tradeoff was solved by producing in a competitive framework rather than lobbying for privilege. No virtue was necessary to do that – the cost of enforcing a privilege outdid that of the competition.

The interplay of natural and human factors defined a set of institutional conditions that were at the same time evolving as the relationship between those factors changed. Habits and customs that had been accepted as good, or were too costly to eradicate as their usefulness was wearing out, called for a new definition of property rights, which would still be dependent upon a tradeoff between the gains introduced by such potential redefinition and the cost of undertaking it.

Alsina's questions, the landowners' answers, and the Rural Code taken together show how rights over goods and services were changing in mid-nineteenth-century Buenos Aires. Public goods were appropriated, on paper at least, and the violation of regulations was discouraged by fines. The use of property remained unchecked (barring hunting blackouts), but externalities were now properly taken care of. Law enforcement remained problematic, but Alsina did not introduce that element of doubt into the Code. Although the cost of law enforcement was not entirely removed from the landowners' minds, there is no explicit reference to that issue in the Code, which implicitly relied on fines to help meet the expenses.

Regulations, laws, and the Code were perhaps poorly enforced and largely disregarded, but the issues they dealt with were a reflection of real problems affecting rural production. As such, they can be considered as photographs, freezing an existing reality that can later develop in numerous directions. The 1865 Rural Code was an expression of institutional change in the countryside, but change did not stop when it was passed. Godofredo Daireaux, in the fourth edition of his treatise on "cattle-raising on the modern estancia," published in 1908, underscored that the expansion of agriculture, the multiplication of railroads, the development of cattle and frozen-beef exports, the importation of bulls, and the division of landholdings had turned the provisions of the Code obsolete.[31] The "general progress of the country" required, like four decades before, a redefinition of property rights and a further improvement of law enforcement. This chapter has examined the issues debated by hacendados and the government from the mid-1850s to the mid-1860s to show how the tradeoff between property rights and externalities was then expressing a particular institutional development affecting rural production in the Buenos Aires countryside.

31 Daireaux (1908), 545–548.

PART III

Human action

8

Labor

In *La ciudad indiana*, a classic on colonial Buenos Aires read by many generations, Juan Agustín García says that slaves were introduced into the colonial estancia because they were cheaper than peons. By investing a few hundred pesos on a slave who would work 15 to 20 years, he argues, estancieros could save thousands in peons' salaries. As a result peons could not easily find jobs, and when they did find one, monthly wages of 6 to 8 pesos were sufficient to cover only "their most pressing needs." All estancias, however, were "full of gauchos with no regular wage because rich men, instead of hiring all the peons they need, keep on only foremen and slaves."[1] How was it, then, that these gauchos without a regular salary did not offer to work for under 6 pesos a month? If they had done so, why should landowners still invest in slaves? If they did not do so, why did slaves not take the place of peons completely? García does not answer these questions. The idea prevailing in his writing is that free labor was unstable, so slaves had to be introduced into rural work to compensate for that instability, due in turn to the peons' lack of industriousness. More recent contributions have also singled out the unstable nature of free labor as the reason for the increasing use of slaves in rural work in late-eighteenth-century Buenos Aires. Free labor was unstable, it has been argued, because of a subsistence sector to which peons could turn after taking on casual work simply to earn money for those needs that could not be satisfied in that sector.[2]

The solution to García's riddle lies in the seasonality of rural production. As in all other agrarian economies, in Buenos Aires there were periods of low demand when estancias only required labor for upkeep and basic livestock operations. The coexistence of forced and free labor in late-eighteenth- and early-nineteenth-century Buenos Aires was actually due to that pattern of labor demand as well as to factors such as the price of slaves

---

1 García (1966), 179–180.
2 Halperín Donghi (1975), 457–459; Mayo (1984), 614–615.

(which was presumably falling) and the cost of coercion (which was probably higher for peons).[3]

Recent studies on rural labor in Buenos Aires in the late colonial and early national period have been concerned with the social relations of production. Whether trying to identify peasants working in agriculture, vagrants, or proletarian peons, these studies share a concern for those workers' social condition rather than for their economic role as suppliers of labor for the estancia.[4] This chapter focuses upon the demand and supply of rural labor, that is, upon the economic relations of production on the Buenos Aires estancias.

It has always been clear that agriculture is a seasonal undertaking. Wheat, corn, any grain, should be sowed at some time of the year and harvested months later. Cattle raising also has a seasonal pattern. A factor accounting for the seasonality of cattle production, thistles, has been studied in Chapter 6. Other factors were also present: Calving, branding, and gelding could not take place all year round. There was a season for calving, and branding and gelding were performed when cooler weather had reduced the number of flies and therefore the risk of infection. So both agriculture and cattle production had a seasonal pattern of labor demand. Money, to some extent, could be used to offset that pattern. When funds were necessary, cattle had to be sold, so peons were hired during off-season periods or for longer spans. But that was clearly a last-resort occurrence. A well-managed estancia, such as the López Osornio estancia, tended to avoid higher off-season expenses (Figure 2.6). But if thistles could be countered at some expense, biological factors were harder to deal with. Rosas recommended avoiding roundups of newly born calves and their mothers, and he set up clear rules for branding and gelding operations.[5] Seasonality was therefore a characteristic feature of all pre-industrial rural economies, and Buenos Aires, in spite of its differences with other European and Latin American rural landscapes, could not escape from that pattern. The analysis is focused here upon the late eighteenth and early nineteenth centuries, although conditions of production did not change on the pampas until the expansion of wire fencing, railroads, and commercial agriculture, from the 1870s onward. The aim of this chapter is to test the arguments of labor scarcity and labor instability – Was labor scarce? When was it scarce? Was labor unstable? Why was it so?

3 The peons' and slaves' productivity and daily profit have been compared in Chapter 2 to explain the demand for both kinds of labor on López Osornio's estancia.
4 For peasants, see Gelman (1989a), (1989b), and (1992a); for vagrants, see Mayo (1984), (1987a), (1987b), and (1989); for would-be proletarians, see Salvatore and Brown (1987) and (1989), and Salvatore (1992). García's chapter on rural labor was entitled "el proletariado de las campañas," the rural proletariat.
5 Rosas (1942), 36–41.

Labor scarcity

In order to determine whether there was any labor scarcity, the demand for and supply of labor should be estimated. An estimate of total labor demand should start with the potential production per worker, both in agriculture and cattle raising. Then the total output of both sectors should be divided by the output per worker. This will give us an estimate of the annual demand of labor for both sectors, irrespective of seasonal fluctuations, which will be introduced later.

According to Azara, one agricultural worker could harvest 46.5 Buenos Aires fanegas of wheat in 1.5 years. Although he does not advance any reason for using such a time span, it can be assumed that 31 fanegas could have been 1 years' product.[6] In the cattle-ranching sector, one foreman and ten peons could tend 10,000 head, making an average of 909 head of cattle for each man. Leaving aside for a while the seasonality of rural tasks, and therefore how many weeks or months a rural worker should work to meet Azara's sectoral output per worker, the number of workers required by Buenos Aires wheat production is estimated assuming they should work year-round to meet such goals. Agricultural labor demand is therefore equivalent to the total number of fanegas of wheat divided by the number of fanegas produced by each worker in that sector. Consequently, a total output of 84,000 fanegas of wheat supposedly produced in Buenos Aires at the end of the eighteenth century would have required 2,710 workers, and 3,774 workers by the 117,000-fanega peak harvest. A parallel estimate of the number of workers required by cattle ranching is obtained by dividing the total number of cattle head by the number of head tended by a peon. A total cattle stock of 857,600 head would have required 943 workers.[7]

The demand for labor, however, was not homogeneous year-round, since rural tasks followed a marked seasonal pattern. On the López Osornio estancia in the 1790s, actual demand fluctuated according to seasonal requirements. In a 60-month period, from February 1787 to January 1792, no peon was hired in 10 months, only one peon or less was hired in 17 months, between one and less than three peons were hired in 19 months,

---

6 In the mid-1850s, it was estimated that three men had to work during eight days to sow wheat on one square cuadra. One man might have done so in 24 days, but even if the season for sowing was longer than that, it is doubtful that he could have done much more, on the one hand, because working by himself the task might well have demanded more time, and on the other, because of delays caused by rains. As the yield of that plot could vary from 20 to 30 fanegas according to the type of seed, that might well have been the result of one man's work if he could do the job by himself at harvest time. For this estimate, see REBA (1855), 2:35–37; for Azara's, Azara (1943), 7–8.

7 That number of head is estimated according to the maximum tithe paid between 1776 and 1804 (see Chapter 5) and according to the reproduction rate on the López Osornio estancia (Chapter 2).

Human action

Table 8.1. *Seasonal demand for temporary labor on the López Osornio estancia, 1787–1791 (average man-days worked per month)*

	Summer	Fall	Winter	Spring
1787	–	20.3	118.7	122.0
1788	38.3	5.3	5.7	138.0
1789	30.7	46.3	124.0	34.0
1790	38.3	78.3	47.7	21.7
1791	22.7	45.7	26.0	79.3
X_d	27.5	41.2	64.4	79.0
X_t	0.92	1.37	2.15	2.63

Notes: Summer: December to February. Fall: March to May. Winter: June to August.
Spring: September to November. X_d = average man-days worked per month; X_t = average temporary workers per month ($X_d/30$).
Source: Table 2.8.

and three or more peons were hired in 14 months. To move forward in the analysis of labor scarcity, it is therefore necessary to determine the permanent and seasonal labor demand and what proportion of the potential labor supply was actually demanded in each season.

Between February 1787 and January 1792, there were five men working on a permanent basis on the López Osornio estancia: the foreman and four slaves. To determine seasonal demand, each month is considered separately, even though some tasks perhaps required more than one peon working simultaneously in a way that dividing the number of man-days worked by 30 may not represent correctly. Seasons are also taken as fixed, even though it is quite clear that they do not start and end according to the calendar.

Temporary peon hiring for seasonal tasks during the same period went from an average of 0.92 peons per month in summer to 1.37 peons in fall, to 2.15 in winter, and to 2.63 in spring (Table 8.1). Demand peaked in the spring of 1788, with 4.6 peons per month, and reached its lowest figure in the fall and winter of that year, with 0.2 peons per month. Temporary labor demand in 1789 (the year with the highest overall demand, since data for the summer of 1787 are not complete) was 35% higher than that of 1791, the year with the lowest demand. But it should be noted that variations in 1788, 1790, and 1791 are within an 8% range. These figures underscore the fact that annual labor demand was fairly homogeneous, but the seasonal peak of labor demand varied from year to year. In 1788 demand peaked in spring; in 1789, in winter; in 1790, in fall; and in 1791, in spring again.

Table 8.2. *Head of cattle per temporary worker on the López Osornio estancia, 1787–1791*

	Cattle stock	Summer	Fall	Winter	Spring	Average
1787	1,630	–	2,409	412	401	1,074
1788	1,796	1,407	3,522	9,453	391	3,693
1789	1,978	1,933	1,282	479	1,746	1,360
1790	2,180	1,708	835	1,372	3,014	1,732
1791	2,402	3,175	1,577	2,772	909	2,108
Mean	1,997	2,056	1,925	2,898	1,292	2,043[a]

[a] Average of the seasonal figures in the bottom row. The average of the figures in the right column is 1,994 head.
Note: The number of head of cattle for each temporary worker (H) has been estimated as

$$H = \frac{s\,t}{X_d}$$

where s = cattle stock on the López Osornio estancia; t = number of days in a month; and X_d = monthly average of man-days worked in each season.
Sources: Tables 2.4 and 8.1.

Temporary labor demand and the number of cattle head on the López Osornio estancia provide an estimate of the number of cattle head per temporary worker (Table 8.2). From 1787 to 1791, there were 1,997 head on average, making an average of 2,043 head per peon, with seasonal peaks of 2,898 head per peon in winter and 1,293 head per peon in spring. There were, however, wide seasonal and annual fluctuations in labor demand, from a low of 9,453 head per peon in the winter of 1788 to a high of 391 head per peon in the spring of the same year.

Seasonal labor demand for a stock of 857,600 head can be estimated using the ratio of cattle head per peon on the López Osornio estancia (Table 8.3). As seasonal demand varied from year to year according to each year's conditions of production, the seasonal mean for 1787–1791 is more relevant than each year's figures. The total demand for temporary labor for that stock fluctuated, therefore, from 456 men in summer to 1,210 in spring (Table 8.3).

The demand for permanent labor should be added to the seasonal demand for temporary labor in order to find the total labor demand for cattle ranching (Table 8.4). On the López Osornio estancia in 1795, there were five permanent workers and 4,581 head, equivalent to 916.2 head per worker.[8] The permanent labor demand for 857,600 head was, therefore,

8 This figure is extremely close to that of 909 head per worker stemming from Azara's estimates. Azara, therefore, was not taking into consideration temporary labor demanded by seasonal tasks.

Table 8.3. *Seasonal demand for temporary labor in Buenos Aires,*
1787–1791

	Summer	Fall	Winter	Spring
1787	–	356	2,082	2,139
1788	610	243	91	2,193
1789	444	669	1,790	491
1790	502	1,027	625	285
1791	270	544	309	943
Mean	456	568	979	1,210

Note: Seasonal demand for temporary labor (L_t) is

$$L_t = \frac{S\,X_d}{s\,t} = \frac{S}{v}$$

where s = cattle stock on the López Osornio estancia; t = number of days in a month; X_d = monthly average of man-days worked in each season (Table 11.3); S = total cattle stock, 857,600 head (see Table 5.9); and v = head per temporary worker.
Sources: Tables 2.8 and 8.2.

749 workers. Adding this figure to the temporary labor seasonal average, the total labor demand for cattle ranching would have been 1,205 workers in summer, 1,317 workers in fall, 1,728 workers in winter, and 1,959 workers in spring.

The demand for labor for agriculture should be added to the demand for labor for cattle ranching in order to find the total demand for labor (Table 8.4). Based upon Azara's information on output per worker, the demand of labor for wheat farming was 3,226 workers for a total output of 100,000 fanegas. Since off-season permanent tasks were almost non-existent for wheat farming, no labor demand has been assigned to fall and spring, since sowing took place in winter and harvesting in summer. Total demand for labor fluctuated therefore between 1,317 workers in fall and 4,954 workers in winter.

The total demand for labor should be compared to the potential supply of workers in order to ascertain whether labor was scarce or abundant. For that comparison the potential supply of workers should be found first (Table 8.5). The potential supply of workers is equivalent to the active male population present in the countryside. Total demand for labor has been estimated using the average for 1787–1791, and the estimate of labor supply should start with an estimate of total rural population in those years, which can be done using the 1778 and 1815 censuses and the annual rate of intercensal growth. There were 15,080 rural inhabitants in 1778 and 42,053 in 1815; therefore, the annual rate of growth was 2.81% (Table

Table 8.4. *Seasonal demand for temporary and permanent rural labor in Buenos Aires around 1800*

	Summer	Fall	Winter	Spring
Cattle ranching: Permanent (L_p)	749	749	749	749
Temporary (L_t)	456	568	979	1,210
Subtotal (L_g)	1,205	1,317	1,728	1,959
Wheat farming (L_a)	3,226	–	3,226	–
Total (L)	4,431	1,317	4,954	2,995
Potential supply (S_l)	5,944	5,944	5,944	5,944
Employment rate (%)	74.5	22.2	83.3	50.4

Note: Cattle-ranching permanent labor demand (L_p) is estimated as follows

$$L_p = \frac{S \; N}{V}$$

where S = total cattle stock: 857,600 head (see Table 5.9); V = maximum cattle stock on the López Osornio estancia: 4,581 head in 1795 (see Table 2.4); N = the number of permanent workers on the López Osornio estancia in 1795: 1 foreman and 3 slaves (see Chapter 2). Cattle-ranching temporary labor demand (L_t): see Table 8.3. Wheat-farming temporary labor demand (L_a):

$$L_a = \frac{T}{F}$$

where T = wheat produced in Buenos Aires (estimated at 100,000 fanegas); and F = fanegas of wheat produced by one worker [31 fanegas, according to Azara (1943), 7–8]. Total labor demand, $L = L_p + L_t + L_a$. S_l: see Table 8.5. The employment rate (E) is

$$E = \frac{L}{S_l}$$

8.6).[9] Using the 1778 rural population figure as the base year, total rural population grew from 19,352 inhabitants in 1787 to 21,620 inhabitants in 1791. Males accounted for 52.4% of total rural population in 1778, and active males for 69.1% of that figure.[10] Some of those men (officials,

9 Total rural population according to the 1778 census was 12,925, but Luján was not included. Diego G. de la Fuente, director of the first national census (1869), corrected that figure by adding 1/6 to that total, since there were seven districts and only six had been taken into account. The method may not be that accurate, but the resulting figure, 2,155 inhabitants, cannot be too far from the actual figure if later estimates and census are considered. See de la Fuente (1872), 10, 13.

10 Figures for male (as well as female) population in the 1778 census are aggregated in four categories: married; widowers; single; and children. The first three categories have been considered here as active population. Usually, active population is somewhat lower than 69.1% of total population. For 1869, Recchini de Lattes's estimate is 62% of all males and 43% of all females. Unfortunately, no methodological details are given there. See Recchini de Lattes (1975), 150, and de la Fuente (1872), 632–633.

Table 8.5. *Potential supply of rural labor in Buenos Aires,*
1787–1791

	P	P_m	P_{am}	S_l
1787	19,352	10,140	7,007	5,620
1788	19,896	10,425	7,204	5,778
1789	20,455	10,718	7,406	5,940
1790	21,029	11,019	7,616	6,107
1791	21,620	11,329	7,828	6,278
Mean	20,470	10,726	7,412	5,944

Notes:
P = total population: estimated according to an annual growth rate of 2.81%.
See Table 8.6 for the intercensal growth rate between 1778 and 1815.
P_m = male population (52.4% of P).
P_{am} = active male population (69.1% of P_m).
S_l = potential supply of rural labor (80.2% of P_{am}).
Sources: For population estimates, see Table 8.6; for male population and
active male population, see the 1778 census in REBA (1856), 2:7; and for an
estimate of active male population in the rural sector, see the 1744 census in
REBA (1858), 1:64.

Table 8.6. *Buenos Aires urban and rural population, 1744-1869*

Year	Urban population	Annual growth	Rural population	Annual growth	Total population	Annual growth
1744	11,600	–	7,154	–	18,754	–
1778	24,363	2.2	15,080	2.2	39,443	2.2
1810	42,872	1.8	–	–	–	–
1815	–	–	42,053	2.8	–	–
1822	55,416	2.2	63,230	6.0	118,646	2.5
1836	62,228	0.8	142,957	6.0	205,185	4.0
1854–1855	90,076	2.0	180,257	1.3	270,333	1.5
1869	177,787	5.0	317,230	3.8	495,017	4.3

Note: annual growth = annual growth rate between censuses (percentage).
Sources: Comadrán Ruiz (1969); de la Fuente (1872); García Belsunce (1976); Maeder
(1969).

military, landowners, and priests) should be excluded to find the potential
supply of rural labor. In the 1744 census (no occupational data are available
for 1778), those excluded occupations accounted for 13.7% of the male
population. Since most of them were probably at an active age, the potential supply of rural labor was 80.2% of the active male population. Consequently, between 1787 and 1791, the potential labor supply was on
average 5,944 men (Table 8.5).

A comparison of labor demand and potential labor supply shows that the rate of employment fluctuated between 22.2% in fall and 83.3% in winter (Table 8.4). Given the imperfections of the labor market, the winter labor demand could have easily meant scarcity. This scarcity could be offset by female and child labor, especially in agriculture (no record of the use of female and child labor in cattle ranching has been preserved, but there is no reason to rule them out). If female and child labor are added up, unemployment and underemployment rates are higher.[11]

The values for the different variables may be changed, but this model remains valid in defining the limits of arguments related to the characteristics of rural workers and their working habits. Vagrancy, cattle rustling, and the condition of agregado were the result of a pattern of labor demand that in its seasonal peak left about 17% of the active male population without a salaried job, and in the seasonal low, about 78%. As women and children were probably engaged in rural activities as well, the rate of unemployment could have been even higher. It should be noted also that seasonal estimates conceal the fact that there was no steady demand for labor throughout the season but rather peaks of demand within it on each rural establishment.

Rather than outright unemployment, underemployment was probably more common. That explains the turnover of peons, who worked for short periods and then were forced to leave for another job. Labor market imperfections, such as the lack of access to information, distance, lack of proper means of communication (other than word of mouth) and transportation (other than horses), all operated in favor of mobility, but it is clear that peons were on the move due to a marked seasonality of labor demand and, probably, of excess labor supply. There is no hint leading to an estimate of labor demand far in excess of potential supply. Zorraquín Becú also supports the view that there was an excess labor supply in eighteenth-century Buenos Aires, which explained for him the reason for vagrancy.[12]

This model of rural labor demand may be extended to later periods, but due to the lack of information on the agricultural output, the demand of labor for agriculture cannot be estimated. Wheat farming did not disappear in Buenos Aires after 1820, but there are no proper records of total output, and qualitative evidence points to a decline.[13] According to an

---

11 In 1778, female rural population totaled 6,154 women, including 1,906 children. As these figures do not include Luján, following de la Fuente's method that total is 7,180 women (including 2,224 children). See de la Fuente (1872), 10, 13.

12 Zorraquín Becú (1968), 163–165.

13 According to Robert Montgomery, a British merchant residing in Buenos Aires, wheat production declined after 1816 and in the early 1820s was not enough to meet urban demand. See his report to Woodbine Parish in Barba (1978), 37, and Humphreys (1940).

English report, the introduction of wheat from the countryside into the city fell from 95,000 fanegas in 1836 to about 61,000 fanegas on average between 1838 and 1840, and to 31,000 fanegas in 1841. That decline was accompanied by rising prices, both nominal (in paper pesos) and real (in specie).[14] Around 1850 real wheat prices tended to be at the mid-1830s' level, and we can assume that wheat output was also at the same level. Population was growing, but it is also true that there were no restrictions on imports.[15] Because there had been no significant technical improvements in wheat farming since Azara's times, there is no reason to look for different estimates of output per worker than those already used. Therefore, assuming a wheat output of 100,000 fanegas, 3,226 workers would have been required.[16]

Labor demand for sheep breeding can be estimated from the total stock and the number of sheep tended by each shepherd. The average wool export for 1849–1853 was 711,000 arrobas. Maxwell estimated wool output at 3.5 lbs of wool per sheep, but since 20% of the sheep were not sheared, that output is reduced to 2.8 lbs per sheep. For that export, therefore, a stock of 6,348,214 sheep would have been required. Estimated at 1,500 sheep per shepherd, that stock would have required 4,323 shepherds.[17]

---

14 For total introduction of wheat into Buenos Aires, see Mandeville to Viscount Canning, Buenos Aires, 25 March 1842, in PRO, Foreign Office 6/83. For the evolution of wheat prices, see Gorostegui de Torres (1962–63), 152–153, 157–159. This author mentions an English report (no proper reference) giving a total output of almost 100,000 fanegas. Total introduction was 62,711 fanegas in 1840, and that year's was an abundant harvest according to a letter from another English diplomat. Cf. Griffiths to Palmerston, Buenos Aires, 31 March 1840, in PRO, Foreign Office 6/76.

15 U.S. wheat producers took easy advantage of scarcities in Buenos Aires, according to the same English envoy. Cf. Griffiths to Palmerston, Buenos Aires, 31 December 1835, in PRO, Foreign Office 6/49, 119v. Distress caused by civil wars was then the main obstacle to agriculture, according to the same source.

16 Information from an estancia in Colonia, Banda Oriental, shows an average demand of 15 workers for seven days to produce on average 120 fanegas. Gelman estimated therefore a demand of 12,500 workers for 100,000 fanegas. Salvatore and Brown pointed out those workers were demanded for a week and not for a whole month and that harvest did not take place at the same time all over the region. Assuming harvest could take place along a whole month and a perfect mobility of workers, only one-quarter of the demand estimated by Gelman would have been required. Therefore only 3,125 workers were necessary for a 100,000-fanega output – a figure not too far from the 3,226 workers estimated according to Azara's information. See Gelman (1989b), 727; Salvatore and Brown (1989), 736.

17 For export figures, see Table C.1. For the average wool yield of a sheep, see Maxwell (1863), 3. For another estimate of the output per sheep, see REBA (1855), 2:42. For the average number of head per shepherd, see Brabazon (1981). That number does not seem too high. On an estancia belonging to Juan Miller in Saladillo in 1852, there were four sharecroppers who tended on average 2,290 sheep each. See AGN, Sucesiones, 6811, Juan Miller. For a similar estimate of labor demand for sheep breeding, see Sabato (1989), 104. She estimates labor demand at 3,000 permanent workers and 2,000 temporary workers in 1850, and 4,700 permanent workers and 3,100 temporary workers in 1855. She does not estimate labor demand for agriculture and cattle ranching.

Labor demand for cattle ranching can also be estimated from the total cattle stock and the number of head tended by each worker. The average hide export for 1849–1853 was 2,237,300 units per year. At the 22% reproduction rate estimated for the López Osornio estancia, the total cattle stock required for that output would have been 10,169,545 head. Although not all hides exported from Buenos Aires were from the countryside, let us assume here that they were. Using the same procedure as in Table 8.4, the demand for permanent labor would have been 8,840 workers, and the seasonal peak for temporary labor would have been 11,137 additional workers (using the spring 1791 figure from Table 8.2).[18]

The total demand for labor (agriculture, cattle ranching, and sheep breeding) in the peak season, assuming that no workers shifted from one rural activity to another within that season, would have been 27,526 workers. Total rural population around 1850 can be estimated at 170,000 inhabitants. Estimating the potential supply of labor in the same way as in Table 8.5, a figure of 49,367 potential male workers is reached. In the seasonal peak, therefore, demand was equivalent to 55.8% of the potential labor supply.

The evidence for the mid-1850s presented by Sabato does not depart from this picture.[19] She estimates the potentially active rural population at 126,802 people. Rural workers (including among them those employed in livestock raising and agriculture as well as those described as peons and day-workers) accounted for 28.5% of the potentially active rural population, non-rural workers (people in the secondary and tertiary sectors as well as those described as employees or in sundry jobs) for 12.6%, and people of unknown occupation for 58.9%. Leaving aside the latter category (assuming that their occupation was not listed because of recorders' carelessness rather than because they did not have any occupation at all), actually active population falls to 51,775 workers, with peons and day-workers accounting for 39.2% of it. Consequently, there was a large pool of potentially or actually active people who did not have a proper occupation or a stable job.

These estimates fail to capture other types of labor demand that were also present in the countryside around 1850. First, a growing number of the rural population was actually working in the towns and villages that had emerged in the countryside. Second, increasing production and increasing exports meant also an increasing demand for labor in the transportation sector to carry the rural produce to the port. Finally, the army was

---

18 For hide exports, see Table C.1. As for the usefulness of Azara's figures for later periods, Daireaux reports that in the late 1880s, one peon was required to tend 1,000 to 1,500 head of cattle, provided no artificial supply of water was necessary. See Daireaux (1908), 387.
19 Sabato (1989), 90–91.

also tapping into the same resource.[20] By 1850, therefore, the potential labor pool was much smaller than that previously estimated – but only at the peak of labor demand, assuming that rural activities were not complementary at all, and that all hides exported by Buenos Aires were produced in the countryside.

Was labor scarce in Buenos Aires? Labor was scarce or plentiful according to the seasonal demand for it. Hacendados complained about labor scarcity when they were demanding labor, but it was not their business to care about its abundance when they did not need it. Seasonal labor demand was, therefore, at the root of the problem of labor instability.

Labor instability

Rural labor has been deemed "unstable" because peons did not work for long periods on the estancias. That was actually the case and has been attributed to the character of the rural inhabitants and to the easiness of life on the pampas.[21] According to this view, rural workers did not work for long periods because they did not like to work, and the pampas generously supported their lack of industriousness. The landowners' complaints about the difficulties in obtaining temporary free workers and travelers' reports on the lack of diligence of the rural inhabitants ("Oh! incurie des Argentins," complained a Frenchman in the 1830s) led to "labor instability," the euphemism for peons' laziness.[22]

The question of why those apparently conscious leisure maximizers did any work at all (for there were wage peons after all) has been answered by pointing to their need to get cash to pay for "vices" (yerba mate, alcoholic beverages, tobacco). Once that cash had been obtained, they would leave

---

20 Salvatore ([1992], 33–34, 42) underscores the army recruiters' preference for rural people, attributing it to a class bias. He disregards the fact that the army could have had a legitimate interest in recruiting people already acquainted with riding horses and handling knives.

21 For Mayo (1984) "labor instability" was due to a subsistence sector and to the non-Calvinistic mentality of the rural inhabitants. After the existence of that subsistence sector was questioned (Amaral [1987b]), Mayo (1991b) dropped it but still supported the view that "labor instability" was due to cultural factors (now an "attitude vis-à-vis work" rather than a "non-Calvinistic mentality"). Salvatore and Brown (1987) also pointed to cultural factors as the explanation for what they see as the peons' preference for mobility. Salvatore (1992) has emphasized the opportunities to earn a living offered by the pampas and the ineffectiveness of labor control regulations but has not backed down from that supposed preference. Mayo's "attitude vis-à-vis work" and Salvatore's "preference for mobility" are both cultural factors. There are no sources originated in the rural workers, however, to account for their culture. All sources are from outside the rural workers' world. By accepting those outside views, both Mayo and Salvatore fail to filter the cultural bias of their sources. Moreover, they implicitly consider culture as pre-determined rather than as a result of human activity in a particular setting at a particular time.

22 The quotation is from Isabelle (1835), 265.

their jobs. These arguments fail in two ways: (1) the cultural determination of leisure maximization (laziness) cannot be proved; and (2) the actual conditions of rural production on the pampas are not taken into account. Indeed, only by disregarding the seasonality of rural tasks, and therefore of labor demand, can the mobility of workers from job to job after short terms of work be turned into labor supply instability.

Most workers did actually work short spans on each estancia during the peak season, had to move from job to job during that season, and did not have a salaried job during the off-season. If some cultural trait affected their behavior, that was consequence rather than cause of that pattern of labor demand. The instability of free labor was not due to either the laziness of the rural inhabitants or to the easy conditions of life on the pampas. It was due to that particular pattern of labor demand determined by the marked seasonality of rural production. Pre-industrial agrarian economies failed to generate year-round employment. That was the case in Europe as well as in Buenos Aires. There was labor instability, but it was labor demand that was unstable rather than labor supply. A closer examination of rural tasks would shed light on that pattern of labor demand.

The seasonality of rural production (and consequently of labor demand) was due to biological and ecological factors. Wheat was the main cereal cultivated in Buenos Aires around 1800. For wheat production, land was tilled by the end of fall and the beginning of winter (May, June, and even July), and harvest took place in late spring and early summer (December and January). Cattle was rounded up, branded, and gelded in late summer and fall, or in late winter and early spring; calving and thistles were among the main factors accounting for such a pattern. There were, therefore, peaks of labor demand but also periods of steep decline. These fluctuations depended upon the weather conditions of a particular season (rain, frost, hail, wind, temperature) rather than upon the calendar. For a normal year (if any), it could be expected that labor demand for cereal agriculture would be lower from February to April and from August to November, and labor demand for cattle ranching would be lower from November to February and from May to August – March, August, and November being therefore "idle" months. The expansion of sheep breeding in the 1840s complicated this simple picture in two ways. On the one hand, the main lambing took place in late March and April with a secondary one in November, and shearing was carried out from mid-October to November. On the other hand, a new type of labor demand appeared, for sheep should be cared for year-round; consequently, a new type of sharecropping worker appeared – the medianero.[23] It should be noted, however, that the heyday

23 Hutchinson (1865), 243–244; and Sabato (1989), 117–123.

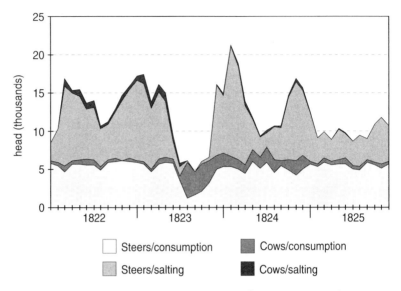

Figure 8.1. Cattle introduced into Buenos Aires for consumption and salting, 1822–1825. *Source*: REBA, 1822–1825.

of wool production would not come until the 1860s, and that there was an increasing differentiation between the sheep-breeding and cattle-ranching areas.[24]

There is a gap, however, between this model and the real world. Two factors should be mentioned in that regard. First, the pampas are a fairly homogeneous region, but minor differences account for different timing for rural tasks. The northern districts are better drained than the southern ones, and due to a slightly higher average temperature in the former, thistle growing and harvesting took place earlier than in the latter. Second, there was a steady demand for beef in the city, and cattle flowed to the urban market year-round. But there was also a growing overseas demand for hides and to a lesser extent for jerked beef. Because of these factors, the seasonal pattern of rural tasks, and consequently of labor demand, took a different turn – but did not disappear.

In the early 1820s, there was a stable demand for beef cattle and a seasonal demand for salting cattle (Figure 8.1). The number of head of

24 For wool exports, see Chapter 12. For the increasing differentiation between the sheep-breeding and cattle-ranching areas, see Latham (1868), 34, and the descriptions of the Buenos Aires province *partidos* (counties) in Martin de Moussy (1860–1864), 3:46–75, and Mulhall and Mulhall (1875), 108–147.

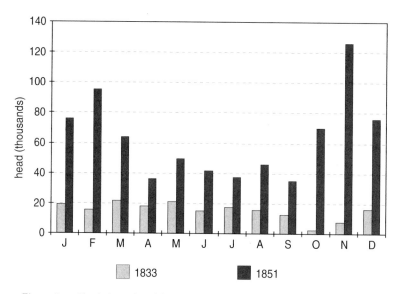

Figure 8.2. Cattle introduced into Buenos Aires: Monthly distribution, 1833 and 1851. *Source: La Gaceta Mercantil,* 1833 and 1851.

cattle introduced into Buenos Aires displayed this seasonal pattern in 1833, and even more markedly in 1851 (Figure 8.2). From April to September 1851, the floor was at about 40,000 head per month; in the seasonal peaks, this figure doubled or even tripled. In 1833 there was also a seasonal decline, but the lowest level was reached in October and November due to political problems affecting both city and countryside.

The demand for cattle varied from month to month and, consequently, so did the aggregate demand for labor. Furthermore, labor demand on each estancia was not continuous throughout the season. Rural tasks, related to either cattle ranching or agriculture, were performed within the appropriate season but only in short periods not spanning the full season. Some tasks required the hiring of temporary workers for a few days. Permanent workers (usually slaves up to the 1820s) would then go on performing the regular tasks until the hiring of temporary workers became necessary again.

Livestock raising demanded labor in a discontinuous fashion. The aquerenciamiento of 1,000 head of cattle, 1,000 sheep, and 600 horses required three peons and one foreman for 2 or 3 months, and only two peons and the foreman after the third month.[25] The branding of 400 to 500

25 For a description of the technique of aquerenciamiento, see Vicuña Mackenna (1936), 120.

calves required 16 to 18 peons for one day. Since other tasks were also required by livestock raising (cattle roundups, sortings, gelding, sheep shepherding and shearing, horse breaking) peons were hired by the day, by the month, or for longer periods. Other tasks, not directly related to livestock raising, but necessary for it, such as ditch cutting, were performed by peons hired for piecework. All types of contracts could be present on one estancia at the same time due to a different type of demand for different tasks.[26]

Peon hiring at an estancia in Monsalvo in the 1820s followed the same pattern of short intra-seasonal periods. In 1822 José Lastra and Green and Hodgson formed a partnership to buy and operate an estancia located in Kakel, south of the Salado River. The estancia was in an area still being settled, 80 leagues southeast of Buenos Aires. There are peon hiring accounts from 7 May 1822 to 6 September 1825.[27] In that 1,219-day period, 34 peons were hired for 47 terms of work. There was one "flight," or maybe two, and two peons "left." The rest remained on the estancia for as long as they were needed. There is one case of advanced payment, but it was to a peon who had worked twice on the estancia, for two long periods. Nine peons worked more than once and 25 peons only once. The former worked 2,431 days, equivalent to 45% of the 5,406 days worked by all peons. There were 23 terms of work lasting less than 3 months, and 24 terms were longer than that. The former accounted for 1,075 days and the latter for 4,331 days, 20% and 80% of the total days worked. On average, each term of work lasted for 115 days, and each peon worked for 159 days. The longest-serving peon, Manuel Antonio, was on the estancia for 514 continuous days, and the second longest-serving peon, Julián Aponte, worked for 470 days in two terms, one lasting 276 days and the other 194 days.

The pattern of peon hiring displays seasonal peaks and lows. The former took place in the winter of 1822 and the springs of 1823 and 1824; the latter occurred in the fall of 1823 and the summers of 1824 and 1825. Although peons were hired and dismissed almost every month, most of the work was done by peons who stayed on the estancia for more than 1 month (Figure 8.3). There were some key moments of peon hiring and dismissal. On 3 June 1822, four peons were hired; on 22–23 July 1822, two; on 12–15 August 1823, four. In the second half of October 1823, three peons

---

26 See Manuel Morillo's letters to Juan José Anchorena, 22 October 1830, 24 October 1830, 24 November 1830, 10 January 1831, 25 January 1831, 2 March 1832, in AGN, VII–4–4–2, VII–4–4–3, and VII–4–1–6. Salvatore ([1992], 36–37) interpreted Anchorena's order to hire peons per month rather than per day as an expenditure-cutting device, as if those peons were performing exactly the same job. The two types of contracts meant different jobs, so the shift from day-peons to monthly-peons meant that some tasks should be postponed.

27 JRM, Green and Hodgson Ranch Accounts, 1822–1825.

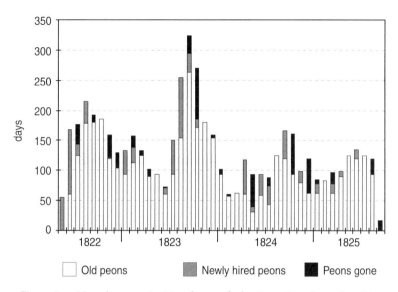

Figure 8.3. Monsalvo estancia: Man-days worked, 1822–1825. *Source*: See this chapter, n. 27.

were dismissed, and the same number were dismissed on 23 October 1824 and 6 September 1825. Most of the terms of work overlap or are distant enough (more than 2 weeks) one from the next to reject the idea of replacements being hired due to flights. That could have happened in only two cases.

The peon hiring accounts of Tambito, an estancia in southern Córdoba, where production was similar to that of Buenos Aires, also show the pattern of intra-seasonal fluctuations.[28] The amount of money spent in labor from August 1857 to July 1873 varied from month to month. A seasonal pattern can be discerned, but the active season is not the same every single year. The summer and winter of 1858 registered a higher expense in peons' wages than the fall and spring of that year. Conversely, in 1859 those expenses were higher in fall and spring than in summer and winter. Some years, such as 1865 and 1869, do not present a remarkable seasonal difference, but others do, such as 1867, 1870, 1871, and 1872. Intra-seasonal gaps are observed when considering monthly expenses in peons' wages compared to the monthly average per quarter (Figure 8.4).[29]

The agricultural sector also presented the same pattern of peon hiring

28 JRM, James Hodgson Papers, Wage Accounts (1857–1865) and Tambito Journal (1865–1873).
29 In Figure 8.4, as in Figure 8.3, quarters go from December through February (summer), March through May (fall), June through August (winter), and September through November (spring).

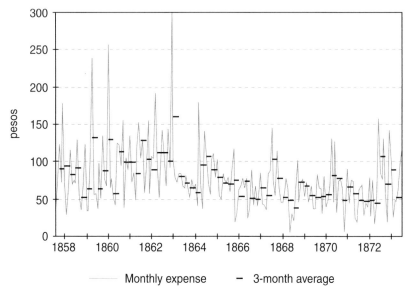

Figure 8.4. Tambito estancia: Peons' wages, 1857–1873. *Source*: See this chapter,
n. 28.

for short intra-seasonal periods. According to information supplied by
rural producers in the 1850s, three peons should work for 8 days to sow
wheat on 1 square cuadra.[30] If one peon could do the job by himself, it
would have taken him 24 days to sow 1 square cuadra, and during the
sowing season, from mid-May to early-July, he could have sown 2 square
cuadras. But disregarding other factors, rain could have easily delayed his
work, reducing the extension of land sown by that peon. That is why rural
producers needed three peons for 8 days rather than one peon for 24 days
to sow 1 square cuadra. Although unlikely, one peon could have sown 2
square cuadras during the sowing season, thereby finding employment on
one estancia for the whole period. The need for more peons during shorter
periods was even more marked during the harvest season. In the 1850s,
harvest work was paid for according to the extension of the plot, not to the
time demanded by the job. There is no estimate, therefore, of the number
of days one peon would have to work to complete 1 square cuadra, since
that was relatively irrelevant to the rural producer. After the wheat had
been reaped, peons where hired by the day for thrashing and winnowing.
For those tasks, six peons were hired for 3 days to process the wheat from
1 square cuadra. Then the sowing and harvesting seasons on one estancia

---

30 REBA (1855), 2:35–37.

meant high demand for short periods within them, rather than a sustained demand throughout them. That was a good reason for peons' mobility or instability.

Labor demand was seasonal but varying within the season for each estancia. Individual hirings seldom lasted for the whole season, and the end of a labor relationship came generally due to a decision made by the employer, not by the worker. That was the pattern on the López Osornio estancia in the 1780s and 1790s, on Miguel de Riblos's estancias in Areco in the 1720s, and on Lastra's and Anchorena's estancias in the 1820s, as well as on the Tambito estancia from the late 1850s to the early 1870s.[31]

During the inter-seasonal gaps, would-be workers did not have a salaried job. In order to get one, they had to move to the other sector (from cattle ranching to agriculture, or vice versa), increasingly distant from each other as the expansion to the south was taking place, or even to the city (since there was a fluid relationship between the city and the immediate countryside, where most of the wheat output was obtained). During intra-seasonal gaps they had to move from place to place looking for a job, or they could tend their own production, whether legal or illegal.

Labor instability was due to the seasonal rhythm of rural tasks, and only landowners' complaints could lead one to think that it was due to the rural inhabitants' peculiar character. Lazy workers would not feel any urgency to produce beyond the satisfaction of their needs, so they would not represent any threat to the landowners' property. But far from that, free workers – partly salaried and partly independent producers – were producing (modest amounts maybe) for the market. On their way to becoming fully independent producers, there were (leaving aside each individual's own abilities) a series of obstacles such as the dimension of the market, the conditions of production, and non-economic restrictions. The first two factors were valid for all producers, but the latter only for free workers. The repression of vagrancy was aimed at restricting the legal and illegal activities of free workers, without putting an end to them, since they were part of the informal agreements between landowners and free workers for protection and labor.

Landowners and vagrants derived a mutual advantage from that forced coexistence. "Vagrancy: here is the origin of all evil," wrote Valentín Fernández Blanco, one of the landowners reporting to Valentín Alsina in 1856 on rural working conditions. Because of the "lack of continuous employment, and the easiness to go from one district or village to another,"

---

31 On the López Osornio estancia, see Chapter 2; on Riblos's estancia, see Mayo and Fernández (1991), 312. Mayo ([1991b], 212–213, 224–227) still fails to differentiate the instability of labor supply and demand.

he said, the so-called peones por día (day-peons) were responsible for most of the damage and wrongdoings experienced in the countryside. But "they are necessary," he reluctantly acknowledged, for the seasonal tasks of the estancias.[32]

Vagrancy, therefore, was easier to identify than individual vagrants. For Patricio Linch, another landowner reporting to Alsina, only those whose behavior was harmful and criminal should be considered vagrants. For them he had a solution: They, like Martín Fierro, should be sent to the frontier.[33] Stray cattle, wild dogs, ostriches, and pulperías were singled out as responsible for the vagrants' existence. Accordingly, the solutions were to bring cattle under control, to ban dog- and ostrich-hunting parties, and to eliminate itinerant pulperías. But Linch also suggested other even less realistic measures, such as the banishment of agregados to the towns, the reorganization of the police, and a yearly registration of all people "useful for the service of the state."

Other landowners, more realistic, more pessimistic, or not quite attracted by such an array of controls that could easily backfire, restricted themselves to vaguely pointing out the lack of enforcement of the many anti-vagrancy laws and regulations already existing. That was the key issue: It was not the lack of regulation but that of enforcement that kept vagrancy alive. Vagrancy was a social disease, but vagrants were potential workers. "Vagrants and rustlers live as agregados, pretending they are workhands," wrote a royal official in 1788, stopping short of identifying landowners as those who allowed them to live as agregados and pose as workers.[34] Vagrants, peons, and agregados were all the same people. During the high-demand season, they worked for a salary, and there were more workers than jobs. Market imperfections and demand peaks accounted for occasional, punctual scarcities.[35]

"Labor instability," meaning labor supply instability, is a concept stemming from the demand side of the labor relationship. From the viewpoint of those who supplied labor, demand was unstable and scarce. The fact that

32 "No obstante, ellos son necesarios a las faenas periódicas de los establecimientos" [However, they are necessary for the periodical tasks of the establishments]. See ACR, 174–175. An analysis of the landowners' testimonies on labor is found in Sabato (1989), 94–99.

33 ACR, 166.

34 The quotation is from José de la Rosa's appointment as Alcalde de la Santa Hermandad for the districts of Matanza and Conchas, 2 February 1788, in AGN, IX–30–4–1. There is ample evidence linking *agregados* with cattle rustling. See, for instance, the note from the Fiel Ejecutor to the Cabildo on 2 May 1783, in DHA, 4:49; Viceroy Arredondo's *bando* (decree) of 17 November 1792, in AGN, Biblioteca Nacional, leg. 303, doc. 4878; the letter from Juan Lorenzo Castro to Chascomús's Alcalde de la Hermandad, dated 19 January 1808, in AGN, IX–19–5–9, 64v., quoted by Frías and Levaggi (1977), 192; and Manuel Belgrano's contributions to *El Correo de Comercio*, Belgrano (1954), 180–182.

35 ACR, 141–203.

the same workers did not come back to the same estancia year after year was a consequence neither of an attitude toward labor nor of the appeal of open lands. It was due to the seasonality of rural tasks, producing gaps in labor demand between seasons, to the discontinuity of labor demand on each estancia during peak seasons, producing gaps in labor demand within them, and to the different meaning of seasonality for each individual estancia, producing a different timing of tasks on each one.

As livestock production grew over time, labor became relatively scarce. But the seasonality of rural tasks and consequently of labor demand did not disappear. Only in the late nineteenth century did the combined production of wool, cattle by-products, and grain for export help to offset the marked seasonality of each activity individually considered. Even then, the concept of labor instability should be related to the seasonal pattern of demand for rural labor.

Conclusion

Juan Agustín García's riddle is not impossible to solve. Either those peons who refused to work for low salaries were conscious maximizers of leisure, or his picture blends two different situations occurring in different seasons. In the peak season, those peons might have refused to work for a low salary if their bargaining position was strengthened by a relative scarcity of labor; in the off-season, they were idle due to a low labor demand, and they might well have been still on the estancia as agregados or settlers.

At the end of the eighteenth century, the Buenos Aires countryside was inhabited mainly by free people, neither bound to the land nor to other men, who worked to earn a living. Some of them might have been involved in criminal activities, others (or the same) might have succeeded as independent producers, but most had to combine seasonal work for a salary with working for themselves on land that might or might not have belonged to them. With that combined income, they had to meet their food, clothing, housing, and ceremonial expenses. Some of them may have been keener than others on drinking alcoholic beverages, playing cards and other games, and playing the guitar – the picturesque elements used to depict the rural inhabitants. But witnesses perhaps missed the less colorful elements of that picture. Travelers were from social and economic environments, some of them already affected by the Industrial Revolution, where rural tasks were performed under conditions different from those found in Buenos Aires. Their testimonies are useful, provided that cultural bias is skipped. Brackenridge noted, as other travelers did, the laziness of the Buenos Aires rural people. But he reminded his readers "that we also of the north [he was American] are reproached by Europeans for our carelessness of time and our lazy habits." MacCann attributed the habits and feelings of the "peons or creole workers" to the very shape of the countryside.[36] Those habits and feelings were not due to "laziness," therefore, but to the seasonality of rural tasks, to the discontinuity of labor demand even within the peak season, to primitive methods of production, to the low degree of labor specialization and non-existent education, and, up to 1810, to regulated local markets for agricultural goods and not yet developed overseas markets.

Labor supply was probably scarcer after 1806. It has been pointed out that landowners' complaints on that problem saw an upsurge after the process of militarization due to the English Invasions.[37] How many people were mobilized then and later by the armies fighting the wars of independence, the war with Brazil, and the many civil wars is still unknown. Recruitment and the fear of recruitment played a role in the labor scarcity brought about by those wars.[38] Foreigners spared from recruitment into those armies were not enough to offset the consequences of continuous conflicts.[39] Immigration into Buenos Aires both from the Interior and from abroad steadily increased from the 1820s to the 1860s, as shown by high rates of population growth, far above what could have been expected from natural reproduction.[40] A French traveler estimated in the 1830s that 33% of the Buenos Aires rural population and 20% of the urban population were foreigners.[41] His figures may not be accurate, but they underscore what was then a visible trend.

Estancias went on demanding temporary as well as permanent labor. The slow vanishing of slavery between the 1810s and the 1840s due to the prohibition of slave imports and the effects of the Free Birth law made room for permanent free workers in the countryside. Working conditions changed in the countryside as a result of the increasing demand for Buenos Aires produce in overseas markets. But these changes did not change the pattern of seasonal labor demand.

36 Brackenridge (1820), 1:250, and 2:29–30; MacCann (1969), 116.
37 Gelman (1989b), 729.
38 The fear of being recruited was a cause of peons' mobility. See Marcelo Ignes to Juan Pedro Aguirre, San Nicolás, 29 August 1820, in ABP, 031–5–3–14; and *ibid.*, San Nicolás, 6 March 1827, in ABP, 031–5–3–16.
39 That might have been the reason for Rosas to hire foreigners as peons for his estancias. If Rosas was to enforce his own rulings, he hardly could have violated them as a private citizen. Salvatore, however, attributes such decision to the supposed impossibility of hiring natives as permanent workers. That fits his argument regarding the cultural determination for such mobility. The cultural difference between Spaniards and natives is taken for granted rather than explained. If it was rational for the natives to behave in such a way, the Spaniards' irrationality should be explained. See Salvatore (1992), 37–38.
40 From 1822 to 1869, total population grew at an annual rate of 3.1%, and rural population at 3.5%. For population figures, see Table 8.6.
41 Isabelle (1943), 144.

The recent literature on rural Buenos Aires has focused upon what can be called, using the language of some contributors, the social relations of production. In this chapter the economic relations of production have been emphasized. The lack of continuous and reliable information on salaries and output has prevented us from following a different path to analyze the demand for and supply of estancia labor, or labor productivity beyond what has been estimated in Chapter 2. Two issues related to labor demand and supply, labor scarcity and labor instability, have been examined here. It has been argued that labor demand was determined by seasonal factors, so both scarcity and instability were due to that uneven pattern of demand.

9

Management and entrepreneurship

As with any type of business concern, estancias required different sets of tasks. Roundups, brandings, sortings, geldings, and dehornings were performed by peons on the fields. It is clear what that meant, and there are abundant descriptions produced by both travelers and experts on how they were carried out. But those peons had to be hired, supervised, and dismissed; food and tools for them had to be supplied; cattle had to be bought and sold; and improvements had to be maintained and expanded. Those were the tasks of management. A different set of tasks, aiming at the accomplishment of the overall business objectives, corresponded to entrepreneurship: decisions related to land purchases and sales, the obtention of title deeds, and the resolution of legal and fiscal problems. Rural production is cyclical, and so were the tasks demanded from peons, but natural and unnatural calamities made management and entrepreneurship far from automatic and repetitious. Droughts, rain, floods, locusts, and wild dogs affected production as much as Indians, bandits, rustlers, and montoneras. Action was required from managers and entrepreneurs to counter these calamities as well as to take advantage of favorable conditions. Estancias were a profitable business, but profit did not stem just from the workings of nature and the labors of peons. Profit stemmed from the skills of managers and the initiative of entrepreneurs, from their ability to combine the different factors of production and to cope with unexpected threats.

This chapter studies estancia management and entrepreneurship. The scarcity of sources and an ideological bias toward labor have kept scholars away from these key aspects of rural production. One of the few sources available for the managerial and entrepreneurial history of the estancia is used here – the letters sent by a manager-entrepreneur in the countryside to his partner in the city in the mid-1820s. These letters serve as a testimony to both the overall managerial-entrepreneurial side of rural production and the particular history of that business.[1]

1 Marcelo Ignes sent 69 letters to Juan Pedro Aguirre from 7 December 1823 to 28 October 1828.

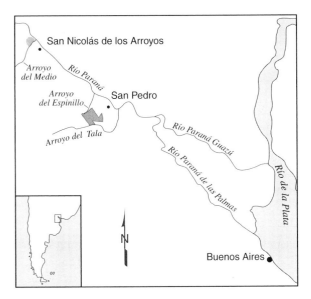

Map 9.1 Location of the Aguirre and Ignes estancias: Arroyo del Tala and Arroyo del Espinillo, San Pedro, Buenos Aires, and Arroyo del Medio, Santa Fe. *Source*: See this chapter, n. 3.

Setup: 1823–1824

In December 1823 Juan Pedro Aguirre and Marcelo Ignes signed a contract to operate an estancia in San Pedro, 150 km northwest of Buenos Aires (Map 9.1). Aguirre was an important Buenos Aires merchant in the early 1820s.[2] Because his commercial and banking activities retained him in town, a partner had to manage the estancia. No information is known about Ignes, but his elegant handwriting and proper use of the language reveal an educated man. According to their contract, he would be in charge of the on-site management, but he was barred from making any deal on his own. Aguirre would lead the partnership, with his partner's consent. He contributed two-thirds of the down payment, and Ignes the remaining

These letters are in ABP, 031–5–3–8 to 17. Twenty-two letters were sent from 7 December 1823 to 11 November 1824; forty-six letters, from 1 September 1825 to 20 September 1827; and one letter in October 1828.

2 In 1825, Aguirre, a general-store owner paying 80 pesos for direct tax, was the president of the Buenos Aires legislature. He had held positions in government in the late 1810s, and after a brief exile in 1820–1821, he became the most prominent Buenos Aires banker, presiding over three different banking institutions between 1822 and 1826. For Aguirre's political activities during the 1820 crisis, see Pérez (1950); for his banking activities, Amaral (1977a) and (1977b); for his taxes and commercial activities, *Lista Alfabética . . .* (1970), 1, and Blondel (1968), 92, 155; and for other information, ABP, 031–4–1 and 031–5–1.

Table 9.1. *Aguirre and Ignes's land purchases, 1823–1826*

Date	Seller	Place	Area front	length	Price
Dec. 1823	M. P. Ruiz Moreno	Tala	13,032.5	?	60,000
June 1824	T. Banegas	Espinillo	1,000	?	1,300
July 1824	A. P. Ruiz Moreno	Espinillo	2,630	3,479	swap
July 1824	T. Taybo	Espinillo	5,000	?	2,500
Jan. 1826	M. F. Aguirre	A. del Medio	3,940	9,000	3,000
Aug. 1826	T. Fernández	A. del Medio	1,333.3	9,000	2,000
Nov. 1826	The Banegas minors	Espinillo	500	?	?

Note: Area is given in varas; price, in pesos.
Source: ABP, 031–5–3–9 to 17.

third. After paying the remainder of the estancia total price, the annual profit would be split equally among the partners. The partnership would last for 6 years but could be extended with both partners' agreement.

On 13 December 1823, Ignes arrived in San Pedro after inspecting Manuel Pacífico Ruiz Moreno's estancia, which the partners were about to buy. That estancia was 13,032.5 varas wide and probably 9,000 varas long (Table 9.1), equivalent to 8,797 hectares.[3] Arguing that thistles prevented roundups, the inspection was not eased by Ruiz Moreno, who presumably wanted to keep some unmarked head for himself. As Ignes was not an expert in rural matters, he and Aguirre relied upon Juan Lorenzo Castro's advice concerning the condition of the estancia. Castro found it so convenient as to urge an immediate takeover, without a previous headcount. Ignes followed this recommendation, and trouble ensued later as a result. The title deed was extended in February 1824.[4]

Summer 1824

As cattle had not been rounded up before the takeover, roundups and sortings were the first task for Ignes to carry out on the estancia. It was mid-summer, and thistles were fully grown, so more peons than usual were hired for those tasks. After the sortings, according to Castro's estimate, there would be about 2,000 3-year-old steers, 500 steers between 2 and 3

3 For the successive sales of Ruiz Moreno's estancia, see MOP, San Pedro, Survey Duplicate No. 58, Facundo Quiroga's heirs, 1881. Aguirre sold that estancia to José Tomás de Isasi; Isasi to Dolores Fernández de Quiroga; and Facundo's widow to her son Facundo Jr. His heirs commissioned that survey.
4 Marcelo Ignes to Juan Pedro Aguirre, Buenos Aires (?), 7 December 1823; San Pedro, 13 December 1823, ABP, 031–5–3–8.

years old, and many old bulls and yearlings. Mares, horses, and colts seemed to exceed the "budget" (a rough estimate made at the time of the sale), but sheep were below its figures, and corrals and ranchos were poorly kept. Buying an estancia the way Aguirre and Ignes had done was an investment as much as a gamble. Ignes, however, thought there was an overall difference in their favor.

Castro left for Buenos Aires, leaving instructions on what to do next. Ñandubay poles were bought to build new corrals, and poles from the old corral were sent to the Espinillo puesto, where a new rodeo would be established with cattle from roundups. Castro had selected the location for a new estancia to be developed there. "Everything is moving along according to Castro's plans," wrote Ignes.

In order to move along, funds were necessary. Ignes took cash from one of Aguirre's debtors who was in the neighborhood, but Aguirre had to send some goods also: carts, tools, and foodstuffs, as well as three slaves to prepare building materials and plant trees. In late January Ignes was building ranchos and corrals without disregarding daily operations. He had already formed a new rodeo with cattle recently bought for wintering.

Since Aguirre had the final word on cattle sales, he was kept informed about market conditions in the countryside. In January 1824 cattle were selling at 10 pesos per head including 2-year-old steers, and from 11 to 12 pesos per head if sorted out by the buyer. Ignes expected to sell 2,500 head at these prices. In February Aguirre sold cattle to José María Coronell, whose foremen took away 600 steers at three different times between mid-February and mid-March (Table 9.2).

Estancia operations were hindered by natural and unnatural factors. In January steers still in poor shape had to be sold because locusts were ravaging the countryside. Sortings were suspended by mid-March due to the threat of an Indian invasion. Invasions could delay rural operations and even cause some actual losses, but there could also be positive consequences. Producers whose lands were directly affected by invasions sold their cattle at bargain prices. Both sortings and Indian invasions were possible in mid-March because the previous year's thistles had already gone down and the new ones were still at floor level.[5]

Fall 1824

Restoring productive conditions on an estancia after a period of relative abandonment required investment in wood for new corrals and buildings,

5 Marcelo Ignes to Juan Pedro Aguirre, San Pedro, 7 January 1824; Tala, 23 January 1824; Tala, 28 February 1824; Tala, 3 March 1824; Tala, 19 March 1824, ABP, 031-5-3-9.

Table 9.2. *Cattle sales by and purchases for the Tala, Espinillo, and Arroyo del Medio estancias, 1824-1827*

Date	Buyer-seller	Operation	Head	Price	Origin-destination
31 Jan. 1824	Julián Rodríguez	P	?	4.4	T
28 Feb. 1824	J. M. Coronell	S	200		T
3 Mar. 1824	J. M. Coronell	S	200		T
19 Mar. 1824	J. M. Coronell	S	200		T
25 Mar. 1824	J. M. Coronell	S	100		T
29 June 1824	T. Banegas	P	84		E
29 June 1824	I. Irazoqui	P	250		E
29 June 1824	R. Gallegos	P	1,259		E
29 June 1824	I. Irazoqui	P	47		E
29 June 1824	M. F. Aguirre's heirs	P	126		AM
11 Nov. 1824	J. M. Coronell	S	200		T-E
10 Oct. 1825	?	S	81	14	T-E
20 Nov. 1825	Ubaldo Ortega	P	300	6.6	AM
22 Dec. 1825	Tiburcio Olmos	P	500	6.4	AM
20 Jan. 1826	Bartola Albandea	P	[a]250	6	AM
16 Feb. 1826	José Santiago Sosa	P	[b]900	5	AM
19 Feb. 1826	Juan M. Ruiz Moreno	P	200	4.4	AM
25 Feb. 1826	Roque Carcoche	P	100	6	AM
11 Feb. 1826	P. Hidalgo	S	100	9	T-E
25 Feb. 1826	P. Hidalgo	S	102	9	T-E
8 May 1826	M. Chaparro	S	168	10	T-E
3 Aug. 1826	P. Hidalgo	S	100	10	T-E
21 Mar. 1827	P. Hidalgo	S	250		T-E
29 May 1827	P. Hidalgo	S	120		T-E
16 Feb. 1827	Ramón Gaona	S	119	17	AM
16 Feb. 1827	Felipe Navarro	S	20		AM

[a] 300 head according to the October 1827 inventory.
[b] 800 head according to the October 1827 inventory.
Notes:
Operation: P = purchase; S = sale.
Head: number of head sold or purchased.
Price: per head in pesos of 8 reales up to January 1826; paper pesos afterward.
Origin-destination: T = Tala; E = Espinillo; AM = Arroyo del Medio.
Source: ABP, 031-5-3, Folders 6, and 9 to 17.

and higher salary expenses. As Ignes was also establishing a new estancia on Arroyo del Espinillo, more than 1,000 laurel poles for a big corral were bought in San Pedro. Aguirre had sent two carts, but Ignes asked for a third one to carry 900 ñandubay poles for the Espinillo corral. Cattle from sortings and purchases had to get used (aquerenciado) to their new place. "Otherwise," said Ignes, boasting of his newly acquired expertise, "it is necessary to reconcile oneself to suffer all the losses, damages, and expenses brought about by the old and stubborn tactics of the miserable cattleowners who for not turning loose one peso all at once quietly lose one hundred in open-field grazing." Ignes set himself apart from investment-reluctant traditional cattleowners, but he could do so because he had access to an outside source of funds: Aguirre. Barring outside sources the main financial device for any estancia was its own cattle stock.

Cattle purchases for the new estancia went on, but the partners some-times disagreed on them. When Aguirre bought cattle from Ilario Irazoqui at 1 peso 6 reales, 3 pesos 4 reales, and 4 pesos 4 reales, Ignes complained that he did not have information on the number of head bought for those prices, or the quality of Irazoqui's cattle, or the time of delivery. Without this information it was impossible for him to determine the advantages of such purchase. This misunderstanding should be attributed less to faulty communications than to Aguirre's ignorance of his new trade as estancia owner. Ignes was still waiting to get news about the cattle on sale due to the Indian invasions. Referring to that operation, but no doubt to Aguirre's purchase as well, Ignes assured that he "would not act hastily regarding important matters without consulting you, even at the expense of paying for a messenger." Ignes was indirectly recriminating Aguirre for not doing so.

Misunderstandings among partners could frustrate the economic result of an estancia as much as Indian invasions or locusts, but these were just temporary inconveniences. Banditry and cattle rustling were permanent ones. Ignes complained about "the afflictions and damages suffered because of the disorder in which this county finds itself," getting comfort from the news about the good will of the government to put an end to them, as well as from Aguirre's efforts on those matters. Some thieves had been caught while stealing on their estancia, but they still had to be arraigned. This problem would linger for years.

Other legal problems were due to the blurred boundaries of properties on the old pampa. The original grants had been split up and sold many times without a proper survey. On July 7, while complaining about the "tiresome and expensive" measurement, Ignes reported that it had resulted in less land than expected, according to the "budget." But surveys did not put an end to conflicts: The boundaries of the Tala estancia were still a matter of legal disputes more than 50 years later.

Rural operations were increasing "as winter gets closer." Sortings sus-pended because of the Indians were resumed, more than 100 bulls had already been gelded, and brandings would follow suit. By late March Ignes discontinued cattle sales. No more head would be sold until June because they were too lean. Moreover, the herds needed some rest to protect the calves. After devoting some time to the legal procedures required by the theft they had suffered, Ignes would start branding the bigger head result-ing from sortings that had been carried out in the neighborhood to retrieve stray cattle. Meanwhile more bulls were gelt, mares rounded up, and colts broken. These were the early fall tasks.

In early April Ignes bought about 900 ñandubay poles. The new corral at Espinillo was badly needed, for the sortings had yielded more than 300 head, and a similar number was expected from future gatherings. Meanwhile, brandings went on at Tala and Espinillo and would be done before Easter. Then Ignes would terminate Negrete, who had been in charge of sortings and brandings, to "reform the abuses introduced by him [Negrete], that were impossible to redress without risking further harm." After a few months' learning, Ignes was ready to assert his authority.

On April 5 Ignes was in San Pedro to file a petition for the cattle theft at Tala. The judge's indifference, Ignes feared, was due to a bias against him. Six days later he reported that nothing had been done, so right after the brandings, he would go to San Pedro again to file another complaint for damages and injuries caused by the criminals' impunity.

Brandings, delayed by rains, were completed by mid-April. Ignes expected about 1,300 head from that fall branding and 600 to 700 head from the October branding, but the actual outcome of both brandings was 1,330 head. Sortings and roundups in the late summer, after the downfall of thistles, were followed by a main branding in the early fall, and a smaller branding was carried out in late winter or early spring, before thistles grew again.

Barely 6 months after the beginning of the partnership's estancia operations, Ignes was ready for expanding them. He urged Aguirre to buy a neighboring tract. That operation failed, but a month later he was after another neighboring tract, the "thin guy's widow's little estancia." The widow, Tomasa Banegas, had allowed Ignes to count the head of cattle on her estancia and send his peons to take it over. The widow had asked for 1,000 pesos, but, tempted by someone coming from Buenos Aires, she raised the price by 30%. Ignes's last chance was to match that bid. Legally, neighbors were preferred in that case. That was a traditional right devised to prevent the proliferation of small plots, unsuitable for cattle ranching.[6]

In late May Ignes went to Buenos Aires to renew his bills at the bank but went back to San Pedro by late June to oversee the surveys. He had succeeded in his bid for the widow's land, which had already been taken over (Table 9.1). The judge overseeing her late husband's estate took 500 pesos out of the amount paid for the estancia and gave it to Ignes as a deposit for the charges that might result against her for the cattle-rustling suit, since her late husband was apparently responsible for it. Ignes par-

---

6 *Retracto* (retraction) was "the right someone has to keep something for the same amount it has been sold to other person; or the right granted by law, custom, or pact to someone to cancel a sale and keep for himself for the same price what has been sold to another person." See Escriche (1852), 1442.

tially used that money for the down payment of another tract of land and to buy a slave. Two years later, in October 1826, he would run into trouble for spending that money, instead of keeping it liquid.[7]

Winter 1824

In early July the partnership expanded their landholdings again (Table 9.1). Angel Pío Ruiz Moreno and Ignes traded two similar parcels after the survey in order to regularize their holdings.[8] And Tomás Taybo sold them a 5,000-vara tract at 4 reales per vara. Those tracts, added to the 1,000-vara Banegas estancia and a similar one Ignes expected to buy soon, would make – Ignes said – a 7,000-vara "wonderful" estancia, with "famous" grasses and vacant contiguous tracts for further expansion.[9]

A few weeks later, Ignes found a new opportunity to enlarge their holdings. Juan Ortega's sons and daughters were about to split their late father's land. This tract, 3,000 varas wide, was contiguous to their estancia, on the same side of the Arroyo del Tala. If split in small plots, overstocking would be unavoidable. They should buy it to prevent that. In spite of Ignes's sound reasons, they did not buy it. The Ortega brothers probably agreed to keep their father's property, for in 1864 there were large tracts in the area still owned by some Ortegas.[10]

By late July a 3-day storm halted the sortings, but the corral at Espinillo had been completed. Cattle were easily locked up and their shape was improving. A headcount was carried out in early September to determine the actual number of cattle on the estancia. The result was 4,087 head, including 436 head from sortings on the new Espinillo estancia, as well as 1,330 steers branded that year in April (1,200) and August (130). Because the newly branded steers should be discounted from the "budget" total, the actual number of cattle on the estancia at the time of its purchase was 2,757 head. This figure, well below Castro's estimates, proved for Ignes that he and Aguirre had been the victims of a fraud, taking advantage of his own "absolute lack of expertise" at that time.

The headcounter, Irazoqui, wrote a letter to Aguirre a few days later reporting the result of his labors. "Regarding the deception you have suffered, I believe in good faith that where a mistake is found it is corrected," he said in a cryptic way (using the wrong tense), "and I wish at

---

7 Marcelo Ignes to Juan Pedro Aguirre, Tala, 22 March 1824; Tala 25 March 1824, ABP, 031–5–3–9; and Marcelo Ignes to Juan Pedro Aguirre, San Pedro, 5 April 1824; Tala, 11 April 1824; Tala, 12 May 1824, ABP, 031–5–3–10.

8 Ignes did not elaborate on that swap. Information on it comes from the survey duplicate (San Pedro, No. 58). Facundo's widow had also bought Angel Pío Ruiz Moreno's estancia, later sold to her son-in-law Antonio Demarchi.

9 Quiroga's survey duplicate does not mention these later purchases.

10 See Buenos Aires, *Registro Gráfico* (1864).

the same time you may amend it without a big loss." Was he suggesting
Aguirre should get rid of Ignes? Probably, since Irazoqui was looking for
a tract of land for Aguirre. Ruiz Moreno blamed Ignes for mismanagement,
but Ignes complained about "the nonsense they are talking to give an
honest appearance to their fraud when selling the estancia." Those rumors
might have had no effect on Aguirre's mind, but he was looking for land
anyway.[11]

Aguirre had asked Irazoqui to inspect a tract on Cerrito Colorado, south
of the Salado River. Irazoqui's report was positive: a high dune, with a
freshwater creek springing from its foot and flowing into the Salado, and
a whole-day journey to the north, forming a chain of lagoons on its way.
Aguirre had to hurry to apply for that tract in emphyteusis, since many
people coveted it. The emphyteusis system, established in 1822, was a way
for the government to obtain revenues from public land, while using it as
collateral for the public debt. Sixty-three percent of the 6.7 million hectares obtained by individuals under that system was located, as was Cerrito
Colorado, south of the Salado River.[12]

Spring 1824

In late September Ignes was also looking for land, but for the partnership.
He expected to buy a neighboring tract on Espinillo creek by matching the
highest bid, as had been done with the Banegas tract. Ignes had learned
that the tract was on sale because some people had been refused permission
to settle there. Informal settlements were a way for landowners to secure
labor for seasonal tasks, but they could turn into a liability at sales time. In
March Ignes had to pay for an informal settler's ranchos when ousting him
from the Espinillo estancia.

Ignes's spring chores were just the daily cattle roundups. The number of
peons had been streamlined according to the actual number of head, so
expenses had gone down. There were two peons at Tala and one at
Espinillo, and "everything is well served." As there were 4,087 head of
cattle on the estancia according to that month's enumeration, the average
was 1,000 head per man if Ignes is taken into account, and 1,362 head per
man if not. These averages, however, do not consider the slaves that might
have been on the estancia.

11 Marcelo Ignes to Juan Pedro Aguirre, San Pedro, 29 June 1824, ABP, 031–5–3–10; and Marcelo
    Ignes to Juan Pedro Aguirre, Tala, 7 July 1824; Tala, 21 July 1824; Tala, 5 September 1824, ABP,
    031–5–3–11.
12 Ilario Irazoqui to Juan Pedro Aguirre, Tala, 5 September 1824, ABP, 031–5–3–11. For the
    legislation on emphyteusis, see Cárcano (1972) and Coni (1927); for land distributions under that
    system, see Infesta (1991) and (1993). On the public debt, see Burgin (1946), 53–55; Amaral
    (1982); and Nicolau (1988), 150–159.

In April Ignes had acknowledged reception of "four horses for the blacks," indicating neither how many blacks were there, nor their legal status – slaves or freemen. On July 7 he reported a "fieldhand slave" had been bought for 250 pesos. Two weeks later he made a proposal to two brick-making slaves, who had already accepted it: They would obtain their freedom at the end of 1829 (the partnership's expiration date) if they served on the estancia until then. These slaves were owned by someone else, so they had to buy them before implementing the agreement. "The labor and honesty of those servants (*criados*) promise considerable advantages to these rural establishments," wrote Ignes to convince Aguirre of the benefits expected from that operation. Ignes estimated that the annual expenses of the estancias could be met by selling bricks. Maybe Aguirre rejected that deal, but other slaves were bought instead since at the end of August Ignes drew a bill on Aguirre to obtain cash to pay for a male "fieldhand slave" and a female servant for his wife. There were slaves on the estancia, but how many and how good they were for rural work cannot be determined. In February 1826 Ignes asked Aguirre to send him a slave to tend the fruit-tree grove on the Tala estancia. A few days later, a runaway slave, too "vicious" for field work, was captured in Baradero. Ignes sent him to Aguirre just to get rid of him.

In late September cattle were ready to be sold, but the market was bearish. Some neighbors had sold their steers at 10 pesos each, in spite of falling prices in Buenos Aires. Ignes himself had been offered 9 pesos per head for all cattle, fat or lean. The beginning of the spring, before thistles grew up, was a good time for cattle sales, but their abundance meant lower prices. Aguirre's preference for old customers (Coronell, Hidalgo) was a way to cope with this uncertainty.

On November 11 Ignes reported that 200 steers had been sorted out by Coronell's foreman. "I expect Coronell would send for the remaining cattle as soon as possible," Ignes wrote, "for the pressing circumstances in the countryside at present are requiring so." Twenty days earlier the Indians had been only 6 leagues away from their estancia, forcing him to work all night to move the horses to a safe place. The Indians finally left for Arrecifes, some 40 km southwest of Tala, but they could come back again. There were other threats as well. By the end of November, Ignes complained about "the inevitable locust pest [which] will leave the fields without a single root."

Ignes had told Aguirre that he would ride to Buenos Aires to see him when the Indians were gone. They had to talk about the headcount and the future safety of their cattle if events "keep being so threatening as they have been so far."[13] Ignes had been at Tala since December 1823, spending

---

13 Marcelo Ignes to Juan Pedro Aguirre, Tala, 19 March 1824, ABP, 031–5–3–9; Marcelo Ignes to

that summer in restoring the productive capacity of the estancia. By the end of the winter of 1824, operations seemed normal, but by mid-spring Indians and locusts threatened their cattle. There are no letters available for the summer and fall of 1825.

Expansion: 1825–1827

Ignes's correspondence resumed at the end of the winter of 1825 and lasted for 2 whole years. In that period the long-run expansion of the cattle business was hindered by short-run calamities. Among the latter the Brazilian blockade, lasting from January 1826 to August 1828, and inflation fueled by increasing issues of inconvertible paper money, should be singled out. For these and other reasons, Aguirre went broke, and his cattle business failed dramatically in October 1828.

Spring 1825

In the spring of 1825, Ignes was selling fattened steers from Tala and buying young, lean cattle for a new tract of land that the partners were about to buy.[14] He sold 81 head on 10 October 1825 at 14 pesos each and he bought 300 head at 6 pesos 6 reales each on November 20 and 500 head at 6 pesos 4 reales each on December 22 (Table 9.2). On September 23 Ignes had received 1,000 pesos from Aguirre to buy neighboring lands. No tract was bought then, but a few months later, they purchased an estancia on the Santa Fe side of the Arroyo del Medio, close to San Nicolás (Table 9.1). This estancia was 2,500 to 3,000 varas wide and 9,000 varas long. Improvements were a brick house with double wall, three rooms, thatched roof, and a wooden attic; an adjacent adobe room and kitchen; a contiguous two-room house; a rancho "made of mud"; a brick water-well; a mill; a corral with more than 100 ñandubay poles and some willow poles; and a small fruit-tree grove. The total inventory value was around 3,000 pesos; the land accounted for half of it.[15]

Summer 1826

Ignes went to San Nicolás in late January 1826 to purchase the Arroyo del Medio estancia. The partners planned to enlarge their landholdings in that

Juan Pedro Aguirre, Tala, 26 September 1824, ABP, 031–5–3–11; and Marcelo Ignes to Juan Pedro Aguirre, Tala, 20 October 1824; Tala, 22 October 1824; Tala, 11 November 1824, ABP, 031–5–3–12.

14 Jarvis (1974) presents a model of this behavior.

15 Marcelo Ignes to Juan Pedro Aguirre, San Pedro, 1 September 1825; San Pedro, 12 October 1825; San Pedro, 24 November 1825, ABP, 031–5–3–12.

region in order to sell the Tala and Espinillo estancias, which were not well watered. They would soon discover that the Arroyo del Medio region was not drought-free, and, worse than that, other threats were present there.

By mid-February Ignes had already taken over the new estancia and was sending poles from the Espinillo corral to rebuild it at Arroyo del Medio for the head they had been buying and those resulting from sortings. Rains had flattened the thistles down, so roundups were about to start there. That was the end-of-summer routine: waiting for the thistles to go down so that roundups, sortings, and brandings could be carried out in March and early April.

On 19 February Ignes bought 200 head of "big cattle from the branding" at 4 pesos 4 reales per head. These were yearlings to be fattened on the new estancia. A few days earlier, Aguirre had bought 900 head at 5 pesos each. At the same time, Ignes was selling 100 head at 9 pesos each, a price due to the drought affecting Tala. Cattle were lean, therefore he would discontinue sales until April. A further decline of cattle prices was feared, however, since exports were halted by the Brazilian blockade established on 31 December 1825.

By the end of February, rain at Tala left the fields ready for sortings. Ignes sent his peons to Arroyo del Medio to drive cattle and sheep, so sortings were delayed until they were back. Neighbors were about to carry out their own sortings, delivering cattle Ignes had bought from them for the new estancia. As usual, while buying yearlings he was selling steers: Hidalgo's foreman took away 102 steers at 9 pesos each. By mid-March sortings were almost over, and branding would start on April 15.

Legal problems stemming from the purchase of the Tala estancia still lingered. The argument was about the number of cattle on the estancia at that time. Ruiz Moreno, the seller, had assured that there were 10,000 head of branded cattle plus 1,800 head to be branded. At the usual 30% reproduction rate, this calving figure meant a branded stock of 6,000 head. Ruiz Moreno's figures proved both his deception and Aguirre and Ignes's ignorance of the usual cattle reproduction rate. The appraiser, Castro, could not have been ignorant of the rate, so he was to blame for the success of Ruiz Moreno's scheme.[16]

Fall 1826

On March 21 Ignes left for Arroyo del Medio, but a week later he was back at Tala. Bulls were being gelded and preparations for branding were

16 Marcelo Ignes to Juan Pedro Aguirre, San Pedro, 22 December 1825, ABP, 031–5–3–12; Marcelo Ignes to Juan Pedro Aguirre, 2 February 1826; San Pedro, 11 February 1826; San Pedro, 19 February 1826; Tala, 25 February 1826; San Nicolás, 26 February 1826; Tala, 18 March 1826; San Pedro, 20 March 1826, ABP, 031–5–3–13.

underway, but sortings were not over yet because two neighbors had
refused cooperation. At Arroyo del Medio, Ignes had left everything ready
to receive 1,000 head of cattle and brand them at once. By mid-February
Aguirre had bought 900 head, but Ignes advised him to delay their
delivery until August because they would still be too small. At the same
time, Ignes was worried by some buyers' delays in taking cattle away from
Tala: Fat cattle should not stay on the estancia over the winter. Finding the
right time to sell fat head and buy lean head was a key factor for successful
estancia management.

On April 8 Ignes arrived in San Nicolás from Arroyo del Medio to draw
a bill on Aguirre for 1,200 pesos to pay for cattle, horses, and tools. News
about inflation had already reached the countryside, so the bill had to be
paid in gold. The Arroyo del Medio estancia had received all the cattle
bought for it, and they had already been branded. That estancia was in
good productive condition as proven by an attractive offer Ignes had
received for it. Far from accepting it, Ignes urged Aguirre to buy a
neighboring tract belonging to Tomás Fernández. The paralyzation of "our
speculations in the countryside" and the impossibility of selling the "old
estancias" would be the consequences of failing to get that tract. It would
take them a few months to get the Fernández tract.

On April 10 Ignes left San Nicolás for Tala and Espinillo to start
branding. By May 1 he was still busy at it because calving had been
abundant and peons were scarce. When branding was completed, Ignes left
for Arrecifes to receive 500 head of cattle, drive them to Arroyo del Medio,
and brand them there. Later, he would go to Buenos Aires and pay a visit
to Aguirre. An inventory dated on May 15, recording sales, purchases,
brandings, and cattle stock since December 1823, was probably prepared
for that visit.[17]

Winter 1826

On June 24 Ignes was back at Espinillo to drive 500 head of cattle to
Arroyo del Medio. Mid-winter storms kept Ignes at Arroyo del Medio for
20 days. He tended the cattle recently delivered and prepared the defense
of the estancia due to the threat of a new Indian invasion. A ditch was cut
to protect the fruit-tree grove, the buildings, and the big corral. The ditch
was reinforced with ñandubay poles from the corral and more than 2,000
laurel poles. Ignes also asked Aguirre for a dozen rifles and ammunition
and to get an order from the Ministry of War for the military commander

17 Marcelo Ignes to Juan Pedro Aguirre, Tala, 28 March 1826; San Nicolás, 9 April 1826; Tala, 23
   April 1826; Tala, 1 May 1826; Tala, 5 May 1826, ABP, 031-5-3-13.

of the region to give him one or two of the many unused cannons. In case of attack, neighbors would bring their cattle to that fortification and help defend it. That was the practice in the region, where many estancias were already fortified.

Ignes left for Tala and Espinillo for the August branding, but the fortification works forced him back to Arroyo del Medio. Always looking for land, once there he resumed his talks with one Ramírez over the sale of a tract and made a new attempt to purchase the Fernández tract. Because their tract would be surveyed in August, Ignes wanted to make a deal soon to get all tracts surveyed at the same time. Cattle recently introduced into the Arroyo del Medio estancia were already used to their new place and therefore demanded less intensive labor. Ignes expected to sell them soon since they were getting fat at a good pace.

A fiscal problem pending for 2 years reappeared at the end of July. The 1821 fiscal reform substituted a tax on capital invested in rural establishments (contribución directa) for the tithe. In July 1824 the San Pedro police had asked Ignes to pay his dues, but he had argued that Aguirre's statement might have already included his share of the capital invested in the Tala estancia. Ignes was not on the 1825 rural taxpayers' roll, and Aguirre was on the urban list paying 80 pesos for a commercial capital of 10,000 pesos. Consequently, Aguirre was not paying for Ignes's share. In July 1826 Ignes asked for Aguirre's advice. Should he be forced to file his statement, he said, he would be unable to declare less than 30,000 pesos "without being ashamed." To pay for what could not be concealed – that was the taxpayer's logic.

The government was asking for a separate statement for rural concerns to prevent "scandalously low statements from some rural capitalists," who were only filing in Buenos Aires. The tax forms asked for the capital of the partnership at the end of the previous year, including the value of the land, slaves, and livestock. The figure should be as fair as possible, Ignes was reminded by the taxman, "if you do not want to jeopardize me, and to jeopardize yourself, for if you are not fair, I will not act as a friend but as the tax collector. I hope you will not force me to do that, considering the great advantage cattleowners enjoy by the substitution of this tax for the tithe." Under the old system, a 60,000-peso estancia (as Tala was originally worth) producing 1,000 head of cattle would pay 100 head (the tithe was 10% of annual production), equivalent to 400 pesos (the average small or lean head of cattle were at 4 pesos per head). Under the new system, assuming that the value of the livestock necessary to produce 1,000 head per year was included in the total value of the estancia, the tax would have been 140 pesos. The taxman was right: The tithe was almost three times higher than the new tax. His pressure had some moral, if not practical, effect. On August 17 Ignes demanded a quick answer from Aguirre on that matter, for "meanwhile I am having quite a shameful part."[18]

A storm kept Ignes in San Pedro and disbanded the cattle at Arroyo del Medio. Once back there he managed to round them up but had to fire the foreman for his incompetence. Cattle were fattening so they had to be put into the corral again to prevent them from going back to their old *querencia.*[19] Cattle purchased in February were expected by the beginning of September. Those head were bought at 5 pesos each, but similar head were selling at 10 to 12 pesos then. Cattle and land prices were soaring, but only as a result of inflation. Tracts on Pavón creek, close to Arroyo del Medio, were at 10 reales per vara, and Fernández was asking 12 reales per vara for his tract, three times higher than the pre-inflation price. Ignes had already bought a 1,333.33-vara "remainder" at that price (Table 9.1) and had reached an agreement to buy Ramírez's tract. Ignes would pay a visit to him to close the deal once the Indian threat was over.

Levies due to the war with Brazil added to Ignes's worries by late August. The lack of peons in San Nicolás forced Ignes to carry out round-ups himself. Calving at Tala and Espinillo was abundant, so a few weeks later, before thistles were fully grown, the steers would be driven out of those estancias to make room for calves. A bill was due on September 6 in Buenos Aires, but Ignes asked his compadre Castro to discount a new one at the bank to pay for it. Land purchases, roundups, calving, labor shortage, and thistles retained Ignes on his estancias.[20]

Spring 1826

Ignes had suggested the sale of Tala and Espinillo. Back at Tala he found two letters from Aguirre concerning that proposal. Ignes backed down, however, due to changing circumstances in the countryside. He had taken for granted that lean cattle for the establishment of the Arroyo del Medio estancia would be available, but they were not. Consequently, they had to keep Tala and Espinillo as their own breeding grounds. By doing so, Ignes said, they would make "a gigantic fortune." Ignes's expectations were based on the illusion of inflation rather than on any change in relative

---

18 On the Buenos Aires direct tax, see Estévez (1960), and for a list of 1825 taxpayers, see *Lista Alfabética . . .* (1970). For an estimate of the effects of tithe and direct tax on cattle producers, see de Angelis (1834), 80–94.

19 This behavior is reported in Marcelo Ignes to Juan Pedro Aguirre, San Nicolás, 29 August 1826, ABP, 031-5-3-14.

20 Marcelo Ignes to Juan Pedro Aguirre, Espinillo, 24 June 1826; San Pedro, 28 June 1826, ABP, 031-5-3-13; Marcelo Ignes to Juan Pedro Aguirre, San Nicolás, 27 July 1826; Espinillo, 3 August 1826; San Nicolás, 17 August 1826; San Nicolás, 29 August 1826; San Pedro, 10 September 1826, ABP, 031-5-3-14.

prices. Prices of agricultural goods were soaring due to the abundance of paper money, but import prices were rising at a faster pace because of the blockade.[21]

By late September the arms had arrived in Arroyo del Medio and the fortification was close to completion. No further Indian invasions were reported, but soon other threats would disrupt rural operations. Meanwhile, operations were normal: Cattle would be driven from Giles to Tala for branding and then to Arroyo del Medio for fattening; 300 head had already been branded at Tala and Espinillo in September, and because of the abundance of calves, as many as 3,000 head were expected from the fall branding. Sortings had been taking place on those estancias, so there were head ready for sale. Ignes, according to Aguirre's instructions, had been asking 15 paper pesos per head, but "bank notes in general are not being received for cattle." Convertible bank notes had been turned into inconvertible paper money in January 1826, and 4 months later, paper money was declared the only legal means of payment. Those bank notes could not be legally rejected, but specie was still preferred in the countryside, where the government's law enforcement ability was quite weak.

Ignes left for Arroyo del Medio on September 25 in order to close the deal for Ramírez's tract and to oversee the survey of all their land there. Ignes drew two bills on Aguirre in September to pay for those land purchases. Those bills were drawn for cash advanced by Ramón Mosquera and Manuel Almadana, who had been regular sources of cash for Ignes in the past to meet the estancia expenses.[22] As cattle sales were usually cashed in by Aguirre, Ignes could only obtain funds by drawing bills over his partner to the order of local merchants. Ignes's cash requirements served those merchants to transfer funds to the city to pay for goods for their countryside stores.

In early October Ignes insisted that Aguirre should drop the idea of selling Tala and Espinillo, at least until the Arroyo del Medio estancia was fully established. The Espinillo estancia could be sold "once thistles are down" and after counter-branding its cattle and moving them to Arroyo del Medio. The deal for Ramírez's tract failed, because he asked for 17,420 pesos in "gold or silver." Ignes thought the price was too high, so he sent a detailed appraisal for Aguirre to learn the reasons of that failure.

The Melincué garrison had been reestablished by the Santa Fe govern-

21 On changes in relative prices due to inflation in late 1820s Buenos Aires, see Amaral (1989).
22 Twelve bills were drawn to the order of Mosquera for a total of 8,121 pesos 4 reales between 29 August 1824 and 3 December 1827, and four to the order of Almadana, for 3,500 pesos between 1 September 1825 and 10 September 1826. All these bills were drawn for cash advanced to Ignes. Twenty-six bills for a total of 25,853 pesos 3 reales are mentioned by Ignes, but only those drawn to the order of Mosquera and Almadana were due to cash advances. See ABP, 031–5–3–9 to 17.

ment, Ignes reported on October 7, due to his efforts and those of other producers. He had donated 50 head of cattle to help in covering the expenses. Echagüe, the Santa Fe acting governor, had paid a visit to the region to reassure producers of his government's commitment to protect them. Ignes was sure about the "wishes of that government to attract capital to its beautiful province, nowadays ruled [*sic*] and in the best possible order." Soon, however, he was forced to change his mind about the Santa Fe government.

The 800 head of cattle purchased in February finally arrived at Arroyo del Medio and were about to be branded. The construction of corrals had been finished, so after the branding, a ditch would be cut for the cannons. But all tasks were subject to delays due to a labor shortage. By mid-October Ignes went back to San Pedro, where new legal problems awaited him. The Justice of the Peace ordered him to produce at once the 500-peso deposit made when buying the neighboring Espinillo tract from Tomasa Banegas in June 1824. Ignes, taking that amount as compensation for cattle stolen from their properties, had immediately spent it. This case shows how justice worked in the Buenos Aires countryside: The theft had occurred in April 1824, 2 months later Ignes had obtained the deposit, and the next legal action took place 2 years and 4 months later.

In spite of his pessimism regarding the availability of lean cattle, Ignes learned that about 500 breeding cows with their calves were on sale at Cañada de la Cruz at 7 pesos per cow. He made an offer to their owner, but it was up to Aguirre to close the deal. The owner had to tell Aguirre how many head were on sale and when they could be taken away. Ignes wanted to pick those head up after thistles fell down, in February or March. By late October they could not be driven without incurring extraordinary expenses. Thistles were also delaying the sale of more than 700 steers from Tala.

By mid-November Ignes came back from San Nicolás for a formal headcount at Espinillo, where a new foreman was in charge. The old foreman had been sent to Arroyo del Medio because he was honest, hardworking, and intelligent. The ineptitude of the last two foremen had forced Ignes to keep an eye on them constantly. He could not afford that, since the expansion of their landholdings was taxing his time. The survey of the original tract at Arroyo del Medio had resulted in an extension larger than expected, and an additional 500-vara tract was added to their Espinillo holdings in late November (Table 9.1).

At that time the drought was disbanding their cattle at Tala and Espinillo due to the lack of an artificial watering station there, and more peons were hired at Arroyo del Medio to prevent cattle dispersion. The drought continued throughout December, and, as usual, fires razed the fields. At Espinillo cattle had to walk a league every day to get water, but evening roundups kept them together. No roundups were possible at Tala because of "immense thistleries," so the drought was not allowing cattle to fatten as expected.

Ignes intended to ride to Buenos Aires by the end of December to settle his accounts with Aguirre "before they get more complicated," but the drought retained him in the countryside. Since a bill was then due, he asked Aguirre to help him discount a new one to pay for it. On December 11 he drew a bill on Aguirre for 2,500 pesos to the order of Ramón Mosquera, for cash needed to meet the usual expenses of their estancias and to cancel pending balances for land purchases. After those payments the deeds would be extended, so he would carry them to Buenos Aires by mid-January.[23]

Summer 1827

Ignes probably did go to Buenos Aires that summer. Back at Tala and Espinillo in early February, he found that the three rodeos had kept together in spite of the drought. Sortings would start soon in the region, from the more distant estancias to the closer. The Arroyo del Medio estancia was doing fine, but there were problems in its neighborhood – montoneras this time, rather than Indians. A month later, a levy would be carried out in San Pedro, so peons had vanished. Some of them were at the Arroyo del Medio estancia. Ignes would take them back to San Pedro to complete the sortings.

Tala and Espinillo soon recovered from the drought, but it lasted longer at Arroyo del Medio. Cattle were too lean there, but regular rains would let them improve rapidly. Sortings at Tala were over by mid-March and would be over at Espinillo before April 2, when branding would start.[24]

Fall 1827

Brandings at Tala yielded 1,800 head, but rains delayed those at Espinillo and Arroyo del Medio. Production had remarkably improved in the summer and early fall, but there were clouds on the political horizon. Ignes urged Aguirre to sell the Arroyo del Medio estancia due to lawlessness in

23 Marcelo Ignes to Juan Pedro Aguirre, San Pedro, 24 September 1826, ABP, 031–5–3–14; Marcelo Ignes to Juan Pedro Aguirre, San Nicolás, 7 October 1826; San Nicolás, 13 October 1826; Arroyo de Ramallo, 17 October 1826; San Pedro, 19 October 1826 (two letters); San Pedro, 20 October 1826; San Nicolás, 13 November 1826; San Nicolás, 22 November 1826; San Nicolás, 3 December 1826; San Pedro, 11 December 1826, ABP, 031–5–3–15.

24 Marcelo Ignes to Juan Pedro Aguirre, San Nicolás, 23 December 1826, ABP, 031–5–3–15; Marcelo Ignes to Juan Pedro Aguirre, San Nicolás, 6 February 1827; San Nicolás, 6 March 1827; San Pedro, 15 March 1827, ABP, 031–5–3–16.

Santa Fe, for which no remedy could be expected soon. They had suffered no losses yet, due both to his care and to the cattle's poor shape, but it was just a matter of time. Aguirre should look for a buyer for that estancia without revealing their reasons for selling it. Contradicting his previous views, Ignes assured Aguirre that their business would not be damaged by such a sale since Tala was an establishment "of great importance," as Espinillo would also be if given an aguada. Ignes expected to brand 200 head by the end of the winter, to make a total of 2,000 head for that year. This figure was larger than in previous years, but it could be even larger in the future, since that estancia was good enough for 4,000-head annual brandings. They should take advantage of the presence of agents in San Nicolás who were buying estancias for Buenos Aires investors. Ignes himself had been appraising estancias for them. In mid-March he had made an estimate for an estancia holding 4,500 to 5,000 head of cattle, 150 horses, 500 mares, and 500 sheep. If for some reason the potential investor decided not to buy it, Aguirre should not miss that opportunity.

In mid-May Ignes recovered his optimism regarding the situation at Arroyo del Medio. He had asked some influential person in Santa Fe to pressure Governor López into action against bandits pestering the region. (The influential person's name was mentioned by Ignes, but that portion of the letter has been lost to rodents.) The Arroyo del Medio estancia had not suffered any damage yet, but in case of a new emergency, Ignes would sell its cattle.

The brandings at Espinillo and Arroyo del Medio had yielded 600 and 300 head, respectively, making a total fall branding, including Tala, of 2,700 head. He expected it to be over 3,000 head after the August branding. Good weather had helped to fatten the cattle at Tala, so in a few days' time, he would go from San Nicolás to San Pedro to look for buyers for those steers. Some steers had already been sold at 16 pesos per head, but Ignes reversed that sale because current prices were ranging from 20 to 30 pesos per head. When sales were resumed, however, he only got 17 pesos per head

By mid-May the taxman made a further attempt to collect Ignes's overdue direct tax for 1825 and 1826. The first attempt had been made in July 1824, and almost 3 years later, Ignes was still evading it. Passive resistance to that tax seems to have been widespread in the countryside. Even Rosas failed years later to collect it from otherwise supportive cattleowners.[25] Maybe they knew taxes bore on them while inflation bore on everyone, so it was better to spread their burden.

Since the Arroyo del Medio estancia was on the Santa Fe side of that creek, it was subject to the 4% Santa Fe sales tax. On May 29 he asked

---

25 Estévez (1960), 174; de Angelis (1834), 91.

Aguirre to be sent the title deed for one of the tracts they had purchased. He would go with it to Rosario to pay that tax. The Buenos Aires direct tax had been dodged for 3 years, but he could not do the same with the Santa Fe sales tax. Such different behavior was probably due to Ignes's request for help against banditry to the Santa Fe governor, or maybe the title deed was only effective after paying that tax. Dodging the Buenos Aires direct tax did not affect their title to the land.[26]

Winter 1827

A storm gave Ignes extra work in mid-June, so he suspended the moving of the big corral at Arroyo del Medio – a move necessary to make it larger in order to accommodate fattened head. A month later, on July 16, Ignes reported that there were 1,400 steers on the three estancias. He expected to sell 800 head, 600 from Arroyo del Medio and 200 from Tala and Espinillo. Another 600 from the latter estancias would be sent to the former for fattening. Because the Tala cattle were too lean, he would not sell them until November. At Arroyo del Medio, sales would start in September.

By mid-August Ignes already had many bidders for the Arroyo del Medio cattle. Among them, their old customer Paisano Hidalgo would match any offer. Ignes had told him to deal with Aguirre. Since late June Aguirre had tightened his control over their business. There had been some malevolent comments on Ignes's management, but even without them Aguirre could easily think his partner was cheating on him: He only knew about cattle output by Ignes's reports. Aguirre would soon lose control if Ignes was allowed to make a deal on his own, as he had done on several occasions. Moreover, Ignes had suggested several times (twice when they were considering selling their estancias, and once regarding cattle sales) that it would be better for customers to deal directly with him. When Aguirre tightened his grip, however, Ignes quietly submitted, informing Aguirre on the shape of their cattle and current prices. By mid-August those prices were 30 pesos per head for big steers, and 25 pesos per head for lean cattle.

Four hundred steers had been sent from Tala to Arroyo del Medio. Ignes rounded up other steers from sortings to send another 200 head there. After gelding, that year's second branding would start. On August 25 he reported gelding and dehorning of the Tala steers was over at Arroyo del Medio, as well as the branding of stray yearlings rounded up there. Many people were interested in those steers, but his advice to Aguirre was to sell

26 Marcelo Ignes to Juan Pedro Aguirre, San Nicolás, 18 April 1827; San Nicolás, 19 May 1827; Tala, 29 May 1827; San Nicolás, 15 June 1827, ABP, 031-5-3-16.

them for specie in Córdoba and Santa Fe. Perhaps Ignes had realized that Buenos Aires high paper-money prices were illusory. In February 1827 more than 100 steers had been sold to a buyer from Santa Fe, who paid for them both in specie and paper money. This mixture in the means of payments shows both Ignes's difficulties in finding more customers ready to pay in specie, and Aguirre's reluctance to go into such deals. The government's law enforcement ability was weak in the countryside, but certainly stronger in the city, where Aguirre was. He could neither make such deals without breaking the law nor allow Ignes to make them without running the risk of being cheated.

In late September the Arroyo del Medio cattle were ready to be sold, and cattle brought there from the other estancias would be ready in January. One old customer had offered 20 pesos per head for 3-year-old steers to be taken away at once. If Aguirre could not get a better price, that was a good deal for Ignes. They had to sell the steers before thistles prevented them from being driven to Buenos Aires.

Ignes had complained several times about the lack of aguadas at Espinillo. Water was one of the main factors determining the price of land. The old pampa north of the Salado River was well watered, but the northwestern districts of San Pedro, Arrecifes, and San Nicolás were less so than Magdalena, in the southeast of that region. While in Magdalena there were many creeks, depressions, and lagoons, in the northeast there were mainly creeks, not all good as a water source. Occasional droughts worsened the problem. Around 1825 a new invention was introduced to the Buenos Aires countryside to cope with the water problem. The bottomless bucket, created by one Vicente Lanuza, was a very simple machine: a rope, a bucket made out of hide, a sheave, and a horse for power.[27] After learning about it, Ignes asked Aguirre to order one for their Espinillo estancia. On 13 August 1827, he was preparing the new aguada for the "newly invented machine," and 12 days later he insisted that he had seen a bottomless bucket and that was what he needed.[28]

On September 20 Ignes rejected Aguirre's renewed proposal to sell the Tala and Espinillo estancias. At that time those establishments were just about to start repaying his efforts. Aguirre wanted to focus upon improving the Arroyo del Medio estancia, but that establishment, Ignes argued, was inferior to Tala and Espinillo, and its further expansion was checked by the unavailability of land. Ignes had been in favor of selling Tala and Espinillo while land was still available to extend their holdings there. But

27 Sbarra (1973), 45–63. See drawings of several different bottomless bucket models in Moreno (1991), 88–93. For a contemporary description, see MacCann (1969), 52.
28 Marcelo Ignes to Juan Pedro Aguirre, San Pedro, 13 August 1827; San Nicolás, 25 August 1827; and San Nicolás, 20 September 1827, ABP, 031-5-3-16.

Table 9.3. *Cattle stock at the Tala, Espinillo, and Arroyo del Medio estancias, September 1824–October 1827*

Cattle	El Tala	Espinillo	Arroyo del Medio	Total
Existing	3,651	520	–	4,171
Bought	–	1,556	2,326	3,882
Branded	4,916	1,189	300	6,405
Subtotal	8,567	3,265	2,626	14,458
Sales[a]	1,824	696	139	2,659
Consumption[b]	398	152	100	650
Losses[b]	207	79	114	400
Subtotal	2,429	927	353	3,709
Total	6,138	2,338	2,273	10,749

[a] The Tala and Espinillo cattle sales are not differentiated. The distribution has been made according to the proportion of cattle stock on each estancia over the total stock for both of them.
[b] Consumption and loss figures have been distributed according to the same procedure, except the 50 head donated to the Santa Fe government which are included among the Arroyo del Medio losses.
Source: October 1827 inventory, ABP, 031–5–3–6.

the situation had changed, so he had already backed down. If selling, Ignes pointed out, Aguirre should sell everything but should let him choose his new partner. He wanted to discuss that personally with Aguirre, but his wife's illness and the installation of the bottomless bucket had delayed his trip to Buenos Aires. In the meantime, Ignes would make an inventory of the three estancias to carry with him to Buenos Aires, "just in case you [Aguirre] insist with your project."[29]

Collapse: 1827–1828

On 22 October 1827, Ignes prepared the inventory of the three estancias (Table 9.3). He estimated 8,567 head of cattle for Tala, 3,265 head for Espinillo, and 2,626 head for Arroyo del Medio, making a total of 14,458 head (Maps 9.2 and 9.3).[30] Sales accounted for 2,659 head, and consump-

29 Marcelo Ignes to Juan Pedro Aguirre, San Pedro, 16 July 1827; San Nicolás, 1 August 1827; San Pedro, 13 August 1827; San Nicolás, 25 August 1827; San Nicolás, 20 September 1827, ABP, 031–5–3–16.
30 The Tala figure results from adding 1,300 head branded in 1825; 1,616 head branded in 1826; and 2,000 head branded in 1827 to the 3,651 head existing in 4 September 1824, when an inventory was carried out at Tala. When Espinillo was organized as a separate estancia, 436 head were introduced there from the Tala sortings and 84 head were bought from Tomasa Banegas; 1,556

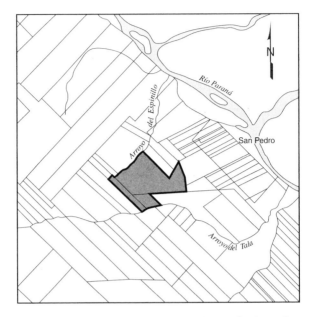

Map 9.2 The Tala and Espinillo estancias, San Pedro, 1864. *Source*: Buenos Aires
(province). *Registro Gráfico* (1864).

tion for 650 head, while 400 head had been lost, stolen, donated, or had
died. The total number of cattle on the three estancias was therefore
10,749 head, plus an unknown number of stray cattle. The proportion of
sales over the total number of head results in a rate of extraction of 18.4%
for all the estancias from December 1823 to October 1827. As 4.5% had
been consumed on the estancias and 2.8% had been lost, the overall rate of
extraction rises to 25.7%.

The Arroyo del Medio estancia was listed with an extension of 5,273.3
varas by 9,000 varas, equivalent to 3,559.5 hectares. There were 2,273
head of cattle, 80 horses, 40 mares, and 500 to 600 sheep, making a total
of about 2,492 LU. The livestock density was, therefore, 1.25 h/LU. The
extension of Tala and Espinillo was not recorded in that inventory and
cannot be determined with enough precision to carry out a similar estimate.

As no value was recorded in that inventory for any item, a quantitative
analysis of the capital structure cannot be carried out either. Cattle raising
was the predominant occupation on the three estancias. Horses were kept

head were bought later; and brandings yielded 74 head in 1825, 515 head in 1826, and 600 head
in 1827. There was only one branding at Arroyo del Medio, in 1827, yielding 300 head. See the
inventory of 22 October 1827, ABP, 031–5–3–6.

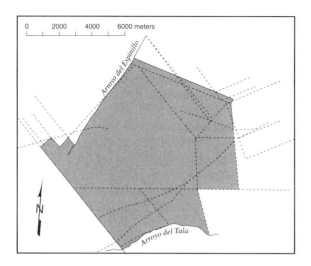

Map 9.3 The Tala and Espinillo estancias, San Pedro, 1881. *Source*: See this
chapter, n. 3.

just for their service, and sheep probably for their own consumption, since
no sheep, sheepskin, or wool sales were recorded. There was a mill on one
estancia but no record of sowing, harvesting, or any agricultural equipment or activity. Agriculture was probably practiced anyway, but just for
estancia consumption.

No letter accompanies that inventory, probably because Ignes handed it
to Aguirre while paying the visit announced in his letter of 20 September
1827. This is the last extant letter from Ignes to Aguirre for the period
September 1825 to September 1827. There are four pieces of evidence
accounting for what happened later.

The first piece is a statement of income and expenditure prepared by
Ignes on 7 January 1828.[31] Whereas total expenditure was 3,858 pesos,
total income was only 1,358 pesos, leaving a negative balance of 2,500
pesos covered by drafts on Aguirre. Labor expenses amounted to 2,222
pesos for foremen's and peons' salaries, that is, 57.6% of total expenses,
plus another 610 pesos spent in temporary workers' salaries, that is,
another 15.8%. Labor expenses accounted, therefore, for 73.4% of total
expenses on the three estancias in 1827. Either the estancias were over-
staffed because of Ignes's inexperience, Ignes was cheating Aguirre regarding the number of permanent peons on the estancias, or the low-income
figure was just due to the cattle capitalization of their estancias. Without
dismissing the first two factors, the third was true: Total reproduction had

31 ABP, 031–5–3–6.

been 6,405 head while sales, consumption, and losses made only 3,709 head, leaving 2,696 head as cattle capitalization. At an average price of 10 pesos per head, it would have been necessary to sell just 10% of those head to balance the account. Those head were kept to capitalize their estancias, not because of any expectation regarding future cattle prices. The 1827 loss could also be related to a depressed cattle market due to the Brazilian blockade.

The second piece is a contract dated 13 August 1828 selling 4,000 calves "from this calving" to Diego Martínez at 5 pesos each, to be taken away in March 1829. The low price perhaps reflected the size of those head – calves, rather than yearlings or steers. But that figure was 38% higher than the 2,900 head branded in 1827. About 3 years were necessary to turn those calves into steers, but the loss in that period was not as high as that. So the 1828 calving estimate reflected expectations of continuous growth.

The third piece is an undated agreement dissolving their partnership.[32] Aguirre would keep the Tala and Espinillo estancias, while Ignes would keep the Arroyo del Medio estancia. As part of the agreement, 1,500 head of cattle from the former would be sent to the latter. Aguirre would also be responsible for the Diego Martínez contract, for another deal made with Juan Pedro Varangot for 1,590 yearlings, for a 5,000-peso bill accepted by Ignes, and for 2,000 pesos advanced by Juan Carlos Benavente for cattle yet to be delivered. Aguirre would also be responsible for bills he had re-quested Ignes to draw and endorse, probably due to his business failure. It is not known when this agreement was carried out, but it was certainly carried out since Ignes was not mentioned when Tala and Espinillo were sold to José Tomás de Isasi in 1838.

The fourth piece of evidence brings this story to a dramatic end. On 28 October 1828, Ignes sent a letter from Arroyo del Medio to Juan Pedro Aguirre, Juan José de Larramendi, and José Matías Gutiérrez.[33] "I have just received yours dated on the 25th instant," he said, "in the most bitter circumstances for me, since the condition of this countryside is such that I am forced to move all livestock out of this establishment, as all cattleowners from the other side of the creek are doing since yesterday, so I will not be able to proceed there as you have requested but after eight days at least." No mention is made of the reasons for such hurried depar-ture, but it could have been any of the unnatural calamities affecting rural production: Indians, bandits, or political disruptions. Ignes's obliquity points to the latter as the most likely explanation.

32 ABP, 031-5-3-7.
33 Marcelo Ignes to Juan Pedro Aguirre, José Juan de Larramendi, and José Matías Gutiérrez, Arroyo del Medio, 28 October 1828 ABP, 031-5-3-17.

Conclusion

Ignes's letters to Aguirre provide information both on the history of their partnership and on rural operations in the Buenos Aires countryside in the 1820s. Their partnership evolved thanks to a heavy investment by Aguirre, to Ignes's industry, and to cattle capitalization. The partners' holdings had expanded from their original investment on the Tala estancia to three neighboring tracts on the Espinillo creek and two tracts on the Arroyo del Medio. Cattle sales were still far from paying for regular annual operations, let alone capital investment. Land was plentiful, but profitability was not assured. Estancia profits were probably high, but only after a period of organization of production. By the beginning of 1828, after 4 years of operation, the Aguirre–Ignes estancias were not producing at full strength yet. Management skills were required to make a profit out of that business, but Ignes's correspondence does not reveal the stage of normal operations at which their skills could be assessed. It does show, however, what the operational skills were that were required to manage an estancia. Those skills had a final result: fat cattle. The ability to produce fat cattle depended upon the repetitive performance of rural tasks such as roundup, branding, sorting, and gelding. It also depended on the aptitude of making good decisions regarding cattle: to look for better pasture, to move them in case of drought, and to keep the fields with the right stocking rate according to their quality. It also required the ability to look for and take care of horses to work the cattle, and the ability to match labor demand and supply, combining slaves and permanent and temporary peons.

All those skills were required from Ignes and from all managers in the countryside. But as partners and owners, he and Aguirre had to have other skills in order to turn their estancias into a profitable concern. Information on prices of land, cattle, labor, and supplies was necessary, as well as the ability to make decisions based upon that information: when to buy a new tract of land and how much to pay for it; when to hire more peons, at what salary, or when to buy another slave; when to sell cattle, to whom, and for how much; and what supplies to buy for estancia consumption and where to buy them. For Aguirre and Ignes, such decisions were complicated by the upsurge of inflation in Buenos Aires in 1826.

Other skills not directly related to cattle ranching were also necessary to survive and make a profit out of an estancia. Land surveys, cattle rustling, taxes, Indian invasions, banditry, and political disorder were sources of problems as much as locust, diseases, droughts, and excessive rain. To counter non-natural threats, it was necessary to look for protection from the authorities. But protection was expensive: It meant paying taxes and making donations. If the Santa Fe government was at some stage effective against bandits in the Arroyo del Medio area, Ignes's flight from his land was probably due to political disorder not controlled (maybe even supported) by that government. Government protection, therefore, had some limitations. No authorities are mentioned in the San Pedro area other than the justice of the peace and the tax collector. And Ignes's letters show that their law enforcement efforts were less than successful. After 3 years, cattle thieves had not been punished, and taxes had not been paid.

Cattle did not breed themselves, so human action was necessary to turn the different factors required by rural production into wealth. For any rural enterprise to succeed, management skills were required to deal with the operational and administrative aspects of that business, and entrepreneurial skills to deal with its commercial, legal, and political aspects. Success was guaranteed neither by vast tracts of land and large herds nor by the right political connections. All those elements were necessary, but it was up to the individual entrepreneur to combine them to make a profit. As Richard Napp put it in 1876, "an estancia offers a vast and productive field to an active and far-seeing man."[39] These traits should be emphasized, for without them neither production nor profit were possible.

39 Napp (1876), 309.

PART IV

Results

10

Profit

Estancia operations, their capital structure, the conditions of production, and the human action required by livestock raising on them have been described in the preceding Chapters. The economic results of all those factors should be considered now. At a microeconomic level, estancia operations resulted in profit; at a macroeconomic level, the overall result of estancia production can be traced by the ability of estancia-produced goods to reach overseas markets. Estancia profits are the subject of this chapter, and the markets for estancia-produced goods are the subject of Chapter 12. Linking both levels are prices and marketing conditions, which are dealt with in Chapter 11.

The traditional vision of Latin American rural estates as prestige-oriented rather than profit-oriented concerns has been increasingly challenged in recent decades. Studies of haciendas for both the late colonial period and the nineteenth century have shown that criteria used to run them were not necessarily different from those used to run other businesses. Eighteenth- or nineteenth-century business criteria may differ from present ones but still be sound in their day. Belgrano's criticism of the Río de la Plata merchants who would "buy at four and sell at twenty" was the view of an intellectual, a merchant's son but not a merchant himself, a man trained at Salamanca rather than behind the store counter. The overpricing practice of those merchants may have spared them some customers and markets, but it was not out of place in a world with poor communications, affecting both the dissemination of information and the transportation of goods. News arrived late; goods were delivered in poor shape or were lost. Merchants may have been overpricing when considering a single good, a single transaction, but when all costs were taken into account in the long run, their struggle to make a profit becomes apparent. Those who were lucky enough to get rich (in a modest way, since even large fortunes were modest in Buenos Aires when compared with those in Lima and Mexico) did so due to the application of both their shrewdness and their skills in a fairly competitive environment.[1]

---

1 For a study of the literature on Mexican haciendas, see Van Young (1983). Belgrano's quote is in

Business conditions were different for each economic activity, but that does not mean that merchants or landowners did not mean business. Accounts may be difficult to obtain and then difficult to decode, but when both conditions are overcome, the result may well be similar to that of Clemente López Osornio's estancia, studied in Chapter 2. The criteria to run that estancia were inferred from the three periods undergone by its administration. The existing accounts are those required by the courts, which might not have been the only ones kept at that time, but they are explicit enough. That was a profit-oriented concern, specializing in cattle production for urban consumption. Not all Buenos Aires estancias at that time or later might have been devoted to that particular purpose, but from the analysis of the capital structure of the 1820 and 1850 estancias, from their evolution over that period, and from the analysis of the management of Juan Pedro Aguirre and Marcelo Ignes's estancias, it is clear that estancias were business concerns. They might have been successful or unsuccessful, but as with any business, profit was the paramount aim around which factors were organized to carry out the production of certain goods.

Profit was the main business concern of estancias, but this is not equivalent to saying that they were all successful or that the rate of profit was similar for all producers. As with any other business, natural, market, labor, technical, and management factors affected the rate of profit in the short run. Because the combination of those factors is never stable, profit should necessarily fluctuate. In the case of the López Osornio estancia, operations and consequently profit were affected first by the owner's death and later by droughts, and even when operations were stabilized, from 1791 onward, the rate of profit fluctuated from 7.3% to 11.5% over the following 5 years. In the case of the Aguirre and Ignes estancias, there are no accounts left for us to estimate the rate of profit, but Ignes's letters show the range of problems affecting rural production – from locusts to law enforcement.

The amazing territorial expansion of Buenos Aires from the 1780s to the 1870s proves that the private enterprises carrying out livestock production

Belgrano (1954), 167, and paraphrased by Halperín Donghi (1972), 42. For the long-run rate of return vis-à-vis the single operation approach, I am indebted to Javier Balsa, who made that point in a paper written in 1986 for my Argentine History course at the University of La Plata. Using data from Socolow (1978b) on merchants' wealth, Balsa showed that for an 8-year period after marriage the average rate of return for a set of twelve merchants was 8.1% per year. This figure is close to the current interest rate and even closer to the profit rate estimated for the López Osornio estancia, and very far indeed from the windfall profits made from single successful operations. The same estimate for a period going from the merchants' marriage to their deaths results in profit rates ranging from 2.8% to 25% per year. Disregarding three extreme cases, Balsa finds that the annual profit rates for the remaining nine cases range between 4.2% and 15%. See Balsa (1986).

on those lands were as a whole profitable. An estimate of their rate of profit seems in order to explain why they were attracting capital and labor. The study of the López Osornio estancia has already shown that in the 1790s the reason was a rate of profit that was well above the usual rate of interest. (But even below that rate, rural investment could have been attractive since the lack of financial institutions restricted both the availability of credit and the gainful placement of idle funds.) Our estimate was, however, for the 1790s, when the process of expansion was just beginning. The steady continuation of that process requires an examination of the evidence on estancia profits. As the analysis of the evolution of the capital structure of estancias from 1820 to 1850 shows, profit making was complicated by the fact that land value was on the rise while cattle values were declining. If estancias continued to expand, it was necessarily due to healthy returns in spite of such negative conditions.

The rate of profit for the Buenos Aires estancias during the process of territorial expansion has been estimated at around 30%, and even nominal annual profit rates of 50% to 100%, which some landowners claimed to have achieved over 1- to 3-year terms, have been mentioned.[2] These are mere claims, however, not proper estimates. In order to make a proper estimate, capital investment and capital growth must be known. The evidence is not plentiful. In Chapter 2 the rate of profit made by the Lóez Osornio estancia in the late eighteenth century has been estimated. Because no other sources like that have been found so far, the evolution of profit rates in the nineteenth century is examined according to three contemporary estimates. The first section of this chapter presents a study of the different economic results of agriculture and livestock production in 1801, according to Félix de Azara, aiming at explaining why (apart from market reasons) the latter prevailed on the Buenos Aires pampas in the first half of the nineteenth century. The second section studies an estimate made in 1831 by Pedro Trapani, a well-known landowner, at the request of Woodbine Parish, the British minister in Buenos Aires from 1824 to 1832. The third section deals with an estimate made in 1856 by Manuel Castaño, at the request of Justo Maeso, the head of the Buenos Aires Statistical Department.[3]

As pointed out by other rural producers at that time, profit making was dependent upon so many conditions that estimates would be impossible to generalize. The study of Azara's, Trapani's, and Castaño's estimates is carried out just to compare their knowledgeable estimates with other hacendados' claims.

---

2 Halperín Donghi (1963), 69; Brown (1979), 154–155.
3 Trapani's and Castaño's estimates were first studied by Barba (1967) and Infesta de Guerci (1983).

Estancia profitability, 1801

The most exhaustive analysis of estancia profitability at the beginning of
the process of territorial and productive expansion is due to Félix de Azara.
In his *Memoria sobre el estado rural del Río de la Plata en 1801*, he analyzes the
output expected from agriculture and livestock production from the
double viewpoint of labor demand and human consumption.[4] For a man
educated in the enlightened and physiocratic ideas of the eighteenth
century, it was an amazing discovery to find that the loose way in which
cattle was raised on the Río de la Plata plains was more profitable than
agriculture. Azara, however, disregards two factors: the capital investment
required by agriculture and livestock production, and the cost of labor.
Those two factors will now be introduced into Azara's analysis to explain
why cattle raising prevailed and why agriculture was possible around 1800
in spite of its critical condition stressed by Azara and other observers of
rural practices.

According to Azara, a Spanish farmer after 1.5 years of labor obtained 50
Castilian fanegas of wheat, equivalent to 23.25 Buenos Aires fanegas.
Considering a yield double that of Spain, a Buenos Aires farmer would have
obtained for 1.5 years of labor 46.5 fanegas, 31 fanegas per year. If Buenos
Aires wheat yields were 1 : 16, as Azara himself says, 1.94 fanegas should be
sown to obtain 31 fanegas. If 0.75 fanegas were sown in a cuadra cuadrada
($16,874\,m^2$), 1.94 fanegas would have required 2.59 cuadras cuadradas,
equivalent to 4.37 hectares.

The average price for a fanega of wheat was 2.54 pesos for 1791–1800.
So, at the average price, 31 fanegas would have had a market price of 78.74
pesos. That amount of money could only be obtained after meeting certain
expenses, such as land rental, labor, and seed. Simple tools were used also,
but they are left aside here because their amortization period was very long,
and consequently their eventual rental fee quite low. So in order to estimate the rentability of wheat agriculture, those expenses should be compared with the income produced by those 31 fanegas.

Land required by those fanegas could have been purchased or rented. In
any case the rent or the alternative use of that amount of money should not
be too distant from the usual rate of interest, 6%. Land values in the 1790s
were around 2 reales per vara (i.e., for every front vara with a 9,000-vara
length). So, if 2 reales bought 9,000 square varas and one hectare is
equivalent to 13,334 square varas, 2.96 reales would have been required to
purchase one hectare. As 4.37 hectares were required for 31 fanegas, they
would have had a cost of 1.62 pesos. A 6% rent over that amount was 0.10
pesos.

<hr/>

4 Azara (1943), 7–8.

According to Azara's estimate, 31 fanegas of wheat were the product of 1 year of labor. Labor could be estimated at 7 pesos per month. But agriculture does not require full-time employment. So the product of one year of labor probably was the product of actual labor for 2 months or less: one for sowing, another for harvesting. Labor cost was then 14 pesos.

To obtain, therefore, 78.74 pesos for 31 fanegas of wheat after a year of labor, it was necessary to spend 0.10 pesos for land, 14 pesos for labor, and 4.93 pesos for seed (1.94 fanegas at the average price of 2.54 pesos). Total expenses were then 19.03 pesos, so profit was 59.71 pesos, equivalent to a 314% return.

That high return can be sized down by increasing the rent for land. The land value used corresponds to the López Osornio estancia, but a plot of land closer to Buenos Aires was probably ten times more expensive. It can also be assumed that labor was needed to sow and harvest for a few weeks and also to take care of a plot on a permanent basis to maintain ditches and fences in good shape. For another 2 months, there could have been demand for labor at the same salary, but for the rest of the year, salaries could drop to half or one-third of the seasonal-peak level. So expenses could rise to 1 peso for land and 54 pesos for labor (another 2 months at 7 pesos each, and 8 months at 2 pesos each). Total expenses would amount in this case to 59.93 pesos, leaving a profit of 18.81 pesos, equivalent to a 31% return. That return could be further reduced by the inclusion of transportation, storage, and marketing expenses, but on the basis of the available information, it is not possible to estimate them. The crucial factor in making a profit is, therefore, the amount of labor needed and its cost.

That estimate is for a single year, without considering the many problems that agricultural production met in the long run, such as floods, droughts, livestock invasions, locusts, and hail. Since natural calamities did not affect all producers in the same way, some farmers might have taken advantage of high prices in times of scarcity, but others might not have been able to do so. Average prices reflect all those factors that affect agricultural production, but on average, not for actual producers. So actual producers could not expect to have such returns, whether they were as high as 314% or as low as 31%, for a long period. But they could expect that return for a normal year, at average prices, during the 1790s.

Cattle raising is a different type of business. Whereas wheat agriculture has an annual cycle, a complete cattle cycle takes 4 years, the period necessary to go from dry cows to fully grown steers. Azara took into account neither this factor nor the cost of land and livestock to produce steers or seed to produce wheat. Labor (physical labor, not its cost) was the only factor considered by Azara. Considering the cattle cycle and the cost of land, livestock, and labor, his profit estimate can be substantially improved. Although based upon information supplied by Azara and the study of the López Osornio estancia, what follows is a model. Its aim is not to determine the profitability of cattle raising but rather to show the evolution of profit rates in the long run.

According to Azara, one man could take care of 1,000 head of cattle. At a reproduction rate of 22% (the López Osornio estancia average for 1791–1795, see Table 2.4), these head would yield 220 calves in one year (Table 10.1). Assuming the 1,000-head herd included head of different ages, a 7% extraction rate (the López Osornio estancia average for 1791–1795, in Table 2.4) would mean the sale of 70 head. At the average price of 3 pesos per head (Table 2.3), that sale would produce 210 pesos. As 220 calves were born and 70 head were sold in the first year, 150 head were added to the original herd. The capitalization of these head, at the average head value of 1 peso $1\frac{1}{4}$ reales (1.281 pesos, the average value of the López Osornio stock, see Table 2.3), generates 192 pesos as non-cashed income. Total income (sales + capitalization) was 402 pesos for the first year.

For this model, capital is just the cattle stock. At the same average head value, the original 1,000-head herd was worth 1,281 pesos. At a stocking rate of 3 hectares per head, 1,000 head required 3,000 hectares. At 2.96 reales per hectare, the value of that extension was 1,110 pesos. Estimating the rent as the opportunity cost of retaining that capital on land, at the usual 6% interest rate the annual rent for that tract is 67 pesos. Assuming that labor costs are 0.087 peso per head (the average expenses in peons and slaves on the López Osornio estancia for 1791–1795, see Table 2.5), labor expenses for 1,000 head are 87 pesos. Total expenses (rent + labor) are 154 pesos. Profit (sales + expenses) is 56 pesos. The profit rate (profit as percentage of capital) is 4.4%. Considering a 15% capitalization rate, the total profit rate (profit + capitalization as percentage of capital) is 19.4% for the first year.

In the second year, the stock is 1,150 head, as a consequence of the addition of 150 head to the original 1,000-head herd. The reproduction and extraction rates are the same as for the first year. Because averages were used, they are assumed to be constant. Assuming an increasing productivity of the land, the rent does not change. The cost of labor increases in proportion to the number of head because labor productivity is assumed to be constant. The profit rate in the second year is 5.2% and, as the capitalization rate is constant, the total profit rate is 20.2%.

Following the same procedure, the profit rate grows from 5.7% in the third year to 7.6% in the eighth year, and the total profit rate grows from 20.7% to 22.6% in the same period. For further years the model should take into account the stocking rate. In the first year the stocking rate was 3 h/LU but, in the eighth year, as an increasing productivity of land was assumed, the stocking rate is 1.13 h/LU. This figure is in between the

Table 10.1. *Estancia profitability around 1800: An elaboration of Azara's model*

Year	Stock N	Reproduction N	Income Sales N	Income Sales V	Capitalization N	Capitalization V	Income V
1	1,000	220	70	210	150	192	402
2	1,150	253	81	243	172	220	463
3	1,322	291	93	279	198	254	533
4	1,520	334	106	318	228	292	610
5	1,748	385	122	366	263	337	703
6	2,011	442	141	423	301	386	809
7	2,312	509	162	486	347	445	931
8	2,659	585	186	558	399	511	1,069

Year	Capital	Rent	Labor	Expenditure and Profit Total expenses	Profit	Profit rate	Capitalization rate	Total profit rate
1	1,281	67	87	154	56	4.4	15	19.4
2	1,473	67	100	167	76	5.2	15	20.2
3	1,693	67	115	182	97	5.7	15	20.7
4	1,947	67	132	199	119	6.1	15	21.1
5	2,239	67	152	219	147	6.6	15	21.6
6	2,576	67	175	242	181	7.0	15	22.0
7	2,962	67	201	268	218	7.4	15	22.4
8	3,407	67	231	298	260	7.6	15	22.6

Note: N = number of head; V = pesos of 8 reales. Stock = previous year's stock + previous year's capitalization. Reproduction = 22% of a year's stock. Sales (extraction rate) = 7% of a year's stock. Capitalization = reproduction – sales. Income = sales + capitalization. Capital = stock at the average head value of 1 peso 2¼ reales. Rent = 6% over the estimated price of 3,000 hectares at 2.96 reales per hectare. Labor: estimated expenses according to the number of head. Total expenses = rent + labor. Profit = sales – total expenses. Capital, rent, labor, total expenses, and profit are in pesos of 8 reales. Profit rate: profit as percentage of capital. Capitalization rate: capitalization as percentage of capital. Total profit rate: profit + capitalization as percentage of capital.
Sources: for cattle reproduction and extraction rates, see Table 2.4 (the average for 1791–1795); for the average head value, see Table 2.3; for rent, see this chapter; for labor expenses, see Table 2.5 (average expenses in peons and slaves, 1791–1795).

average stocking rates found in the North, 1.01 h/LU, and the Center, 1.24 h/LU, in 1820 (Table 5.7). That 3,000-hectare estancia, therefore, had reached the limit of its expansion. Consequently, capitalization would not be possible and the extraction rate (sales) should be equivalent to the reproduction rate. From the ninth year onward, a total profit rate of 22.6% is expected.

For this estimate it has been assumed that: (1) land was bought or rented; (2) its productivity increased (the same extension for a growing number of head); (3) labor productivity was constant, so labor expenses grew in proportion to the number of head; (4) the prices of an average head and a finished head remained constant; and (5) there were no expenses other than rent and labor, and no income other than the sale of finished head. Varying any of these assumptions, the outcome also varies. Labor expenses do not include the amortization of slaves. Only the actual labor expenses (excluding the foreman) on the López Osornio estancia in 1791– 1795 were considered. If the amortization of slaves is taken into account, labor expenses would be higher and, consequently, profit and the profit rate would be lower. This model requires increasing land productivity, but if land productivity remained constant at 3 hectares per head, the eighth year's stock would require 7,272 hectares, which would raise the rent to 161 pesos and lower the profit rate to 4.8% and the total profit rate to 19.8%.

In a real estancia, there were other expenses and other sources of income, and prices could vary according to the quality of cattle and market conditions. This model, moreover, also assumes perfect managerial and entrepreneurial skills – since wrong decisions are dismissed – as well as perfect conditions of production, because fires, droughts, and other natural and non-natural factors are not considered. This model shows, however, that no windfall immediate return could be expected from cattle raising but, in the long run, there were substantial and steady profit rates. It remains clear, therefore, that the economic logic of wheat agriculture and cattle raising were different. The former required a smaller capital investment for a quick but volatile return; the latter, a larger capital investment for a larger profit in the long run.

These are the economic reasons for the survival of agriculture around 1800 in spite of Azara's dooming analysis. Survival was not easy, since other factors contributed to the crisis. Price regulation, adopted to favor urban consumers, affected wheat production to a larger extent than cattle raising. Whereas wheat producers saw the price of their final product frequently regulated by the Cabildo, cattle ranchers were less affected by the regulation of beef prices because hide, tallow, grease, mane, and bone prices, which accounted all together for about 40% to 50% of a head's final price, were not regulated.[5] Moreover, although fresh beef could be sold only in Buenos Aires, other cattle by-products were steadily demanded in overseas markets. Around 1800, therefore, wheat agriculture was attractive for small and occasional producers, while cattle raising required a larger investment and a longer commitment to make a profit out of it.

This analysis, an elaboration of Azara's model, aims at explaining the economic rationality of both types of production. Models are not to be

5 Beef accounted for 39% to 53% of the final price of a head of cattle, according to three different estimates made in 1834, 1836, and 1846. See de Angelis (1834), 179; RO (1836), 114–119; Mackinnon (1957), 157–158.

confused with reality. In the real world, for example, there were also small cattle ranchers, as shown by the 1789 estancia return. Whatever the size of the cattle enterprise, however, its economic foundations were those already outlined. No quick profits, a long-run capitalization by keeping a healthy difference between the rates of cattle reproduction and extraction, and increasing land productivity were characteristic of all cattle enterprises.

Wheat farming around 1800 was profitable but in critical shape, as Azara and many other enlightened observers pointed out.[6] What happened after 1810 remains unclear: An economic analysis of the evolution (perhaps stagnation, or even decline) of agriculture is still missing. Estancia inventories show that agriculture was still practiced in the 1820s and the 1850s as a complementary activity. Chacras around Buenos Aires did not disappear, even when the opening of the port made room for foreign flour, mainly Brazilian and American.[7] The consumer-oriented approach was not completely abandoned, so bread and beef prices suffered regulations from time to time. But agriculture, even without those restrictions, could not develop as cattle ranching did. Foreign demand, not local consumption, was pushing the frontier to the south, opening up new lands for cattle ranching. No foreign markets existed in the early nineteenth century for Buenos Aires wheat. Agriculture survived, but cattle ranching was the leading economic activity since the time of Azara's analysis, for the sound reasons explained by him.

Estancia profitability, 1831

Woodbine Parish's inquisitive spirit prompted a memorandum on the Buenos Aires trade, submitted to him by the local British merchants, and reports on agricultural and livestock production in Buenos Aires, San Juan, and La Rioja.[8] The report about Buenos Aires was written by Pedro Trapani, a well-known merchant and estanciero in the 1820s and early 1830s. Parish posed several questions to him in order to understand how estancias were run and what their profits were. Another set of questions inquired about chacras. Trapani did not answer those questions in strict order, but he presented a budget for the establishment of an estancia.

6 Belgrano (1954) and Vieytes (1956). See also Weinberg (1956). Garavaglia (1985) and (1989), García Belsunce (1988), and Gelman (1992a) have emphasized the importance of agricultural production in the Buenos Aires area during the late colonial period, but the economic reasons of the crisis of agricultural production in the early nineteenth century remain unexplained.
7 For the location of chacras around 1790, see Borrero (1911), 4.
8 The British merchants' report has been published in Humphreys (1940), 26–62. For a Spanish translation, see Barba (1978). Pedro Trapani's report is in the PRO, Foreign Office 354/8, Woodbine Parish Papers, 66v–67. See also Barba (1967), 65–68. On Woodbine Parish's mission in Buenos Aires, see Kay-Shuttleworth (1910), 266–380. The author was Sir Woodbine's granddaughter.

Table 10.2. *Pedro Trapani's model estancia, 1831: Capital structure*

	Initial investment		After 6 years	
	pesos	%	pesos	%
Land	24,000	41.1	24,000	19.8
Improvements	7,000	12.0	5,000	4.1
Tools	1,750	3.0	1,050	0.9
Cattle	21,960	37.6	70,900	58.5
Horses	2,450	4.2	10,680	8.8
Sheep	1,250	2.1	9,500	7.8
Total	58,410	100	121,300	100

Source: PRO, Foreign Office 354/8, Woodbine Parish Papers, 67.

Parish asked Trapani (1) what could be considered the average price of land suitable for an estancia, and on what terms land was granted on emphyteusis; (2) what the number of cattle considered as fair stock was on any estancia of a given extent, and what the fair price of cattle to stock an estancia was; (3) what the yearly increase of cattle was; (4) what the number that could be killed every year was; and (5) what the usual estimates of expenses and profit were.

Trapani's budget for the establishment of an estancia included 24,000 pesos for 1.5 square leagues of land; 6,000 pesos for wood for corrals and buildings; 1,000 pesos for ditches; 750 pesos for tools, furniture, and utensils; 21,000 pesos for cattle of all ages and types; 700 pesos for mares and 1,750 pesos for horses; 1,250 pesos for sheep; 960 pesos for oxen; and 1,000 pesos for carts (Table 10.2). Land accounted for 41% of the initial investment; improvements (woods and ditches) for 12%; tools (including carts) for 3%; cattle (including oxen) for 38%; horses for 4%; and sheep for 2%. This estimate was an intermediate step in the evolution of the capital structure from 1820 to 1850, since land accounts for more and cattle for less than in the 1820s.

Annual expenses for that estancia amounted to 3,200 pesos: 840 pesos for a foreman; 2,160 pesos for six peons; and 200 pesos for foodstuffs (salt, green peppers, yerba mate, etc.). It should be noted that no slaves are mentioned.

Profit resulted, according to Trapani, from a 30–35% annual reproduction rate for cattle and horses, and 80–90% for sheep. From that reproduction would come the steers to be sold at 25–30 pesos (those from 2 to 3 years old) and at 34–38 pesos (those from 3 to 4 years old). The average price for a head of cattle according to the budget was 7 pesos. It should be noted that the difference between those head and finished, 3- to 4-year-old steers is 1 : 4.8, the same as that found in the López Osornio estancia, where cattle of all types and ages were sold in 1785 at 5 reales, while several years later finished cattle reached 3 pesos per head. Profit would also come from the hides of cattle consumed on the estancias, and from tallow and grease from those head. It should also be noted that no income is estimated for the sale of sheep, wool, or sheepskins. The consumption of mutton on the estancia seems to have been the main reason for the existence of that flock of sheep.

In order to make clearer for Parish the result of the operations of that model estancia, Trapani presented an account of income and expenditure for a 6-year period, "not taking into account droughts and other unexpected events." According to Trapani's estimate, after 6 years the value of land, livestock, improvements, and all other items on the estancia, plus the sales of estancia products during those 6 years, would have amounted to 189,220 pesos. Taking away the original investment, 58,410 pesos, and labor expenses for 19,200 pesos, a profit of 111,610 pesos is reached. Dividing this figure by the number of years, Barba estimated that the resulting 18,601-peso average annual profit mentioned by Trapani was equivalent to an annual profit rate of 31.4%.[9] According to Trapani's estimate, the annual profit should rise to 25,000 pesos in the seventh year, and in subsequent years the annual "increase" (cattle reproduction?, profit?) should be from 30% to 35% (of cattle stock?, of capital investment?). A closer look at those accounts of income and expenditure yields a different result, although still quite positive. First, those accounts should be rearranged; then, the cumulative rate of profit should be estimated for the 6-year period; and, finally, price fluctuations should be considered.

A rearrangement of those accounts shows that after 6 years, land value is still at 24,000 pesos, accounting for 20% of total value; improvements are worth 5,000 pesos, and account for 4% of total value; tools, for 1,050 pesos and 1%; cattle, for 70,900 pesos and 58%; horses, for 10,680 pesos and 9%; and sheep, for 9,500 pesos and 8%. The capital structure after 6 years of operations was, therefore, quite similar to that of the Azul estancias in 1839 (where land accounted for 26% and cattle for 66%). In Trapani's model estancia total value stood at 121,130 pesos, which, compared to the original investment of 58,410 pesos, means an increase of 62,720 pesos, mainly due to cattle capitalization (78% of the increase was due to that factor).

Over the 6-year period, cattle sales would have produced 54,000 pesos; hides, 10,080 pesos; tallow, 1,800 pesos; grease, 1,890 pesos; and horns, 320 pesos. Total income was estimated at 68,090 pesos (Table 10.3). Total

9 Barba (1967) used the arithmetical mean rather than the cumulative rate.

Table 10.3. *Pedro Trapani's model estancia, 1831:*
6-year income and expenditure accounts

Income	pesos	Outlay	pesos
Steers	54,000	Peons' wages	19,200
Hides	10,080	Sheep losses	1,250
Tallow	1,800	Sheep consumed	3,000
Lard	1,890	Steers consumed	6,300
Horns	320	Subtotal	29,750
Subtotal	68,090		
Livestock capitalization	62,720	Profit	101,060
Total	130,810	Total	130,810

Source: See Table 10.2.

expenditure was estimated at 29,750 pesos due to peons' salaries (19,200 pesos), the loss of sheep (1,250 pesos), sheep consumption (3,000 pesos), and cattle consumption (6,300 pesos). The difference between income and expenditure was 38,340 pesos. Adding this figure to 62,720 pesos of non-cashed profit, total profit rises to 101,060 pesos, which represents a profit rate of 173% for the 6-year period, equivalent to 18.2% per year.

The 25,000-peso profit estimated by Trapani for the seventh year was equivalent to 20.6% of the total value of the estancia at the end of the sixth year. A higher figure can be obtained, however, following Trapani's previous estimate for the first 6 years. The implicit rate of reproduction for that period was 29.7% for cattle, 28.7% for horses, and 49% for sheep. Using these rates the 4,670 head of cattle found on the estancia at the end of the sixth year would have produced 1,387 head in the seventh year; 682 horses would have produced 196 colts; and 3,800 sheep, 1,862 lambs. Some of those head (or others previously held) would be sold, being then cashed profit, and the rest would be non-cashed profit. Following the pattern of the first 6 years, 300 steers would be sold at 30 pesos each, for a total of 9,000 pesos; 75 hides (resulting from beef cattle consumption on the estancia) at 22.5 pesos each, for 1,687.5 pesos; 37.5 arrobas of tallow at 8 pesos each, for 300 pesos; 22.5 arrobas of grease at 14 pesos each, for 315 pesos; and 150 horns at 40 pesos per hundred, 60 pesos. Total income for the seventh year would have been 11,363 pesos. To that amount should be added a total non-cashed profit of 22,935 pesos resulting from 1,087 calves at 14 pesos each (15,218 pesos); 1,862 lambs at 2.5 pesos each (4,655 pesos); 118 colts at 7 pesos each (826 pesos); 52 entire horses at 35 pesos each (1,820 pesos); and 26 foals at 16 pesos each (416 pesos). From that amount, 5,149 pesos for expenses should be taken away. Following the pattern of the first 6 years, that amount would have been formed by peons' wages for 3,200 pesos; beef cattle consumption, 1,050 pesos (75 head at 14 pesos each); mutton consumption, 500 pesos (200 sheep at 2.5 each); depreciation of tools and improvements, 191 pesos; and the loss of sheep, 208 pesos (83 sheep at 2.5 pesos each).

Adding cashed income (11,363 pesos) and non-cashed income (22,935 pesos), the total income would have been 34,298 pesos. Taking away expenses for 5,149 pesos, total cashed and non-cashed profit would have been 29,149 pesos, equivalent to 24.1% of the total value of the estancia at the end of the 6-year period. That rate of profit is negatively affected by a factor neither taken into account in this estimate nor in Trapani's: increasing land productivity, since the number of livestock grew but the size of the estancia remained unchanged. The limit of livestock density could have been reached already and overpassed, so that the estancia could not continue to rely on cattle capitalization. Livestock would have had to be sold at prices conceivably as high as their inventory value, which might explain the lower figure for the rate of profit for the seventh year given by Trapani.

These estimates, as Trapani remarked, referred to an ideal case, not to the real world. In the real world, there were droughts, such as the one plaguing Buenos Aires at that very time, and fluctuating prices. Although in nominal terms price fluctuations, according to Broide's composite livestock price index, were not so dramatic, paper money itself lost 21% of its value vis-à-vis the ounce of gold from December 1831 to December 1837. Estimating livestock prices in ounces of gold, the composite price index dropped 12% in December 1837 and 43% in December 1838 when compared with December 1833 (there are no figures for 1831 and 1832). The figure for 1838 was due to the interruption of the export trade by the French blockade – war, civil or foreign, was also a factor affecting prices.[10]

In constant money, ruling out natural and political factors that could disturb rural production or exports, or both, 18.2% per year was the return that an expert thought could be expected from estancia operations. But neither Trapani nor anybody else could predict the evolution of those unexpected factors, unrelated to production itself, which could easily bring down the expected rate of return.

That rate of return, however, when compared to the current rate of interest, bears a striking resemblance to the one found for the López Osornio estancia. For the period of normal operations (1791–1795), the average rate of profit was 8.7%, a rate that stood 45% above the 6% usual rate of interest. The rate of profit estimated here from Trapani's accounts, 18.2%, is 40% above the effective rate of interest yielded by the 6%

10 Broide (1951), 165, 169, 174.

provincial bonds, which were on average at 46% of their nominal value in 1832.[11] That extra profit, 40–45% above the rate yielded by loans in the 1790s and bonds in the 1830s, explains the expansion of cattle ranching on the pampas – a highly profitable undertaking if, as Trapani remarked, natural and political factors did not interfere.[12]

Estancia profitability, 1856

In 1856 the result of an inquiry on rural production carried out by Justo Maeso, head of the Buenos Aires Statistical Department, was published in the *Registro Estadístico de Buenos Aires*.[13] A circular had been sent to the justices of the peace in the countryside asking for their cooperation in getting information on the rural economy. The inquiry was divided into three parts: pastoral questions, agricultural questions, and industrial questions. Unlike Alsina's inquiry, which dealt with rural habits and customs affecting rural production, Maeso's focused upon rural production itself.

One of Maeso's questions was about the "result and product" of an estancia, "holding 10,000 head of cattle, in five good years, on fertile land with good watering places, at around 40 leagues from Buenos Aires." That was the distance to Dolores, beyond the Salado River, a region settled around 1820. Maeso also asked the same information for a sheep-breeding estancia, 30 leagues from Buenos Aires, the distance to the Salado River. Related to those questions, there were others on the most adequate time of the year for rural operations and on the profitability of cattle raising and horse, mule, and sheep breeding.

Three answers to that inquiry were published in the *Registro Estadístico*: those of Manuel Castaño, from Vecino; Bernardo Gutiérrez, from Mercedes; and the same Gutiérrez and Félix García, also from Mercedes. The second report referred to agricultural matters only; the first and the third, to livestock production. Gutiérrez and García gave detailed information on cattle raising and sheep breeding but refused to estimate "the product of an estancia of a determined number of head," as requested by Maeso. Such calculation "is subject to so many conditions and depends

11 For the quotation of the 6% bonds, see Burgin (1946), 210.
12 Parish also asked about the expenses to set up a chacra, and its economic result. Trapani responded that "according to the best information, the farmer would have to sow six consecutive years, after which he will obtain a 25% annual profit over any capital invested in such labor," assuming the countryside remained peaceful. Trapani's figures still show, as do Azara's, that agriculture required less capital than cattle raising but obtained a higher, more volatile return in the short run.
13 The circular was dated on 1 January 1856, but it was published, along with some of the results of the inquiry, in the issue of the *Registro Estadístico de Buenos Aires* dated in the second semester of 1855. Maeso's inquiry has been analyzed by Infesta de Guerci (1983).

Table 10.4. *Manuel Castaño's model estancia, 1856:*
Capital structure

| | Initial investment | | After 1 year | |
	pesos	%	pesos	%
Land	80,000	22.9	80,000	27.9
Improvements and tools	18,000	5.6	18,000	5.6
Cattle	168,000	52.2	126,600	44.1
Horses	20,500	6.3	18,400	6.4
Sheep	36,000	11.1	44,000	15.3
Total	323,100	100	287,000	100

Source: REBA (1855), 2:34.

upon so many circumstances that we abstain to deal with it." There were estancias, they continued, on rented land, paying a high rent, which in spite of that could get "more advantages" than other estancias with the same number of head on owned land. They said they would supply information, but not in a quantitative format, to let other, more learned people make their own estimates. Their refusal was not the result of ignorance but of the reliance on managerial and entrepreneurial skills to obtain a positive result of estancia operations.

Castaño was more forthcoming and went along with Maeso's exercise, analyzing, as requested, the expenses incurred by the establishment and operation of an estancia, albeit smaller than the one imagined by the inquirer. One square league was worth 80,000 pesos; improvements (buildings, wooden poles) and tools (including a cart), 18,000 pesos; 1,500 head of cattle at 110 pesos each, 165,000 pesos, and 6 oxen at 600 pesos each, 3,600 pesos; 2,000 mestizas sheep at 18 pesos each, 36,000 pesos; 200 breeding mares at 40 pesos each, 8,000 pesos; and 50 broken-in horses at 250 pesos each, 12,500 pesos (Table 10.4). Total investment to set up such an estancia was 323,100 pesos, of which 25% corresponded to land, 6% to improvements and tools, 52% to cattle, 11% to sheep, and 6% to horses.

Expenses for 1 year amounted to 20,000 pesos (Table 10.5). Of that amount 3,600 pesos were for the foreman; 5,400 pesos for three permanent peons at 150 pesos per month each; 6,000 pesos for two temporary peons for 10 months at 300 pesos per month each; 3,000 pesos for foodstuffs; and 2,000 pesos for extraordinary expenses. Cash income would come from the sale of 500 finished steers and cows at 280 pesos each, for a total of 140,000 pesos. And there would be a non-cash income, or livestock capitalization, of 13,000 pesos for 225 calves (the reproduction of the original 1,500 head of cattle at a reproduction rate of 15%) at 80 pesos each; 8,000 pesos from

Table 10.5. *Manuel Castaño's model estancia, 1856:*
1-year income and expenditure accounts

Income	pesos	Outlay	pesos
Cattle sold	140,000	Livestock decapitalization	57,500
Wool in storage	5,000	Foreman	3,600
Livestock capitalization	21,400	Permanent peons	5,400
Total	166,400	Temporary peons	6,000
		Foodstuffs	3,000
		Extraordinary expenses	2,000
		Subtotal	77,500
		Profit	88,900
		Total	166,400

Source: See Table 10.4.

1,000 lambs (the reproduction of the original 2,000 sheep at a 50% rate) at 8 pesos each; and 400 pesos for 20 colts (the reproduction of the original 200 mares at a 10% rate) at 20 pesos each.

Therefore, a cash income of 140,000 pesos and a non-cash income of 21,400 pesos, after taking away expenses for 20,000 pesos, left a profit of 141,400 pesos. To that amount 5,000 pesos should be added for 200 arrobas of mestiza wool at 25 pesos each. That wool was half the product of the existing sheep, the other half being used to pay for the shearing of the whole flock. Total profit, consequently, was 146,400 pesos. That figure did not, however, take into account cattle decapitalization, resulting from the sale of 500 head (while only 225 had been born) and the loss of 10 horses at 25 pesos each. The total value of the estancia at the end of the first year of operations had dropped, consequently, from the initial 323,100 pesos to 265,600 pesos. Taking away the difference, 57,500 pesos, from total profit, the new figure for total profit is 88,900 pesos, equivalent to a profit rate of 27.5%.

An analysis of the capital structure of that model estancia casts doubts on that rate. After 1 year the value of that square league of land remained the same, but the number and value of cattle had dropped, while the number and value of sheep had risen. In the second year, land accounted for 28% of total value, improvements and tools still for 6%, cattle for 44%, horses for 6%, and sheep for 15% (Table 10.4). That proportion of land value over total value looks very low when compared with the 51% average found in the 1850 inventories (Table 3.4). The difference is due to a higher livestock density in Castaño's model estancia. If its 1.3 h/LU density is lowered to 5.0 h/LU, as was the case for estancias in the New South in 1850

(Table 5.7), it can be assumed that the value of all LU could have been 27% of the value estimated by Castaño, since 3.7 times more land would have been necessary per head. In that case livestock value would have dropped from 189,000 (Table 10.4, right column) to 51,030, therefore land value (80,000 pesos) would have amounted to 54% of total value. Then, by lowering the livestock density on Castaño's model estancia, it is possible to place it within the same range found in the 1850 inventories for the New South, where land value was 64% of total value (Table 3.4). Castaño was therefore using for his estimate livestock densities found in the older regions and land values found in the New South. That can be one of the reasons for such a high profit rate. Higher land values, as in the older regions, or lower stocking rates would have brought his profit rate down.

From a different perspective, it should be noted that Castaño's 1-year estimate looks more realistic than Trapani's 6-year account. The sale of finished cattle was designed to prevent an excessive increase of livestock density, already at 1.3 h/LU in the first year. That factor was not taken into account at all by Trapani, whose model estancia goes from an initial density of 2.3 h/LU to another of 0.7 h/LU 6 years later. For Castaño, maintaining the proper stocking rate (el campo desahogado) was the only secret for better development of all breeds, better hides, and faster finishing of livestock. And for him the proper density was 1,500 head of cattle, 2,000 sheep, and 200 horses on 1 square league, equivalent to 1.35 h/LU. This difference may be due to the fact that Trapani could still rely on vacant neighboring land to relieve his own estancia from excess head, but for Castaño, 25 years later, that was no longer an option.

Conclusion

Annual profit rates of 30% for the Buenos Aires estancias by the mid-nineteenth century were considered the usual rates, but some producers greatly exaggerated their returns. Few detailed contemporary estimates are available to assess those guesses properly. Two of them have been analyzed here: Pedro Trapani's of 1831, and Manuel Castaño's of 1856. According to information provided by the former for a 6-year period, an annual profit rate of 18.2% has been estimated here, and according to the latter's information for just 1 year, the rate has been estimated at 27.5%. These figures were obtained by rearranging data from models, not from actual accounts and inventories. It is clear in both cases that many factors operating in the real world, but not taken into account for those estimates, would have brought those figures down.

Estancia operations were profitable, but profit was neither stable nor assured. Favorable natural and political conditions and the appropriate managerial and entrepreneurial skills were necessary. When all those conditions were present, cattle raising and sheep breeding were a prosperous business, although annual profit rates were lower than 30%. Another case – this one belonging to the real world, that of estancia "Los Merinos," studied by Infesta – does not depart from that pattern. Inventories and accounts for a 32-month period, from February 1838 to September 1840, show an annual profit rate of 16.5%. There was no cash income due to the French blockade, but the estancia increased its livestock. This case also proves how political factors could affect production. The accounts ended in September 1840 because that estancia was one of the many rural properties seized by the Rosas government.[14] It should be stressed that values were estimated in paper money, and paper money was fluctuating at a rate different from that of other goods. Broide's composite livestock index rose 13.6% in paper pesos in those 32 months, but the quotation of an ounce of gold (specie was the ultimate means of payment) increased 170% in paper pesos in the same period. Although profit was negative in terms of specie, taking away 4.9% per year (as the depreciation of paper money in terms of livestock by-products) from the 16.5% profit rate (in paper money), there still is an 11.6% annual profit rate for the estancia during that brief period.

Profitable as it was, livestock production was far from yielding those fantastic returns found in some contemporary sources or even those more moderate estimates from rural producers such as Trapani or Castaño, whose ideal conditions were hard to get in this world. Legend, however, seemed more powerful than truth, as had been the case with Potosí's riches, which declined to the point of extinction after the wars of independence but were still attracting the attention of British investors. Those interested in bringing European immigrants to the still sparsely populated pampas fostered the legend. That seems to be the case with Louis Guilaine, who in 1889 estimated an average profit rate of 45% per year for a cattle-raising estancia over a 4-year period. His estimate, however, while requiring ideal natural and political conditions, did not take into account the cost of land and improvements. Whether Guilaine's book misled any Frenchmen regarding the conditions of production and profit rates prevailing on the pampas is not known to us. It is difficult, however, to believe that it had any other purpose.[15]

A much more balanced view on this issue is that of Richard Napp, whose book, published in 1876, also described the country's wealth. Although not directly aimed at attracting immigration, he insisted that more immigrants were badly needed. For a Buenos Aires sheep-breeding estancia, Napp estimated an annual profit of 20% on the capital invested,

14 Infesta de Guerci (1983).
15 Guilaine (1889), 138–139.

including livestock capitalization. He pointed out also that a 25% profit was more usual and even 35% was not uncommon. His estimate remarks on the entry cost due to high land values but disregards natural and political factors affecting production in the long run.[16]

Even Napp's profit rate estimate is high when compared to some estimates of actual estancia operations in the late 1870s. Juan Fair's "El Espartillar," in Chascomús, valued at 14.3 million pesos, yielded an annual profit ranging from 1.9 to 2.4 million pesos, equivalent to a profit rate ranging from 13.3% to 16.8%. And Samuel B. Hale's "Tatay," in Carmen de Areco, valued at 15,950,000 pesos, yielded 2,167,019 pesos, equivalent to an annual profit rate of 13.6%. Both were described as model establishments, so these profit rates corresponded to some of the better-managed and better-organized estancias.[17]

The best summary of the issue of estancia profitability is Gutiérrez and García's answer to Maeso's inquiry: Profit depended so much upon natural, political, market, and entrepreneurial factors that general estimates would mean little for understanding individual cases. On the whole, however, when considering the amazing territorial and commercial expansion that started in the late eighteenth century and accelerated after 1820, it seems clear that the cattle-raising business was certainly highly profitable. Whether it was so for a particular enterprise during a particular period is a different matter.

Rural producers enjoyed no rents. As beneficiaries of no privilege, they had to compete for overseas markets producing livestock by-products at a cost low enough to bear the handling, transportation, insurance, and other expenses incurred in order to reach those markets. Because their products were esteemed but not strategic, and because those markets were supplied by other producing regions, international prices were for the Buenos Aires producers a given factor, which they were in no position to alter. Markets for hides, tallow, and wool were certainly expanding, but profits were not guaranteed. This chapter has been devoted to the analysis of profit of rural enterprises. The next chapter, dealing with overseas market conditions, studies the framework within which the Buenos Aires entrepreneurs prospered.

16 Napp (1876), 307–308, 335.

17 Jurado, Newton, and Jurado (1878), 500; and Jurado, Almeida, and Jurado (1879), 135. Sabato's profit rate estimates for a 10,000-hectare sheep-breeding estancia in the 1860s and 1870s are 13% and 11%. Those declining rates (when compared to her higher estimates for previous decades) are due to land valorization. See Sabato (1989), 156.

11

Prices and marketing

Ships arriving in Buenos Aires in the seventeenth and early eighteenth centuries carried people more interested in the riches of Upper Peru than in the meager return that local goods provided for such a long and risky trip. But hides were abundant in Buenos Aires as a consequence of the proliferation of wild cattle on the pampas and the hunting activities of the natives, the vaquerías. So hides were, if not so profitable a return as silver, at least a convenient load for ships sailing back on ballast.

The annual average number of hides exported from Buenos Aires in the second half of the seventeenth century was 26,000 units, but due to the progressive extermination of wild herds, it fell to 16,000 hides between 1721 and 1738.[1] For 1756–1766 the average rose to 87,600 hides per year, and during the following decade, 1767–1776, it only remained at 88,700 hides per year. A sharp contrast is offered by the figures for exports after the 1778 free trade regulations came into force. The annual average for 1777–1786 was 173,400 hides, and 331,500 hides for 1787–1796 (Figure 11.1).[2] Those figures are for Buenos Aires only, without taking contraband into account. The remarkable growth rate should be stressed over the absolute figures. There was a 278% increase from the 1756–1766 average to that of 1787–1796, equivalent to a rate of growth of 4.5% per year.

Other sources put total hide exports at 447,000 hides per year (53% supplied by the Banda Oriental and 47% by Buenos Aires) for 1777–1784, and 743,000 hides for 1793–1796.[3] This represented a 66% increase in about 13 years, equivalent to a 4% annual rate of growth. If the proportion of total hide exports contributed by Buenos Aires (and the other regions whose share cannot be accurately determined, except for the Banda Orien-

---

1 For 1648–1702, see Moutoukias (1988), 178. For 1721–1738, see Coni (1979), 56–58.
2 Moutoukias (1995).
3 For 1779–1784, see Garavaglia (1977), 97; for 1793–1796, see Haenke (1943), 86, quoted by Montoya (1984), 301.

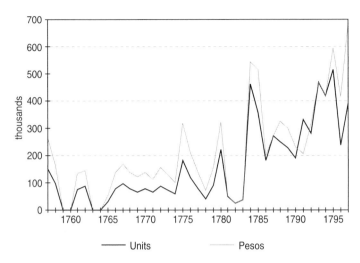

Figure 11.1. Buenos Aires: Hide exports, 1756–1796. *Source*: See Appendix C for the sources of all figures in this chapter.

tal) had remained unchanged, it would have amounted to 349,000 hides in the early 1790s.

The consequences of the free trade regulations can also be observed through the figures for Cádiz hide imports. Although the origin of those is not given, it can be safely assumed that most were from Río de la Plata. In 1729–1738 the annual average (repeating the previous year's figures when data are not available) of hides imported into Cádiz was as low as 1,900 hides; in 1751–1760 it was 42,600; in 1761–1770, 79,200; in 1771–1777, 161,800; and the estimated annual average imports for 1782–1791 and 1792–1796, based upon a constant price of 3 pesos per hide, were 319,000 and 460,000 hides. This estimate might be too low, however, since on average 712,000 hides were exported from the Río de la Plata to Spain from 1790 to 1794, according to the Buenos Aires Royal Customs administrator.[4] The disparity of such figures may be explained by a different price for hides imported into Cádiz and by exports to other Spanish ports.

After 1810 complete free trade was introduced, and hide exports went up. Figures for hide exports after 1810 are more precise than those for the colonial period. Buenos Aires exported an average of 570,000 hides per year in the 1810s, 620,000 in the 1820s, and 2,700,000 around 1850. In

4 García-Baquero González (1976), 2:228ff.; Fisher (1985), 74; and Barba (1955a), 279.

all those cases, Buenos Aires's own share over total exports was much higher than in the 1780s.[5]

Hide exports, and later the export of other livestock by-products, were possible because of adequate conditions of production present on the pampas and steady overseas demand for those products, but also because of profitable conditions of commercialization. The right conditions of production or the steady overseas demand did not necessarily bring about the expansion of production and trade that Buenos Aires experienced from the late eighteenth century onward. The right conditions of commercialization had to be present also.

Consequently, this chapter is devoted to the study of prices and other market conditions that made possible (from an economic perspective) the commercialization of Buenos Aires livestock by-products.[6] First, the evolution of hide prices in Buenos Aires and some of the main markets for its products is analyzed. The right marketing conditions meant nothing without a price gap between Buenos Aires and potential markets, and, in the absence of abundant information on marketing conditions, observing the evolution of prices in different markets is a way to understand why that trade was possible. Second, marketing conditions, the actual or potential profits from the hide trade, are considered. An estimate of the profit expected from hide exports in 1768 shows the result of an export operation to Spain before that process of expansion began, and estimates of the cost of exporting livestock by-products to Britain around 1830 and 1850 are studied to estimate the potential profit that could be expected from such operations. The estimates carried out in this chapter underscore the factors involved in the hide trade and its rationality.

Prices

The commercialization of hides (or other livestock by-products) was possible due to a price differential between Buenos Aires and overseas markets. The price paid for hides by the Buenos Aires merchants had to be enough for them and for producers to pay for their costs and make a profit. Obviously, the same can be said for overseas importers. The behavior of Buenos Aires and overseas prices shows the reasons for the continuation and intensification of the hide trade from the 1790s onward.

---

5 Data for 1811–1823 are from Humphreys (1940), 59–60; and those for 1825, 1829, and 1849–1851, from Parish (1852), 353–354. For estimates of the share of the Buenos Aires countryside over total hide exports, see Chapter 5, this text.

6 For the mechanisms of commercialization, see Brown (1978) and (1979), passim; Reber (1978) and (1979), 55–109; Sabato (1989), 203–251.

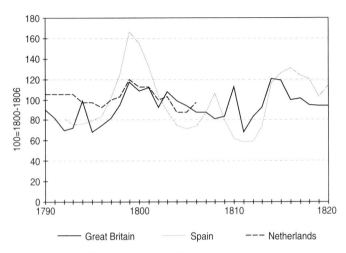

Figure 11.2. Hide prices in three European countries, 1790–1820.

European hide prices from 1790 to 1820 behave in a way that partially anticipates the reasons for the Buenos Aires hide-export success. Whether those prices were remunerative or not is not possible to tell, but fluctuations were not similar for all countries. So, in a context of complete free trade (only true after 1810), exporters could have taken advantage of such differences to get a better price for their hides. Hide prices peaked in Spain (Cádiz) around 1800, and again after 1814 (Figure 11.2).[7] On the other hand, with the exception of 1809–1813, hide prices did not reach a depression in Spain, Britain, and the Netherlands at the same time. During that period French prices had skyrocketed due to the Napoleonic wars, but because of that very reason, Buenos Aires hides could not reach that market. The pattern, however, is clear: Hide prices varied in different markets according to different local conditions affecting demand. It was up to local importers and the Buenos Aires exporters to take advantage of such fluctuations. Considering the 6-month delay (at least) from the moment of placing an order to the moment of receiving the hides, as well as the fact that averages could be far from single-transaction prices, it becomes apparent that the ability to take advantage of favorable market conditions was always accompanied by uncertainty.

For a few years, from 1792 to 1796, there are figures for Cádiz and

7 Hide prices for Spain, Britain, and the Netherlands are from Cuenca Esteban (1990), 391–395.

Table 11.1. *Hide prices: Cádiz and*
Buenos Aires, 1792–1796 (in reales)

	Cádiz	Buenos Aires	
	35 lb	30 lb	35 lb
1792	45	8	9.4
1793	41.7	8	9.4
1794	42.3	12	14
1795	43.8	14	16.3
1796	46.3	14	16.3

Note: 8 reales = 1 peso.
Sources: For Cádiz, Cuenca Esteban (1990), 391; for
Buenos Aires, Moutoukias (1995), passim.

Buenos Aires prices.[8] The former are market prices, whereas the latter are
implicit prices obtained by dividing the total value of hide exports by the
total number of hides. The implicit price of a hide in Buenos Aires was 1
peso for 1792 and 1793, 1.5 pesos for 1794, and 1.75 pesos for 1795 and
1796. Buenos Aires hide prices are per unit, whereas Cádiz prices are for
35 lbs. Assuming that Buenos Aires hides weighed on average 30 lbs, the
average price in Buenos Aires for each 35-lb pesada would have been 1.17
pesos for 1792–1793, 1.75 pesos for 1794, and 2.04 pesos for 1795–1796.
Prices in Cádiz ranged from a low 5.2 pesos in 1793 to a high of 5.8 pesos
in 1796 (Table 11.1). Although the price differential was substantial,
transportation expenses from Buenos Aires to Cádiz were also significant.
The Marqués del Real Thesoro estimated that the cost of hides in Buenos
Aires was 18.2% of total expenses for heifer hides, 22.9% for cow and steer
hides, and 32.5% for ox hides.[9] An ox hide of an average weight of 36 lbs
6 ounces cost 13 reales in Buenos Aires. So 35 lbs would cost 12.5 reales in
Buenos Aires and 41 reales in Cádiz. In spite of the Cádiz price being 3.3
times higher than that of Buenos Aires, profit left by ox hides was rather
low due to transportation expenses. Profit was better for cow, steer, and
heifer hides. Converting their prices into 35-lb pesadas, the former were at
9.1 reales in Buenos Aires, and the latter at 7.1 reales, whereas their price
in Cádiz was 48 reales for both. Cádiz prices were therefore 5.3 times and
6.8 times higher than Buenos Aires prices. In those cases profits left by
cow, steer, and heifer hides were handsome. In 1792 and 1793, Cádiz
prices were 4.8 times higher than Buenos Aires prices, but in 1794 the
former were only 3 times higher, and in 1795 and 1796, only 2.7 and 2.8

8 For Cádiz, see Cuenca Esteban (1990), 391; for Buenos Aires, see Moutoukias (1995).
9 AGN, Biblioteca Nacional 184/1284.

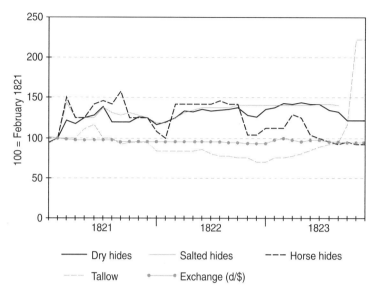

Figure 11.3. Current price of Buenos Aires produce and exchange rate,
1821–1823.

times higher. If transportation expenses remained the same as in 1768,
Cádiz prices for the last 3 years of that sequence were not too attractive.

Hide prices in Buenos Aires also varied as a result of the fluctuation of
overseas prices and supply conditions. Those fluctuations affected not just
hide prices, but the prices of all agricultural goods. For a short span of 3
years, from 1821 to 1823, it can be seen that dry and salted cow hides,
horse hides, and tallow (all of them export products with a limited domestic demand) suffered fluctuations in spite of a stable exchange rate (Figure
11.3).[10] When attention is paid to the evolution of the price of one product,
dry hides, taking into account both high and low monthly averages, those
fluctuations become more marked. The highest monthly price is on average
13% higher than the lowest monthly price during those 3 years, but it was
5% higher in October 1821 and 32% higher in November and December
1823. Such fluctuations cannot be attributed to sudden outbursts of foreign demand or to a drastic variation of the amount of money in circulation, which would have affected the rate of exchange. Bank notes were
issued in Buenos Aires as of September 1822, but they remained convertible up to January 1826. Even before conversion was abandoned, credit

10 PRO, Foreign Office 354/8, ff. 34v–35, Woodbine Parish Papers, "Price current of produce in
Buenos Ayres in the years 1821, 1822, 1823." See also Humphreys (1940).

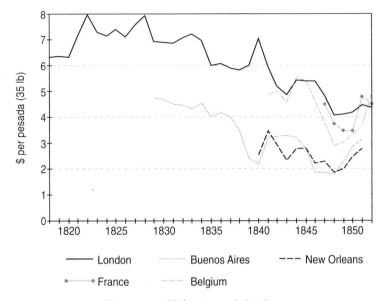

Figure 11.4. Hide prices, 1818–1852.

(and, consequently, non-specie means of payment) expanded, but that expansion took place in 1824 and 1825, not in 1823. So price fluctuations in 1823 were due to market conditions. The peak was reached in the first months of 1823, when Indian incursions were perhaps disrupting the normal flow of agricultural goods to the Buenos Aires market. Price fluctuations are a regular feature of all economies and do not necessarily mean inflation. In that case, if the early-1823 peak was due to Indian activity, high prices were reflecting an increasing cost of transportation from the countryside to Buenos Aires.

The advantage that Buenos Aires hides enjoyed in overseas markets is revealed when Buenos Aires and overseas prices are compared (Figure 11.4). Hide prices in London remained fairly stable until the early 1830s, when a downturn lasting to the late 1840s began. A new stability was reached then, but at a much lower level than in the 1820s. Hide prices in Belgium and France, available from 1841 and 1847 onward, show a pattern very similar to British prices. Buenos Aires prices also followed a curve similar to that of British prices, but at a lower level. That gap between local and overseas prices was the main reason for the hide trade. The correspondence between Buenos Aires and European prices is altered more by the 1838–1840 blockade than by the blockade of 1845–1847. The trend for Buenos Aires hide prices was downward from 1829 to 1840;

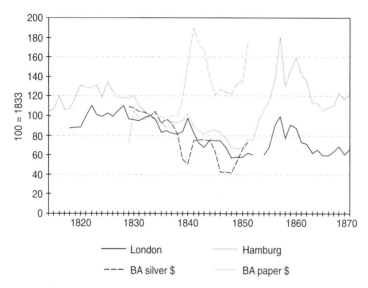

Figure 11.5. Buenos Aires hides: Price indexes, 1814–1870.

there was a rise from 1841 and 1844, with a new decline reaching the lowest level from 1846 to 1848, and a recovery from 1849 to 1851. New Orleans prices, available from 1840 onward, followed a pattern similar to those of Buenos Aires, at about the same level. The U.S. south was not the final destination of Buenos Aires hides. Rather, New York was, but those prices are not available.[11]

Other price series for Buenos Aires hides and other livestock by-products display declining or stable curves. The price of hides in Hamburg declined from the mid-1820s onward, and the same behavior is observed for London prices (Figure 11.5).[12] In both cases there was a recovery in the

11 London prices are from Halperín Donghi (1963). Those prices are for dry hides, although Britain imported mainly wet hides (see Appendix C). Buenos Aires prices are from Broide (1951). Hide prices for France and Belgium are from the *Tableau générale du commerce* for each country and for every year; and New Orleans prices are from Cole (1938). All values have been converted into pesos and all weights into 35-lb pesadas.

12 For London prices from 1814 to 1852, see Halperín Donghi (1963). Implicit prices of British hide imports are used for 1854 to 1870 (see Table C.3). For Buenos Aires prices, see Broide (1951). Hamburg prices are from Jacobs and Richter (1935), 68–69. Chiaramonte [(1991), 216] gives the quotation for Hamburg prices from 1814 to 1845 taken from the same source. As Jacobs and Richter also quote Buenos Aires and Montevideo salted hide prices from 1843 to 1870, there is a 3-year overlapping (1843–1845) used in Figure 11.5 to combine both series. For that reason the level reached by Hamburg hide prices after 1845 might be too high. But it should be noted that the pattern of price behavior is very similar to that of London prices.

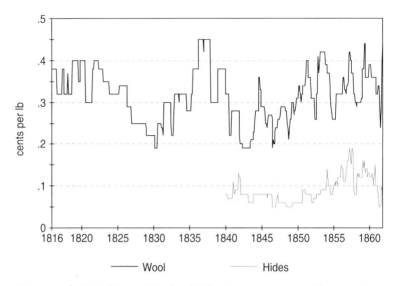

Figure 11.6. United States: Wool and hide prices; average monthly quotation,
1816–1861.

early 1850s, lasting until 1860 for London and until 1870 for Hamburg.
On average London prices in the 1860s were at about 60% of the level
reached in the 1830s. At that time, however, Britain was not the main
market for Buenos Aires hides. Declining prices in some markets (unfortunately, there are series for just a few markets) do not mean that other
markets had a similar behavior, as shown by the steady rise of hide prices
in the United States from the early 1850s to the late 1860s (Figure 11.6).[13]
It does not mean either that those lower prices were not remunerative for
Buenos Aires producers. Hide prices in Buenos Aires had also gone down
from 1830 to 1850 when converted into specie, but in paper money they
were far above the 1830 level from the late 1830s onward. A "profit
inflation" argument can hardly be made for nineteenth-century Buenos
Aires, as Hamilton did for sixteenth-century Spain. In order to do that, the
extent (in territorial terms) of paper money circulation should be known
before arguing that producers were taking advantage of those inflated
prices. That argument depends upon the people's perception of paper
money and specie as the ultimate means of payment. Paper money was the
only means of payment for local transactions in both the 1830s and the
1850s, but to argue that all traces of specie had vanished may be too

13 For U.S. prices, see Cole (1938).

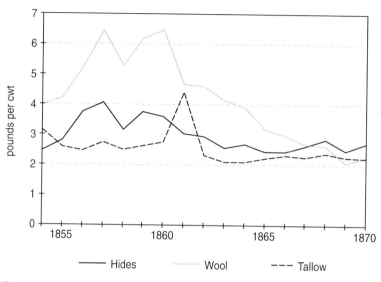

Figure 11.7. Great Britain: Imports from Argentina; implicit prices, 1854–1870.

farfetched. From September 1827 onward, the parts of a contract could freely determine the means of payment. Although specie was not used any longer as a means of payment for retail transactions in the city, the penetration of paper money into the countryside was much slower.

The prices of other Buenos Aires exports should also be taken into account since the share of hides over total exports declined from the 1840s onward. Wool and tallow exports grew, and that expansion served (as shown later) to develop new markets. Prices had different behaviors in different markets. Wool prices rose in the United States from the mid-1840s to the late 1850s, but the curve has a serrated pattern (Figure 11.6). There is no information for the 1860s. In Britain wool prices rose up to 1860 but had a steady decline in that decade, to reach a low in 1870 that was about one-third of the 1860's peak (Figure 11.7).[14] The tariff rate of wool in Belgium started to go down in 1856, and in 1870 it was less than half of the 1856 level (Figure 11.8).[15] Wool exports to Belgium, however (as discussed later), were steadily growing. The tariff price of wool in France also shows a decline from 1863 onward (Figure 11.9), but wool exports to France were also growing.

The behavior of tallow prices is less marked than that of wool. It

---

14 For the implicit prices of Argentine imports into Britain, see Table C.3.
15 Wool prices for Belgium are from the *Tableau générale du commerce de la Belgique* (see Appendix C).

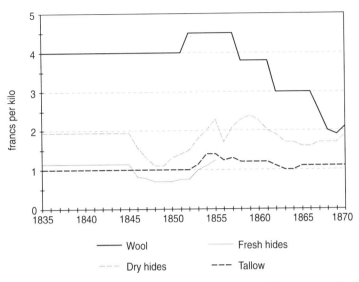

Figure 11.8. Belgium: Imports from Río de la Plata; tariff rates, 1835–1870.

declined in Britain from 1854 to 1870 (excepting a peak in 1861), but only from about £2.5 to about £2.25. It rose in Belgium in the early 1850s but had a slow decline to the mid-1860s. The difference between peaks and depressions was also small. Almost the same pattern can be seen in French prices. Tallow price rose in the early 1850s, remained at about the same level up to 1864, and experienced a small decline from 1865 onward (Figures 11.7, 11.8, and 11.9).

   Prices do not mean anything by themselves. Wool production in Buenos Aires might have been encouraged by rising U.S. prices, but Belgium developed as the main market in spite of declining prices there. On the one hand, marketing conditions could be different for the different markets. An increasing share of European vis-à-vis American goods in the Buenos Aires market could have resulted in lower freight rates to Europe. On the other hand, price curves show yearly averages, and they are not representative of single transactions. The serrated pattern of the U.S. wool price curve meant uncertainty in the short run in spite of the long-run rising trend. Wool prices were declining in Belgium (at least tariff rates were, which are not the same thing as market prices), but plateaus lasting several years could have reduced the degree of uncertainty when single operations are considered, in spite of a long-run downward trend.

   Rising or declining international prices are just one element to take into account when studying conditions of production. They do not reveal

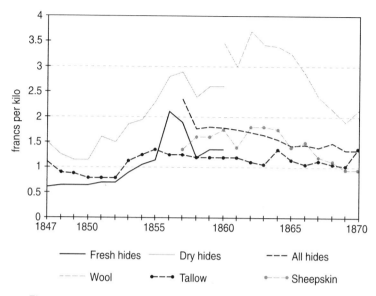

Figure 11.9. France: Imports from Argentina; tariff rates, 1847–1870.

anything about local conditions of production, which could be pushing local prices upward or downward unrelated to international price fluctuations. In spite of uncertain or declining prices for the main Buenos Aires products, their exports were firmly rising, which is indicative of a positive adjustment of local conditions of production to overseas market conditions. How those changing conditions affected the expectations and the actual results of the hide trade is the subject of the next section.

Marketing

An estimate of the profitability of the Buenos Aires hide trade was made by the Marqués del Real Thesoro in Cádiz on 16 December 1768.[16] The aim of such an estimate seems to have been to ascertain whether the taxes levied on those hides should be changed or kept as they were. It showed, however, at that early stage, before the implementation of the Bourbon reforms, and before the process of expansion began, what the economic reasons were that made expansion possible.

Prices in Buenos Aires were 13 reales de plata for ox hides, 8 reales de

16 AGN, Biblioteca Nacional 184/1284. For an estimate based upon different sources but with a similar outcome, see Saguier (1991), 111–112.

plata for cow and steer hides, and 6 reales de plata for heifer hides.[17] Taxes
levied in Buenos Aires, plus loading expenses, were equivalent to 4 reales
de plata per hide. Freight plus taxes levied in Cádiz and expenses there
added up to 23 reales de plata per hide. Cow, heifer, and steer hides (all
hides weighing less than 35 lbs each were considered steer hides) were at
$48\frac{1}{2}$ reales de plata for 35 lbs. Ox hides were at 41 reales for 35 lbs.

   Using an operation involving 462 hides of all four kinds dispatched
from Buenos Aires to a Cádiz merchant, an estimate was made of the
different profits made out of them. There were 84 ox hides, with an average
weight of 36 lbs 6 ounces each; 357 cow and steer hides, with an
average weight of 30 lbs 15 ounces each; and 21 heifer hides, with an
average weight of 29 lbs 4 ounces each.

   The 84 ox hides had cost 1,092 reales de plata, and expenses in Buenos
Aires were 336 reales, for a total cost on board in Buenos Aires of 1,428
reales. Freight, taxes, and expenses in Cádiz amounted to 1,932 reales, for
a combined total of 3,360 reales. The total weight of those hides was
3,059 lbs. At 41 reales for 35 lbs, the total market price obtained for them
was 3,597.75 reales. Profit was then 237.75 reales de plata. The rate of
profit over the capital invested in that operation was therefore 7.1%. By
discounting the interest corresponding to the time that that amount of
money had been invested in that operation, and assuming that the operation was carried out in less than 1 year, we find that the merchant making
the investment was obtaining a higher return than the usual 6% interest
rate. Time has been taken into account, but not risk. No insurance was
mentioned among the cost either in Buenos Aires or Cádiz. If it was not
included, the operation was not brilliant, unless the amount of money
invested in Buenos Aires could be recovered within 6 months or so, and the
amount spent in Cádiz within a few weeks. This might have been the case,
since the Marqués estimated profit over the amount of money invested in
Buenos Aires. So freight expenses were probably met in Cádiz, and there
might have been a certain grace period for meeting them as well as to pay
for taxes and other expenses there. A profit of 16% was mentioned in that
estimate for the ox-hide section of the operation, although if those were the
actual conditions, profit was in fact 16.6%.

   If there was any risk of not breaking even in that operation, it was just

---

17 The Spanish "national" silver real or real de plata was 1/68 of a mark and contained 11 dineros
(91.7%) of pure silver. (There were lighter and baser provincial reales.) According to Hamilton, the
national real was equivalent to 85 maravedíes de vellón, being 34 maravedíes equivalent to one real
de vellón. Twenty reales de vellón were equivalent to one Spanish American 8-real peso. The
national silver real and the Spanish American real were both worth, therefore, 2.5 reales de vellón.
See Hamilton (1947), 56–57, and Senillosa (1835), 26.

concerning ox hides. Regarding cow and steer hides, there was a total cost in Buenos Aires of 4,284 reales de plata (2,856 reales for hides, and 1,428 reales for expenses). Freight and expenses in Cádiz amounted to 8,211 reales de plata, for a total investment of 12,495 reales. The total weight of those 357 hides was 11,060 lbs, which at 48 reales de plata for 35 lbs had reached a market price of 15,168 reales de plata, leaving a profit of 2,673 reales de plata, equivalent to a 62.4% return over the amount invested in Buenos Aires and a 21.4% return over the total investment.

The 21 heifer hides had cost 126 reales de plata, and other expenses amounted to 84 reales, for a total investment in Buenos Aires of 210 reales. Expenditure in Cádiz was 483 reales, for a total expenditure of 693 reales. Those hides weighed 614 lbs and had a market price, at 48 reales for 35 lbs, of 842 reales. The difference of 149 reales de plata represented a 71% return over the investment in Buenos Aires and a 21.5% return over total investment.

The Marqués del Real Thesoro estimated the return over the investment made in Buenos Aires because, as already suggested, expenses in Cádiz could be met after selling the hides. To the amount invested in Buenos Aires, considering that it had to be sent from Cádiz, a 6% annual rate of interest should be added. Six months were necessary for the return trip, and the ships had to stay for about 3 months in Buenos Aires, so 4.5% should be added for that 9-month period. In that case total expenditure in Buenos Aires would have been 1,492.3 reales de plata for ox hides, 4,476.8 reales de plata for cow hides, and 219.5 reales de plata for heifer hides. So the return on those amounts would have been 15.9%, 59.7%, and 67.9%, respectively.

For the whole operation, there was a total investment in Buenos Aires (including interest over the amount invested for 9 months) of 6,188.6 reales de plata and a total return of 3,059.75 reales, equivalent to 49.4% over total investment. If the 10,626 reales de plata spent in Cádiz are added to the amount invested (with no interest charged), the rate of profit drops to 18.2%. If 9 months were enough to complete that operation, an annual profit rate of 24.3% was realized.

That was an estimate based upon an actual operation carried out by a Cádiz merchant. Consequently, the import of Buenos Aires hides into Spain revealed itself as a very attractive proposition. If from a single-operation estimate a full-fledged trade developed, even considering that losses could be expected, the proposition still looked good – so good that the import of hides into Cádiz (it can be safely assumed they were mainly from Buenos Aires) had a sixfold increase between the 1760s and the 1790s.

An anonymous Spanish bureaucrat made another estimate of the profit-

ability of the Buenos Aires hide trade in the 1790s.[18] His name is unknown, maybe because his writing was so clearly aimed against the free
trade policies then prevailing that he preferred to remain in obscurity. His
name, however, could not have been ignored by those to whom his report
was sent, so maybe it is missing because only an unfinished copy of his
report is known. He was against the Bourbon free trade policies as well as
other freedoms. More control was his solution for the wrongdoings caused
by contraband in the Banda Oriental, but he did not answer the obvious
questions that had pushed the Crown in that direction: How effective
could that control be, and how much would it cost?

Because free trade was hurting the Cádiz merchants dealing in Río de
la Plata hides, the report recommended its suppression. Its author was
concerned by the profit that changadores, hacendados, and merchant-
estancieros were making out of that business, so he wanted to restrict their
access to the market in a compulsory way.

Hides, the anonymous bureaucrat says, were bought in the Banda Oriental at 16 reales per pesada (35 lbs). There were 3 reales for sales and war
taxes and loading expenses, 8 reales for freight, and 5 reales for storage,
handling, brokerage, and insurance expenses. Total expenses for 1 pesada
to reach Cádiz were 32 reales, while the current price in Cádiz was at that
time from 28 to 32 reales. His solution to the prospect of a loss was to
prevent the contraband of hides and cattle from the Banda Oriental to Rio
Grande do Sul. That was for him the reason for the rise of hide prices in the
Banda Oriental. But not just that. Local merchants in Montevideo were
taking advantage of those very prices, unsuitable for Cádiz merchants, in
order to expand their cattle-ranching activities. So the anonymous bureaucrat thought that the Montevideo merchants should be barred from that
business.

Less interested in the business than in the fiscal aspects of the hide trade,
he mentions seven taxes levied on the different transactions of a hide from
Buenos Aires to its final destination in Spain, resulting, he says in awe, in
an annual income for His Majesty of 1 million pesos. From those transactions shippers would obtain another million; brokers 25 thousand,
estancieros 2.5 million, and the transportation and storage sectors 0.5
million.[19] So, he says, the hide trade yielded 4 million pesos annually, but
he was disregarding the fact that estancieros, according to his own report,
were obtaining a greater profit by selling their cattle in Brazil, and that the
cost of enforcing control should be discounted from those taxes.

18 Brito Stífano (1953), 367–377.
19 Brokers are mentioned as getting 25 pesos, but 25 thousand appears more reasonable than the 25
    million attributed to them by Martínez Díaz, who republished the document first published by
    Brito Stífano. Cf. Brito Stífano (1953), 370; and Martínez Díaz (1988), 97.

His plea in favor of regulation is rich in detail but poor in analysis of the profitability of the hide trade. The hide trade was presented as highly profitable, both for individuals and for the Crown, but some distortions – contraband to Brazil and vertical integration of that business by the Montevideo merchants – affected what he considered the natural order of things: a profitable business for the Cádiz merchants. If his views were representative of those of other Spanish bureaucrats in the Río de la Plata area in the late eighteenth century, one can see why independence from Spain was so popular in the countryside of the Banda Oriental just a few years later.

The problems referred to by that bureaucrat for the Banda Oriental were not similar to those on the western shore of the river. That bureaucrat's main concern was the hunting of orejano cattle by cattle rustlers (changadores) either for themselves or for Montevideo merchants. The only orejano cattle left in Buenos Aires were the annual offspring of domestic cattle. Conditions of production were different on both shores of the river, but marketing conditions for hides were in both cases those described by that anonymous bureaucrat.

A further look at the marketing conditions for hides is provided by the ledgers and correspondence of British merchants operating in Buenos Aires. From John Gibson's papers, it is possible to estimate the result of a hide-export operation.[20] On 15 July 1824, 273 hides weighing 189.9 pesadas were bought in Buenos Aires at 5 pesos 3 reales per pesada, making a total of 1,020 pesos 6 reales. Carting, taxes, and commission added 85 pesos 2 reales, for a total cost in Buenos Aires of 1,106 pesos. Those hides were sold in Liverpool in November 1824 for £270 12s. 11d. (£253 5s. 1d. for 6,234 lbs at 9.75 d. each, and £17 7s. 1d. for 506 lbs at 8.25 d. each). "Charges at Liverpool" and insurance were £54 19s. 3d. The net income of that operation was therefore £215 13s. 8d. Freight is not mentioned. If freight was included among those "charges at Liverpool," the result of this operation, exchanging the net income into pesos at a rate of 46.8 d. per peso (as mentioned in Gibson's accounts), would have been 1,108 pesos 3 reales. Unless those "charges at Liverpool" included profit also, that operation was only good to transfer funds from Buenos Aires to Liverpool at no cost.

James Hodgson's papers supply an example of another export operation. He was a British merchant who resided in Buenos Aires for 26 years and retained his interest in the Río de la Plata until his death, probably in the 1870s. James Hodgson arrived in Buenos Aires in January 1818 and left for good in June 1844. Apart from a trip to Britain from July 1828 to October 1830, he remained in Buenos Aires for the rest of that

20 NLS, Gibson Papers, 10326, f. 104.

period.[21] Hodgson probably started as a junior partner of Joseph Green, a Liverpool merchant, who through him and other associates opened up branches in Buenos Aires and Valparaíso. On 25 October 1830, Green and Hodgson (the name under which they were conducting their businesses in Buenos Aires, including the ownership of an estancia in Monsalvo in partnership with José Lastra) shipped 1,187 "prime dry ox hides" to John Dugdale and Brothers, of Manchester.[22] Those hides weighed 35,000 lbs, and their cost was 31.5 pesos for each 35-lb pesada, making a total of 31,500 pesos. Export duties on 1,143 hides at 1 peso each amounted to 1,143 pesos (it is not clear why the remaining 44 hides were not taxed). Brokerage, storage, inspection, loading, carting, and launch expenses amounted to 1,114 pesos, and their 2.5% commission amounted to 787.5 pesos. Total expenses amounted to 3,044.5 pesos, which, added to the cost of hides, made a total of 34,544.5 pesos. Freight and insurance were not mentioned.

Because of the difference between the Buenos Aires lb (459.4 grams) and the British lb (453 grams), those hides had a total weight of 35,494 British lbs.[23] In the first quarter of 1831, the average price for dry hides in London was 9.375 pence per pound.[24] At that price those hides could have been sold for £1,386.5 (using decimals instead of shillings and pence to simplify the operation). In October 1830 the rate of exchange in Buenos Aires was 6.75 d. per paper peso, so 34,544.5 pesos were equivalent to £971.6. There was therefore a difference of £414.9 to pay for freight, insurance, and expenses in Liverpool. The overseas freight rate was at 0.006 pesos fuertes per ton per league in 1834, according to the Buenos Aires business newspaper *La Gaceta Mercantil*.[25] Since that quotation was in specie, and no technical improvements were introduced between 1830 and 1834, that was probably the rate in 1830 as well. At that rate the transportation of 1 ton from Buenos Aires to Liverpool, about 7,000 miles (2,156 leagues), would have cost 12.93 pesos. Those hides weighed 35,000 lbs, equivalent to 17.5 tons, so the freight would have been 226.3 pesos, equivalent to £45.3. Taking away that amount from the difference between total expenses in Buenos Aires and the estimated sale price in London, there are still £369.6 to pay for insurance and expenses in Liverpool. If charges at Liverpool and insurance are estimated at 20.5% of the sale price, as was the case for John Gibson's operation in 1824, they would have amounted to

21 See Green and Hodgson Outgoing Letterbook, 1817–1821; James Hodgson Outgoing Letters, 1828–1830 and 1831–1846, in JRM, Hodgson and Robinson Papers.
22 Green and Hodgson, Shipments to Liverpool, 1823–1834, f. 65, in JRM, Hodgson and Robinson Papers.
23 See Senillosa (1835), 23–24.
24 For the average price of dry hides in London, see Halperín Donghi (1963), 65.
25 Burgin (1946), 117.

£284.2, and Green and Hodgson's operation would have left £85.2 as a profit. Expenses in Buenos Aires and for freight added to £1,016.9, so that profit was equivalent to an 8.4% profit rate on a single operation. Again, single operations are not representative of the long-term profit a merchant could make out of that trade, but considering that return as the outcome for a 6-month operation, it can be argued that the Buenos Aires hide trade was founded upon solid arguments.

Better than this estimate (as a source at least, since the economic result was a bit lower) is the actual result of an export operation carried out by the same Green and Hodgson in 1833, for the account of Fielden Brothers, of Liverpool.[26] Seven hundred prime ox hides were shipped on 22 August 1833. Their cost was 28,686 pesos 2 reales, and 2,475 pesos 4 reales were added for duties, carting, and commissions. The total cost in Buenos Aires was therefore 31,161 pesos 6 reales, equivalent to £857 11s. 8d., at a rate of exchange of 6.625 d. per paper peso. On 9 May 1834, those hides were sold in Liverpool for £928 10s. 6d. Profit "less premium of insurance" (but freight is not mentioned) was £70 18s. 10d. That amount meant an 8.3% profit over an 8.5-month period, equivalent therefore to a 12% annual profit rate. Although less profitable than the operation previously described, it was still good enough to sustain the interest of Liverpool merchants in the Buenos Aires hide trade.

A further estimate is possible for 1852. British merchant George W. White reported several of his operations to Baring, the London merchant bankers, to show them the actual costs of the hide trade.[27] On 1 March 1852, White shipped 4,689 dry hides to Britain. Those hides weighed 111,138 lbs and had cost 197,201.7 pesos. Duties and expenses in Buenos Aires amounted to 15,695.5 pesos, and the 2.5% commission was 5,322.4 pesos. Total expenses were therefore 218,220 pesos. In the second quarter of 1852, the average price for dry hides in London was 4.875 d. per pound. The weight of those hides was equivalent to 112,708 British lbs, so at the average price for that quarter, they would have reached a price in Britain of £2,289.4. On 1 March 1852, the gold ounce was at 261 paper pesos in Buenos Aires, so the peso fuerte may be estimated at 16.3 paper pesos. Total cost and expenses in Buenos Aires were therefore equivalent to 13,387.7 pesos fuertes, or £2,677.5. For that operation, then, without taking into account freight, insurance, and expenses in Britain, there was a loss of £388.1. The average price of dry hides, however, improved in the third quarter of 1852 to 6.25 d. per pound. Assuming that that was the selling price for those hides, the total income was £2,935.1. Assuming the

26 JRM, Green and Hodgson Papers, Shipments to Liverpool, 1823–1834.
27 George W. White to Baring Brothers, Buenos Aires, 1 July 1852, in Baring Archives, London, HC 4.1.24.8.

same rate as in 1830, the freight would have been 718.7 pesos, or £143.7. That leaves £113.7 to pay for insurance and expenses in Britain. If they are estimated again at 20.5% of the final sales price, that operation would have left a loss of £488. Perhaps freight rates, insurance, and expenses in Britain were down compared to those of the 1830s. But it could have been just a bad operation due to a fluctuating exchange rate in Buenos Aires and fluctuating hide prices in London.

This estimate does not mean that a loss actually occurred from that operation, but it shows that marketing conditions were much tighter, for hides at least, than in 1830. That might have been the reason for the discontinuity of the dry hide trade with Britain. Only 3% of all Buenos Aires hides imported into Britain were dry hides at the beginning of the 1850s, and there were no imports after 1854.[28] The salted hide trade with Britain went on strong, and it was much stronger with continental countries.

Although little is known about the long-run evolution of freight rates between Buenos Aires and its main trade partners' ports, freight rates were a key factor in allowing the Buenos Aires export trade to prosper. It has been argued that navigation improvements sent freight rates down in Europe and the United States after 1815.[29] Whether that was the case for Buenos Aires as well is open to question, but it is difficult to imagine too different a behavior. A firm statement on this issue, however, is not possible without a study of the Buenos Aires freight rates (which in turn depends upon sources not yet identified).

Conclusion

From the late eighteenth to the mid-nineteenth centuries, the Buenos Aires hide trade was based upon a price differential between Buenos Aires and overseas markets. That difference, irrespective of price fluctuations, was large enough to pay for export expenses, freight, insurance, and import expenses. It was large enough to make a profit as well out of the hide export–import trade.

The first section of this chapter studied the evolution of prices in Buenos Aires and overseas markets. In spite of a decline of hide prices in the long run in the main markets for Buenos Aires hides, and consequently falling local prices, hides remained as the main Buenos Aires export until the early 1860s. The Buenos Aires cattle ranchers successfully adjusted to those

28 See Appendix C. There were no imports in 1855, and from 1856 onward, figures for dry and wet hide imports are not given separately.

29 Harley (1988). The same long-term decline of freight rates in the nineteenth century had already been observed by North (1958).

conditions by expanding their operations, increasing land and labor productivity, and developing new livestock by-products. The Buenos Aires
exporters also adjusted themselves by looking for new markets for old and
new livestock by-products.

The second section of this chapter focused upon marketing conditions.
If exporters were to make a profit out of the hide trade, expenses had to be
kept under control within that price differential gap. A few hide-export
operations from 1768 to 1852 were analyzed in order to explain the
feasibility of the hide-export trade. Single operations say little about the
long-term evolution of a merchant's business, but the handsome profit
rates made out of those operations justify, from the exporter's perspective,
the expansion of that trade. A glimpse of the arguments of a Spanish
colonial bureaucrat who wanted to keep economic forces at bay also helps
to explain the role of these forces in the transition from colonial times to
independence, from mercantilism to freedom.

The overseas trade was a risky business. Many merchants suffered losses
on individual operations due to their failure in forecasting market conditions given the delay in communications and transportation between
Buenos Aires and the overseas markets. On the whole, however, profitable
operations offset those losses, since the hide trade and the trade of other
livestock by-products boomed after 1810, as the next chapter shows.

12

Markets

Except for specially authorized ships (navíos de registro) sailing from
Spain, the port of Buenos Aires was legally closed from 1620 to 1778.
Contraband trade was widely practiced, however, especially after the establishment of a Portuguese outpost in Colonia do Sacramento in 1680. Some
barriers fell down in 1778 with the enactment of the Free Trade regulations, but true free trade was not implemented before the May 1810
revolution. After the revolution merchants were free to send their goods to
any destination and to receive them from any place. That had not been the
case in the past. After 1810 Spain vanished as Buenos Aires's main trading
partner. Great Britain, continental Europe, and the United States soon
emerged as the main suppliers of goods ranging from textiles to wine and
from iron tools to trinkets. These countries were also the main destination
of Buenos Aires exports.[1]

The overall result of the aggregate estancia activity can be seen by
paying attention to the evolution of products and markets. This chapter
shows that in spite of producing a limited range of products for a few main
markets, the Buenos Aires producers successfully adjusted their production
to the evolving pattern of overseas demand for livestock by-products. In
order to show the evolution of markets and products from the 1810s to the
1870s, the first section of this chapter studies Buenos Aires's main customers according to export value figures; the second section studies the evolution of markets for the different Buenos Aires products, according to
import figures into those countries; and the third section studies the
markets for each product.[2]

---

1 For an examination of the industries demanding for Buenos Aires hide, wool, and tallow in the
United States and Britain, see Brown (1979), 50–68.
2 For a discussion of problems concerning the trade statistics of each country and for the sources of
Figures 12.1 to 12.35, see Appendix C.

Main customers

When hide exports expanded in the late eighteenth century, the destination of all exports was Spain. Those hides were probably re-exported to other European countries, but there is no way to trace their final destination. The process leading to a direct contact between Buenos Aires and the customers for her products started with the French Revolutionary wars. That global war affected Buenos Aires in two ways: First, the only legal market for her products, Spain, was beyond reach (especially after Trafalgar); second, the English Invasions of 1806–1807 briefly put Buenos Aires in direct contact with the country that would emerge soon as her main customer. In May 1810 the barriers to foreign trade fell down, and soon ships and merchants from other countries, especially Britain, arrived in Buenos Aires.

There is no precise information on the destination of exports in the 1810s, but in 1822 Buenos Aires's main customer was Great Britain, with at least 46.6% of the total value of exports. Goods shipped to Gibraltar came in second place with 10.6%. The final destination for those goods could have been Spain, or maybe Italy or Great Britain. Italy accounted for 1.4%, the United States for 8%, and France for 3.7%. Goods shipped to Anvers accounted also for 3.7%. Brazil and Cuba accounted for most of the 9.6% of total value represented by the jerked-beef trade (Figure 12.1).[3] These figures are each country's share of Buenos Aires's most important exports – hides, wool, tallow, sheepskins, horse hides, hair, and jerked beef. The remaining 6.4% correspond both to exports of those products to other countries and to exports of other products (chinchilla and beaver skins, for instance) to those and other countries.

Twenty years later, in 1842, Buenos Aires's main customer was France, accounting for 23.5% of the total export value. That seems to have been the case along the 1840s, according to an official British report.[4] France was closely followed by Great Britain, with 22.6%; the United States accounted for 19.3%; and Spain for 8.7%. Several minor destinations accounted for 23% of export value: German ports for 3.8%, Italian ports for 5.1%, Brazil for 4.4%, Belgium for 3%, and "to order" for 6.9%. All other destinations accounted for only 2.7%.

In 1851 France's share of Buenos Aires exports had gone down to 9.9% of their total value. The leading customers were Great Britain with 27.6% and the United States with 27.1%. Belgium and German ports are listed

3 Figures for 1822 are from AGN, III–22–5–9 through III–22–5–20; for 1842, MAE, Correspondance commerciale, Buenos Aires, 2; for 1851, from Parish (1958), 512, 514–515; and for 1872, from REBA (1872), 173–179, 184–186.
4 Great Britain, Parliamentary Papers, 1847, 64(2):397–400.

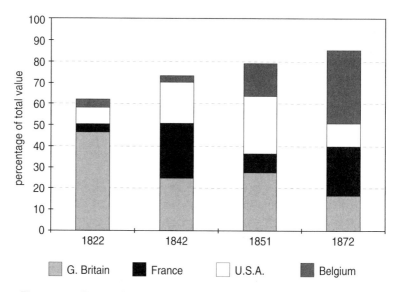

Figure 12.1. Buenos Aires exports: Main destinations, 1822–1872. *Source*: See
Appendix C for the sources of all figures in this chapter.

together, and they accounted for 15.4%. Cuba accounted for 5.5%, Italy
and Spain for 5.3% each, and Brazil for 3.1%.

In 1872 Belgium was the leading Buenos Aires customer, with 34.4%
of the total export value, due to a shift in the pattern of exports – wool and
sheepskins accounted then for about one-half of the total export value.
Because of the same reason, France was in second place with 23.3%. Great
Britain's share had declined to 16.7%, and that of the United States to
11%. Spain and Italy accounted for 3.4% each, Germany for 1.7%, Brazil
for 1.5%, and Cuba for 1.4%; all other destinations accounted for 3.1%.

The overall pattern emerging from the distribution of export value
according to destination for the 4 years from 1822 to 1872 is one of
concentration and dispersion: concentration of exports in a small number
of countries, but at the same time dispersion among them. From 1822 to
1872, Great Britain, France, the United States, and Belgium accounted for
the largest share of Buenos Aires exports, but none of them maintained a
constant lead. This dispersion among the main customers is better seen
later in the chapter, when the destination of exports for each product is
considered. The focus upon those four countries is justified by the fact that
together they accounted for 62% of Buenos Aires exports in 1822, for
73.4% in 1842, for 79.1% in 1851, and for 84.5% in 1872.

Exports to those main trading partners present different patterns along
time. Published statistics or information collected to build them are not

homogeneous. For each of those countries, the following elements are considered here: (1) value of imports and exports; (2) evolution of imports from Argentina; and (3) market share of each of the main products imported from Argentina. In that way it is possible to figure out what the overall result of each bilateral trading relationship was and what the position of Buenos Aires exports was in the overseas markets for each of its products.

Market shares

The livestock by-products exported by Buenos Aires were not native to the pampas, enjoying therefore no particular advantage in overseas markets other than their prices.[5] Those products had to compete with products from other regions, some of them closer than Buenos Aires to those main markets. None of the Buenos Aires exports opened up a new market; on the contrary, all products were demanded by overseas markets before the Buenos Aires exports reached them. But demand for those livestock by-products was on the rise, so the Buenos Aires producers and exporters could take advantage of that rise to capture a portion of those markets. Two remarkable facts should be stressed: None of the Buenos Aires products could be considered strategic in any way, and they seldom enjoyed a dominant position in any significant market.

The value of British imports is not available until 1854. From that year until 1863, the balance of trade was roughly even, but from 1864 onward the value of exports to Argentina were about double the value of imports (Figure 12.2). That situation was only reversed in 1895, and for the next 75 years, the balance of trade was favorable to Argentina. The composition of imports between 1854 and 1870 shows a declining share of hides, a roughly stable share of wool, and an increasing share of tallow in the late 1860s (Figure 12.3). Another important feature of the composition of British imports from Argentina in that period is the sizeable share of all other goods, which accounted for about one-third of the total value of imports in both 1854 and 1870, although there were in-between years with a larger and a smaller share.

Because quantities of British imports are available from 1814 to 1870,

---

5 Sources for British, French, American, and Belgian statistics are listed in Appendix C. Estimates are affected by the evolution of freight and insurance rates, since import statistics into those countries expressed CIF values. In the long run, according to Harley's (1988) figures, freight rates declined from the 1820s to the 1860s by around 40%. This long-run decline, however, conceals short-term fluctuations. Harley did not include any series for South American freight rates, so no year-to-year correction of import statistics have been attempted assuming that the long-run trend was similar to North Atlantic freight rates, but not necessarily the short-term fluctuations. North [(1958), 551–552] did include figures for South America but only after 1887.

Results

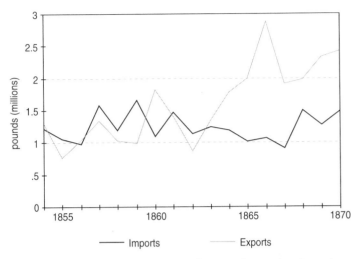

Figure 12.2. Great Britain: Imports and exports from and to Argentina, 1854–1870.

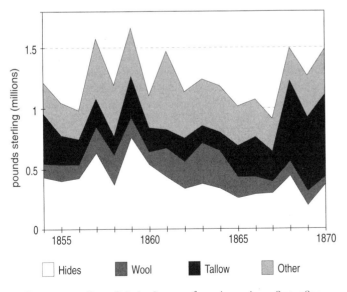

Figure 12.3. Great Britain: Imports from Argentina, 1854–1870.

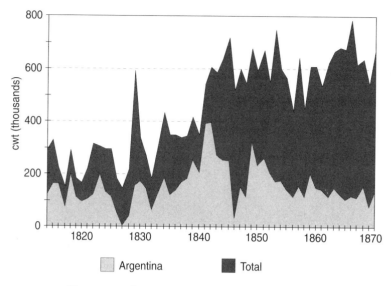

Figure 12.4. Great Britain: Hide imports, 1814–1870.

it is possible to estimate the share of British imports corresponding to each of the main Buenos Aires products. From the early 1830s to the early 1850s, Buenos Aires hides accounted generally for more than 40% of total British hide imports (Figure 12.4). In the late 1830s and early 1840s, that share was always above 50%; the peak was reached in 1841, with 70% of total imports. From the mid-1850s to 1870, that share declined from 40% to 20%.

Wool presents a completely different case from that of hides. Buenos Aires wool imports into Britain started in the mid-1830s and lasted for the whole period, but they never accounted for more than a small portion of total British wool imports (Figure 12.5). The peak was reached in 1841, with 9% of total imports, but Buenos Aires wool imports seldom accounted for more than 3%. In fact, wool imports from Buenos Aires had grown from about 1 million pounds in the mid-1830s to about 5 million pounds in the late 1860s (Figure 12.6); that increase did not translate into a larger share of the market, however, due to a sustained increase of British wool imports from other countries. In the late 1860s, wool imports from Buenos Aires accounted for around 2% of total wool imports.

Tallow imports from Buenos Aires became significant in the early 1830s (Figure 12.7). They accounted for about 10% of all imports in the early 1840s, for about 15% in the early 1850s, again for about 10% in the mid-1860s, and for more than 20% in the late 1860s. There was a constant

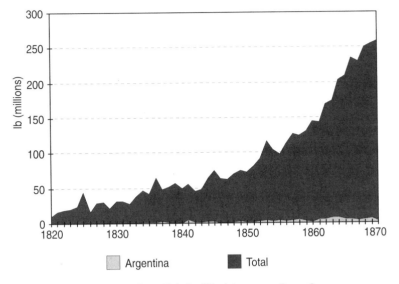

Figure 12.5. Great Britain: Wool imports, 1820–1870.

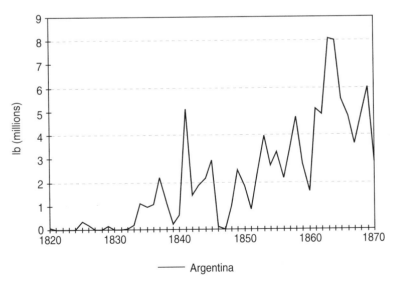

Figure 12.6. Great Britain: Wool imports from Argentina, 1820–1870.

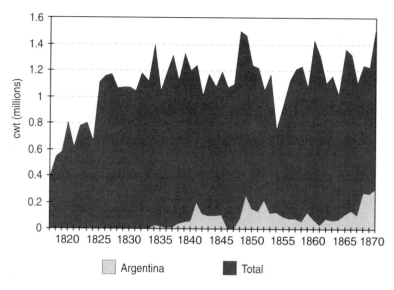

Figure 12.7. Great Britain: Tallow imports, 1817–1870.

growth of Buenos Aires tallow imports into Britain up to the early 1850s (except for the two blockades), a decline up to the mid-1860s, and growth again in the late 1860s (Figure 12.8), but, as with the case of wool, imports from other countries were also growing at the same or even a faster pace.

French statistics are, like those of Great Britain, marred by the use of official (fixed) rates rather than market prices for the estimate of import values. Unlike British statistics, based upon rates determined in 1696, those for France were based up to 1846 upon rates determined in 1826. From 1847 onward average prices based upon market prices were used. The balance of trade between Buenos Aires and France was roughly even up to the mid-1860s. In the late 1860s, that balance turned in favor of Buenos Aires (Figure 12.9).

The official values used up to 1863 depict the evolution of quantities in terms of the structure of relative prices existing in 1826. Hides were the main import from Buenos Aires up to the early 1850s, but then wool imports started to grow (Figure 12.10). From 1847 onward the evolution of import values can be observed. In the late 1860s, there was a significant increase of tallow imports, and by 1870 more than one-third of total French imports from Buenos Aires was wool (Figure 12.11). When compared with British imports, the salient feature of French imports from Argentina is the irrelevance of goods other than hides, wool, and tallow.

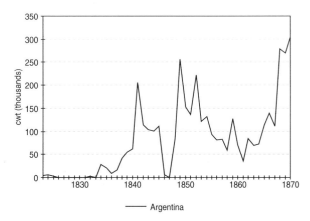

Figure 12.8. Great Britain: Tallow imports from Argentina, 1823–1870.

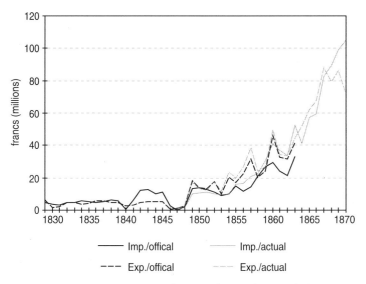

Figure 12.9. France: Imports and exports from and to Río de la Plata, 1829–1870.

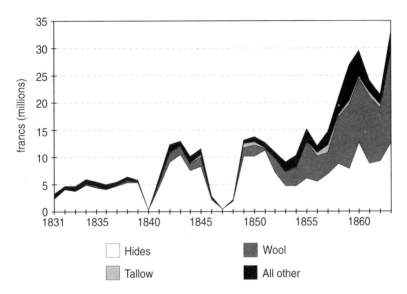

Figure 12.10. France: Imports from Argentina; official value, 1831–1863.

Hide imports from Buenos Aires accounted for about 30% to 35% of total French hide imports between the early 1830s and the early 1850s (Figure 12.12). There were three peaks, in 1832, 1849, and 1850, with figures between 40% and 50% of total hide imports. From 1850 onward there was a steady decline of the Argentine share of total hide imports into France, reaching 10% in 1868. That trend was partially reversed in 1869, and in 1870 the figure was just above 15%. French statistics show an increase of hide imports in the 1860s, but that growth was due to sheepskin imports. (In Figure 12.11 sheepskins were included among hides, but they have been excluded in Figure 12.12.)

Wool imports from Buenos Aires into France had a slow start (Figure 12.13). There were imports in the early 1830s, but they did not account for more than 1% of total imports up to 1841. Total wool imports into France grew about sixfold from the late 1840s to the mid-1860s, but only in the late 1850s did Buenos Aires imports become significant. From 1858 to 1866, they accounted for 10% to 15% of total imports, and from the latter year onward, they grew to reach 25% of total imports in 1870.

Tallow imports from Buenos Aires into France also started in the early 1830s. Although they did not account for a large portion of total imports, there were two peaks of about 8% in 1834 and 1845. In 1850 they were above 25%, but from then onward up to 1863 (except for 1857 and 1859),

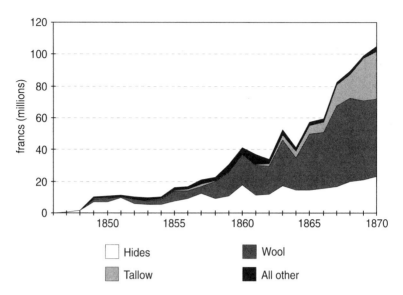

Figure 12.11. France: Imports from Argentina; actual value, 1847–1870.

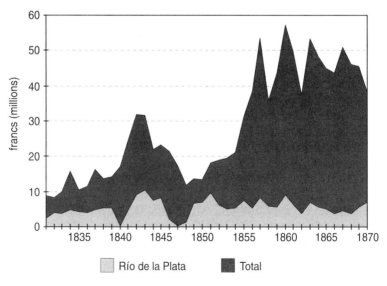

Figure 12.12. France: Hide imports, 1831–1870.

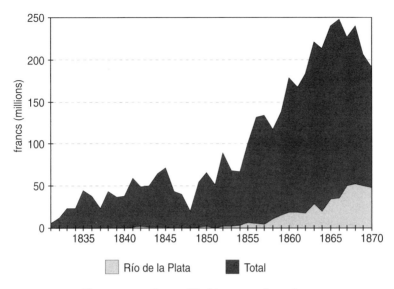

Figure 12.13. France: Wool imports, 1831–1870.

they fell to below 10% (Figure 12.14). From 1864 onward there was a steady growth. In 1870 Buenos Aires tallow accounted for 60% of total tallow imports. In fact, Buenos Aires tallow imports into France had been growing since 1862, but their share over total imports was affected by a pattern of tallow imports altered by two peaks, in 1863 and 1867.

The balance of trade between the United States and the Río de la Plata (up to 1837) or Argentina (from 1838 onward) was favorable to the latter from the early 1830s (Figure 12.15). The gap between the value of imports from and exports to Argentina increased in the early 1840s and was even more marked after 1850. It might have been even greater after 1862, since export values were given in inconvertible currency while import values were given in convertible currency. In that way, the growing value of exports to Argentina after 1863 might be a consequence of those inflated prices. It should be remarked that tallow was not regularly imported from Argentina (rather, the United States was an exporter of that commodity) and that, unlike the case of Great Britain, other goods never had a large share of the total value of United States imports from Argentina.

From 1830 until 1870 the main item imported from Buenos Aires into the United States was hides (Figure 12.16). Wool imports began in the late 1830s, grew in the early 1840s, and leaving aside the periods of blockade, maintained from then up to the early 1860s a fairly constant value. From

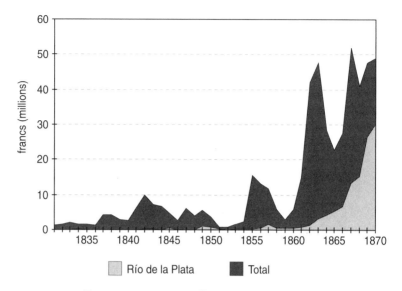

Figure 12.14. France: Tallow imports, 1831–1870.

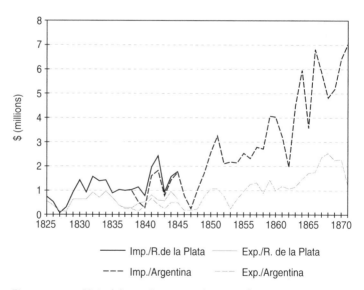

Figure 12.15. United States: Imports and exports from and to Argentina, 1825–1871.

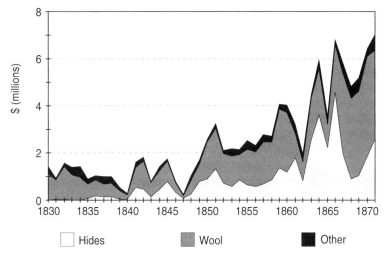

Figure 12.16. United States: Imports from Argentina, 1830–1871.

1863 onward, due to the Civil War, the value of wool imports from Argentina saw an amazing increase. By 1870, however, due to a similar increase in hide imports, hides accounted for about 60% of total imports into the United States from Argentina.

Hide imports from Argentina into the United States saw a steady growth, but that was a reflection of the growth of total hide imports from 1848 onward (excepting the early 1860s). Hide imports from Argentina as a proportion of total imports followed an uneven pattern. They accounted for 45% of total imports in 1830 and for more than 70% in 1834, but they fell below 30% from 1831 to 1833 and below 20% from 1835 to 1840. After 1846 Argentine hide imports into the United States had a share of about 20% of total imports, with occasional peaks above 30%, as in 1850. The late 1860s saw a rise in that share to just above or below 30% (Figure 12.17).

Argentine wool imports into the United States began in the 1830s, but it was only after 1841 that their value became significant. From the early 1840s onward, there was a fairly constant rise that was even more marked during the Civil War. After the war wool imports from Argentina again reached the same level they had before it (Figure 12.18). Due to the uneven pattern of wool imports, imports from Argentina did not have a constant share of the market. In the long run, they seem to have accounted for about

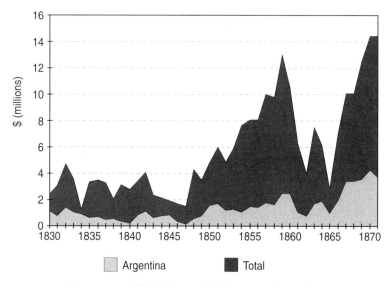

Figure 12.17. United States: Hide imports, 1830–1871.

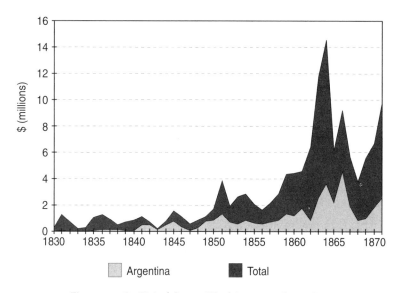

Figure 12.18. United States: Wool imports, 1830–1871.

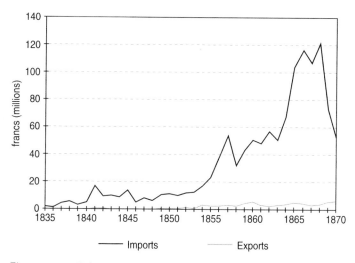

Figure 12.19. Belgium: Imports and exports from and to Río de la Plata, 1835–1870.

30% of total imports, but there were peaks of about 65% in 1842, 1843, and 1849, of 40% in 1861, and of 50% in 1866. There were also depressions, however, such as those of 1840 (about 5%) and 1846 (about 15%), due to the blockades imposed on Buenos Aires; 1853, when Argentina's share was about 25%; 1861, about 15%; and 1868, just below 20%.

The balance of trade between Belgium and the Río de la Plata was extremely favorable to the latter (Figure 12.19), especially from the mid-1850s onward. In 15 years, from 1850 to 1865, the value of Río de la Plata imports into Belgium rose to more than twelve times its original value. The value of exports to the region also grew, but exports did not account for more than 10% of the value of imports at any one time from 1850 to 1870.

Hides were the main item imported from Río de la Plata into Belgium until the mid-1850s. From then onward there was an amazing growth of wool imports, which in the mid-1860s reached a peak of more than five times the value of hide imports. Although there were some tallow imports in the mid- and late 1860s, as well as a marginal presence of other goods, Río de la Plata imports into Belgium were mainly hides and wool (Figure 12.20).

Río de la Plata hides accounted for a large share of Belgium hide imports. From 1837 to 1870, with the exception of 1846, 1859, and again

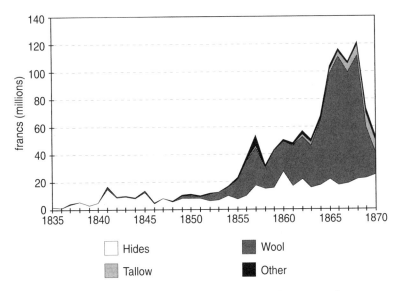

Figure 12.20. Belgium: Imports from Río de la Plata, 1835–1870.

in the late 1860s, the Río de la Plata share was always above 50% of total hide imports. There were peaks, as in 1838, with just below 80%, 1841 with 80%, and 1854 with 70%. From the mid-1850s onward, hide imports had a sustained increase, and the Río de la Plata region retained its share of the market (Figure 12.21).

The amazing increase of wool imports into Belgium, however, was the salient feature of that trading partnership. From the early 1850s to the late 1860s, Belgian wool imports increased fourfold, and the Río de la Plata wool again retained its share of the market. That share was below 10% of total wool imports up to 1851, but it rose to 30–40% during the mid-1850s and early 1860s, reached a peak of almost 60% percent in 1866, sharply declined in the late 1860s to below 20%, to reach only above 10% in 1870. Those years also saw a decline of Belgium total wool imports, but the decline of Río de la Plata wool imports was more marked than that of total imports (Figure 12.22).

Tallow imports from the Río de la Plata into Belgium also grew from the early 1850s onward. After a decline from 1858 to 1860, there was a renewed growth along the 1860s. The share of the Río de la Plata over total Belgium tallow imports was extremely uneven. It reached about 25% in 1841 but declined to below 10% in 1842 and 1843. There was a new peak of about 35% in 1850, but from 1853 to 1856, it was below 10%. Another

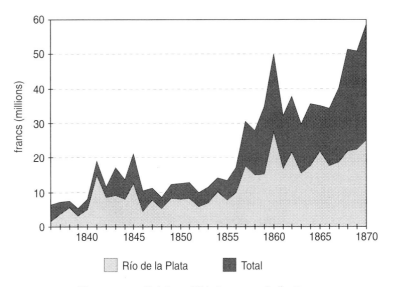

Figure 12.21. Belgium: Hide imports, 1836–1870.

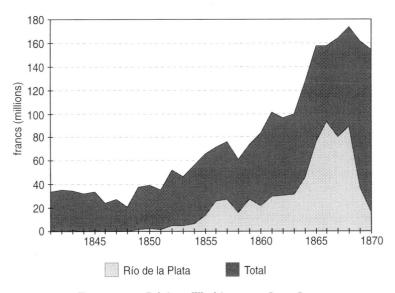

Figure 12.22. Belgium: Wool imports, 1841–1870.

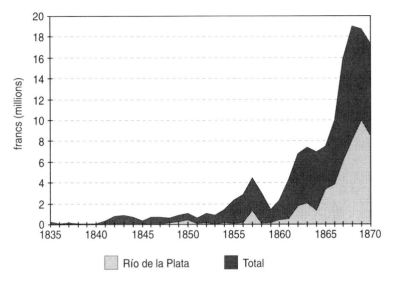

Figure 12.23. Belgium: Tallow imports, 1835–1870.

peak of 30% in 1857 was followed with another depression below 5% in 1858. From that year onward, there was a sustained increase (marked also by some minor decreases) that reached the all-time peak in 1869, with more than 50% of total tallow imports (Figure 12.23).

When Argentina's trade with her four main trading partners is considered, the remarkable expansion of exports from 1820 to 1870 becomes evident. No country, however, remained the main market for Argentine products for the whole period. Great Britain was the main customer in the 1820s; France led in the 1840s but was closely followed by Great Britain and the United States, which shared the lead in the 1850s; and Belgium led in the early 1870s.

Buenos Aires hides retained an important although declining share of the British hide market, a growing but not relevant share of wool imports, and an increasing although moderately significant share of tallow imports. The British market offered good opportunities for products other than those three, however, a characteristic not shared by Argentina's other main trading partners.

France remained a good market for Buenos Aires hides throughout the period, but wool imports from the mid-1850s, and tallow imports a decade later grew faster than hides. Although the French demand for hides was growing, Buenos Aires hide imports did not follow the pace, and wool and tallow imports soon became much more valuable than hides.

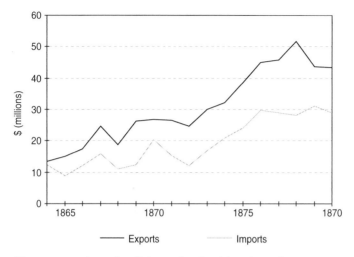

Figure 12.24. Argentina: Balance of trade with main trading partners,
1854–1870.

Argentine hide imports into the United States kept on growing until
1870, excepting the years of the American Civil War. That decline was
compensated by wool imports, which grew during those years and later.
Argentina's share of American hide and wool imports fluctuated, but it
remained within the same range for the whole period.

Trade with Belgium had an impressive development from the mid-
1850s onward. Hide exports to that market grew, but most of the growth
was due to wool exports. The position of Argentine products in the Belgian
market was better than in any other market. Hide, wool, and later tallow
imports from Argentina accounted for an important share of the Belgian
market throughout the period.

The balance of trade with Great Britain was negative for Buenos Aires,
but it was even with France and highly favorable with the United States
and Belgium. Considering Argentina's four main trade partners, the balance of trade from 1854 to 1870 was favorable (Figure 12.24). Even more
important, Argentine exports to its main markets increased and were able
to buy an increasing value of imported goods.

Products

Argentine imports into the four countries that were Argentina's main
customers have been studied in the previous section from the viewpoint of
each country, to see what the share was of its export products in overseas

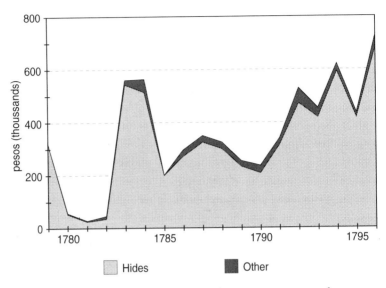

Figure 12.25. Buenos Aires: Non-silver exports, 1779–1796.

markets. In this section Argentine exports are studied from the viewpoint of each product, to see what proportion of the main export products was imported by each of those main customers.

Buenos Aires exports in the late eighteenth century consisted mainly of silver from Alto Peru. From 1779 to 1796, produce accounted for 10% to 15% of the total value of exports, and produce exports were overwhelmingly hides (Figure 12.25).[6] That situation changed in the first two decades of the nineteenth century due to the export of other livestock products, such as tallow, hair, and jerked beef, as well as furs and skins from wild animals, such as chinchilla and beaver.

In 1822 hides accounted for 64.9% of the Buenos Aires total export value (Figure 12.26).[7] Jerked beef accounted for 9.6%, tallow for 3.4%, hair for 3.1%, and wool for 0.9%; all other products accounted for 18.1%. Among the latter, horse hides and to a lesser extent furs and skins of different wild animals accounted for most of that figure. No export of sheepskins was recorded in Parish's statistics, but according to customs records, 5,002 dozen were exported that year.

6 See Moutoukias (1995).
7 For 1822, see Parish (1958), 511; for 1842, MAE, Correspondance commerciale, Buenos Aires, 2 (the values given in this report for each product were corrected according to price and quantities given there); for 1851, Parish (1958), 512; for 1872, REBA (1872), 173–179, 184–186 (only exports through the Buenos Aires and San Nicolás customs are included in this record).

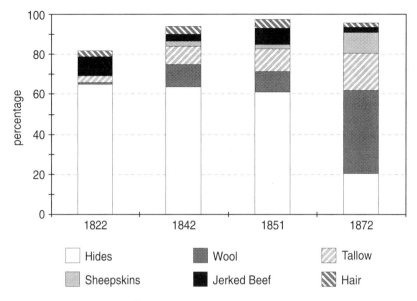

Figure 12.26. Buenos Aires: Main exports, 1822–1872.

In 1842 hides retained the largest share of the Buenos Aires exports. They accounted for 63.7% of the Buenos Aires total export value. Wool was then in second place, accounting for 11%. Tallow accounted for 9.4%, jerked beef for 3.6%, hair for 3.7%, sheepskins for 2.4%, and eleven other products for 6.2%.

In 1851 hides still accounted for 61.2% of the Buenos Aires total export value. Tallow had taken second place with 11.3%, and wool captured third place with 10.3%. Jerked beef accounted for 8.1%, hair for 4.3%, sheepskins for 2%, and all other products for 2.8%.

In 1872 the picture was somewhat different. The same six products that had led export values in 1842 and 1851 were leading then, accounting in all for 95.8% of the Buenos Aires total export value. The share of total value corresponding to each product, however, had changed. Wool was in first place, accounting for 41.8% of total export value. Hides were in second place with 20.2%, and tallow was third with 18.6%. Sheepskin exports had grown to 10.3% of total export value, jerked beef had fallen to 2.8%, and hair had also fallen to 2.1%. All other products accounted for a mere 4.2% of total export value.

A comparison of the total value of Buenos Aires exports for 1822, 1842, 1851, and 1872 is possible, but more difficult is to ascertain the precise meaning of those monetary values along that 50-year span. Since the

British pound remained unchanged (its intrinsic value at least, since relative prices, including those of different goods vis-à-vis specie, are always changing although not necessarily upward), values have been converted into pounds sterling. Accordingly, the value of Buenos Aires exports in 1822 was £728,223; in 1842, £1,402,989; in 1851, £2,126,705; and in 1872, £7,008,048.[8] The annual growth rate of the value of exports was, therefore, 3.3% between 1822 and 1842, 4.7% between 1842 and 1851, and 5.8% between 1851 and 1872. For the whole 1822–1872 period, the annual growth rate was 4.6%.

Another estimate of the growth of Buenos Aires exports can be made by converting pounds and francs into pesos fuertes. Values estimated only according to fixed rates rather than market prices are available for France up to 1846 and for Great Britain up to 1853, but it is clear that there was an amazing growth of Buenos Aires exports to its four main customers from 1854 to 1870 (Figure 12.27).[9] From less than 15 million pesos fuertes in 1854, export value reached a peak in 1868 with more than 50 million pesos fuertes. It went down in 1869 and 1870, but total export value to those countries remained above 40 million pesos. It can be seen also that the value of imports from Argentina into France and Belgium grew in the 1850s and 1860s at a faster pace than the value of imports into the United States and Great Britain. These figures are consistent with those given previously for 1872, at which time the total value of exports from Buenos Aires and San Nicolás to all destinations was about 35 million pesos; in 1870 the value of imports from all Argentine ports into those four countries (which in 1872 accounted for 85% of total exports) was just above 40 million pesos. The difference is small and can be explained by a continuation of the decline of total export value, by the absence of information for 1872 for other Argentine ports (notably those of Entre Ríos), and by the different origin of those figures (exports from Buenos Aires, imports into its four main trading partners) and the consequent exchange problems arising from that difference. It is surprising that in spite of all those factors, the difference between the 1870 and 1872 figures is so small.

8 For the rates of exchange, see Appendix C. It has been assumed that values given by the Buenos Aires *Registro Estadístico* were recorded in pesos fuertes, equivalent to one ounce of silver, therefore £0.20. Paper money was convertible from 1867 to 1876 at the rate of 25 paper pesos for 1 peso fuerte, and peso fuerte became the monetary unit.

9 To estimate the value of British imports from 1830 to 1852, figures for the weight of hide imports (Table C.2) and Halperín Donghi's (1963) prices have been used. It has been assumed that hides accounted for 50% of all British imports from Buenos Aires. As pointed out in Appendix C, British imports did not always differentiate Buenos Aires and Río de la Plata. Figure 12.27 represents, therefore, a maximum estimate for British imports from Buenos Aires from 1830 to 1852. Halperín Donghi's (1963) hide price averages are slightly higher than those from Gayer, Rostow, and Schwartz (1953), but the trend is the same in both cases. I thank Carlos Newland for sending me a copy of Gayer's hide price averages.

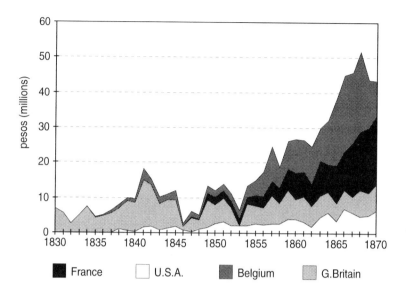

Figure 12.27. Value of Argentine imports into main customer countries, 1830–1870.

New markets for Argentine hides emerged, and the old ones either remained firm or had a small decline, so the overall result from the 1850–1870 period was an expansion of hide exports (Figure 12.28). An earlier concentration of demand in Great Britain and the United States (French data are also missing before 1847), was soon challenged by Belgian demand in the early 1840s. Great Britain accounted for most of the expansion of hide exports in the 1850s (although that may be only a consequence of the use of market prices to estimate the value of imports after 1854), but in the 1860s Belgium again accounted for most of the expansion of the demand for Buenos Aires hides. Comparing the mid-1850s, when import values for all those countries were based upon market prices, with 1870, the total value of hide imports into those countries was doubled.

Wool imports from Argentina into those four countries show an even more shocking pattern of development (Figure 12.29). Although these data suffer also from the lack of estimates based upon market prices for France before 1847 and for Britain before 1854, from the mid-1850s to the late 1860s, there is an amazing growth also led by Belgian demand. This figure clearly shows that in spite of an increasing U.S. demand, French and Belgian demand accounted for the growth of Argentina's wool exports. It also shows that leaving aside the mid-1860s peak, from the early 1850s to

Results

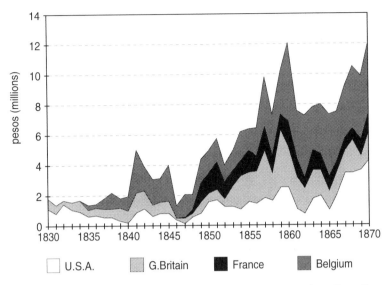

Figure 12.28. Argentine hide imports into main customer countries, 1830–1870.

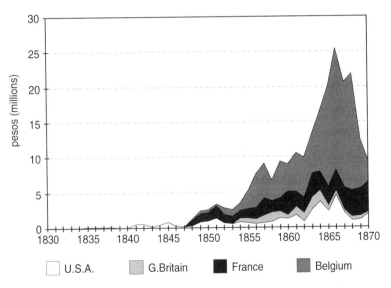

Figure 12.29. Argentine wool imports into main customer countries,
1830–1870.

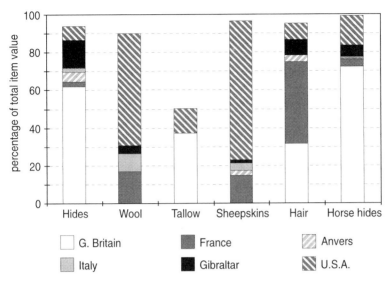

Figure 12.30. Buenos Aires exports: Main destinations, 1822.

1870, there was a threefold increase of wool imports from Argentina into those four countries.

The evolution of different markets for the different Buenos Aires exports can be better seen (although sacrificing the detailed evolution shown by Figures 12.28 and 12.29) from Argentine export statistics. These statistics allow us to examine the share of each of the main destinations over total export value (1842, 1851, and 1872) or total export quantity (1822 and 1862) for each of the main products.

In 1822, 61.9% of the total number of hides exported from Buenos Aires went to Great Britain (Figure 12.30).[10] Great Britain accounted for 58.9% of total dry hide exports and for 96.6% of total salted hide exports. The latter, however, accounted for only 7.9% of the total number of hides exported in that year. The second main destination for Buenos Aires hides was Gibraltar, 15%. There is no record of exports to Spain, so Gibraltar might have been the port where hides for that country were sent, or those hides might have ended up in Italy or Great Britain. Italy accounted for 1.9% of the total number of hides, the port of Anvers (later part of Belgium) for 5.5%, France for 2.4%, the United States for 7.1%, and other destinations for 6.2%. Horse hides were the second most valuable export in

---

10 The source for Figure 12.30 is AGN, III–22–5–9 to 20. For the value of those exports, the quotation for each product given by Parish has been used. See Parish (1958), 511.

1822. Most of them, 72.3%, were exported to Great Britain, 15.9% to the
United States, 5.9% to Gibraltar, 4.1% to France, 1% to Italy, 0.2% to
Anvers, and 0.7% to all other destinations. The third most valuable export
was then jerked beef; jerked-beef destinations were different from those of
other products, however, and they are dealt with separately for the whole
period. Tallow and hair came in fourth and fifth. The main destination for
hair was France, where 43.2% of Buenos Aires hair exports were sent.
Great Britain accounted for 31.6%, the United States for 8.6%, Gibraltar
for 8%, Anvers for 3.6%, and all other destinations for 4.9%. The main
destination for tallow was Great Britain, with 37.1% of Buenos Aires
tallow exports. Brazil accounted for 34%, the United States for 13%, the
Banda Oriental for 4.6%, Chile for 3.4%, and other destinations for 7.9%.
Wool and sheepskins were worth at that time less than 1% each of total
export value. The United States was the main destination for wool exports,
with 59.6% of its total volume. France accounted for 17%, Italy for 9.4%,
Gibraltar for 4.2%, and other destinations for 9.8%. There were no exports
to Anvers, and only 4 lbs were sent to Great Britain (equivalent to 0.01%
of total exports). Not much greater was Great Britain's share of total
sheepskin exports (0.04%). In this case the main destination was the
United States, with 73.7%; then France with 14.6%; Italy, 4%; Anvers,
2.5%; Gibraltar, 1.6%; and other destinations, 3.6%.

In 1842 horse hide exports had all but disappeared. They accounted for
just 1% of total export value. Great Britain was still the main destination,
accounting for 54% of that meager figure. Another difference regarding
1822 is found in the proportion of dry and salted hides to the total number
of hide exports. The former accounted for 72.6%, and the latter for 27.4%.
As the value of the latter was slightly higher (58 pesos against 50 pesos for
the former), its share of total hide export value was 30.4%. The main
destination for Buenos Aires dry hides was the United States, with 25.2%
(Figure 12.31).[11] France accounted for 16.5%, Great Britain for 5%,
Belgium for 4.3%, and other destinations for 49%. Among the latter,
exports to Falmouth (waiting for orders) accounted for 14.1% of total
exports, those to Spain for 17.4%, to Italy for 7.4%, and to Germany for
6.1%. The main destination for salted hides was Great Britain, with
43.6%. France accounted for 36.4%, the United States for 6%, Italy for
4.1%, Belgium for 3.6%, and other destinations for 6.3%. Wool was in
1842 the most important export after hides. The main destination for wool
was France, with 40.6% of total exports. The United States accounted for
37.6%, Great Britain for 11.3%, Italy for 4.5%, and Belgium, later the
main customer, for only 2%. Tallow exports were almost as valuable as
wool exports. The main destination for tallow was Great Britain, with

11 MAE, Correspondance commerciale, Buenos Aires, 2.

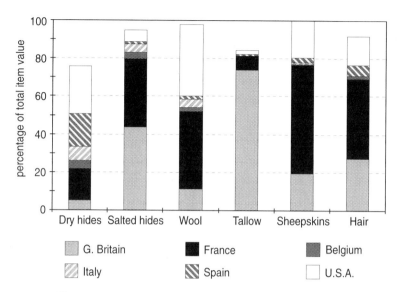

Figure 12.31. Buenos Aires exports: Main destinations, 1842.

74.2% of total exports. France accounted for 7.2%, Brazil for 8.1%, the
United States for 2.1%, and other destinations for 8.4%. Hair and sheepskins accounted for a similar share of total exports – the former for 3.7%,
and the latter for 3.3%. The main destination for hair was France, with
42% of total exports. Great Britain accounted for 27.4%, the United States
for 15%, Germany for 6.7%, Italy for 5.6%, Belgium for a mere 1.8%, and
other destinations for 1.5%. The main destination for sheepskins was again
France, with 57.5%. Great Britain and the United States accounted for
19.3% each, Spain for 2.7%, and other destinations for 1.2%.

In 1851 Great Britain was the destination of 22.9% of total hide exports
(Figure 12.32).[12] The United States accounted for 26.8%, Germany (including Belgium and the Netherlands) for 23.7%, France for 10.8%, Spain
for 8.2%, and Italy for 7.4%. The United States was also the destination of
most of the Buenos Aires wool exports, with 83.2% of the total. Great
Britain accounted for 5.8%, France for 4%, and Italy and Spain for 3.5%
each. Tallow was exported mainly to Great Britain, which accounted for
94.8% of total exports. France accounted for 2.2%, Germany for 0.5%,
Italy and Spain for 0.2% each, and the United States for 0.1%. Sheepskins
were exported mainly to France, accounting for 56.2% of total exports.
The United States accounted for 31.7%, Great Britain for 10.3%, Italy for

12 Parish (1958), 512, 514–515.

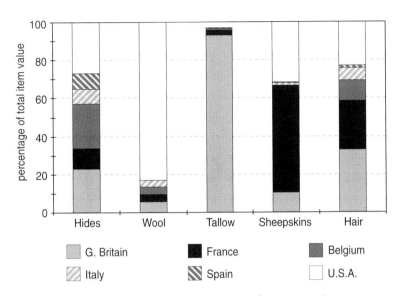

Figure 12.32. Buenos Aires exports: Main destinations, 1851.

1.2%, Germany for 0.3%, and Spain for 0.1%. Finally, hair was exported to Great Britain, accounting for 33% of total exports. France accounted for 25.4%, the United States for 23%, Germany for 10.5%, Italy for 6.6%, and Spain for 1.1%.

In 1862 dry and salted hides are again listed separately. To the former corresponded 79.9% of total hide exports in that year, and to the latter 20.1%. The United States was the main destination for dry hides, with 32.4% of total exports (Figure 12.33).[13] Germany (with Belgium and the Netherlands) accounted for 25.7%, Spain for 18.1%, Italy for 11.7%, France for 10.7%, and Great Britain for 1.4%. The main destination for salted hides was Germany, with 50.7%. Great Britain accounted for 38.5%, France for 7.9%, Italy for 2.5%, and Spain for 0.3%. There were no salted hides exported to the United States in that year.

During the previous decade, from 1849 to 1862, the United States had maintained the lead as the main destination of the Buenos Aires dry hide exports. Exports to the United States accounted for 35.6% of total exports in 1849–1852, 31.8% in 1853–1857, and 29% in 1858–1862. The second place in the three periods was for Germany, with 30.6%, 26.8%, and 25.8%. The share of Great Britain was always low, not rising beyond

13 Maxwell (1863).

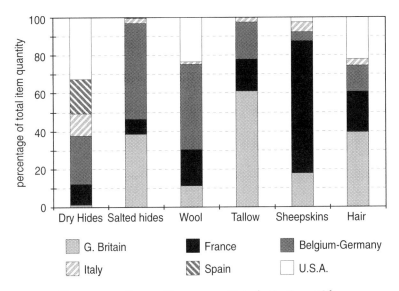

Figure 12.33. Buenos Aires exports: Main destinations, 1862.

3% in any of those three periods. The French share remained between 10% and 12%. That of Italy rose from 7% to 13% from the first to the third period, and that of Spain from 12% to 18%. Throughout that decade the main destination for salted hides was Great Britain, with 59.3% in 1849–1852, 57.3% in 1853–1857, and 63.1% in 1858–1862. The U.S. share fell from 14.7% in the first period to 2.6% in the third. France's share rose from 10% to 13%, but Belgium's rose even more, from 9% to 17.9%. The main destination for wool exports was Germany (rather, the port of Anvers, in Belgium), with 45.2% of total exports. The United States accounted for 23.3%, France for 18.9%, Great Britain for 11.4%, Italy for 1.2%, and Spain for 0.1%. Belgium had evolved into the main exporter in the late 1850s. In 1849–1852 the United States was still the main customer for Buenos Aires wool, with 63.2% of total exports. In 1853–1857 the U.S. share fell to 27.1%, and in 1858–1862 it fell again to 21.1%. Belgium rose from 8% in 1849–1852 to 30.8% in 1853–1857, and to 39.8% in 1858–1862. The share of France also rose from 12.2% in the first period to 27.5% in the third.[14]

In 1872 there were changes both in the leading products exported from Buenos Aires and in the leading trading partner. Wool, as seen earlier,

14 For each country's share of dry hides, salted hides, and wool exports in those three periods, see Maxwell (1863), 14.

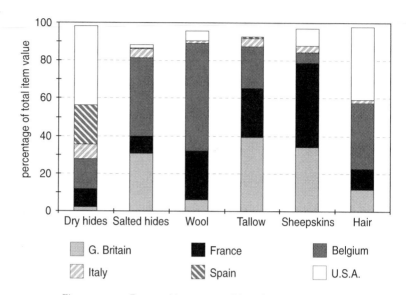

Figure 12.34. Buenos Aires exports: Main destinations, 1872.

accounted then for the largest share of Buenos Aires exports, and Belgium was the main customer. Belgium accounted for 57.2% of total wool exports, and France accounted for 26%. The remainder was distributed among Great Britain, with 6%; the United States, with 5.1%; Germany, with 2.2%; Italy, with 1.4%; and other destinations, with 2.1% (Figure 12.34).[15] Belgium was also the main destination for salted hides, with 41.3% of total exports. Great Britain was in second place, with 30.6%. France accounted for 9.2%, Germany for 7.3%, Italy for 4.7%, the United States for 1.7%, Spain for 0.6%, and other destinations for 4.6%. The main destination for dry hides was the United States, with 42.2% of total exports, followed by Spain with 20.6%. Belgium accounted for 15.6%, France for 9.8%, Italy for 8.1%, Great Britain for 2.1%, Germany for 0.4%, and other destinations for 1.2%. Great Britain was the main destination for tallow, with 39.2% of total exports, but France accounted for 26%, and Belgium for 22.1%. Chile and Italy accounted for 4.6% each, and other destinations accounted for 3.5%. Hair and sheepskin exports presented a pattern similar to that of tallow exports, but with two main customers. The main destinations of hair exports were the United States with 38.4%, and Belgium, with 35.2%. Great Britain accounted for 11.8%, France for 10.6%, Italy for 1.9%, and other destina-

15 REBA (1872), 173–179, 184–186.

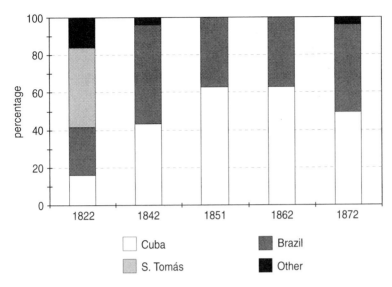

Figure 12.35. Buenos Aires jerked-beef exports: Main destinations, 1822–1872.

tions for 2.1%. In the case of sheepskins, the main customers were France, with 44.6% of total exports, and Great Britain, with 34%. The United States accounted for 9.2%, Belgium for 6%, Italy for 3.1%, and other destinations for 3.1%.

Jerked beef was from the 1820s to the 1860s one of Buenos Aires's leading exports. Markets for jerked beef were, however, different than those for other livestock by-products. Brazil and the Antilles, mainly Cuba, accounted for the bulk of total exports throughout the period (Figure 12.35).[16] It is known that jerked beef was destined for slave consumption and that efforts to find different markets for it were not successful. Of the 5 years studied between 1822 and 1871, only in 1822 is there a destination more important than Cuba or Brazil – Santo Tomás, probably the Caribbean island of Saint Thomas. This destination may have been for customs purposes, due to the still unsettled state of the diplomatic and commercial relations between Spain and Buenos Aires. The final destinations of jerked-beef exports to Santo Tomás might well have been Havana. The share of Buenos Aires jerked-beef exports of the Brazilian and Cuban markets is unknown. The only possible estimate according to the available evidence is for Cuba between 1849 and 1854. Cuban jerked-beef

16 For the sources of Figure 12.35, see nn. 8 to 11 and 13.

imports for those years added up to 7,437,139 arrobas. Buenos Aires jerked-beef exports to Cuba during the same years added up to 6,296,276 arrobas. So if the Buenos Aires arroba was equivalent to the Cuban arroba, Buenos Aires exports accounted for 84.7% of Cuban jerked-beef imports during that 6-year period.[17]

Conclusion

Hides were Buenos Aires's most important export from the 1820s to the 1850s. In the early 1870s, however, they had been displaced by wool. Tallow exports grew throughout the whole period, and other products retained a visible share of Buenos Aires exports, such as jerked beef through the 1850s and sheepskins in the 1860s. Whatever the leading product was, Argentine exports grew at an astonishing pace throughout the period.

That growth was possible due to the emergence of new markets for a new product, such as France and Belgium for wool, and the consolidation of old markets for old products, such as the United States for hides. But the overall picture cannot be summarized just in those two factors. Dry hides were demanded in the United States, salted hides in Great Britain, sheepskins in France, and tallow in Belgium. There were a few main products and a few main customers, but the combination of products and markets did not remain constant, except for jerked beef.

Buenos Aires exports had different markets, and those markets evolved over time for its different products. There was no single pattern for the evolution of overseas markets for the Buenos Aires export products. Some markets had developed before any significant export left Buenos Aires, so its products failed to capture a sizeable share of them, but, in other cases, a late arrival did not prevent Buenos Aires exports from capturing a large market share. Finally, demand from other markets was met by Buenos Aires products as soon as it developed.

An example of the first case is the British wool market. Buenos Aires exports increased, but the market had developed before any sizeable amount of wool from the pampas reached it. An example of the second case is the development of tallow exports to Great Britain. Demand was present well before Buenos Aires tallow had any meaningful presence in the British market, but an increasing share of that market was captured. An example of the third case is the Belgian wool market. When demand emerged in

17 For Cuban jerked-beef imports, see *Merchant's Magazine*, 1859, 40:283. For Buenos Aires jerked-beef exports to Cuba, see Maxwell (1863). As two different sources are used for this estimate, and there was a lag of several months between the record of an export in Buenos Aires and of an import into Cuba, the aggregate for that 6-year period, rather than figures for single years, has been preferred.

Belgium, Buenos Aires wool production was growing, so its wool exports to Belgium accompanied the evolution of that market.

In some cases the Buenos Aires exports to a market stagnated or declined. But in the long run, growth was the rule for all products and most markets. Hide exports to Great Britain and France declined from the mid-1850s onward, but that decline was offset by hide exports to other markets. Hide exports, in fact, doubled from 1850 to 1870.

Prices were right, conditions of commercialization were right, and markets were growing. These key conditions account for the process of expansion undergone by Buenos Aires from 1820 to 1870, but, as stressed in previous chapters, other conditions were also necessary to explain that process.

The amazing growth of Buenos Aires exports is not a statistical illusion. The quality of statistics produced in Buenos Aires and in her main trading partners improved in the 1850s, and for that reason it is easier to picture the growth of exports from then onward. That process of export growth, although more difficult to trace, had started much before. The 1850s, however, were a watershed. It can be attributed both to the development of new markets for new products and to the improved conditions of production in Buenos Aires as a result of the removal of arbitrary rule, accompanied by an effort to clarify and enforce the rules of the game.

In spite of a specialization in the production and export of livestock by-products, Buenos Aires responded in a flexible way to changing patterns of demand in different markets. Four countries accounted for most of the exports from 1820 to 1870, but none of those countries was the main destination for all products at any one time. That was not the result of a planned export diversification but rather the answer to different stimuli originating in different overseas economies within a legal context that allowed local producers to take full advantage of those opportunities.

13

Conclusion

The estancia was a type of economic organization that led the process of economic expansion in nineteenth-century Buenos Aires. Estancias had existed since the early days of Spanish settlement in the region, but it was only in the late eighteenth century and during the nineteenth century that they turned into a dynamic type of organization. This change was partially due to external factors – a growing European demand for hides – affecting the local structure of relative prices. But it was also due to human endeavor aimed at the search for profit. The number of cattleowners and head of cattle at the beginning of that process made it impossible for any of the former to attempt the exclusion of actual and potential competitors by means of regulation for privilege. Moreover, an increasingly ineffectual authority, due both to the weakness of the Spanish crown and the new challenges posed by the opening up of new land, turned any such attempt into an unthinkable proposition. So when estancias started to spread over the pampas and their main product turned out to be hides for export, estancieros had to compete with each other and to organize factors of production in a way leading to the survival of the firm. Demand was steady, but there were no guarantees of profit. Individual estancieros had to cope with political insecurity, the Indian threat, the weather, price fluctuations, and many other factors generating uncertainty. It was only their ability to do so that could lead to making a profit out of estancia operations. Estancia operations were therefore guided by market signs. Insofar as the prevalence of market mechanisms is a definition for capitalism, the rise of capitalism on the pampas took place as soon as estancias began to spread over them.

The internal structure, operations, and economic aims of estancias, and the conditions surrounding their evolution, have been dealt with in this book. First, the combination of factors on one estancia at the end of the eighteenth century was studied. Free and forced labor were used on that estancia to raise cattle for urban consumption. The different cycles undergone by that estancia underscore the entrepreneurial skill required by that kind of firm to turn a profit. And profit rates were sound. The economic foundations for the process of expansion that had already started, but which would boom in the nineteenth century, were then in place. The financial mechanism used for that expansion was also present – cattle liquidation or cattle capitalization.

After 1810, particularly after 1820, and for decades to come, the process of territorial expansion to the south was fostered by the rapid growth of exports. Estancias turned then into "the principal wealth and better hope" of Buenos Aires, but their capital structure showed no striking variations.[1] Land, livestock, improvements, a few tools, and few other goods were found on estancias both around 1820 and 1850. By the latter year, however, slaves had disappeared, and there were changes in the value of the other items as proportion of the capital structure. Land value went up, and cattle value went down. Changes in the conditions of production and in managerial and entrepreneurial skills can only explain the estancias' continued expansion and growth in spite of those changes.

Conditions of production did change in the first half of the nineteenth century. They would change in a more radical way in the second half with the introduction of new technology, but in the previous period, no new technology was introduced apart from the bottomless bucket. Nor were radical changes present in the material conditions of production. Yields and reproduction rates do not change in the short run, and there were no incentives to introduce new breeding techniques in a massive way – the cost of refining cattle was higher than the expected return from better hide, tallow, and jerked-beef exports. Wool production would change that situation, but wool would not prevail over cattle by-products until the early 1860s. By 1850 the pampas were still populated mainly by cattle, since they had not yet been pushed south of the Salado River by sheep.

Environmental changes were the inevitable company for such an expansion of production. By the mid-eighteenth century, cattle had been instrumental in spreading thistleries, and as long as cattle prevailed, thistles covered vast extensions of the pampas. Only sheep and later agriculture would help to bring them under control. Due to their seasonal cycle, thistles emphasized the seasonality of rural tasks.

Production changes brought about institutional change as well. Old habits die hard, but by mid-century they were a burden for rural producers. The still open fields were overcharged when compared to the 1820s, and hunting and transit rights that had been advantageous or neutral for most producers turned into a nuisance. An effort aiming at a proper definition of property rights began in the 1850s. Laws, however, were difficult to enforce. Anti-vagrancy laws were defeated by the same interests that claimed them. And the state was in no position to enforce such laws in

1 REBA (April 1822), 54.

spite of so many free-riders. But even if the law could not be easily enforced, there were underway two parallel processes of institutional change. On the one hand, institution building in the countryside – both state institutions (police, justice, army) and local institutions (militia and local administration, but also schools and voluntary associations) – was taking place in and around old and new villages and towns.[2] On the other hand, there was an internal institutional change within the estancia, as shown by Rosas's 1819 set of managerial rules.[3] Those rules are a clear-cut case of internalization of externalities, a redefinition of the role of the firm. There was, therefore, institutional change, but its peculiarities and effects have only been suggested here to point out that estancias did not operate in an institutional vacuum but rather within a changing setting that their own expansion was forcing to redefine.

Material, environmental, and institutional conditions of production were only a long-term framework for human action. No good produces itself – only human action can turn nature into a good, even if that action is just hunting or gathering. Beyond that primitive stage of production, more than labor is required for production. Firms require not only workers but also managers and entrepreneurs.

Slaves and later free permanent workers were necessary to perform the regular estancia tasks – tending livestock, and the upkeep of improvements. Temporary workers were hired for short periods for special tasks such as gathering, sorting, branding, gelding, and dehorning head of cattle. Biological, climatic, and environmental factors (calving, heat, thistles) determined a seasonal pattern of rural work and, therefore, a seasonal pattern of labor demand. Tasks, however, were irregular even within the peak season, so labor demand was uneven during inter-seasonal as much as during intra-seasonal periods. Labor instability has been elsewhere attributed to the workers' character or cultural traits (laziness or independence), but that character and those cultural traits were the consequence (not the cause) of such pattern of labor demand. Labor instability was therefore not related to labor scarcity but rather to that seasonal pattern of labor demand, characteristic of all agrarian economies.

Peons alone did not raise head of cattle. Estancias required managers and entrepreneurs as well. On the one hand, managers were in charge of overseeing estancia operations. Workers and foremen came and went, but managers (the owner, a partner, a mayordomo) had to decide when to carry out those operations, when to hire more workers, when to sell head of cattle, and what head would be sold. On the other hand, entrepreneurs (estancieros) were in charge of devising a proper combination of inputs: the

2 See Cansanello (1994) and (1995).
3 As remarked by Halperín Donghi (1963), 97ff.

right extension of land, the right number of head, the right number of permanent and temporary workers. Entrepreneurs had to take care as well of the overall administration of estancias, paying taxes and bribes, providing legal and extra-legal protection to the firm and its employees. As the institutional framework evolved and property rights were better defined, the role of entrepreneurs became more differentiated from that of simple managers.

Entrepreneurial skills were necessary, but they were not always present in people going into the estancia business. The case analyzed here, the Aguirre–Ignes partnership, points to moderate managerial and poor entrepreneurial skills. The vilified Anchorenas did have those skills, which were surely more appreciated in a society that had not yet become contemptuous of success. Land was granted to them, as well as to many other people, and they turned those barren tracts into successful enterprises, under Rosas's dictatorship and later as well.

The recollection of the Anchorena case serves another purpose also. Land was granted to them, but rents (in the sense used by Tullock, not Ricardo) did not stem from that fact.[4] As soon as cattle spread over a tract of land, as soon as it was populated and secured, its value increased. Because capital could be realized and put to a different use, a return was therefore expected from its application to rural production. In order to make a profit, such managerial and entrepreneurial skills were required. Otherwise, there was no profit. Land could be left unused, but no rent would derive from it in that case. If a land grant was sold, the original beneficiary could make a windfall profit (or, rather, cash in a one-time rent), but subsequent owners, those who had paid a price for a piece of land, had to obtain a positive return from their investment. The market for land was far from closed, and many grants were sold. Landownership (if rural production was involved) was not therefore tantamount to rent seeking, since land produced rent only once. After that, land and landowners were subject to market mechanisms.

The result of estancia operations was estimated here for one estancia at the end of the eighteenth century. Since no similar sources have been found yet to reproduce that analysis for a later period, other sources were used for this purpose. At a microeconomic level, the result of estancias as business concerns was analyzed on the basis of three profitability estimates. They are not as high as some contemporaries guessed, but they were more than reasonable to convince anyone to go into that business. These estimates fail, however, to take uncertainty (risk for which there is widespread disagreement, according to Demsetz) into account.[5] Over a period of years, those optimistic estimates would turn into a lower profit rate due to

---

4 Tullock (1967) and (1993); Buchanan, Tollison, and Tullock (1980).
5 Demsetz (1988).

unforeseen factors such as prolonged droughts (as in the late 1820s and early 1830s), civil wars, revolutions, and Indian invasions – factors that we know about today but which were not then forecastable with any degree of precision.

Prices and marketing conditions were also the result of human activity. For the estancia business to be profitable, the combination of international prices, freight rates, and marketing expenses had to translate into internal prices remunerative enough of the estancieros' endeavors. The export of cattle by-products started to grow at a time of rising prices in Europe, but falling prices after 1820 did not prevent an even larger growth of the Buenos Aires exports. It has been argued that one of the reasons for that response was the estancieros' ability to take advantage of local inflation to pay their workers' salaries with depreciated paper money while getting hard currencies for their exports. This argument implies that, as relative prices do not fluctuate homogeneously, the price of labor relative to export-able goods changed in favor of estancieros and against the rural workers. But this argument fails to take into account many factors. First, it is true that there was paper money inflation from 1826 onward, but apart from the two blockade periods (1838–1840 and 1845–1847), according to the paper peso–gold ounce exchange rate, there was stability in the 1830s, deflation in the early and late 1840s, and a slow depreciation of paper money from the early 1850s onward. Therefore, if there was a deterioration of real salaries in the long run, the short-run consequences are an open question. Second, it is known that the Buenos Aires paper money was not accepted in the Interior provinces, but the rhythm of its spread over the Buenos Aires countryside has still to be established. And third, even if it spread fairly rapidly, a considerable proportion of export hides came from regions where no paper money was used. If real salaries were deteriorating in Buenos Aires but not in the Interior, a migration should have taken place from Buenos Aires to the Interior. As there was migration, but from the Interior to Buenos Aires, the argument based upon the deterioration of real salaries should be ruled out until further evidence can be produced to support it.

Prices, marketing conditions, and managerial and entrepreneurial skills turned the estancia into a profitable concern. At a macroeconomic level, the consequence was a remarkable growth of exports. There were just a few products and a few main markets, but the combination of products and markets shifted during the nineteenth century. Against those who saw Argentine rural production in the twentieth century as homogeneous, Carlos Díaz Alejandro argued that there were many rural products with many different markets.[6] In the nineteenth century, there were fewer

6 Díaz Alejandro (1970), 17–21.

products and fewer markets, but the prevailing institutional conditions let the adjustment be made in a successful way by individual entrepreneurs following the signs posted by markets.

In nineteenth-century Buenos Aires, during the period considered here, resources were not allocated according to any other mechanism than the firm, and the structure of those firms was fairly simple. Land grants created a one-time rent, but no other rents were created along the road for business concerns that had no protection from outside risk factors and that looked for none. This was not due to an excess of public virtue lacking before or after those estancieros were around. Rent seeking was too costly in a place where entry barriers were impossible to establish, where a monopoly was unthinkable, and where regulations of any kind were hard to enforce. Because of that and a set of right exogenous conditions combined with personal skills, estancieros sought for profit instead of rents, seeking no interference with market mechanisms. Capitalism had risen on the pampas.

There was no writing on any wall. Market conditions are not known beforehand. It is up to individuals to act (or not) according to those signs, to push for institutional change, and to be able to take advantage of new conditions. Growth, as remarked by North, is the result of the coincidence of the private and social rates of return.[7] Because of exogenous conditions (steady demand for her products) and endogenous conditions (too many producers, an environment hostile to regulation enforcement, a declining law enforcement ability of governments), the Buenos Aires economy began growing at the end of the eighteenth century. That growth was led by a type of economic organization, the estancia, under conditions of increasing freedom. This book contributes to the understanding of that process by shedding light on the estancia as a type of economic organization.

7 North and Thomas (1973), North (1990).

A

Profit rates and present value

In Tables 2.6 and 2.7, the rate of profit (b) has been estimated as follows:

$$\left(M + i\right) = P$$

$$P = \left(K_t + I\right)$$

$$M = K_{t-1} + E$$

$$\left[\left(K_{t-1} + E\right) + i\right] = K_t + I$$

$$i = \left(K_t + I\right) - \left(K_{t-1} + E\right)$$

$$i = \left(K_t - K_{t-1}\right) + \left(I - E\right)$$

$$i_n = K_t - K_{t-1}$$

$$i_c = I - E$$

$$i = i_n + i_c$$

$$b = i\left(100\right)/K_{t-1}$$

where M is the amount of initial investment; i, total profit; P, present value; K_t, capital according to inventory; K_{t-1}, capital according to the previous year's inventory value; I, income; E, expenditure; i_n, non-cashed profit; i_c, cashed profit; and b, the annual rate of profit.

The inventory variation (V) and return on investment (R) have been estimated as follows:

$$V = i_n\left(100\right)/K_{t-1}$$

$$R = i_c\left(100\right)/K_{t-1}$$

The slaves' present value (P_s) has been estimated in Chapter 2 as follows:

$$P_s = M + A + \frac{A}{\left(1 + d\right)} + \frac{A}{\left(1 + d\right)^2} + \ldots + \frac{A}{\left(1 + d\right)^{19}}$$

where M is the amount of initial investment (cost of a slave); A, the annual expenditure on a slave (clothing, food, and other expenses); and d, the interest rate (6%). A peon's present value has been estimated in the same way, but in this case there is no M, and A includes both salary and food.

B

Probate inventories

Probate inventories from 1820 and 1850 have been chosen in order to analyze the evolution of the capital structure of rural properties at the onset and at the end of the first wave of territorial and economic expansion.[1] These inventories are found in *sucesiones*, the legal procedures carried out to split the estate between the heirs of a deceased person.[2] Only estancia inventories are used here; personal belongings, urban property, quintas, and chacras are not considered. Chapters 3 and 4 focus upon the estancias, not on their owners. Personal wealth has not been a concern here, so personal items not directly related to production – such as clothing, religious images, and musical instruments – have been excluded from those inventories. Furniture and cutlery have been retained, since they were necessary for people involved in productive activities.[3] For unknown reasons some inventories were not complete. They have been disregarded.

The 1820 sample includes inventories from 1818 to 1822 (Tables B.1 and B.2). From 382 probate records corresponding to those years, 83 inventories were collected, 66 of which were used in the first section of Chapter 3. The 1850 sample includes inventories from 1848 to 1851 (Tables B.3 and B.4). From 587 probate records corresponding to those years, 94 inventories were collected, 63 of which were used in the second section of the same chapter. These totals include all probate records, not just those with estancia inventories. Probate records with estancia inventories are only a fraction of all probate records. No attempt has been made to determine this fraction precisely. These samples were collected at random, taking 1820 and 1850 as the base years. Only for those two years were all extant estancia inventories collected.[4]

---

1 For a broader discussion of methodological issues related to probate inventories, see Smith (1975) and Lindert (1981), as well as the books mentioned in Chapter 3, n. 1.

2 For a study of the Buenos Aires inventories as a source, see Garavaglia (1993), 125–127.

3 Urban property, chacras, quintas, and items not related to production were also disregarded by Garavaglia (1993).

4 Garavaglia (1993) took into account all estancia inventories from 1750 to 1815 (the title of his article mentions 1850 as the closing year, but that is a printing error since no information is found there beyond 1815). He used 281 inventories for a 65-year period, while I have used here 66 for a 5-year period (1818–1822) and 63 for a 4-year period (1848–1851).

Table B.1. *Inventories of estancias on owned land, 1818–1822*

Name	Legajo[a]	Year	Place
1. Burgos, Luis	3920	1818	Pilar
2. Burgos, Santiago Felipe	3920	1820	Cañada de la Cruz
3. Cano, Bautista	4842	1819	Luján
4. Cavrera, María Antonia	4842	1819	Magdalena
5. Caxaravilla, Andrés	4843	1820	Magdalena
6. Chaves, Gerónima	4843	1821	Salado
7. Figueroa, Mariano	5692	1822	San Antonio de Areco
8. Garay, Mercedes	5910	1821	Guardia de Salto
9. Gómez, María R.	5910	1821	San Pedro
10. González, Dámaso Tadeo	5910	1821	Quilmes
11. Guerra y López, Sebastián	5909	1818	Pilar
12. Gutiérrez, Bonifacio	5910	1821	Navarro
13. Lara, Manuela	6499	1822	Magdalena
14. López, Cipriano	6498	1818	Luján
15. López, Margarita	6499	1822	Pilar
16. López Olivera, María G.	6499	1820	Pilar
17. Navarro, Juan	7206	1822	San Pedro
18. Noriega, Manuel	7206	1819	San Andrés de Giles
19. Pacheco, Bartolo	7389	1822	Cañada de la Cruz
20. Palomeque, Gerardo	7388	1818	Luján
21. Pardo, Bernardina	7389	1822	Pilar
22. Parodi, Andrés	7388	1820	Pilar
23. Piñero, Andrés	7389	1822	Luján
24. Rocha, Gabriel	7782	1818	Pergamino
25. Rodríguez, Antonio	7782	1818	Luján
26. Rodríguez, Juan de la Rosa	7782	1819	Luján
27. Rodríguez, Pascual	7784	1822	Pilar
28. Rodríguez, Petrona	7784	1822	San Antonio de Areco
29. Rodríguez, Severino	7782	1819	Luján
30. Rodríguez Berón, Alejandro	7784	1821	San Vicente
31. Rojas, Santiago	7784	1821	Chascomús
32. Romero, María Mercedes	7782	1818	Baradero
33. Tito, Pedro	8458	1822	Arrecifes

[a] AGN, Tribunales, Sucesiones.

Regions

North: Arrecifes, Baradero, Cañada de la Cruz, Capilla del Señor, Chivilcoy, Exaltación de la Cruz, Fortín de Areco, Fuerte Federación, Guardia de Salto, Pergamino, Rojas, Salto, San Andrés de Giles, San Antonio de Areco, San Nicolás, San Pedro.

Center: Cañuelas, Flores, Guardia de Luján, La Matanza, Las Conchas, Lobos (in 1850 only), Luján, Merlo, Morón, Navarro (in 1850 only), Pilar, San Isidro.

South: Chascomús, Ensenada, Magdalena, Monte, Quilmes, Ranchos, San Vicente.

Frontier: Lobos, Navarro.

New South: Ajó, Azul, Bahía Blanca, Bragado, Chapaleofú, Dolores, Las Flores, Lobería, Mar Chiquita, Monsalvo, Montes Grandes, Mulitas, Pila, Saladillo, Tapalqué, Tordillo, Tuyú, Vecino.

Table B.1a. *Estancias on owned land, 1820: Capital structure*

Region	Land (ha) A	Land B	Imp. C	Tools D	Cattle E	Horses F	Sheep G	Slaves H	Other I	Total J	Land B/J	Imp.+Tools[a] (C+D)/J	Livestock (E+F+G)/J
North													
2	338	188	129	238	980	94	52	0	24	1,704	0.11	0.215	0.661
7	338	125	564	178	5,345	134	333	845	29	7,551	0.017	0.098	0.77
8	810	225	58	54	1,429	48	851	190	33	2,888	0.078	0.039	0.806
9	17,499	5,330	1,048	186	57,791	725	403	2,675	10	68,167	0.078	0.018	0.864
17	1,245	389	147	71	470	147	0	450	26	1,249	0.311	0.175	0.494
18	675	250	481	365	4,616	351	823	415	165	7,500	0.033	0.113	0.772
19	878	488	115	105	707	80	49	795	12	1,969	0.248	0.112	0.425
24	1,856	1,375	434	157	5,982	428	208	430	199	9,578	0.144	0.062	0.691
28	1,013	375	50	92	4,443	77	357	1,415	63	5,886	0.064	0.024	0.829
32	4,059	3,006	1,449	207	3,040	115	238	250	521	9,992	0.301	0.166	0.34
33	62	46	134	80	1,585	75	151		30	2,349	0.02	0.091	0.771
Mean	2,616	1,072	419	157	7,853	207	315	679	101	10,803	0.099	0.053	0.775
Center													
1	169	63	48	127	355	42	382	0	56	1,072	0.059	0.163	0.727
3	675	250	54	70	806	70	269	200	12	1,722	0.145	0.072	0.665
11	5,648	1494	1999	242	1747	233	171	100	25	6,011	0.249	0.373	0.358
14	1,637	492	1750	277	4886	588	222	800	360	9,375	0.052	0.216	0.608
15	757	338	816	125	2117	86	468	250	126	4,324	0.078	0.218	0.618
16	4,759	1772	922	342	2133	303	1,110	420	116	7,118	0.249	0.178	0.498
20	1,703	545	885	225	2153	431	196	730	451	5,616	0.097	0.198	0.495
21	405	225	57	116	437	109	0	0	25	970	0.232	0.178	0.563

22	135	50	100	171	104	77	920	229	171	1,822	0.027	0.149	0.604
23	2,025	1125	378	294	8845	231	733	1,450	28	13,084	0.086	0.051	0.75
25	24	18	216	191	2919	198	783	0	28	4,353	0.004	0.093	0.896
26	338	129	9	18	1176	48	3	0	23	1,406	0.092	0.019	0.873
27	763	424	248	451	1430	219	216	800	179	3,966	0.107	0.176	0.47
29	169	63	83	138	1991	47	303	0	30	2,655	0.024	0.083	0.882
Mean	1,372	499	540	199	2221	191	412	356	116	4,535	0.11	0.163	0.623
South													
4	360	102	188	156	1,017	184	447	530	3	2,626	0.039	0.131	0.628
5	31,500	8,750	4,320	391	53,903	1,665	1,755	340	967	72,090	0.121	0.065	0.795
10	338	250	1,730	195	572	82	300	0	65	3,194	0.078	0.603	0.299
13	4,253	3,330	1,136	357	18,915	552	806	930	419	26,445	0.126	0.056	0.767
30	5,130	300	344	43	7,437	448	563	400	50	9,585	0.031	0.04	0.881
31	3,105	2,300	120	105	522	143	0	280	68	3,536	0.65	0.064	0.188
Mean	7,448	2,505	1,306	208	13,727	512	645	413	262	19,579	0.128	0.077	0.76
Frontier													
6	4,725	237	651	57	520	74	63	0	30	1,632	0.145	0.434	0.402
12	10,800	117	258	333	1,873	13	0	450	130	3,174	0.037	0.186	0.594
Mean	7,763	177	455	195	1,197	44	32	225	80	2,403	0.074	0.27	0.53
Mean	3,278	1,035	634	187	6,129	246	399	466	136	9,231	0.112	0.089	0.734

[a] Imp = Improvement

Table B.1b. *Estancias on owned land, 1820: Livestock*

Region	Land	Cattle	Horses	Sheep	LU	h/LU
North						
2	338	229	116	112	387	0.87
7	338	1,389	102	841	1,622	0.21
8	810	545	89	2,357	951	0.85
9	17,499	15,226	1,029	1,260	16,670	1.05
17	1,245	138	197	0	384	3.24
18	675	1,360	506	2,350	2,286	0.3
19	878	169	97	78	300	2.93
24	1,856	1,992	649	748	2,897	0.64
28	1,013	1,210	56	1,043	1,410	0.72
32	4,059	762	223	535	1,108	3.66
33	62	388	107	554	591	0.11
Mean	2,616	860	288	897	2,601	1.01
Center						
1	169	89	34	1,110	270	0.63
3	675	292	72	808	483	1.4
11	5,648	802	296	808	1,273	4.44
14	1,637	1,666	636	825	2,564	0.64
15	757	635	92	1,436	930	0.81
16	4,759	622	753	3,140	1,956	2.43

20	1,703	530	567	590	1,313	1.3
21	405	74	140	0	249	1.63
22	135	15	55	2,130	350	0.39
23	2,025	2,258	153	2,118	2,714	0.75
25	24	763	321	1,829	1,393	0.02
26	338	355	75	10	450	0.75
27	763	346	361	620	875	0.87
29	169	434	104	868	673	0.25
Mean	1,372	634	261	1,164	1,106	1.24
South						
4	360	280	226	1,021	690	0.52
5	31,500	14,557	1,432	2,980	16,720	1.88
10	338	140	85	1,000	371	0.91
13	4,253	4,714	507	3,345	5,766	0.74
30	5,130	2,348	537	2,500	3,332	1.54
31	3,105	229	163	0	433	7.18
Mean	7,448	3,711	492	1,808	4,552	1.64
Frontier						
6	4,725	134	30	200	197	24.05
12	10,800	517	7	0	526	20.54
Mean	7,763	326	19	100	362	21.47
Mean	3,278	1,673	297	1,128	2,186	1.5

The reason for restricting the 1820 sample to 1818–1822 and the 1850 sample to 1848–1851 is the price difference between the first and last year of each sample compared to the previous and following years (1817 and 1823; 1847 and 1852). Prices were not stable in either period, but price variations do not necessarily mean inflation. For that reason no attempt has been made to correct the values for 1818–1822 and 1848–1851 according to any price index.[5]

How representative these samples are can be determined in two ways: first, by estimating the proportion of the total productive area covered by these estancias; and second, by estimating the area needed by the number of livestock units found on these estancias. In order to estimate the total area of the 1820 estancias, the area covered by estancias on non-owned land in each region should be found (Table B.5). First, investment per hectare is estimated for each region (column C). Second, the value of land is estimated for estancias on non-owned land (column E). And third, the total value of estancias on owned land and non-owned land (column F) is divided by the average investment per hectare for each region. The result is the estimated area for all estancias in all regions, 144,587 hectares (column G). This figure rises to 153,562 hectares when estimates for each region are added up. Since the productive area around 1820 was about 4.5 million hectares (all regions north of the Salado River, plus Ajó and Tuyú), the area estimated for those 66 estancias ranged from 3.2% to 3.4% of the total area.

The second way to estimate the area covered by the 1820 estancias is based upon the livestock density (Table B.6). The number of head in each region has been multiplied by the average number of hectares required by one livestock unit in the same region. A total of 99,767 head found on those 66 estancias in 1820 would have required a total area ranging from 149,650 hectares to 167,793 hectares. These figures are equivalent to 3.3% and 3.7% of the 4.5 million hectares estimated for the whole productive area.

Estimating the area covered by 63 estancias in 1850 according to the value of estancias on owned land (Table B.7) results in a range of from 279,038 hectares to 288,930 hectares, equivalent to 2.4% of the 11.8 million hectares of the total productive area (the same as in 1820 plus Rojas, Saladillo, Azul, and Lobería). According to the total number of livestock units, the results range from 282,523 hectares to 283,690 hectares (Table B.8), equivalent also to 2.4% of the same productive area.

---

5 Inflation, understood as the rapid upward surge of nominal prices, is a complex phenomenon that does not affect all sectors, actors, and goods in the same way. The perception of price variations did not provoke immediate reactions from economic actors. For the consequences of paper money fluctuations on monetary obligations in the long run, see Amaral (1989). For the lack of reaction to changes in exchange rates, see MacCann (1969), 30.

Table B.2. *Inventories of estancias on non-owned land, 1818–1822*

Name	Legajo[a]	Year	Place
1. Abrego, Petrona	3475	1818	Luján
2. Acosta, Sebastián Damián	3475	1818	San Vicente
3. Alvarez, Paulino	3475	1820	Luján
4. Balmaceda, Juan	3920	1818	Salto
5. Cainzo, Benedicta	4842	1820	Arrecifes
6. Canales, José Joaquín	4843	1821	Magdalena
7. Casco, Gregorio	4842	1819	San Antonio de Areco
8. Dias, Casimiro	5401	1819	San Antonio de Areco
9. Escobar, Petrona	5590	1821	Navarro
10. Frías, Toribio	5691	1819	Cañada de la Cruz
11. Hernández, Miguel	6317	1818	Pilar
12. López, Baleria	6499	1822	San Antonio de Areco
13. López, Gregorio	6498	1818	Cañada de la Cruz
14. Mansilla, Elena	6781	1821	Pilar
15. Molina, José León	6781	1822	Luján
16. Montero, Marta	6781	1821	Pilar
17. Montero, Narcisa	6781	1822	Luján
18. Moreno, Felisa	6781	1819	Magdalena
19. Navarro, Fernando	7206	1821	San Andrés de Giles
20. Ortega, Juan Manuel	7275	1822	San Vicente
21. Peñalva, Isabel	7388	1818	Luján
22. Peres, Placido	7388	1819	Magdalena
23. Ponce, Petrona	7388	1821	Luján
24. Rodríguez, Feliciana	7784	1822	San Nicolás
25. Rodríguez, Raymundo	7783	1820	San Isidro
26. Rojo, Susana	7782	1818	Morón
27. Romero, Marcos	7782	1819	Luján
28. Rosa, Pedro de la	7784	1822	Navarro
29. Salazar, Atanacio	8143	1819	San Vicente
30. Sayas, Marcelino	8143	1820	Las Conchas
31. Silva, Teodora Martina	7784	1820	San Vicente
32. Torre, Clemencia de la	8458	1822	Lobos
33. Zapata, Rosa	8780	1819	Luján

[a] AGN, Tribunales, Sucesiones.

Table B.2a. *Estancias on non-owned land, 1820: Capital structure*

Region	Imp. C	Tools D	Cattle E	Horses F	Sheep G	Slaves H	Other I	Total J	Imp.+Tools (C+D)/J	Livestock (E+F+G)/J
North										
4	22	17	241	99	0	0	25	404	0.097	0.842
5	221	234	207	30	78	0	65	835	0.545	0.377
7	699	275	7,652	1,153	600	650	161	11,189	0.087	0.841
8	137	156	3,388	115	260	250	58	4,363	0.067	0.862
10	37	92	333	144	0	0	149	754	0.171	0.633
12	42	25	569	29	93	0	10	768	0.087	0.9
13	57	174	659	507	319	0	32	1,716	0.135	0.865
19	18	16	535	23	189	0	4	784	0.043	0.953
24	489	66	915	62	0	250	15	1,796	0.309	0.544
Mean	191	117	1,611	240	171	128	57	2,516	0.122	0.804
Center										
1	170	177	1,037	123	0	0	172	1,679	0.207	0.691
3	32	81	4,663	267	0	157	120	5,319	0.021	0.927
11	143	170	797	82	141	1,050	81	2,463	0.127	0.414
14	25	18	799	62	353	0	11	1,267	0.034	0.958
15	28	76	1,124	76	167	0	12	1,482	0.07	0.922
16	78	42	402	68	304	0	6	899	0.133	0.861
17	545	208	5,561	129	177	200	68	6,886	0.109	0.852
21	42	107	443	51	118	0	41	802	0.186	0.763

23	82	75	5,585	139	0	355	40	6,236	0.025	0.918
26	30	40	910	188	1,780	0	21	2,969	0.024	0.969
25	10	0	45	146	66	0	0	267	0.037	0.963
27	2	20	1,291	13	0	0	20	1,345	0.016	0.97
30	240	486	517	172	188	750	956	3,309	0.219	0.265
33	146	191	3,021	35	0	0	19	3,405	0.099	0.898
Mean	112	121	1,871	111	235	179	112	2,738	0.085	0.81
South										
2	1,473	269	8,335	569	925	680	125	12,376	0.141	0.794
6	59	33	719	217	188	0	29	1,244	0.074	0.904
18	20	21	1,742	102	13	0	9	1,906	0.022	0.974
20	302	123	3,874	82	694	250	16	5,341	0.08	0.871
22	8	13	267	53	0	0	5	345	0.061	0.928
29	69	75	1,757	89	484	100	58	2,631	0.055	0.886
31	279	109	1,090	0	368	550	86	2,482	0.156	0.587
Mean	316	92	2,541	159	382	226	47	3,761	0.108	0.819
Frontier										
9	69	85	565	51	15	0	3	787	0.196	0.802
28	70	116	2,398	57	32	0	16	2,688	0.069	0.925
32	27	16	618	40	50	0	8	758	0.057	0.934
Mean	55	72	1,194	49	32	0	9	1,411	0.09	0.904
Mean	171	100	1,945	111	274	137	72	2,806	0.097	0.83

Table B.2b. *Estancias on non-owned land, 1820: Livestock*

Region	Cattle	Horses	Sheep	LU
North				
4	21	116	242	196
5	60	10	375	119
7	1,931	1,905	1,350	4,481
8	775	164	590	1,054
10	77	88	0	187
12	173	49	290	271
13	231	49	1,100	430
19	140	22	422	220
24	267	75	0	361
Mean	408	275	485	813
Center				
1	388	83	0	492
3	1,194	530	0	1,857
11	238	53	395	354
14	233	44	1,031	417
15	324	57	530	462
16	105	80	920	320
17	1,806	124	514	2,025
21	160	65	339	284
23	1,809	149	0	1,995
25	104	434	264	680
26	298	215	6,625	1,395
27	285	14	0	303
30	79	70	878	276
33	899	33	0	940
Mean	566	139	821	843
South				
2	2,113	417	2,902	2,997
6	211	226	700	581
18	532	99	36	660
20	992	97	2,431	1,417
22	89	52	0	154
29	515	143	1,782	917
31	458	0	1,178	605
Mean	701	148	1,290	1,047
Frontier				
9	100	0	102	113
28	687	54	90	766
32	227	22	160	275
Mean	338	25	117	385
Mean	531	168	765	836

Table B.3. *Inventories of estancias on owned land, 1848–1851*

Name	Legajo[a]	Year	Place
1. Agüero, María Ignacia	3505	1849	Pila
2. Aguila, Juan de la	3507	1851	Exaltación de la Cruz
3. Aristegui, Anselma	3507	1850	Azul
4. Arroyo, Alejandro	3507	1851	Quilmes
5. Barrancos, Petrona	3942	1849	Chivilcoy
6. Burgos, Ignacio	3943	1849	Lobos
7. Cabrera, Ana María	4876	1848	Navarro
8. Cainzo, Roque	4876	1849	Pilar
9. Cascallares, Mariano	4878	1850	Lobos
10. Cepeda, Pedro	4877	1849	Lobos
11. Dávila, Rosalía	5410	1849	Rojas
12. Díaz, Petrona	5410	1851	Ajó
13. Falcón, Braulio	3944	1850	Ajó
14. Fernández, Miguel Ciriaco	5706	1851	Chivilcoy
15. Fernández Márquez, Juana	5706	1851	Navarro
16. Figueroa, Marcelina	5706	1850	Arrecifes
17. Gutiérrez, Juan José	5939	1850	Luján
18. Larredia, Ana María	6514	1848	Magdalena
19. Lastra, Domingo	6512	1848	Lobería
20. López, José Ambrosio	6515	1851	San Andrés de Giles
21. López, Manuel	6515	1849	Navarro
22. López de Osorio, Eulalio	6513	1850	Ensenada
23. Llanos, José Benito	6517	1850	Magdalena
24. Manfi, Vicente	6807	1848	San Antonio de Areco
25. Martínez, Ventura	6807	1849	Quilmes
26. Montenegro, José	6807	1849	Monte
27. Morales, Fructuosa	6806	1848	Morón
28. Muñoz, Leandro	6806	1848	Cañuelas
29. Navarro, Pedro	7209	1851	Luján
30. Obligado, Juan José	7281	1849	San Nicolás
31. Páez, María Ascencia	7412	1850	Ensenada
32. Rodríguez de la Torre, Josefa	7806	1850	La Matanza
33. Soler, Ambrosio	8166	1849	Arrecifes
34. Sosa, Francisco	8168	1848	Luján
35. Suárez, Francisco	8169	1851	Mar Chiquita
36. Suárez, Francisco	8169	1851	Ajó
37. Tabosi, Juan	8463	1849	Luján
38. Tobal, Celestina	8463	1850	Chascomús
39. Tobal, Celestina	8463	1850	Pila
40. Vázquez, Cipriano	8614	1851	Vecino
41. Viñas, Rafael	8613	1848	Arrecifes

[a] AGN, Tribunales, Sucesiones.

Table B.3a. *Estancias on owned land, 1850: Capital structure*

Region	Land (ha) A	Land B	Imp. C	Tools D	Cattle E	Horses F	Sheep G	Other I	Total J	Land B/J	Imp.+Tools (C+D)/J	Livestock (E+F+G)/J
North												
2	84	1,250	1,502	322	6,796	1,430	5,778	2,000	19,078	0.066	0.096	0.734
5	2,844	15,800	33,000	14,233	28,462	5,835	330	2,940	100,600	0.157	0.47	0.344
11	3,417	22,550	2,043	0	33,425	7,126	2,411	824	68,378	0.33	0.03	0.628
14	2,700	16,000	0	0	9,000	0	0	1,833	26,833	0.596	0	0.335
16	3,548	105,140	61,732	19,275	121,700	31,585	6,563	1,500	347,495	0.303	0.233	0.46
20	591	1,750	1,403	100	3,700	374	785	150	8,262	0.212	0.182	0.588
24	450	12,000	8,025	255	3,715	855	1,005	0	25,855	0.464	0.32	0.216
30	2,700	80,000	14,011	2,479	54,976	19,160	475	8,000	179,101	0.447	0.092	0.417
33	1,716	30,504	9,264	0	63,495	11,600	5,520	4,000	124,383	0.245	0.074	0.648
41	9,126	169,000	47,697	0	22,100	18,200	600	0	257,597	0.656	0.185	0.159
Mean	2,718	45,399	17,868	3,666	34,737	9,617	2,347	2,125	115,758	0.392	0.186	0.403
Center												
6	506	13,500	1,627	1,447	16,200	4,200	5,175	1,319	43,468	0.311	0.071	0.588
7	2,025	15,000	9,565	1,441	15,798	2,437	2,214	697	47152	0.318	0.233	0.434
8	4,803	148,120	60,153	1,500	94,480	10,995	17,188	1,295	333,731	0.444	0.185	0.368
9	4,482	66,400	61,885	3,999	25,500	12,960	6,665	117	177,526	0.374	0.371	0.254
10	2,700	25,000	5,452	997	33,484	4,940	2,700	412	72,985	0.343	0.088	0.563
15	4,050	60,000	9,653	300	11,800	1,925	0	800	84,478	0.71	0.118	0.162
17	1,620	60,000	13,760	0	28,150	1,250	400	500	104,060	0.577	0.132	0.286
21	5,400	50,000	0	0	1,248	1,960	563	0	53,771	0.93	0	0.07
28	405	9,600	4,785	510	4,088	1,112	75	200	20,370	0.471	0.26	0.259
27	2,023	54,709	17,922	9,953	33,220	5,805	1,428	300	123,337	0.444	0.226	0.328
29	1,416	52,450	4,548	210	40,540	5,226	2,996	600	106,580	0.492	0.045	0.458
32	2,025	60,000	46,286	1,310	28,375	5,902	0	824	142,697	0.42	0.334	0.24

34	945	16,800	544	1,162	12,809	5,998	1,534	850	39,697	0.423	0.043	0.512
37	900	24,000	2,230	4,280	9,490	1,545	1,102	300	42,947	0.559	0.152	0.283
Mean	2,379	46,827	17,029	1,936	25,370	4,733	3,003	587	99,486	0.471	0.191	0.333
South												
4	338	15,000	3,740	479	4,700	4,380	1,290	900	30,489	0.492	0.138	0.34
18	2,025	30,000	25,635	200	1,255	1,515	1,107	500	60,212	0.498	0.429	0.064
22	3,838	91,600	33,098	3,060	30,125	4,398	353	1,721	164,355	0.557	0.22	0.212
23	675	6,250	9,417	317	10,744	3,880	0	230	30,838	0.203	0.316	0.474
25	1,013	10,000	4,380	1,501	18,880	5,926	594	2,705	43,986	0.227	0.134	0.577
26	675	15,000	10,975	109	15,000	5,200	1,005	0	47,289	0.317	0.234	0.448
31	2,183	38,800	29,072	204	2,112	150	482	0	70,820	0.548	0.413	0.039
38	7,335	114,100	55,160	4,648	18,406	6,336	15,993	2,676	217,218	0.525	0.275	0.188
Mean	2,260	40,094	21,435	1,315	12,653	3,973	2,603	1,092	83,151	0.482	0.274	0.231
New South												
1	21,071	195,100	35,495	3,490	103,495	12,541	4,389	2,235	356,745	0.547	0.109	0.338
3	8,100	40,000	3,600	0	44,480	2,273	1,000	425	91,778	0.436	0.039	0.52
12	1,350	15,000	1,000	601	3,200	2,450	0	2,000	24,251	0.619	0.066	0.233
13	4,320	35,200	1,590	436	39,300	1,806	53	150	78,535	0.448	0.026	0.524
19	40,500	45,000	800	120	100,000	1,910	0	0	147,830	0.304	0.006	0.689
35	16,200	210,000	29,469	2,327	13,930	3,585	0	476	259,787	0.808	0.122	0.067
36	30,825	340,500	28,670	1,992	10,800	9,761	1,955	14,160	407,838	0.835	0.075	0.055
39	16,200	140,000	27,895	2,971	55,708	12,276	24,444	1,683	264,977	0.528	0.116	0.349
40	10,800	88,000	15,278	1,198	1,680	5,200	800	1,000	113,156	0.778	0.146	0.068
Mean	16,596	66,060	15,977	1,459	41,399	5,756	3,627	2,459	193,877	0.341	0.09	0.262
Mean	5,559	61,930	17,862	2,132	28,692	6,000	2,902	1,471	126,549	0.489	0.158	0.297

Table B.3b. *Estancias on owned land, 1850: Livestock*

Region	Land	Cattle	Horses	Sheep	LU	h/LU
North						
2	84	227	92	672	426	0.2
5	2,844	1,032	210	165	1,315	2.16
11	3,417	1,310	328	1,607	1,921	1.78
14	2,700	379	0	0	379	7.12
16	3,548	4,868	1,658	1,875	7,175	0.49
20	591	210	47	370	315	1.88
24	450	223	39	670	356	1.27
30	2,700	1,718	667	173	2,573	1.05
33	1,716	2,712	510	2,760	3,695	0.46
41	9,126	1,300	1,040	600	2,675	3.41
Mean	2,718	1,398	459	889	2,083	2083
Center						
6	506	900	310	2,300	1,575	0.32
7	2,025	778	135	1,107	1,085	1.87
8	4,803	4,276	678	4,297	5,661	0.85

9	4,482	879	422	2,962	1,777	2.52
10	2,700	1,522	442	1,800	2,300	1.17
15	4,050	451	109	0	587	6.9
17	1,620	1,225	47	100	1,296	1.25
21	5,400	52	100	250	208	25.93
27	2,023	1,232	189	782	1,566	1.29
28	405	164	35	50	214	1.89
29	1,416	2,098	374	616	2,643	0.54
32	2,025	1,095	291	0	1,459	1.39
34	945	845	422	1,534	1,564	0.6
37	900	466	74	612	635	1.42
Mean	2,379	1,142	259	1,172	1,612	1.48
South						
4	338	235	241	430	590	0.57
18	2,025	81	74	369	220	9.22
22	3,838	1,785	336	235	2,234	1.72
23	675	691	153	0	882	0.77
25	1,013	924	265	297	1,292	0.78
26	675	1,000	440	670	1,674	0.41

Table B.3b. (cont.)

Region	Land	Cattle	Horses	Sheep	LU	h/LU
North						
31	2,183	132	25	482	224	9.77
38	7,335	997	269	4,130	1,850	3.97
Mean	2,260	731	225	827	1,116	2.03
New South						
1	21,071	7,457	923	3,287	9,022	2.34
3	8,100	2,206	261	1,000	2,657	3.05
12	1,350	160	65	0	241	5.6
13	4,320	2,603	123	53	2,763	1.56
19	40,500	5,000	129	0	5,161	7.85
35	16,200	575	108	0	710	22.82
36	30,825	600	651	786	1,512	20.39
39	16,200	4,050	645	3,497	5,293	3.06
40	10,800	70	620	200	870	12.41
Mean	16,596	2,525	392	980	3,137	5.29
Mean	5,559	1,428	330	994	1,966	2.83

Table B.4. *Inventories of estancias on non-owned land, 1848–1851*

Name	Legajo[a]	Year	Place
1. Aguila, Valentín	3505	1848	Exaltación de la Cruz
2. Alvares, Gregorio	3507	1851	Chapaleofú
3. Barrios, Juan Fco	3942	1849	Lobería
4. Balenzuela, Manuel V.	3942	1849	Tapalquén
5. Clark, Eduardo	4878	1850	Quilmes
6. Clavelino, José	4878	1849	Navarro
7. Domato, José María	5410	1850	Fortín de Areco
8. Espinosa, Salvador	5593	1851	Lobos
9. García, Rosario	5938	1849	Cañuelas
10. Hidalgo, Andrés	6321	1851	Chascomús
11. Lucero, Abdona	6513	1850	Monte
12. Lavallen, Lucas	6517	1851	Morón
13. López, Saturnino	6518	1851	Pilar
14. Martínez, Paula	6809	1849	Magdalena
15. Mac Guire, Tomas	6810	1851	Exaltación de la Cruz
16. Pavón, Carmen	7412	1850	Ranchos
17. Prado, Juan Pablo	7413	1851	San Vicente
18. Rojas, Dionicio	7804	1848	Morón
19. Reynoso, Bernabé	7805	1850	Fortín de Areco
20. Roldán, Pedro	7806	1851	Tapalquén
21. Sarate, Marcos	8166	1850	Tapalquén
22. Villarruel, Andrea	8616	1850	Lobos

[a] AGN, Tribunales, Sucesiones.

Table B.4a. *Estancias on non-owned land, 1850: Capital structure*

Region	Imp. C	Tools D	Cattle E	Horses F	Sheep G	Other I	Total J	Imp.+Tools (C+D)/J	Livestock (E+F+G)/J
North									
1	2,200	0	12,094	1,285	0	200	15,779	0.139	0.848
7	13,293	880	11,362	9,645	0	700	35,880	0.395	0.585
15	0	605	0	0	16,800	200	17,605	0.034	0.954
19	68	525	500	1,960	1,200	200	4,453	0.133	0.822
Mean	3,890	503	5,989	3,223	4,500	325	18,429	0.238	0.744
Center									
6	1,262	1,745	13,475	2,396	3,528	668	23,074	0.13	0.841
8	1,078	515	9,680	2,570	1,080	225	15,148	0.105	0.88
9	1,790	848	12,428	3,345	7,200	250	25,861	0.102	0.888
12	271	45	0	2,630	8,036	0	10,982	0.029	0.971
13	1,934	1,002	1,045	1,923	37,602	463	43,969	0.067	0.923
18	407	199	4,525	1,935	3,800	150	11,016	0.055	0.931
22	16,986	4,244	34,106	6,450	4,662	2,466	68,914	0.308	0.656
Mean	3,390	1,228	10,751	3,036	9,415	603	28,423	0.162	0.816

South

5	117,147	4,319	2,730	1,400	3,318	5,000	133,914	0.907	0.056
10	1,723	801	13,000	3,068	3,200	8,592	30,386	0.083	0.634
11	410	286	17,760	1,011	670	0	20,137	0.035	0.965
14	576	327	11,920	876	2,171	0	15,870	0.057	0.943
16	1,500	633	23,575	692	0	0	26,400	0.081	0.919
17	6,152	994	300	2,300	22,855	7,254	39,855	0.179	0.639
Mean	21,251	1,227	11,548	1,558	5,369	3,474	44,427	0.506	0.416

New South

2	5,455	144	13,200	5,348	600	0	24,747	0.226	0.774
3	0	22	3,814	682	0	100	4,618	0.005	0.974
4	50	950	11,640	72	0	0	12,712	0.079	0.921
20	0	760	13,110	416	0	1,160	15,446	0.049	0.876
21	562	0	45,400	1,180	2,748	385	50,275	0.011	0.981
Mean	1,213	375	17,433	1,540	670	329	21,560	0.074	0.911
Mean	7,857	902	11,621	2,327	5,430	1,273	29,410	0.298	0.659

Table B.4b. *Estancias on non-owned land, 1850: Livestock*

Region	Cattle	Horses	Sheep	LU
North				
1	738	42	0	791
7	437	662	0	1265
15	0	0	2400	300
19	25	182	600	328
Mean	300	222	750	671
Center				
6	518	168	1369	899
8	515	176	540	803
9	472	127	1800	856
12	0	299	2134	641
13	25	52	4078	600
18	227	123	2000	631
22	1324	294	1167	1837
Mean	440	177	1870	895
South				
5	22	14	553	109
10	555	170	800	868
11	888	85	670	1078
14	649	44	1447	885
16	943	37	0	989
17	15	190	3265	661
Mean	512	90	1123	765
New South				
2	1100	447	300	1696
3	205	69	0	291
4	776	9	0	787
20	874	30	0	912
21	2270	19	1364	2464
Mean	1045	115	333	1230
Mean	572	147	1113	895

Table B.5. *Area estimated for 66 estancias*
according to estancia value, 1818-1822

| | Estancias on owned land | | | Estancias on non-owned land | | All estancias | |
| | Area | Value | B/A | Value | Value | Value | Area |
	A	B	C	D	E	F	G
North	28,771	118,833	4.13	22,642	25,130	143,963	34,855
Center	19,204	63,494	3.31	38,376	43,119	106,613	32,246
South	44,685	117,476	2.63	26,326	30,190	147,666	56,169
Frontier	15,525	4,806	0.31	4,233	4,571	9,377	30,292
Total	108,185	304,609	2.82	91,577	103,127	407,736	144,587[a]

[a] The figure obtained by adding column G is 153,562 hectares.
Notes:
A Total area of 33 estancias on owned land, in hectares.
B Total value of estancias on owned land, in pesos.
C Total investment per hectare (B/A), in pesos per hectare.
D Total value of estancias on non-owned land, in pesos.
E Total value of estancias on owned land plus the estimated value of land, according to the proportion of land over total investment for each region = D/(1 - L), where L is the average percentage of land in each region (Table 3.1).
F Total estimated value of all estancias, in pesos (B+E).
G Total area of all estancias (F/C), in hectares.

Sources: Tables B.1a and B.2a.

Table B.6. *Area estimated for 66 estancias according to*
livestock units, 1818–1822

| | Density | LU | Area |
	A	B	C
North	1.01	35,925	36,132
Center	1.24	27,289	33,838
South	1.64	34,643	56,815
Frontier	21.47	1,910	41,008
Total	1.50	99,767	149,650[a]

[a] The figure obtained by adding column C is 167,793 hectares.
Notes:
A Livestock density: hectares per livestock unit (Table 5.7).
B Total number of livestock units on all estancias.
C Total area occupied by livestock units of all estancias (A x B), in hectares.
Sources: Tables B.1b and B.2b.

Appendix B

Table B.7. *Area estimated for 63 estancias according to estancia value,*
1848–1851

| | Estancias on owned land | | | Estancias on non-owned land | | All estancias | |
| | Area | Value | B/A | Value | Value | Value | Area |
	A	B	C	D	E	F	G
North	27,177	1,157,583	42.59	73,997	121,706	1,279,289	30,034
Center	33,301	1,392,789	41.82	198,964	376,113	1,768,902	42,294
South	18,080	665,368	36.80	266,560	514,595	1,179,963	32,063
New South	149,366	1,744,897	11.68	107,798	295,337	2,040,234	174,647
Total	227,924	4,960,577	21.76	647,319	1,326,473	6,287,110	288,930[a]

[a] The figure obtained by adding column G is 279,038 hectares.
Notes:
A Total area of 41 estancias with land, in hectares.
B Total value of estancias with land, in pesos.
C Total investment per hectare (B/A), in pesos.
D Total value of estancias without land, in pesos.
E Total value of estancias on owned land plus the estimated value of land, according to the proportion of land over total investment for each region = D/(1 – L), where L is the average percentage of land in each region (Table 3.4).
F Total estimated value of all estancias, in pesos (B+E).
G Total area of all estancias (F/C), in hectares.
Sources: Tables B.3a and B.4a.

Table B.8. *Area estimated for 63 estancias according to*
livestock units, 1848–1851

	Density A	LU B	Area C
North	1.30	23,512	30,678
Center	1.48	28,835	42,547
South	2.03	13,514	27,376
New South	5.29	34,383	181,922
Total	2.83	100,244	283,690[a]

[a] The figure obtained by adding column C is 282,523 hectares.
Notes:
A Livestock density: hectares per livestock unit (Table 5.7).
B Total number of livestock units.
C Total area occupied by livestock units of all estancias (AxB), in hectares.
Sources: Tables B.3b and B.4b.

C

Prices, exchange rates, and trade statistics

Prices and exchange rates

Prices and rates of exchange should be known when dealing with products and currencies from different countries. Although paper money appeared in many countries during the nineteenth century, specie was the ultimate means of payment. Whether used permanently (as in Buenos Aires) or temporarily (as in Great Britain during the Napoleonic Wars, or in the United States during the Civil War), paper money was an aberration. The barbaric habit of using specie (the Buenos Aires government denounced it a whole century before Keynes) faded away only after 1930. Comparisons are easier, therefore, for the nineteenth century. Since the silver or gold content of the coins used as means of payment in Buenos Aires, Great Britain, France, Belgium, and the United States is known, there remains to be known the rate of exchange of the Buenos Aires paper money after January 1826. This section deals with the sources and problems of tables and figures using currencies from different countries.

The information on hide prices in three European countries from 1790 to 1820 (Figure 11.2) has been taken from Cuenca Esteban.[1] The average for 1800–1806 has been used here as the base for estimating the index.

The current price of Buenos Aires produce and exchange rate in 1821–1823 (Figure 11.3) has been taken from a report submitted in 1824 by the local British merchants to Woodbine Parish, the British minister in Buenos Aires. "Dry" means dry hides, and prices are given for the 35-lb pesada used for them; "salted" means salted hides, and prices are given for the 60-lb pesada used for them; "horse" means horse hides, and prices are given per hide. The rate of exchange is given in English pence per peso, meaning then the silver peso. That rate was not referred to the intrinsic (specie) equivalence between the silver peso and the pound sterling, but to

---

1 Cuenca Esteban (1990), 391–395. See Merediz (1966) for the prices of Buenos Aires produce in European markets from 1815 to 1820 according to the letters received by Juan José Cristóbal de Anchorena (then a merchant, later a powerful landowner). Merediz does not explain the method used to obtain his figures.

the bill of exchange over London. The intrinsic rate of exchange remained constant for long periods; the rate of exchange for bills depended upon the availability of funds to be drawn upon in London. In the long run, it could not depart (if convertibility was not suspended) too far from the intrinsic rate, but in the short run, there could be fluctuations due to a temporary scarcity of available funds.

The sources for hide prices from 1818 to 1852 (Figure 11.4) are as follows: (1) London: Halperín Donghi; (2) Buenos Aires: Broide; (3) New Orleans: Cole; (4) and (5) France and Belgium: from their respective *Tableau générale du commerce*.[2] All currencies and weights have been converted into Buenos Aires pesos and 35-pound pesadas.

The rate of exchange between dollars and pesos (both equivalent in theory to one ounce of silver), pounds sterling, and francs has been estimated according to information taken from Shaw and McCusker, confirmed by the reports of the French consuls in Buenos Aires.[3] The specie content of the 1803 silver franc was 5 grams of .900 silver; and that of the 1792 U.S. silver dollar, 371.25 grains of pure silver. Being 1 grain equivalent to 0.0648 grams, the silver dollar contained 24.057 grams of pure silver, while the franc 4.5 grams. In 1601 one shilling was defined as having 92.75 troy grains of silver. Twenty shillings or one sterling pound (£) was therefore equivalent to 120.204 grams of silver. Then £1 was equivalent to U.S. $5.[4] The rate of exchange was therefore 1 peso fuerte = U.S. $1 = £0.20 (48 pence) = 5.35 French francs. Belgian francs were equivalent to French francs.[5]

The sources for the Buenos Aires hide price indices, 1814–1870 (Figure 11.5) are as follows: (1) London: for 1818–1852, quarterly averages estimated by Halperín Donghi for dry hides from prices quoted by the *London Mercantile Price Current*; for 1854–1870, implicit prices resulting from dividing total value by total quantity of dry and wet hide imports for each year; (2) Hamburg: index number taken from Chiaramonte; (3) Buenos Aires, *pesos fuertes*: monthly average prices for hides estimated by Broide, deflated by monthly average prices for the peso fuerte estimated from the daily quotation for the gold ounce given by Espiñeira, at a fixed rate of 1 gold ounce = 16 pesos fuertes; and (4) Buenos Aires, *moneda*

2 Halperín Donghi (1963), 65; Broide (1951), 149; Cole (1938), Statistical Supplement, passim.
3 Shaw (1896); McCusker (1978), MAE, Correspondance diplomatique, Buenos Aires, 1 and 1 bis.
4 The rate quoted by McCusker [(1978), 10], is U.S. $1 = £0.22. But he also mentions that one ounce troy of sterling silver was valued at 5s 2d from 1601 to 1816. In that case the dollar would have been equivalent to £0.258. The value mentioned there for the Spanish American peso is 4s 6d, equivalent to £0.225. In Buenos Aires the rate of exchange before paper money inflation was 1 peso = 48 pence, equivalent to £0.20. This rate meant a 10% difference between the Buenos Aires peso and the U.S. dollar, which would not have significantly altered my estimates.
5 MacGregor (1844), 1:92.

corriente (paper money): the same monthly average prices estimated by Broide.[6] The monthly average for the gold ounce in paper pesos has been estimated from the daily quotations from January 1826 to December 1864 given by Espiñeira. The official rate of exchange of 17 pesos fuertes for one gold ounce established in 1812 vanished in practice (but not legally) when conversion was suspended in January 1826. From then onward the gold–silver rate of exchange tended to fluctuate around 1:16, closer to the international rate of exchange (for 1826–1870, on average, 1:15.62). Sáenz published the daily quotations of both pesos fuertes (equivalent to one ounce of silver) and gold ounces in Buenos Aires paper money from 1826 to 1849, and Shaw published the international silver–gold rate of exchange for the nineteenth century.[7]

Information for U.S. prices (Figure 11.6) has been taken from Cole.[8] For British, Belgian, and French prices (Figures 11.7, 11.8, and 11.9), the sources listed for Argentine imports into Great Britain, Belgium, and France in Tables C.2, C.3, and C.5 have been used. These implicit prices have been obtained dividing total import value by total quantity imported of each product.

Trade statistics

Different official and private sources have been used to collect information for Table C.1, where figures for the main Buenos Aires exports are recorded. Figures from 1810 to 1823 were included as part of a report prepared by British merchants operating in Buenos Aires for Woodbine Parish, the British chargé d'affaires, shortly after his arrival in 1824.[9] Figures for 1825, 1829, 1837, and 1849–1853 were published by Woodbine Parish.[10] Figures for 1829–1833 were recorded by the U.S. consul in Buenos Aires.[11] Figures for 1841–1842 were part of a discontinued effort to keep track of the Buenos Aires foreign trade. Information for 1836 to 1840 was published in the *Registro Oficial*. Information for 1841 and 1842

6 Halperín Donghi (1963), 65; Chiaramonte (1991), 216; Espiñeira (1864); Broide (1951). Chiaramonte's index has been estimated from averages given by Jacobs and Richter (1935).
7 Espiñeira (1864); Sáenz (1850); Shaw (1896).
8 Cole (1938), *Statistical Supplement*, passim.
9 Humphreys (1940), 59–60. For different figures for 1815–1820, see Merediz (1966), 150. Discrepancies between those two sets of export figures, however, are not significant. Merediz's figures are probably more accurate, since he took them from the Buenos Aires customs ledgers. But as they cover only a short period, those of the British merchants have been preferred here.
10 Parish (1958), 515–519.
11 National Archives, U.S. Consular Reports, Buenos Aires, Reel 5. I am grateful to Alejandro Senderowicz for giving me many years ago these figures and information from other sources to which I did not have access at that time.

Appendix C

Table C.1. *Buenos Aires exports, 1810–1870*

	Hides units	Wool arrobas	Tallow arrobas	Jerked beef quintales
1810	1,094,892	5,209	217,398	0
1811	750,147	5,113	109,585	0
1812	301,934	939	111,957	6,800
1813	397,232	1,581	96,662	4,000
1814	583,492	0	128,102	10,715
1815	824,947	5,536	255,493	3,000
1816	584,185	12,249	165,260	3,140
1817	801,534	14,746	96,156	16,000
1818	594,236	40,832	50,105	6,013
1819	464,533	41,697	70,610	53,656
1820	442,357	8,074	52,269	113,110
1821	441,854	15,328	54,762	47,919
1822	590,872	33,417	62,400	87,663
1823	578,225	31,789	15,473	87,879
1824				
1825	655,255	0	12,167	130,361
1826				
1827				
1828				
1829	854,799	30,334	21,757	164,818
1830	910,541	19,809		307,456
1831	777,818	64,157		126,390
1832	915,702	40,551		107,699
1833	674,764	69,704		139,240
1834				
1835	534,213	130,308	59,337	119,017
1836	622,802	132,580	59,618	150,580
1837	823,635	164,706	100,249	178,877
1838	355,993	166,796	146,664	165,229
1839	8,501	25,028	30,190	6,670
1840	72,865	283,101	15,575	12,010
1841	2,310,480	692,942	635,799	120,526
1842	1,256,883	381,791	302,031	136,338
1843	1,978,373	468,790	390,216	162,184
1844				
1845				
1846				
1847				
1848	1,101,093	460,292	503,550	209,435
1849	2,961,342	821,908	798,120	553,478
1850	2,424,251	631,839	446,400	390,731
1851	2,601,320	672,809	519,881	431,873
1852	1,994,197	659,821	718,284	530,960
1853	1,205,252	768,281	523,481	335,615
1854	1,399,353	768,137	628,759	323,059
1855	1,243,288	985,541	267,529	277,447
1856	1,220,204	1,152,116	335,722	287,301
1857	1,359,484	1,216,427	425,491	337,750

	Hides units	Wool arrobas	Tallow arrobas	Jerked beef quintales
1858	1,393,885	1,383,388	198,380	283,600
1859	1,563,076	1,509,439	375,962	492,342
1860	1,576,817	1,571,115	359,186	394,902
1861	1,412,654	1,829,268	439,912	322,106
1862	1,580,740	2,412,674	420,091	370,701
1863	1,726,057	3,018,520	374,829	
1864	1,690,927	3,287,087	341,610	
1865	1,877,603	4,449,240	742,615	
1866	1,776,302	5,115,436	785,521	
1867	2,308,364	5,272,652	1,216,967	
1868	2,142,648	6,085,592	1,822,996	
1869	2,485,921	5,891,452	2,595,496	
1870	2,599,701	5,452,546	2,408,293	

Note: A blank means that no data have been found for an article in a particular year in the sources listed below.
Sources: 1810–1823, Humphreys (1940); 1825, 1829, 1837, 1849–1853, Parish (1958); 1829–1833, National Archives, U.S. Consular Reports, Buenos Aires, Reel 5; 1835–1836, 1838–1839, RO (1836–1841); 1841–1842, AGN, X–42–10–11; 1842, MAE, Correspondance commerciale, Buenos Aires 2; 1843, Great Britain, House of Commons, Sessional Papers, 1847, 64(2):398; 1848–1862, Maxwell (1863); 1862–1870, AGN, Archivo Victorino de la Plaza, VII–4–6–6. For other figures for wool exports from 1829 to 1842, and jerked-beef exports from 1835 to 1851, see Nicolau (1975), 153, 162.

was collected but never published.[12] Slightly different figures for 1842 were recorded by the French minister in Buenos Aires.[13] For 1843 there is information published in the British Parliamentary Papers.[14] For 1848–1862, Daniel Maxwell's *Planillas estadísticas* has been used.[15] And for 1862–1870, the figures were collected by an unknown private merchant house in Buenos Aires.[16]

Figures given by this latter source may be different from those stemming from other sources since years there, instead of following a calendar pattern, go from November 1 to October 31. That was thought to suit better the cycle of production in Buenos Aires.[17]

From 1848 onward tallow figures are given in pipas and marquetas.

12 AGN, X–42–10–11.
13 MAE, Correspondence diplomatique, Buenos Aires 1.
14 Great Britain, House of Commons, Sessional Papers, 1847, 44:2.
15 Maxwell (1863).
16 AGN, Archivo Victorino de la Plaza, VII–4–6–6. My thanks to Adela Harispuru for this information.
17 Maxwell (1863).

Table C.2. *Great Britain: Imports from and exports to Argentina, 1810–1870*

	Exports £ a	Imports £ b	Hides cwt c	£ d	Wool lb e	£ f	Tallow cwt g	£ h
1810			135.8					
1811			281.4					
1812			41.5					
1813								
1814			122.0					
1815			163.9					
1816			161.2					
1817			74.1					
1818			199.4					
1819			112.3					
1820			96.1					
1821			104.1				4.9	
1822			123.6				6.1	
1823			199.3		0.02		3.2	
1824			131.2		0		0	
1825			114.2		0.33		0	
1826			55.8		0.21		0	
1827			3.4		0		0	
1828			40.6		0		0	
1829			156.0		0.16		0.1	
1830			174.4		0.02		0.1	
1831			146.0		0.01		2.5	
1832			65.6		0.03		0.1	
1833			121.6		0.21		18.8	
1834			187.5		1.10		28.1	
1835			123.6		0.97		20.8	
1836			139.9		1.07		8.4	
1837			170.6		2.21		16.8	
1838			181.5		1.11		41.1	
1839			252.9		0.24		55.0	
1840			206.1		0.62		62.7	
1841			394.7		5.11		206.3	
1842			296.6		1.46		113.9	
1843			270.8		1.88		103.1	
1844			254.0		2.19		100.6	
1845			250.3		2.93		110.6	
1846			34.0		0.13		6.4	
1847			149.2		0		0	
1848			114.5		1.01		82.4	
1849			326.9		2.53		257.2	
1850			232.4		1.84		152.8	
1851			261.7		0.85		135.9	
1852			207.8		2.35		221.9	
1853			172.3		3.95		122.3	
1854	1,300.1	1,215.1	176.0	433.6	2.71	107.3	131.9	415.2
1855	769.5	1,052.0	142.1	397.9	3.27	137.8	94.0	242.7
1856	1,042.2	981.2	113.7	424.7	2.19	114.2	81.7	202.1

	Exports £	Imports £	Hides		Wool		Tallow	
	£	£	cwt	£	lb	£	cwt	£
	a	b	c	d	e	f	g	h
1857	1,342.4	1,573.6	155.1	632.1	3.42	219.6	82.4	227.8
1858	1,036.2	1,195.0	115.8	366.4	4.78	252.9	58.9	147.5
1859	987.7	1,664.1	202.0	757.5	2.78	171.5	127.3	336.0
1860	1,820.9	1,101.4	149.2	535.8	1.61	104.4	71.6	197.4
1861	1,403.2	1,471.6	142.9	431.2	5.09	236.9	35.1	154.2
1862	869.3	1,133.1	115.3	338.2	4.86	222.9	84.4	194.2
1863	1,348.1	1,239.7	147.9	378.0	8.08	333.8	69.7	145.5
1864	1,782.1	1,186.2	125.6	338.2	8.00	312.3	73.1	152.3
1865	1,988.6	1,014.3	104.7	254.2	5.54	176.3	114.5	254.4
1866	2,880.8	1,073.0	119.2	290.7	4.80	142.9	140.1	325.0
1867	2,909.9	911.9	113.2	295.5	3.63	97.6	111.5	249.5
1868	1,984.7	1,496.1	155.1	438.8	4.76	124.8	279.5	663.3
1869	2,332.2	1,267.6	77.3	190.8	6.04	124.0	270.2	608.9
1870	2,428.2	1,486.4	136.2	370.9	2.86	63.9	304.6	673.3

Notes: a, b, c, d, f, g, h: thousands; e: millions.
Sources: PRO, Customs 4/6 to 4/25, Customs 5/1 to 5/104, and Customs 8/1 to 8/80.

According to values given in the 1841 and 1842 returns, 3.17 marquetas were equivalent to one pipa. One pipa was equivalent, according to the same returns, to 22.22 arrobas.

Most sources report the quantity of each export rather than its value. Only Parish's and the French minister's figures, as well as those for 1841 and 1842 prepared for the *Registro Oficial*, include both quantity and value. But no reliable series of either the tariff rate or market value of those exports can be established for the whole 1810–1870 period. The value of Buenos Aires exports can therefore be better estimated through statistics produced by the main customer countries.

The quantity and value of British imports from Argentina (Table C.2) have been collected from the ledgers of Customs from 1814 to 1855, and Board of Trade from 1856 to 1870, both located at the Public Record Office. The total amount of British imports from and exports to Argentina have been taken from the Parliamentary Papers. This information has been used for Figures 12.2 through 12.8.

Up to 1853, official rates fixed in 1696 were used for all articles. They are, therefore, useful only to indicate quantities. From 1854 onward real values are given, reflecting real market prices.[18] From 1814 to 1823, the number rather than the weight of hides was recorded. The weight has been estimated taking into account that four 28-lb hides made one 112-lb cwt.

18 On the British trade statistics, see Maizels (1957) and Mitchell (1962).

The difference between the Buenos Aires pound and the British pound has
been discarded, since it was less than 2%.[19] From 1824 onward only the
weight of imported hides was recorded. In Table C.2 figures for 1824 and
afterward correspond to the aggregate of dry and wet hides. From 1824 to
1830, 65.3% of that aggregate correspond to dry hides and 34.7% to wet
hides, but later that proportion is reverted. Between 1831 and 1840,
19.1% correspond to the former and 80.9% to the latter; from 1841 to
1850, 6.5% and 93.5%; and from 1851 to 1855, 3.2% and 96.8%.

For 1822–1823 and 1827–1845, the figures correspond to Río de la
Plata, and for 1810–1821 and 1824–1826, to Buenos Aires. From 1846
onward there are separate accounts for Buenos Aires and Montevideo. Of
the joint imports of dry and wet hides for 1824 and 1825, 86% correspond
to Buenos Aires and 14% to Montevideo; of those for 1849–1855 (leaving
aside 1846–1848 due to the French blockade to Buenos Aires), 83%
correspond to Buenos Aires, and 17% to Montevideo. No correction has
been made, however, to the figures for 1827–1845 either in Table C.2 or
in Figures 11.2 and 11.3.

Figures for French imports from and exports to Argentina (Table C.3)
have been taken from the *Tableau générale du commerce de la France avec ses
colonies et les puissances étrangères*. This was an annual publication starting in
1829. This information has been used for Figures 12.9 to 12.14. Up to
1839 figures corresponding to Río de la Plata included imports from
Buenos Aires and Montevideo. From 1840 onward figures for Uruguay are
given separately, and Río de la Plata means Argentina. Up to 1846 import
values were only estimated according to an official rate established in 1826;
from 1847 to 1863, both official and actual values were given, and from
1864 onward only the latter, which were averages determined on an annual
basis. Therefore, from 1829 to 1863, official values reflect quantity rather
than market value. Wool imports are quoted in francs up to 1855; only
from 1856 onward are both value and quantity given.

Up to 1860 hides were given in two different categories: "Peaux brutes
fraîches" and "Peaux brutes sèches grandes." The former was divided
between "grandes" and "petites," and within "petites" there were four
items, one of them corresponding to "béliers, brebis, et moutons, revêtues
de leur laine." No entries from Río de la Plata were registered there up to
that year. From 1861 onward "Peaux" are only differentiated between

19 For the average weight of hides and the difference between the British and Buenos Aires pound (lb),
see Senillosa (1835), 24 and 41. Senillosa gives an average of 21 to 23 lbs for dry cow hides, 55 to
60 lbs for salted cow hides, 28 to 33 lbs for dry steer hides, and 70 to 80 lbs for salted steer hides.
My estimate has been done on the basis of a 30.5-lb average for dry hides and a 75-lb average
for salted hides, and the figures for dry and salted hides have been estimated according to
the percentages corresponding to dry and wet hide imports into Great Britain from 1824 to
1830.

Table C.3. *France: Imports from and exports to Argentina, 1831–1870*

	Exports a	Imports b	Hides c	d	Wool e	f	Tallow g	h
1831			1.51				0.02	
1832			2.34					
1833			2.08				0.10	
1834			2.70				0.24	
1835			2.62				0.09	
1836			2.47				0.02	
1837			2.97				0.01	
1838			3.34				0.07	
1839			4.04				0.07	
1840			0.20				0	
1841			2.99		0.63	0.89	0.19	
1842			6.22		1.65	1.73	0.33	
1843			8.18		1.38	1.57	0.25	
1844					1.02	1.33	0.24	
1845			5.36		1.05	1.65	0.78	
1846			1.54		0.25	0.25	0.11	
1847	1.0	0.5	0.24	0.31	0.09	0.15	0	0
1848	2.6	1.7	1.09	1.36	0.24	0.22	0.09	0.08
1849	17.4	10.1	6.56	6.78	1.06	1.58	1.17	1.02
1850	13.6	10.8	6.61	6.86	1.00	2.08	1.18	0.93
1851	12.4	11.3	4.40	9.72	0.16	0.38	0.29	0.23
1852	17.7	10.0	5.10	6.11	1.49	2.62	0.10	0.09
1853	11.8	9.4	2.75	5.21	1.19	2.49	0.28	0.32
1854	23.6	10.4		5.37	1.66	3.20	0.24	0.30
1855	19.6	15.9		7.56	3.56	6.62	0.22	0.33
1856	27.0	16.7	2.30	5.30	2.40	5.19	0.53	0.64
1857	38.4	21.1	3.75	8.41	2.00	4.38	1.30	1.50
1858	24.3	22.7	3.46	5.87	6.13	11.03	0.44	0.48
1859	26.9	30.7	3.20	5.56	5.89	15.34	0.55	0.56
1860	49.7	41.2	4.29	9.03	5.85	18.95	0.43	0.46
1861	34.1	36.7	3.60	6.30	6.20	18.61	0.85	0.93
1862	33.7	33.8	2.20	3.74	4.78	17.70	1.18	1.27
1863	44.4	52.5	4.29	7.08	8.42	28.87	2.80	3.08
1864	51.9	41.5	3.64	5.65	5.99	20.37	3.18	4.33
1865	62.0	57.2	3.50	4.97	10.79	35.08	4.33	5.27
1866	67.5	59.5	2.66	3.86	12.44	35.46	6.01	6.68
1867	88.1	82.4	3.17	4.44	21.08	50.59	11.62	13.26
1868	79.2	89.2	2.62	3.88	24.37	52.41	13.99	15.19
1869	86.4	99.2	4.27	5.72	26.33	50.02	25.20	26.47
1870	71.8	105.1	5.10	6.84	22.54	48.47	21.47	30.39

Notes: a, b, d, f, and h: million francs; c, e, and g: million kilos.
Source: France, *Tableau générale du commerce de la France avec ses colonies et les puissances étrangères, 1831–1870.*

"grandes" and "petites," and among the latter were those of "béliers, brebis et moutons." Those from Río de la Plata were the largest entry in that category. In the table summarizing the decade 1857–1866, however, there are records of sheepskin imports from Río de la Plata for 1857–1860. Those sheepskins had neither been registered in the accounts corresponding to "Peaux" for those years nor in the accounts corresponding to "béliers, brebis et mouton." Even after 1861 in the section of the *Tableau* corresponding to imports from Argentina, the value and quantity of "Peaux" include sheepskins.

Figures for U.S. imports (Table C.4) have been taken from the "Foreign Trade and Navigation of the U.S.," an annual report included among the U.S. Congress papers. This information has been used for Figures 12.15 to 12.18. Value and quantity of wool imports from Argentina are given for every year since 1830. Only the value of hide imports was recorded. In both cases those were declared values. Hide imports were usually listed as "Raw Hides and Skins." That category might have included, therefore, horse hides and sheepskins also. U.S. trade statistics are given for the year closing on June 30 of each year. Convertibility was abandoned in 1862 and resumed in 1879, but imports continued to be valued in specie during that period. Imports from Río de la Plata were given without differentiation up to 1837, but from 1838 onward Argentina is listed separately.[20]

Figures for Belgian imports from and exports to Río de la Plata (Table C.5) have been taken from the *Tableau général du commerce de la Belgique avec les pays étrangers*. This information has been used for Figures 12.19 to 12.23. Some articles, such as wool, were subjected to ad-valorem duties, while others were taxed according to average rates based upon current prices. Fixed rates were established in 1833, but in 1850 they were being revised every year. That practice probably started in 1846.[21] Río de la Plata imports included those of Uruguay up to 1866. Adding up wool imports from Argentina and Uruguay, 79.5% correspond to the former and 20.5% to the latter from 1867 to 1880. In the case of hide imports for the same period, 27.3% correspond to the latter and 72.7% to the former, and in the case of tallow imports, 24.6% and 75.4%, respectively.

Figures of total hide, wool, and tallow imports into Great Britain, France, the United States, and Belgium (Tables C.6, C.7, and C.8) have been used for Figures 12.4, 12.5, and 12.7 (Great Britain); 12.12, 12.13, and 12.14 (France); 12.17 and 12.18 (United States); and 12.21, 12,22, and 12.23 (Belgium).

---

20 On U.S. trade statistics, see North (1960), and U.S. Department of Commerce (1975), 2:876.
21 For a description of the method, see Belgium, *Tableau* (1836), vii, and (1850), viii.

Table C.4. *U.S. imports from and exports to Argentina, 1825–1870*

	Exports $ (thousands)	Imports $ (thousands)	Hide $ (thousands)	Wool $ (thousands)	Wool lb (millions)
1825	573.5	749.8			
1826	379.3	522.8			
1827	151.2	80.1			
1828	154.2	317.5			
1829	626.1	915.2			
1830	629.9	1,431.9	1,119.5	0.1	0
1831	659.8	928.1	796.3	44.8	1.05
1832	923.0	1,560.2	1,408.6	18.6	0.34
1833	699.7	1,377.1	1,075.7	1.1	0.02
1834	971.8	1,430.1	944.0	7.1	0.07
1835	708.9	878.6	616.3	78.6	1.43
1836	384.4	1,053.5	698.8	163.2	2.30
1837	273.9	1,000.0	531.7	154.7	2.11
1838	236.7	1,010.9	546.2	160.5	2.54
1839	142.5	525.1	333.0	48.5	0.70
1840	369.3	293.6	181.1	38.9	0.57
1841	661.9	1,612.5	871.2	531.8	8.88
1842	411.3	1,835.6	1,150.6	477.4	7.45
1843	262.1	793.5	633.1	128.4	2.33
1844	504.3	1,421.2	791.5	46.7	8.44
1845	503.0	1,750.7	842.1	798.7	11.77
1846	185.4	799.2	387.7	327.6	4.30
1847	176.1	241.2	108.4	79.9	1.31
1848	233.9	1,026.1	552.7	267.4	4.31
1849	767.6	1,709.8	783.6	769.1	12.60
1850	1,064.6	2,563.9	1,588.0	877.9	10.18
1851	1,074.8	3,265.4	1,714.1	1,328.3	12.11
1852	799.1	2,091.1	1,247.8	701.1	7.08
1853	262.6	2,186.6	1,281.0	588.7	5.75
1854	658.7	2,145.0	1,074.0	854.2	6.26
1855	969.4	2,545.1	1,532.1	627.7	5.97
1856	1,259.9	2,322.2	1,460.8	588.4	5.67
1857	1,313.8	2,784.5	1,782.7	694.7	5.76
1858	904.6	2,725.2	1,613.6	861.2	
1859	1,438.2	4,070.0	2,501.2	1,356.0	
1860	997.7	4,020.8	2,519.5	1,194.6	
1861	1,166.6	3,200.8	1,050.6	1,787.3	
1862	1,084.9	1,973.9	766.8	838.9	5.79
1863	1,148.4	4,501.8	1,740.8	2,577.8	17.46
1864	1,469.7	5,971.2	1,951.7	3,618.4	23.93
1865	1,711.3	3,586.2	1,002.2	2,214.8	16.10
1866	1,740.0	6,832.3	2,022.6	4,557.5	36.92
1867	2,340.6	5,842.8	3,437.0	1,949.1	12.67
1868	2,549.2	4,807.9	3,456.2	876.6	5.84
1869	2,235.1	5,163.0	3,601.7	1,020.7	8.25
1870	2,281.1	6,414.7	4,256.3	1,853.1	16.72
1871	1,216.5	7,040.6	3,740.5	2,606.0	23.33

Source: U.S. Congress. "Foreign Trade and Navigation of the U.S.," 1825–1871.

Table C.5. *Belgium: Imports from and exports to Argentina, 1835–1870*

	Exports a	Imports b	Hides c	d	Wool e	f	Tallow g	h
1835	0.1	1.9	1.0	1.9				
1836	0.1	1.5	0.8	1.5				
1837	0.2	4.2	2.3	3.7	0.10	0.3	0.01	0.01
1838	0.1	5.9	3.5	5.5	0.00	0	0	0
1839	0.1	3.3	1.8	3.2	0.00	0	0	0
1840	0.2	5.2	3.4	5.0	0.01	0	0	0
1841	0.4	16.9	9.2	14.9	0.30	1.2	0.10	0.10
1842	0.4	9.3	5.2	8.7	0.88	0.4	0.07	0.07
1843	0.2	10.2	6.0	9.1	0.15	0.6	0.06	0.06
1844	0.2	8.5	4.4	8.1	0.05	0.19	0.10	0.10
1845	0.2	13.8	7.1	12.7	0.21	0.82	0.09	0.09
1846	0.1	4.8	2.9	4.47	0.04	0.14	0.03	0.3
1847	0.2	8.3	6.2	7.84	0.07	0.27	0	0
1848	0.1	6.3	5.5	5.31	0.10	0.40	0.15	0.15
1849	0.7	10.6	8.2	8.3	0.46	1.82	0.23	0.23
1850	0.4	11.0	7.3	8.10	0.54	2.16	0.41	0.41
1851	0.7	10.2	6.7	8.24	0.33	1.31	0.10	0.10
1852	1.3	11.8	5.0	5.98	1.14	5.12	0.16	0.16
1853	0.8	12.8	4.3	7.06	1.16	5.22		
1854	3.4	17.0	6.1	10.25	1.36	6.14	0.10	0.14
1855	2.6	23.3	4.2	7.75	3.07	13.82	0.09	0.13
1856	2.8	37.4	6.2	9.81	5.66	25.49	0.15	0.19
1857	3.3	53.8		17.67	7.10	26.99	1.03	1.34
1858	2.5	31.6	6.5	14.98	4.17	15.86	0.05	0.06
1859	4.5	43.4	6.4	15.31	7.20	27.38	0.12	0.14
1860	5.8	50.7	12.2	27.71	5.62	21.36	0.36	0.43
1861	3.2	48.4	8.4	16.87	7.79	29.59	0.48	0.57
1862	2.2	56.6	11.5	21.81	10.22	30.66	1.66	1.82
1863	3.0	50.5	9.1	15.42	10.35	31.04	2.01	2.01
1864	3.7	67.3	10.4	17.65	15.33	45.99	1.33	1.33
1865	4.8	103.5	13.7	21.93	25.37	76.12	3.11	3.42
1866	4.5	116.5	11.0	17.59	30.98	92.95	3.48	3.82
1867	3.2	106.8	11.1	18.88	32.17	80.41	5.50	6.05
1868	4.0	121.0	13.0	22.09	44.51	89.01	7.38	8.12
1869	5.6	72.9	13.3	22.58	19.38	36.82	9.06	9.96
1870	6.2	52.6	13.2	25.15	7.47	15.68	7.71	8.49

Notes: a, b, d and h: million francs; c, e, and g: million kilos.
Source: Belgium, *Tableau générale du commerce de la Belgique avec les pays étrangers,* 1835–1870.

Table C.6. *Total hide imports into the United States, Great Britain, France, and Belgium, 1830–1870*

	United States $ (millions)	G. Britain £ (millions)	France francs (millions)	Belgium francs (millions)
1830	2.41			
1831	3.06			
1832	4.68			
1833	3.59			
1834	1.30			
1835	3.37			
1836	3.51			6.43
1837	3.31			7.21
1838	2.04			7.45
1839	3.16			5.23
1840	2.76			7.93
1841	3.46			18.99
1842	4.07			11.44
1843	2.33			17.08
1844				13.57
1845				21.21
1846				10.44
1847	1.53		17.30	11.16
1848	4.26		11.91	8.64
1849	3.51		13.77	12.24
1850	4.80		13.38	12.70
1851	5.96		18.22	12.90
1852	4.82		19.04	9.81
1853	5.92		19.45	11.64
1854	7.62	1.51	21.28	14.16
1855	8.05	1.78	31.36	13.26
1856	8.08	1.48	35.46	17.08
1857	10.01	2.30	53.70	30.63
1858	9.80	1.17	35.91	27.96
1859	13.01	1.98	43.79	34.89
1860	10.52	1.97	57.31	50.17
1861	6.29	1.48	49.85	32.28
1862	3.97	1.61	37.43	37.82
1863	7.51	1.55	53.34	29.76
1864	6.18	1.64	48.31	35.59
1865	2.88	1.44	45.11	35.13
1866	7.15	1.74	43.69	34.31
1867	10.07	1.46	50.79	40.23
1868	10.10	1.68	46.14	51.39
1869	12.48	1.25	45.42	50.89
1870	14.40	1.74	38.39	58.78
1871	14.39			

Sources: See Tables C.2 to C.5.

Table C.7. *Total wool imports into the United States, Great Britain, France, and Belgium, 1830–1870*

	United States $ (millions)	G. Britain £ (millions)	France francs (millions)	Belgium francs (millions)
1830	0.28			
1831	1.28			
1832	0.69			
1833	0.24			
1834	0.32			
1835	1.09			
1836	1.27			
1837	0.89			
1838	0.53			
1839	0.70			
1840	0.85			
1841	1.16			33.92
1842	0.72			35.06
1843	0.19			34.90
1844	0.75			31.94
1845	1.55			33.72
1846	1.11			24.50
1847	0.55			27.51
1848	0.86		0.22	21.02
1849	1.18		1.58	37.38
1850	1.68		2.08	39.13
1851	3.83		0.38	35.73
1852	1.93		2.62	52.16
1853	2.67		2.49	46.77
1854	2.82	6.37	3.20	56.40
1855	2.07	6.35	6.62	65.91
1856	1.66	8.26	5.19	71.61
1857	2.13	9.33	4.38	76.17
1858	2.84	8.65	11.03	60.69
1859	4.36	9.55	15.34	73.73
1860	4.45	10.70	18.95	83.24
1861	4.56	9.37	18.61	101.04
1862	6.42	11.32	17.70	96.31
1863	11.77	11.47	28.87	99.98
1864	14.60	15.16	20.37	127.24
1865	6.16	14.53	35.08	157.37
1866	9.23	16.98	35.46	157.72
1867	5.67	15.76	50.59	163.85
1868	3.78	14.87	52.41	173.58
1869	5.60	14.30	50.02	161.36
1870	6.74	15.36	48.47	154.45
1871	9.78			

Sources: See Tables C.2 to C.5.

Table C.8. *Total tallow imports into Great Britain, France, and Belgium,*
1835–1870

	G. Britain £ (millions)	France francs (millions)	Belgium francs (millions)
1835			0.28
1836			0.10
1837			0.21
1838			0.11
1839			0.13
1840			0.13
1841			0.38
1842			0.78
1843			0.91
1844			0.70
1845			0.37
1846			0.71
1847		6.17	0.67
1848		3.98	0.61
1849		5.73	0.86
1850		3.69	1.08
1851		0.84	0.60
1852		0.84	1.08
1853		1.68	0.86
1854	2.35	2.29	1.40
1855	2.65	15.49	2.29
1856	2.93	13.16	2.87
1857	3.29	11.78	4.50
1858	3.04	5.82	2.99
1859	2.93	3.02	1.39
1860	4.01	5.76	2.32
1861	3.31	15.09	4.32
1862	2.51	41.99	6.79
1863	2.44	47.58	7.37
1864	2.08	28.37	6.98
1865	3.13	22.87	7.54
1866	3.01	27.59	9.99
1867	2.42	51.92	15.88
1868	2.96	41.06	19.03
1869	2.77	47.64	18.75
1870	3.29	49.15	17.30

Sources: See Tables C.2 to C.5.

Glossary

The translation of most technical words has been taken from Haensch and Haberkamp de Antón (1975).

acción: according to the inventories, the right to brand livestock with someone's own branding iron

agregado: someone living on someone else's land or household

aguada: natural waterer for livestock

algarrobo (*Prosopis alba* and *Prosopis nigra*): a native hardwood tree

alzado: *see* ganado alzado

apartes: sortings, to cut a herd [Daireaux (1908), 370]

aquerenciado: livestock used to a particular place (*see* querencia)

aquerenciar: to get livestock used to a particular place

arroyo: creek, stream

atahona: horse- or mule-driven mill

azotea: terrace roof

balde sin fondo: bottomless bucket; a roughly cylindrical piece of hide, tied by its extremes to a single rope, used to pump water up from a well

Banda Oriental: eastern shore of the Río de la Plata, present Uruguay

bando: governor's or viceroy's decree

bañado: lowland, marsh

baqueano: man with a detailed knowledge of a region

cabezadas: tract of land behind the suerte principal

cañada: small, shallow valley on the plains

cardo (*Cynara cardunculus, Silybum marianum*): thistle

chacarero: farmer, chacraholder

chacra: farm; a plot devoted to agriculture, smaller than an estancia, sometimes within the estancia *changadores*: see gaucho

cimarrón, cimarrona: wild (dogs or cattle); fugitive head of cattle [Azara (1801): 1:367]

compadre: the godfather of someone's child

contribución directa: a direct tax paid by merchants and landowners, according to a law passed in 1821

corral: "an inclosure fabricated of the crooked branches of trees – generally of the Nandubaya [ñandubay] wood" [Hutchinson (1865), 29]; the urban cattle markets were called *corrales*

criolla, criollo: native, local born; a criollo slave was one who was born in the Americas; a criolla sheep was a head of an unrefined breed

espinillo (*Acacia praecox*): a thorny, small, native tree

estanciero: estancia owner

ganado alzado: stray cattle

gaucho: in the eighteenth and early nineteenth centuries, a rural criminal; in the late nineteenth century, rural inhabitants

hacendado: cattle owner

Interior: the provinces other than Buenos Aires, especially from Córdoba to the north and west

invernada: wintering place, usually located on a permanent stream where green grasses could be found even in winter

jagüel: watering place for livestock

Litoral: the provinces along the Paraná River (Santa Fe, Entre Ríos, and Corrientes)

mayordomo: estancia manager [Hernández (1953), 358]

medianero: sharecropper; a shepherd who took care of someone else's herd getting half of the annual reproduction as his share

mejoras: improvements, such as dwellings, fences, corrals, ditches, groves

mensura: land survey

mestiza, mestizo: mixed; a mestizo was someone of mixed blood (typically, European and Indian); a mestiza sheep was a mixed breed

moneda corriente: paper money

montoneras: a band of irregular, armed men

ñandubay (*Prosopis algarrobilla* var. *ñandubay*): a hard wood

ombú (*Phytolacca dioica*): a big treelike bush, appreciated for its shadow, but useless otherwise

orejano, ganado orejano: unbranded cattle

pagos: loosely defined rural districts, frequently named after a geographical characteristic

paja: pampas grass

pajonal: a place with a dense concentration of tall, dense pampas grass

palenque: a wooden structure to which to tie the horses

palo a pique: corral made of wooden stakes, one along the other

palo blanco: white stick, used for soft, whitish woods as willow, poplar, paraíso, and even peachwood

pampero: strong southwesterly wind that sweeps the pampas

paraíso (Melia azederach): a tree appreciated for its leaves, which are not eaten by locusts, rather than for its low-quality wood

partido: rural administrative district, usually defined by the presence of judiciary or military authorities

peso fuerte: a Spanish-American coin weighing one ounce of silver

población: "habitations, with their foliaged surroundings" [Latham (1868), 27]

poblar: the action of establishing a rancho on a piece of land

posta: usually a rancho and a corral with fresh horses for travelers

potrero: at present, a fenced subdivision of an estancia; in the nineteenth century, a corral for horses

pozo de balde: a well suited to get water with a bucket

pulpería: a rural general store

puestero: a man in charge of a puesto

puesto: "the huts of the shepherds [or herdsmen], with their 'corrales'" [Latham (1868), 27]

querencia: a place cattle are used to (*see* aquerenciar)

quincha, quincho: a building technique mixing mud and straw

quinta: fruit-tree grove, according to the use of the word made in the 1820 and 1850 inventories; it also means vegetable garden

ramada: a structure of wooden poles with straw roof but no walls

rancho: building, usually made of adobe walls and paja roof, with a wooden structure

real: one-eighth of a peso

redomón: colt in the process of being broken [Azara (1801), 2:317]

rincón: the confluence of two streams, a convenient place to round up cattle

rodeo: place where at certain times the animals are gathered to be inspected or counted (*animales de rodeo* [roundup beasts] are those animals that have been taught to gather at that meeting point [Azara (1801), 1:lxxiii]); the action of rounding up head, but also used for herds [Daireaux (1908), 363]

saladero: jerked-beef factory

sobra: remainder; a portion of land left outside the boundaries of a tract after a survey

suerte de estancia: a tract of land 3,000 varas wide and 9,000 varas long

suerte principal: main tract of land of an estancia, usually facing a river or stream of water

tablada: an office in charge of controlling the introduction of cattle into Buenos Aires [Daireaux (1908), 553]

tala (*Celtis spinosa*): a thorny tree used for fences

vaquería: a hunting expedition looking for wild head of cattle

viscacha or vizcacha: a rodent of the pampas

yerba mate (*Ilex paraguayensis*): a stimulant, also called Paraguayan tea

Bibliography

Abbreviations*

ABP   Archivo y Museo Histórico del Banco de la Provincia de Buenos Aires, Buenos Aires.
ACR   *Antecedentes y fundamentos del proyecto de Código Rural.*
AGN   Archivo General de la Nación, Buenos Aires.
AHP   Archivo Histórico de la Provincia de Buenos Aires "Dr. Ricardo Levene," La Plata.
ASRA   *Anales de la Sociedad Rural Argentina.*
CRBA   *Código rural de la provincia de Buenos Aires.*
DHA   *Abastos de la ciudad y campaña de Buenos Aires (1773–1809).*
JRM   John Rylands University Library of Manchester, Manchester.
MAE   Ministère des Affaires Etrangères, Paris.
MOP   Ministerio de Obras Públicas de la Provincia de Buenos Aires, Dirección de Geodesia y Catastro, Departamento de Investigación Histórica y Cartográfica, La Plata.
NLS   National Library of Scotland, Edinburgh.
PRO   Public Record Office, London.
REBA   *Registro Estadístico de Buenos Aires.*
RO   *Registro Oficial de la Provincia de Buenos Aires.*

Abastos de la ciudad y campaña de Buenos Aires (1773–1809). Buenos Aires: Universidad de Buenos Aires, Facultad de Filosofía y Letras, 1914 (Documentos para la Historia Argentina, v. 4) [DHA].

Acarete du Biscay. "Rélation des voyages du Sieur . . . dans la rivière de la Plate, et de là par terre au Pérou, et des observations qu'il y a faites." In Melchisedech Thévenot, *Rélation de divers voyages curieux.* Paris: André Cramoisy, 1672, IV partie.

Adelman, Jeremy. *Frontier Development. Land, Labour, and Capital on the Wheatlands of Argentina and Canada, 1890–1914.* Oxford: Clarendon Press, 1994.

Aguirre, Juan Francisco. "Diario," *Anales de la Biblioteca,* 1905, 4:1–271, and 1911, 7:1–490. [Reprinted in *Revista de la Biblioteca Nacional,* 1947, 17(43–44); 1948, 18(45–46); 1948, 19(47–48); and 1949, 20(49–50).]

[Alsina, Valentin.] *Proyecto de Código Rural.* Buenos Aires: Imprenta de Buenos Aires, 1865.

Alvarez, Juan. *Las guerras civiles argentinas.* 6th ed. Buenos Aires: Eudeba, 1984.

Alvear, Diego de. "Diario de la segunda partida demarcadora de límites en la América meridional 1783–1791," *Anales de la Biblioteca,* 1900, 1:267–384; 1902, 2:288–360; and 1904, 3:373–464.

* These abbreviations are used in both the text and the bibliography.

335

Alvear y Escalera, Diego. "Diario perteneciente al teniente de navío de la Real Armada . . . ," *Revista de la Biblioteca Nacional*, 1946, 15(40):257–504.

Amaral, Samuel. "El Empréstito Baring y la crisis de 1826." Ph.D. dissertation. Universidad Nacional de La Plata, 1977a.

Amaral, Samuel. "Comercio y crédito en Buenos Aires, 1822–1826," *América*, 1977b, 4:9–49 [Revised version: *Siglo XIX*, 1990, 5(9):105–121.]

Amaral, Samuel. "La reforma financiera de 1821 y el establecimiento del Crédito Público en Buenos Aires," *Cuadernos de Numismática*, 1982, 9(33):29–48.

Amaral, Samuel. "Public Expenditure Financing in the Colonial Treasury. An Analysis of the Real Caja de Buenos Aires Accounts, 1789–91," *Hispanic American Historical Review*, 1984, 64(2):287–295.

Amaral, Samuel. "Rural Production and Labour in Late Colonial Buenos Aires," *Journal of Latin American Studies*, 1987a, 19(2):235–278.

Amaral, Samuel. "Trabajo y trabajadores rurales en Buenos Aires a fines del siglo XVIII," *Anuario del IEHS*, 1987b, 2:33–41.

Amaral, Samuel. "El descubrimiento de la financiación inflacionaria. Buenos Aires, 1790–1830," *Investigaciones y Ensayos*, 1988, 37:379–418.

Amaral, Samuel. "Alta inflación y precios relativos. El pago de las obligaciones en Buenos Aires (1826–1834)," *El Trimestre Económico*, 1989, 56(221):163–191.

Amaral, Samuel, and José María Ghio. "Diezmos y producción agraria: Buenos Aires, 1750–1800," *Revista de Historia Económica*, 1990, 8(3):619–647.

Anderson, Edgar. "Man as Maker of New Plants and New Plant Communities." In Thomas (1956), 763–777.

Andrews, Joseph. *Journey from Buenos Ayres, through the provinces of Cordova, Tucuman, and Salta, to Potosi, thence by the deserts of Caranja to Arica, and subsequently, to Santiago de Chili and Coquimbo, undertaken on behalf of the Chilian and Perubian Mining Association, in the years 1815–1826*. 2 vols. London: John Murray, 1827.

Antecedentes y fundamentos del Proyecto de Código Rural. Buenos Aires: Imprenta de Buenos Aires, 1864 [ACR].

Aparicio, Francisco de, and Horacio A. Difrieri. *La Argentina: Suma de Geografía*. 9 vols. Buenos Aires: Peuser, 1958–1963.

Ardissone, Romualdo. "Datos históricos acerca de las precipitaciones pluviales en la zona de Buenos Aires desde el siglo XVI hasta 1821," *Gaea*, 1937, 5:115–211.

Armaignac, H. *Viaje por las pampas de la República Argentina*. Transl. and prol. Alfredo Amaral Insiarte. La Plata: Ministerio de Educación de la Provincia de Buenos Aires, 1962.

Arnold, Samuel Greene. *Viaje por América del Sur 1847–1848*. Transl. and prol. José Luis Busaniche. Pref. David James. Buenos Aires: Emecé, 1951.

Avellaneda, Nicolás. *Estudios sobre las leyes de tierras públicas* [1865]. In *Escritos y discursos*. Buenos Aires: Compañía Sud-Americana de Billetes de Banco, 1910, vol. 5.

Azara, Félix de. *Essais sur l'histoire naturelle des quadrupèdes de la province du Paraguay*. 2 vols. Paris: Charles Pougens, An IX [1801].

Azara, Félix de. "Diario de un reconocimiento de las guardias y fortines que guarnecen la línea de frontera de Buenos Aires para ensancharla [1796]." In de Angelis (1910), 5:53–87.

Azara, Félix de. "Memoria sobre el estado rural del Río de la Plata en 1801." In *Memoria sobre el estado rural del Río de la Plata y otros informes*. Ed. Julio César González. Buenos Aires: Bajel, 1943, 1–25.

Azara, Félix de. *Viajes por la América meridional*. Madrid: Espasa Calpe, 1969.

Azcuy Ameghino, Eduardo. "¿'Oferta ilimitada de tierras'? Un análisis de caso: Navarro, 1791–1822," *Ciclos*, 1994, 4(6):175–217.

Azcuy Ameghino, Eduardo. *El latifundio y la gran propiedad colonial rioplatense*. Buenos Aires: Fernando García Cambeiro, 1995.

Azcuy Ameghino, Eduardo, and Gabriela Martínez Dougnac. *Tierra y ganado en la campaña de Buenos Aires según los censos de hacendados de 1789*. Buenos Aires: IIHES, 1989.

Balbín, Valentín. *Sistema de medidas y pesas de la República Argentina*. Buenos Aires: Biedma, 1881.

Balsa, Javier. "Tasa de ganancia de los comerciantes porteños durante el virreinato." La Plata, 1986 (ms.)

Banzato, Guillermo, and Guillermo Quinteros. "La ocupación de la tierra en la frontera bonaerense. El caso de Chascomús 1779–1821," *Estudios de Historia Rural*, 1992, 2:37–76.

Barba, Enrique M. "Contribución documental sobre la historia de la ganadería en el Río de la Plata al finalizar el siglo XVIII," *Revista Histórica* (Montevideo), 1955a, 23(67–69):264–336, and 1955b, 24(70–72):318–376.

Barba, Enrique M. "Notas sobre la situación económica de Buenos Aires en la década de 1820," *Trabajos y Comunicaciones*, 1967, 17:65–71.

Barba, Enrique M. (ed.) *Informes sobre el comercio exterior de Buenos Aires durante el gobierno de Martín Rodríguez*. Buenos Aires: Academia Nacional de la Historia, 1978.

Barsky, Osvaldo (ed.) *El desarrollo agropecuario pampeano*. Buenos Aires: Grupo Editor Latinoamericano, 1991.

Bauer, Arnold J. "Rural Workers in Spanish America: Problems of Peonage and Oppression," *Hispanic American Historical Review*, 1979, 59(1):34–63.

Baulant, Micheline, Anton J. Schuurman, and Paul Servais. *Inventaires apres décès et ventes de meubles*. Louvain-la Neuve: Academia, 1988.

Beaumont, J. A. B. *Viajes por Buenos Aires, Entre Ríos y la Banda Oriental, 1826–1827*. Transl. and notes José Luis Busaniche. Intr. Sergio Bagú. Buenos Aires: Hachette, 1957.

Belgium. *Tableau général du commerce de la Belgique avec les pays étrangers*. Bruxelles, 1835–1870.

Belgrano, Manuel. *Escritos económicos*. Intr. Gregorio Weinberg. Buenos Aires: Raigal, 1954.

Bishop, Nathaniel H. *The Pampas and the Andes. A Thousand Miles' Walk across South America*. Boston: Lee and Shepard, 1869.

Bjerg, María Mónica, and Andrea Reguera (eds.) *Problemas de historia agraria*. Tandil: IEHS, 1995.

Blondel, J. J. M. *Almanaque de político y de comercio de la ciudad de Buenos Aires para el año de 1826*. Intr. Enrique M. Barba. Buenos Aires: de la Flor, 1968.

Bonaudo, Marta, and Alfredo R. Pucciarelli (eds.) *La problemática agraria. Nuevas aproximaciones*. 3 vols. Buenos Aires: Centro Editor de América Latina, 1993.

Borrero, Fernando. *Descripción de las Provincias del Río de la Plata*. Buenos Aires: Juan A. Alsina, 1911.

Brabazon, John. [Memoirs]. In Eduardo A. Coghlan (ed.), *Andanzas de un irlandés en el campo porteño (1845–1864)*. Buenos Aires: Ediciones Culturales Argentinas, 1981.

Brackenridge, H. M. *A Voyage to South America*. 2 vols. London: T. and J. Allman, 1820.

Brading, David A. "The Capital Structure of Mexican Haciendas: León 1700–1850," *Ibero-Amerikanisches Archiv*, 1975, 1(2):151–182.

Brading, David A. *Haciendas and Ranchos in the Mexican Bajío, León 1700–1860*. Cambridge University Press, 1978.

Brand, Charles. *Journal of a Voyage to Peru*. London: Henry Colburn, 1828.

Brito Stífano, Rogelio. "Dos noticias sobre el estado de los campos de la Banda Oriental al finalizar el siglo XVIII," *Revista Histórica* (Montevideo), 1953, 18(52–54):301–527.

Broide, Julio. "La evolución de los precios pecuarios argentinos en el período 1830–1850," *Revista de la Facultad de Ciencias Económicas*, 1951, 4(32):113–183.

Brown, Jonathan C. "A Nineteenth-Century Argentine Cattle Empire," *Agricultural History*, 1978, 52(1):160–178.

Brown, Jonathan C. *A Socioeconomic History of Argentina, 1776–1860*. Cambridge University Press, 1979.

Buchanan, James M., Robert D. Tollison, and Gordon Tullock (eds.) *Toward a Theory of the Rent-Seeking Society*. College Station: Texas A&M University Press, 1980.

Bueno, Cosme. *Descripción del Reyno del Perú y de el de Chile por Obispados y Provincias, y en igual conformidad de las del Río de la Plata y sus respectivas dependencias*. Lima, 1763–1778.

Buenos Aires (Province). *Registro Oficial*. Buenos Aires, 1821–1870 [RO].

Buenos Aires (Province). *Registro gráfico de los terrenos de propiedad pública y particular de la provincia de Buenos Ayres*. Buenos Aires, 1830.

Buenos Aires (Province). *Registro Estadístico*. Buenos Aires, 1822–1825 and 1854–1872 [REBA].

Buenos Aires (Province). *Registro gráfico de las propiedades rurales de la Provincia de Buenos Aires construido por el Departamento Topográfico y publicado con autorización del Superior Gobierno de la Provincia. 1864*. Buenos Aires, 1864.

Buenos Aires (Province). *Código rural de la provincia de Buenos Aires*. Buenos Aires: Imprenta de Buenos Aires, 1865 [CRBA].

Buenos Aires (Province). *Censo general de la provincia de Buenos Aires demográfico, agrícola, industrial, comercial, & verificado el 9 de octubre de 1881*. Buenos Aires: El Diario, 1883.

Bunbury, Charles James Fox. "Notes on the Vegetation of Buenos Ayres and the Neighbouring Districts," *Transactions of the Linnean Society of London*, 1855, 21:185–198.

Burgin, Miron. *The Economic Aspects of Argentine Federalism*. New York: Russell and Russell, 1946 [Spanish version: *Aspectos económicos del federalismo argentino*. Transl. Mario Calés. Intr. Beatriz Bosch. Buenos Aires: Hachette, 1960].

Burmeister, Hermann. *Viaje por los estados del Plata*. Transl. Carlos and Federico Burmeister. Buenos Aires: Unión Germánica en la Argentina, 1943.

Cabodi, Juan Jorge. "El reconocimiento de fronteras de Francisco Betbezé." In *Primer Congreso de Historia de los Pueblos de la Provincia de Buenos Aires*. 3 vols. La Plata: Archivo Histórico, 1952, 2:25–101.

Cabrera, Angel. *El perro cimarrón de la pampa argentina*. Buenos Aires: Facultad de Filosofía y Letras, Universidad de Buenos Aires, 1932 (Publicaciones del Museo Antropológico y Etnográfico, Serie A, 2:7–29).

Cabrera, Angel L. (ed.) *Flora de la Provincia de Buenos Aires*. Buenos Aires: INTA, 1963 (Part VI, Compuestos).

Cáceres Cano, Severo. "Algunas consideraciones sobre la ley de aduanas de Rosas (1835) y en qué forma se vio beneficiada Tucumán." In *Quinto Congreso Nacional y Regional de Historia Argentina*. Buenos Aires: Academia Nacional de la Historia, 1987, 179–190.

Caldcleugh, Alexander. *Travels in South America during the years 1819–20–21*. 2 vols. London: John Murray, 1825.

Caldcleugh, Alexander. *Viajes por la América del Sur. Río de la Plata. 1821*. Transl. José Luis Busaniche. Buenos Aires: Solar, 1943.

Campbell, Bruce M. S., and Mark Overton (eds.) *Land, Labour and Livestock: Historical Studies in European Agricultural Productivity*. Manchester and New York: Manchester University Press, 1991.

Cansanello, Oreste Carlos. "Domiciliados y transeúntes en el proceso de formación estatal bonaerense (1820–1832)," *Entrepasados*, 1994, 4(6):7–22.

Cansanello, Oreste Carlos. "De súbditos a ciudadanos. Los pobladores rurales bonaerenses entre el Antiguo Régimen y la modernidad," *Boletín del Instituto de Historia Argentina y Americana Dr. Emilio Ravignani*, 3d ser., 1995, 11:113–139.

Capdevila, Pedro V. *La estancia argentina*. Buenos Aires: Plus Ultra, 1978.

Cárcano, Miguel Angel. *Evolución histórica del régimen de la tierra pública*. 3d ed. Buenos Aires: Eudeba, 1972.

Cardiel, José, S. J. "Diario del viaje y misión al Río del Sauce por fines de marzo de 1748." In Vignati (1956), 113–139.

Carreño, Virginia. *Estancias y estancieros del Río de la Plata*. Buenos Aires: Claridad, 1994.

Carretero, Andrés M. "Contribución al conocimiento de la propiedad rural en la provincia de Buenos Aires para 1830," *Boletín del Instituto de Historia Argentina Dr. Emilio Ravignani*, 2d ser., 1970, 13(22–23):46–92.

Carretero, Andrés M. *La propiedad de la tierra en la época de Rosas*. Buenos Aires: El Coloquio, 1972.

Cascardo, Antonio R., José B. Pizarro, Miguel A. Peretti, and Pedro O. Gómez. "Sistema de producción predominantes." In Barsky (1991), 95–146.

"Censo de propietarios y ganaderos de la frontera del Arroyo Azul levantado en el mes de julio del año 1839 según borrador existente en el archivo del Juzgado de Paz," *Azul*, 1930, 1(3):93–134.

Chiaramonte, José Carlos. *Mercaderes del Litoral*. Buenos Aires: Fondo de Cultura Económica, 1991.

Chijachev, Platon Alejandrovich. "Viaje a través de las pampas de Buenos Aires," *Boletín del Instituto de Historia Argentina Dr. Emilio Ravignani*, 2d ser., 1967, 9(14–15):14–106.

Clark, Andrew H. "The Impact of Exotic Invasions on the Remaining New World Mid-Latitude Grasslands." In Thomas (1956), 737–761.

Coase, R. H. "The Nature of the Firm," *Economica*, 1937, 4(16):386–405.

Coase, R. H. "The Institutional Structure of Production," *American Economic Review*, 1992, 82(4):713–719.

Cole, Arthur Harrison. *Wholesale Commodity Prices in the United States 1700–1861. Statistical Supplement*. Cambridge, Mass.: Harvard University Press, 1938.

Comadrán Ruíz, Jorge. *Evolución demográfica argentina durante el período hispánico (1535–1810)*. Buenos Aires: Eudeba, 1969.

Coni, Emilio A. *La verdad sobre la enfiteusis de Rivadavia*. Buenos Aires: Facultad de Agronomía y Veterinaria, 1927.

Coni, Emilio A. *Historia de las vaquerías de Río de la Plata, 1555–1750*. 2d ed. Buenos Aires: Platero, 1979.

Cortés Conde, Roberto. "Algunos rasgos de la expansión territorial en Argentina en la segunda mitad del siglo XIX," *Desarrollo Económico*, 1968, 8(29):3–29

Cortés Conde, Roberto. *El progreso argentino 1880–1914*. Buenos Aires: Sudamericana, 1979.

Crosby, Alfred W. *The Columbian Exchange*. Westport, Conn.: Greenwood Publishers Co., 1972.

Crosby, Alfred W. *Ecological Imperialism. The Biological Expansion of Europe, 900–1900*. Cambridge University Press, 1986.

Cuenca-Esteban, Javier. "The Markets of Latin American Exports, 1790–1820: A Comparative Analysis of International Prices." In Johnson and Tandeter (1990), 373–399.

Cushner, Nicholas P. *Jesuit Ranches and the Agrarian Development of Colonial Argentina, 1650–1767*. Albany: State University of New York, 1983.

Daireaux, Emilio. *Vida y costumbres en el Plata*. 2 vols. Buenos Aires: Lajouane, 1888.

Daireaux, Godofredo. *La cría de ganado en la pampa*. Buenos Aires: F. Lajouane, 1887.

Daireaux, Godofredo. *La cría de ganado en la estancia moderna.* 4th ed. Buenos Aires: Prudent, 1908.

Daireaux, Godofredo. "La estancia argentina." In República Argentina, Censo Agropecuario Nacional. *La ganadería y la agricultura en 1908.* Buenos Aires: Oficina Meteorológica Argentina, 1909, 3:1–53.

Darwin, Charles. "Journals and Remarks. 1832–1836." In *Narrative of the Surveying voyages of His Majesty's Ships Adventure and Beagle, between the years 1826 and 1836, describing their examination of the southern shores of South America, and the Beagle's circumnavigation of the globe.* London: Henry Colburn, 1839, vol. 3. [Reprinted in New York: AMS Press, 1966.]

de Angelis, Pedro. *Memoria sobre el estado de la hacienda pública.* Buenos Aires: Imprenta del Estado, 1834.

de Angelis, Pedro. *Colección de obras y documentos relativos a la historia antigua y moderna de las provincias del Río de la Plata.* 2d ed. 5 vols. Buenos Aires: Lajouane, 1910.

de la Fuente, Ariel. "Aguardiente y trabajo en una hacienda catamarqueña colonial. La Toma, 1767–1790," *Anuario del IEHS*, 1988, 3:91–121.

de la Fuente, Diego G. (ed.) *Primer censo de la República Argentina.* Buenos Aires: Imprenta del Porvenir, 1872.

Demsetz, Harold. *Ownership, Control, and the Firm.* Oxford: Basil Blackwell, 1988.

de Vries, Jan. *The Dutch Rural Economy in the Golden Age 1500–1700.* New Haven: Yale University Press, 1974.

Dewey, Lyster Hoxie. "The Russian Thistle: Its History as a Weed in the United States, with an Account of the Means Available for its Eradication," *Bulletin*, U.S. Department of Agriculture, Division of Botany, 1894, No. 15.

Díaz, Benito. *Los juzgados de paz de campaña de la provincia de Buenos Aires (1821–1854).* La Plata: Universidad Nacional de La Plata, 1959.

Díaz Alejandro, Carlos F. *Essays on the Economic History of the Argentine Republic.* New Haven: Yale University Press, 1970.

Documentos para la historia del virreinato del Río de la Plata. 3 vols. Buenos Aires, 1912.

D'Orbigny, Alcide Dessalinnes. *Voyage dans l'Amérique méridional.* 7 vols. Paris: Pitois-Levrault, 1835–1847.

Douville, Jean Baptiste. *Viajes a Buenos Aires 1826 y 1831.* Transl. Carlota Podestá. Prol. and notes Bonifacio del Carril. Buenos Aires: Emecé, 1984.

Duplessis, Robert S. "Probate Inventories, Investment Patterns and Entrepreneurial Behavior in the Zaanstreek (Holland) 1690–1709, 1740–1749." In Baulant et al. (1988), 97–108.

Ekelund, Robert B., and Robert D. Tollison. *Mercantilism as a rent-seeking society.* College Station, Tex.: Texas A&M University Press, 1981.

Escriche, Joaquín. *Diccionario razonado de legislación y jurisprudencia.* Paris: Rosa, Bouret y Cía., 1852.

Espalla, J. "La ley de aduana de Rosas y el desarrollo económico," *Kairós*, 1967, 1(1):31–41.

Espiñeira, Mariano F. *Ultimo precio diario al contado de la onza de oro sellada.* Buenos Aires: Pablo E. Coni, 1864.

Estévez, Alfredo. "La contribución directa 1821–1852," *Revista de Ciencias Económicas*, 1960, 48(10):123–240.

Fernández, A. R. *Prontuario informativo de la provincia de Buenos Aires.* Buenos Aires: Compañía Sud-Americana de Billetes de Banco, 1902–1907.

Fernández López, Manuel. "Valor, trabajo y capital. Ensayo sobre *La Riqueza de las Naciones* y el primer pensamiento económico argentino." In Raúl Orayen et al., *Ensayos actuales sobre Adam Smith y David Hume.* Buenos Aires: Instituto Torcuato Di Tella, 1976, 81–116.

Fienup, Darrell F., Russell H. Brannon, and Frank A. Fender. *The Agricultural Development of Argentina*. New York: Frederick A. Praeger, 1969.

Fisher, John. "The Imperial Response to 'Free Trade': Spanish Imports from Spanish America, 1778–1796," *Journal of Latin American Studies*, 1985, 17(1):35–78.

Florescano, Enrique (ed.) *Haciendas, latifundios y plantaciones*. México, D. F.: Siglo XXI, 1975.

Fradkin, Raúl O. "El gremio de hacendados en Buenos Aires durante la segunda mitad del siglo XVIII," *Cuadernos de Historia Regional*, 1987, 3(8):72–96.

Fradkin, Raúl O. "La historia agraria y los estudios de establecimientos productivos en Hispanoamérica colonial: una mirada desde el Río de la Plata." In Fradkin (1993a), 1:7–44 [cited as Fradkin (1993b)].

Fradkin, Raúl O. (ed.) *La historia agraria del Río de la Plata colonial. Los establecimientos productivos*. 2 vols. Buenos Aires: Centro Editor de América Latina, 1993a.

Fradkin, Raúl O. "'Según la costumbre del pays': costumbre y arriendo en Buenos Aires durante el siglo XVIII," *Boletín del Instituto de Historia Argentina y Americana Dr. Emilio Ravignani*, 3d ser., 1995, 11:39–64.

France. *Tableau général du commerce de la France avec ses colonies et les puissances étrangères*. Paris, 1829–1871.

Frías, Susana, and Abelardo Levaggi. *Buenos Aires. 1800–1830. Salud y delito*. Buenos Aires: Emecé Distribuidora, 1977.

Fugl, Juan. *Abriendo surcos*. Buenos Aires: Altamira, 1959.

Gaignard, Romain. *La pampa argentina*. Trans. Ricardo Figueira. Buenos Aires: Solar, 1989.

Gallardo, Guillermo. "La plaga de los perros cimarrones," *Historia*, 1963, 9(31):70–90.

Gallardo, Guillermo. *Joel Roberts Poinsett agente norteamericano 1810–1811*. Buenos Aires: Emecé, 1984.

Gallo, Ezequiel. *La pampa gringa*. Buenos Aires: Sudamericana, 1983.

Garavaglia, Juan Carlos. "El Río de la Plata en sus relaciones atlánticas: una balanza comercial (1779–1784)," *Moneda y Crédito*, 1977, 141:75–101.

Garavaglia, Juan Carlos. "Economic Growth and Regional Differentiations: The River Plate Region at the End of the Eighteenth Century," *Hispanic American Historical Review*, 1985, 65(1):51–89.

Garavaglia, Juan Carlos. "Producción cerealera y producción ganadera en la campaña porteña." In Garavaglia and Gelman (1989), 7–42.

Garavaglia, Juan Carlos. "Las 'estancias' en la campaña de Buenos Aires (1750–1850)." In Fradkin (1993a), 2:124–208 [cited as Garavaglia (1993)].

Garavaglia, Juan Carlos. "De la carne al cuero. Los mercados para los productos pecuarios (Buenos Aires y su campaña, 1700–1825)," *Anuario del IEHS*, 1994, 9:61–95.

Garavaglia, Juan Carlos. "Precios de los productos rurales y precios de la tierra en la campaña de Buenos Aires, 1750–1826," *Boletín del Instituto de Historia Argentina y Americana Dr. Emilio Ravignani*, 3d ser., 1995a, 11:65–112.

Garavaglia, Juan Carlos. "Notas para una historia rural pampeana un poco menos mítica." In Bjerg and Reguera (1995), 11–31 [cited as Garavaglia (1995b)].

Garavaglia, Juan Carlos. "Tres estancias del sur bonaerense en un período de transición (1790–1834)." In Bjerg and Reguera (1995), 79–123 [cited as Garavaglia (1995c)].

Garavaglia, Juan Carlos, and Jorge D. Gelman. *El mundo rural rioplatense a fines de la época colonial: estudios sobre producción y mano de obra*. Buenos Aires: Biblos, 1989.

Garavaglia, Juan Carlos, and Jorge D. Gelman. "Rural History of the Río de la Plata, 1600–1850," *Latin American Research Review*, 1995, 30(3):75–105.

García, Juan Agustín. *La ciudad indiana*. Buenos Aires: Eudeba, 1966.

García-Baquero González, Antonio. *Cádiz y el Atlántico (1717–1778)*. 2 vols. Seville: Escuela de Estudios Hispanoamericanos, 1976.

García Belsunce, César (ed.) *Buenos Aires. Su gente. 1800–1830.* Buenos Aires: Emecé distribuidora, 1976.

García Belsunce, César. "Diezmos y producción agrícola en Buenos Aires virreinal," *Investigaciones y Ensayos*, 1988, 38:317–355.

Gayer, Arthur D., Walt. W. Rostow, and Anna J. Schwartz. *The Growth and Fluctuation of the British Economy, 1790–1850.* 2 vols. Oxford: Clarendon Press, 1953 [Microfilm supplement deposited in the British Library].

Gazaneo, Jorge O. *Estancias.* Buenos Aires: Academia Nacional de Bellas Artes, 1969.

Gazaneo, Jorge O., and Mabel Scarone. *Tres asentamientos rurales.* Buenos Aires: Instituto de Arte Americano e Investigaciones Estéticas, 1965.

Gelman, Jorge. "¿Gauchos o campesinos?," *Anuario del IEHS*, 1987, 2:53–59.

Gelman, Jorge. "Una región y una chacra en la campaña rioplatense: las condiciones de la producción triguera a fines de la época colonial," *Desarrollo Económico*, 1989a, 28(112):577–600 [Reprinted in Fradkin (1993a), 2:7–39].

Gelman, Jorge. "New Perspectives on an Old Problem and the Same Source: The Gaucho and the Rural History of the Colonial Río de la Plata," *Hispanic American Historical Review*, 1989b, 69(4):715–731.

Gelman, Jorge. "Sobre esclavos, peones, gauchos y campesinos: el trabajo y los trabajadores en una estancia colonial rioplatense." In Garavaglia and Gelman (1989), 43–83 [cited as Gelman 1989c. This chapter is an expanded version of 1989b.]

Gelman, Jorge. "Producción campesina y estancias en el Río de la Plata colonial. La región de Colonia a fines del siglo XVIII," *Boletín del Instituto de Historia Argentina y Americana Dr. Emilio Ravignani*, 3d ser., 1992a, 6:41–65.

Gelman, Jorge. "Mundo rural y mercados: una estancia y las formas de circulación mercantil en la campaña rioplatense tardocolonial," *Revista de Indias*, 1992b, 52(195–196):477–514.

Giberti, Horacio C. E. *Historia económica de la ganadería argentina.* 2d ed. Buenos Aires: Solar-Hachette, 1970.

Gibson, Heriberto. "La evolución ganadera." In República Argentina, Censo Agropecuario Nacional. *La ganadería y la agricultura en 1908.* Buenos Aires: Oficina Meteorológica Argentina, 1909, 3:55–102.

Gillespie, Alexander. *Buenos Aires y el interior.* Transl. Carlos Aldao. Buenos Aires: La Cultura Argentina, 1921 [Reprinted in Buenos Aires: Hyspamérica, 1986].

Gómez, Pedro O., Miguel A. Peretti, José B. Pizarro, and Antonio R. Cascardo. "Delimitación y caracterización de la región." In Barsky (1991), 77–93.

González Garaño, Alejo B. (ed.) "Itinerario de Mendoza a Buenos Aires por el camino de las postas. Escrito en Mendoza en 1799," *Anuario de Historia Argentina*, 1940a, 531–542.

González Garaño, Alejo B. (ed.) "Viaje al Río de la Plata y Chile (1752–1756)," *Anuario de Historia Argentina*, 1940b, 518–530.

Gorostegui de Torres, Haydée. "Los precios del trigo en Buenos Aires durante el gobierno de Rosas," *Anuario del Instituto de Investigaciones Históricas*, 1962–1963, 6:141–161.

Graham, María. *Diario de su residencia en Chile (1822) y de su viaje al Brasil (1823).* Madrid: América, n.d.

Grau, Carlos A. *El fuerte 25 de Mayo en Cruz de Guerra.* La Plata: Archivo Histórico de la Provincia de Buenos Aires, 1949.

Grigera, Tomás. *Manual de Agricultura.* Buenos Aires: Imprenta de la Independencia, 1819.

Guilaine, Louis. *La République Argentine physique et économique.* Paris, 1889.

Guzmán, Yuyú. *Estancias de Azul.* Azul, 1976.

Guzmán, Yuyú. *El país de las estancias.* N.p., n.d. [1983?]

Guzmán, Yuyú. *Viejas estancias en el pago de la Magdalena.* Buenos Aires: Librería Sarmiento, 1985.

Haenke, Tadeo. *Viaje por el virreinato del Río de la Plata.* Buenos Aires: Emecé, 1943.

Haensch, Günther, and Gisela Haberkamp de Antón. *Dictionary of Agriculture.* 4th ed. Amsterdam: Elsevier Scientific Publishing Company, 1975.

Halperín Donghi, Tulio. "La expansión ganadera en la campaña de Buenos Aires," *Desarrollo Económico,* 1963, 3(1–2):57–110.

Halperín Donghi, Tulio. "La expansión de la frontera de Buenos Aires (1810–1852)." In Alvaro Jara, *Tierras nuevas.* México, D. F.: El Colegio de México, 1969, 77–91.

Halperín Donghi, Tulio. *Revolución y guerra.* Buenos Aires: Siglo XXI, 1972.

Halperín Donghi, Tulio. "Una estancia en la campaña de Buenos Aires, Fontezuela, 1753–1809." In Florescano (1975), 447–463 [Reprinted in Fradkin (1993a), 1:45–65].

Halperín Donghi, Tulio. *Guerra y finanzas en los orígenes del estado argentino 1791–1850.* Buenos Aires: Editorial de Belgrano, 1982.

Halperín Donghi, Tulio. "La apertura mercantil en el Río de la Plata: impacto global y desigualdades regionales, 1800–1850." In Reinhard Liehr (ed.), *América Latina en la época de Simón Bolívar.* Berlin: Colloquium Verlag, 1989, 115–138.

Hamilton, Earl J. *American Treasure and the Price Revolution in Spain, 1501–1650.* Cambridge, Mass.: Harvard University Press, 1934.

Hamilton, Earl J. *War and Prices in Spain 1651–1800.* Cambridge, Mass.: Harvard University Press, 1947.

Harley, C. Knick. "Ocean Freight Rates and Productivity, 1740–1913: The Primacy of Mechanical Invention Reaffirmed," *Journal of Economic History,* 1988, 48(4):851–875.

Hauman, Lucien. "Les phanérogames adventices de la flore argentine," *Anales del Museo Nacional de Historia Natural,* 1925, 33:319–345.

Head, Francis Bond. *Rough notes taken during some rapid journeys across the pampas and among the Andes.* London: John Murray, 1826.

Head, Francis Bond. *Las Pampas y los Andes.* Transl. Carlos A. Aldao. Buenos Aires: Hyspamérica, 1986.

Hernández, José. *Instrucción del estanciero.* Intr. Alvaro Yunque. Buenos Aires: Peña, Del Giudice Editores, 1953. [First edition: Buenos Aires: C. Casavalle, 1882.]

Hibbert, Edward. *Narrative of a Journey from Santiago de Chile to Buenos Aires in July and August, 1821.* London: John Murray, 1824.

Hinchliff, Thomas Woodbine. *Viaje al Plata en 1861.* Transl. and notes José Luis Busaniche. Intr. Rafael Alberto Arrieta. Buenos Aires: Hachette, 1955.

Holland, W. J. *To the River Plate and Back.* New York and London: G. P. Putnam's Sons, 1913.

Hudson, William Henry. *Far Away and Long Ago.* New York: E. P. Dutton, 1918. [Another edition used: London and Toronto: J. M. Dent and Sons, 1923.]

Humphreys, R. A. *British Consular Reports on the Trade and Politics of Latin America 1824–1826.* London: Royal Historical Society, 1940.

Hutchinson, Thomas J. *Buenos Ayres and Argentine Gleanings.* London: Edward Stanford, 1865.

Hutchinson, Thomas J. *The Parana; with Incidents of the Paraguayan War, and South American Recollections, from 1861 to 1868.* London: Edward Stanford, 1868.

Hutchinson, Thomas. *Buenos Aires y otras provincias argentinas.* Transl. Luis V. Varela. Prol. and notes J. Luis Trenti Rocamora. Buenos Aires: Huarpes, 1945.

Infesta de Guerci, María Elena. "Notas acerca de la instalación de estancias en Buenos Aires, 1830–1860." In *Primeras Jornadas de Historia Argentino-Americana.* Tandil: Facultad de Humanidades, UNCPBA, 1983.

Infesta, María Elena. "Aportes para el estudio del poblamiento de la frontera del Salado." In *Estudios sobre la Provincia de Buenos Aires.* La Plata: Archivo Histórico "Ricardo Levene," 1986, 61–76.

Infesta, María Elena. "Usufructo y apropiación privada de la tierra pública en Buenos Aires, 1810–1850." Ph.D. dissertation. Universidad Nacional de La Plata, 1991.

Infesta, María Elena. "La enfiteusis en Buenos Aires (1820–1850)." In Bonaudo and Pucciarelli (1993), 1:93–120.

Infesta, María Elena, and Marta E. Valencia. "Tierras, premios y donaciones. Buenos Aires: 1830–1860," *Anuario del IEHS*, 1987, 2:177–213.

Isabelle, Arsène. *Voyage a Buénos-Ayres et Porto Alegre par la Banda Oriental, les missions d'Uruguay et la province de Rio-Grande-do-Sul (de 1830 à 1834)*. Havre: J. Morlent, 1835.

Isabelle, Arsenio. *Viaje a la Argentina, Uruguay y Brasil en 1830*. Transl. Pablo Palant. Buenos Aires: Americana, 1943.

Jacobs, Alfred, and Hans Richter. *Die Grosshandelspreise in Deutschland von 1792 bis 1934*. Berlin: Hanseatische Verlagsanstalt Hamburg, 1935.

Jarvis, Lovell S. "Cattle as Capital Goods and Ranchers as Portfolio Managers: An Application to the Argentine Cattle Sector," *Journal of Political Economy*, 1974, 82(3):489–522.

Johnson, Lyman L. "The Price History of Buenos Aires during the Viceregal Period." In Johnson and Tandeter (1990), 137–171.

Johnson, Lyman L. "Perspectivas encontradas: Romano, Johnson y la historia de precios del Buenos Aires colonial," *Boletín del Instituto de Historia Argentina y Americana Dr. Emilio Ravignani*, 3d ser., 1992, 6:163–172.

Johnson, Lyman L., and Enrique Tandeter (eds.) *Essays on the Price History of Eighteenth-Century Latin America*. Albuquerque: University of New Mexico Press, 1990.

Jones, Alice Hanson. "La fortune privée en Pennsylvanie, New Jersey, Delaware, 1774," *Annales E.S.C.*, 1969, 24:235–249.

Jones, Alice Hanson. *American Colonial Wealth: Documents and Methods*. 2d ed. 3 vols. New York: Arno, 1977.

Jones, Alice Hanson. *Wealth of a Nation to Be: The American Colonies on the Eve of the Revolution*. New York: Columbia University Press, 1980.

Jones, Alice Hanson. "Estimating Wealth of the Living from a Probate Sample," *Journal of Interdisciplinary History*, 1982, 13(2):273–300.

Jurado, José M. "La estancia en Buenos Aires," *Anales de la Sociedad Rural Argentina*, 1875, 9(2)33–38; 9(3):65–68; 9(5):153–155; 9(6):185–189; and 9(7):217–221.

Jurado, José M. "Estancia 'Los Manantiales'," *ASRA*, 1879, 13(11):466–472.

Jurado, José M., Antonio J. Almeida, and Nicolás Jurado. "El Tatay," *ASRA*, 1879, 13(4):123–136.

Jurado, José M., and Anastacio Márquez. "Estancia 'El Rosario' de Las Flores," *ASRA*, 1879, 13(1):4–10.

Jurado, José M., Ricardo Newton, and Nicolás Jurado. "Estancia del Espartillar," *ASRA*, 1878, 12(10):495–500.

Kaerger, Karl. *Landwirtschaft und Kolonisation im Spanischen Amerika*. 2 vols. Leipzig: Duncker and Humblot, 1901.

Kay-Shuttleworth, Nina L. *A Life of Sir Woodbine Parish*. London: Smith, Elder and Co., 1910.

Knight, Alan. "Mexican Peonage: What was it and Why was it?," *Journal of Latin American Studies*, 1986, 18(1):41–74.

Korol, Juan Carlos, and Hilda Sabato. *Cómo fue la inmigración irlandesa en Argentina*. Buenos Aires: Plus Ultra, 1981.

L.D[illon]. *A Twelve Months' Tour in Brazil and the River Plate with Notes on Sheep Farming*. Manchester: Alexander Ireland, 1867.

Lapido, Graciela, and Beatriz Spota de Lapieza Elli (eds.) *De Rivadavia a Rosas*. Buenos Aires: Solar-Hachette, 1976.

Larrañaga, Dámaso A. *Viaje de Montevideo a Paysandú.* Prol. J. M. Olsen. Montevideo: Librosur, 1985.

Lastarria, Miguel. *Colonias Orientales del Río Paraguay o de la Plata.* Buenos Aires: Facultad de Filosofía y Letras, Universidad de Buenos Aires, 1914. (Documentos para la Historia Argentina, vol. 3.)

Latham, Wilfrid. *The States of the River Plate.* 2d ed. London: Longmans, Green, 1868.

Le Goff, Jacques. "Le temps du travail dans la 'crise' du XVIe siècle: du temps medieval au temps moderne." In *Pour un autre moyen age.* Paris: Gallimard, 1977, 66–79.

Lemée, Carlos. *El estanciero argentino.* Buenos Aires: Librería del Colegio, 1887.

Lemée, Carlos. *Curso ilustrado de agricultura. IX. Ganadería o cría de animales domésticos.* 2d ed. La Plata: Sesé y Larrañaga, 1905.

León Solís, Leonardo. "Malocas araucanas en las fronteras de Chile, Cuyo y Buenos Aires, 1700–1800," *Anuario de Estudios Americanos,* 1987, 44:281–324.

Levene, Ricardo. *Investigaciones acerca de la historia económica del virreinato del Plata.* In Ricardo Levene, *Obras completas.* Buenos Aires: Academia Nacional de la Historia, 1962, vol. 2.

Líbera Gill, Luis María. *La Magdalena. 23 de Marzo de 1852.* Buenos Aires: Palo a Pique, 1995.

Lima, Miguel A. *El estanciero práctico. Manual completo de ganadería.* Buenos Aires: El Río de la Plata, 1876.

Lima, Miguel A. *El hacendado del porvenir.* Buenos Aires: Juan H. Kidd, 1885.

Lindert, Peter H. "An Algorithm for Probate Sampling," *Journal of Interdisciplinary History,* 1981, 11(4):649–668.

Lista Alfabética de los Señores Capitalistas sujetos al ramo de Contribución Directa en esta Capital y su Campaña, con expresion de la Calle, Número de Puerta o Departamento donde habitan y la cuota que á cada individuo le ha cabido con arreglo a las manifestaciones que han hecho en el año de 1825- la que se publica de orden superior parta conocimiento de los interesados y satisfaccion del encargado. Intr. Ernesto J. Fitte. Buenos Aires: Academia Nacional de la Historia, 1970.

López Osornio, Mario A. *Viviendas de la pampa.* Buenos Aires: Atlántida, 1944.

Loubère, Leo. *The Red and the White. The History of Wine in France and Italy in the Nineteenth Century.* Albany: State University of New York Press, 1978.

Lynch, John. *Argentine Dictator: Juan Manuel de Rosas, 1829–1852.* Oxford: Clarendon Press, 1981.

MacCann, William. *Viaje a caballo por las provincias argentinas.* Transl. José Luis Busaniche and Floreal Mazía. Notes José Luis Busaniche. Append. Félix Weinberg. Buenos Aires: Solar-Hachette, 1969.

McCusker, John J. *Money and Exchange in Europe and America, 1600–1775.* Chapel Hill: University of North Carolina Press, 1978.

MacGregor, John. *Commercial statistics. A digest of the productive resources, commercial legislation, customs tariffs . . . of all nations. . . .* 5 vols. London, 1844–1850.

Mackinnon, Lauchlan Bellingham. *La escuadra anglo-francesa en el Paraná. 1846.* Transl., intr. and notes José Luis Busaniche. Buenos Aires: Hachette, 1957.

Macpheeters, D. W. "The Distinguished Peruvian Scholar Cosme Bueno, 1711–1798," *Hispanic American Historical Review,* 1955, 35(4):484–491.

MacRae, Archibald. *Report of Journeys across the Andes and Pampas of the Argentine Provinces.* Washington, D. C.: A. O. P. Nicholson, 1855.

Maciel, Carlos Néstor. *Las grandes estancias argentinas.* Buenos Aires: n.p., 1939.

Maeder, Ernesto J. A. *Evolución demográfica argentina desde 1810 a 1869.* Buenos Aires: Eudeba, 1969.

Maizels, Alfred. "Oversea Trade." In Maurice E. Kendall (ed.), *The Sources and Nature of the Statistics of the United Kingdom.* London: Royal Statistical Society, 1957, 1:17–33.

Mansfield, C. B. *Paraguay, Brazil, and the Plate. Letters written in 1852–1853.* Cambridge: Macmillan, 1856.

Mariluz Urquijo, José María. "La comunidad de montes y pastos en el derecho indiano," *Revista del Instituto de Historia del Derecho,* 1972, 23:93–121.

Marquiegui, Dedier Norberto. *Estancia y poder político en un partido de la campaña bonaerense (Luján 1756–1821).* Buenos Aires: Biblos, 1990.

Marsh, George P. *The Earth as Modified by Human Action.* New York: Scribner, Armstrong and Co., 1874.

Martin de Moussy, Jean Antoine Victor. *Description géographique et statistique de la Confédération Argentine.* 3 vols. Paris: Firmin Didot, 1860–1864.

Martínez Díaz, Nelson (ed.) *Noticias sobre el Río de la Plata: Montevideo en el siglo XVIII.* Madrid: Historia 16, 1988.

Matossian, Mary Kilbourne. *Poisons of the Past: Molds, Epidemics, and History.* New Haven: Yale University Press, 1989.

Maxwell, Daniel. *Planillas estadísticas de la exportación en los años desde 1849 á 1862.* Buenos Aires: Bernheim y Boneo, 1863.

Mayo, Carlos A. "Estancia y peonaje en la región pampeana en la segunda mitad del siglo XVIII," *Desarrollo Económico,* 1984, 23 (92):609–616.

Mayo, Carlos A. "Sobre peones, vagos y malentretenidos: el dilema de la economía rural rioplatense durante la época colonial," *Anuario del IEHS,* 1987a, 2:25–32.

Mayo, Carlos A. "¿Una campaña sin gauchos?," *Anuario del IEHS,* 1987b, 2:60–70.

Mayo, Carlos A. "Entre el trabajo y el 'ocio': vagabundos de la llanura pampeana (1750–1810)," *HISLA,* 1989, 13–14:67–76.

Mayo, Carlos A. "Landed but not Powerful: The Colonial Estancieros of Buenos Aires (1750–1810)," *Hispanic American Historical Review,* 1991a, 71(4):760–779.

Mayo, Carlos Alberto. *Los betlemitas en Buenos Aires: convento, economía y sociedad (1748–1822).* Sevilla: Diputación Provincial de Sevilla, 1991b.

Mayo, Carlos A. (ed.) *La historia agraria del interior. Haciendas jesuíticas de Córdoba y el Noroeste.* Buenos Aires: Centro Editor de América Latina, 1994.

Mayo, Carlos A. *Estancia y sociedad en la pampa, 1740–1820.* Buenos Aires: Biblos, 1995.

Mayo, Carlos A., and Angela Fernández. "El peonaje rural rioplatense en una época de transición," *Anuario de Estudios Americanos,* 1991, 46:305–319. [Reprinted in Mayo (1994), 65–78.]

Mayo, Carlos A., and Angela Fernández. "Anatomía de la estancia colonial bonaerense (1750–1810)." In Fradkin (1993a), 1:67–81 [cited as Mayo and Fernández (1993)].

Melli, Oscar Ricardo. *Historia de Carmen de Areco, 1771–1970.* La Plata: Archivo Histórico de la Provincia de Buenos Aires, 1974.

"Memorial presentado al ministro D. Diego Gardoqui por los hacendados de Buenos Aires y Montevideo en el año 1794 sobre los medios de proveer al beneficio y exportación de la carne de vaca, etc.," *Revista de Buenos Aires,* 1866, 3(37): 3–20, and 4(39):358–367.

Merchants' Magazine and Commercial Review. New York, 1839–1861.

Merediz, Rodolfo. "Comercio de frutos del país entre Buenos Aires y mercados europeos entre 1815 y 1820," *Trabajos y Comunicaciones,* 1966, 16:136–152.

Miatello, Hugo. *Industrias agrícolas y ganaderas en la República Argentina.* Buenos Aires: Taller Tipográfico de la Penitenciaría Nacional, 1901.

Miers, John. *Travels in Chile and La Plata, including accounts respecting the geography, geology, statistics, government, finances, agriculture, manners and customs, and the mining operations in Chile collected during a residence of several years in these countries.* 2 vols. London: Baldwin, Cradock and Joy, 1826.

Miers, John. *Viaje al Plata 1819–1824.* Transl., intr., and notes Cristina Correa Morales de Aparicio. Buenos Aires: Solar-Hachette, 1968.

Míguez, Eduardo José. *Las tierras de los ingleses en la Argentina (1870–1914)*. Buenos Aires: Editorial de Belgrano, 1985.

Míguez, Eduardo José. "La expansión agraria de la pampa húmeda (1850–1914). Tendencias recientes de sus análisis históricos," *Anuario del IEHS*, 1986, 1:89–119.

Millau, Francisco. *Descripción de la Provincia del Río de la Plata (1772)*. 2d ed. Intr. Richard Konetzke. Buenos Aires: Espasa Calpe, 1947.

Miller, John. *Memoirs of general {William} Miller in the Service of the Republic of Peru*. 2d ed. 2 vols. London: Longman, Rees, Orme, Brown and Green, 1829.

Mises, Ludwig von. *Human Action*. New Haven, Conn.: Yale University Press, 1963.

Mitchell, Brian R. *British Historical Statistics*. Cambridge University Press, 1988.

Mitchell, Brian R., and Phyllis Deane. *Abstract of British Historical Statistics*. Cambridge University Press, 1962.

Molinari, Diego Luis. *La Representación de los Hacendados de Mariano Moreno*. 2d ed. Buenos Aires: Facultad de Ciencias Económicas, Universidad de Buenos Aires, 1939.

Molinari, Ricardo Luis. *Biografía de la pampa*. Buenos Aires: Ediciones de Arte Gaglianone, 1987.

Moncaut, Carlos Antonio. *Estancias bonaerenses. Historia y tradición*. City Bell: El Aljibe, 1977.

Moncaut, Carlos Antonio. *Pampas y estancias. Nuevas evocaciones de la vida pastoril bonaerense*. City Bell: El Aljibe, 1978.

Montoya, Alfredo Juan. *La ganadería y la industria de salazón de carnes en el período 1810–1862*. Buenos Aires: El Coloquio, 1971.

Montoya, Alfredo Juan. *Cómo evolucionó la ganadería en la época del virreinato*. Buenos Aires: Plus Ultra, 1984.

Moreno, Carlos. *Patrimonio de la producción rural en el antiguo partido de Cañuelas*. Buenos Aires: Fundación Arquitectura y Patrimonio, 1991.

Mörner, Magnus. "The Spanish American Hacienda: A Survey of Recent Research and Debate," *Hispanic American Historical Review*, 1973, 53(2):183–216.

Morris, Isaac. "Una narración fiel de los peligros y desventuras que sobrellevó. . . ." In Vignati (1956), 17–109.

Moscatelli, Gustavo N. "Los suelos de la región pampeana." In Barsky (1991), 11–76.

Moutoukias, Zacarías. *Contrabando y control colonial en el siglo XVII*. Buenos Aires: Centro Editor de América Latina, 1988.

Moutoukias, Zacarías. "El crecimiento en una economía colonial de Antiguo Régimen: reformismo y sector externo en el Río de la Plata, 1760–1796," *Arquivos do Centro Cultural Calouste Gulbenkian*, 1995, 34:771–813.

Mulhall, M. G., and E. T. Mulhall. *Handbook of the River Plate*. 2 vols. Buenos Aires, 1869.

Mulhall, M. G., and E. T. Mulhall. *Handbook of the River Plate*. Buenos Aires, 1875.

Mulhall, M. G., and E. T. Mulhall. *Handbook of the River Plate*. Buenos Aires, 1892.

Naciones Unidas. Comisión Económica para América Latina y el Caribe. *Estudio económico de América Latina y el Caribe*. Santiago, 1988.

Napp, Richard. *The Argentine Republic*. Buenos Aires: Sociedad Anónima, 1876.

Newland, Carlos, and Daniel Waissbein. "Una nota sobre Adam Smith, Ulloa y la economía de Buenos Aires," *Revista de Historia Económica*, 1984, 2(1):161–167.

Newton, Jorge. *Cabañas argentinas*. Buenos Aires: Pardo, 1970.

Nicolau, Juan Carlos. *Industria argentina y aduana 1835–1854*. Buenos Aires: Devenir, 1975.

Nicolau, Juan Carlos. *La reforma económico-financiera en la Provincia de Buenos Aires (1821–1825). Liberalismo y economía*. Buenos Aires: Fundación del Banco de la Provincia de Buenos Aires, 1988.

North, Douglass C. "Ocean Freight Rates and Economic Development 1750–1913," *Journal of Economic History*, 1958, 18(4):537–555.

North, Douglass C. "The United States Balance of Payments 1790–1860." In National Bureau of Economic Research, *Trends in the American Economy in the Nineteenth Century*. Princeton: Princeton University Press, 1960, 573–627.

North, Douglass C. *Institutions, Institutional Change and Economic Performance*. Cambridge University Press, 1990.

North, Douglass C., and Robert Paul Thomas. *The Rise of the Western World*. Cambridge University Press, 1973.

Oddone, Jacinto. *La burguesía terrateniente argentina*. 3d ed. Buenos Aires: Ediciones Populares Argentinas, 1956.

Parish, Woodbine. *Buenos Ayres and the Provinces of the Rio de la Plata*. 2d ed. London: John Murray, 1852.

Parish, Woodbine. *Buenos Aires y las provincias del Río de la Plata*. Transl. Justo Maeso. Intr. José Luis Busaniche. Buenos Aires: Hachette, 1958.

Parodi, Lorenzo R. "Las malezas de los cultivos en el Partido de Pergamino," *Revista de la Facultad de Agronomía y Veterinaria*, 1926, 5(2):75–171.

Parodi, Lorenzo R. "Ensayo fitogeográfico sobre el Partido de Pergamino. Estudio de la pradera pampeana en el norte de la provincia de Buenos Aires," *Revista de la Facultad de Agronomía y Veterinaria*, 1930, 7(1):65–271.

Paucke, Florian. *Hacia allá y para acá*. Trans. Edmundo Wernicke. Tucumán: Universidad Nacional de Tucumán, 1942.

Peretti, Miguel A., and Pedro O. Gómez. "Evolución de la ganadería." In Barsky (1991), 261–306.

Pérez, Joaquín. *Historia de los primeros gobernadores de la provincia de Buenos Aires*. La Plata: Archivo Histórico de la Provincia de Buenos Aires, 1950.

Pery-Etchart, Bernardo. *Estado de las variaciones del cambio desde el principio de su alteración, es decir, desde el 8 de Febrero, 1826, hasta el 29 de Febrero, 1832*. Buenos Aires: Imprenta de La Gaceta Mercantil, 1832.

Poinsett, Joel Roberts. "Cartas 1810–1815." In Gallardo (1984), 147–262 [cited as Poinsett (1984a)].

Poinsett, Joel Roberts. "Diario de viaje a Rio de Janeiro, Buenos Aires y Chile 1810–1811." In Gallardo (1984), 81–146 [cited as Poinsett (1984b)].

Queiroz, Juan Pablo, and Tomás de Elía. *Argentina: las grandes estancias*. New York and Buenos Aires: Rizzoli-Brambila, 1995.

Ramón, Armando de, and Jose Manuel Larraín. *Orígenes de la vida económica chilena, 1659–1808*. Santiago de Chile: Centro de Estudios Públicos, 1982.

Randle, P. H., and Nélida Gurevitz. *Atlas de geografía histórica de la pampa anterior*. Buenos Aires: Eudeba, 1971.

Reber, Vera Blinn. "Speculation and Commerce in Buenos Aires. The Hugh Dallas House, 1816–1822," *Business History*, 1978, 20(1):19–36.

Reber, Vera Blinn. *British Mercantile Houses in Buenos Aires 1810–1880*. Cambridge, Mass.: Harvard University Press, 1979.

Recchini de Lattes, Zulma. "Población económicamente activa." In Zulma Recchini de Lattes and Alfredo E. Lattes (eds.), *La población de Argentina*. Buenos Aires: Instituto Nacional de Estadística y Censos, 1975, 149–172.

Robertson, J. P., and W. P. Robertson. *Letters on Paraguay*. 2 vols. London: John Murray, 1838.

Romano, Ruggiero. "De nuevo acerca del movimiento de precios en Buenos Aires en el siglo XVIII," *Boletín del Instituto de Historia Argentina y Americana Dr. Emilio Ravignani*, 3d ser., 1992, 6:149–162.

Rosal, Miguel Angel. "El Río de la Plata en la primera mitad del siglo XIX: las relaciones comerciales entre el interior y Buenos Aires, 1831–1835," *Boletín del Instituto de Historia Argentina y Americana Dr. Emilio Ravignani*, 3d ser., 1992, 5:49–75.

Rosas, Juan Manuel de. *Instrucciones a los mayordomos de estancias*. Buenos Aires: Americana, 1942.

Sabato, Hilda. *Capitalismo y ganadería en Buenos Aires: la fiebre del lanar, 1850–1890*. Buenos Aires: Sudamericana, 1989 [English version: *Agrarian Capitalism and the World Market. Buenos Aires in the Pastoral Age*. Albuquerque: University of New Mexico Press, 1990].

Sabato, Hilda. "Estructura productiva e ineficiencia del agro pampeano, 1850–1950: un siglo de historia en debate." In Bonaudo and Pucciarelli (1993), 3:7–49.

Sabato, Jorge F. *La clase dominante en la Argentina moderna*. Buenos Aires: CISEA-Grupo Editor Latinoamericano, 1988.

Sáenz, Miguel Antonio. *Estado que manifiesta las alteraciones en el precio del metálico en las onzas de oro y en los pesos fuertes*. Buenos Aires: Imprenta de la Independencia, 1850.

Sáenz Quesada, María. *Los estancieros*. Buenos Aires: Belgrano, 1980.

Sáenz Quesada, María, and Xavier Verstraeten. *Estancias argentinas*. Buenos Aires: Larivière, 1992.

Saguier, Eduardo R. "El mercado del cuero y su rol como fuente alternativa de empleo. El caso del trabajo a destajo en las vaquerías de la Banda Oriental durante el siglo XVIII," *Revista de Historia Económica*, 1991, 9(1):103–126.

Saguier, Eduardo R. *Mercado inmobiliario y estructura social. El Río de la Plata en el siglo XVIII*. Buenos Aires: Centro Editor de América Latina, 1993.

Salaman, Redcliffe N. *The History and Social Influence of the Potato*. Cambridge University Press, 1949.

Saldías, Adolfo. *Historia de la Confederación Argentina*. 5 vols. Buenos Aires: Cenit, 1958.

Salvatore, Ricardo D. "Autocratic State and Labor Control in the Argentine Pampas. Buenos Aires, 1829–1852," *Peasant Studies*, 1991, 18(4):251–278.

Salvatore, Ricardo D. "Reclutamiento militar, disciplinamiento y proletarización en la era de Rosas," *Boletín del Instituto de Historia Argentina y Americana Dr. Emilio Ravignani*, 3d ser., 1992, 5:25–47.

Salvatore, Ricardo D. "El mercado de trabajo en la campaña bonaerense (1820–1860). Ocho inferencias a partir de narrativas militares." In Bonaudo and Pucciarelli (1993), 1:59–92.

Salvatore, Ricardo D., and Jonathan C. Brown. "Trade and Proletarization in Late Colonial Banda Oriental: Evidence from the Estancia de las Vacas, 1791–1805," *Hispanic American Historical Review*, 1987, 67(3):431–459.

Salvatore, Ricardo D., and Jonathan C. Brown. "The Old Problem of Gauchos and Rural Society," *Hispanic American Historical Review*, 1989, 69(4):733–745.

Sarmiento, Domingo F. *Campaña en el Ejército Grande*. Prol. and notes Tulio Halperín Donghi. Mexico, D. F.: Fondo de Cultura Económica, 1958.

Sbarra, Noel H. *Historia del alambrado en la Argentina*. Buenos Aires: Eudeba, 1964.

Sbarra, Noel H. *Historia de las aguadas y el molino*. 2d ed. Buenos Aires: Eudeba, 1973.

Scardín, Fr. *La estancia argentina*. Buenos Aires: Compañía Sud-Americana de Billetes de Banco, 1908.

Scarlett, P. Campbell. *Viajes por América*. Transl. Eduardo L. Semino. Buenos Aires: Claridad, 1957.

Schmieder, Oscar. "The Pampa – A Natural or Culturally Induced Grass-land?," *University of California Publications in Geography*, 1927a, 2(8):255–271.

Schmieder, Oscar. "Alteration of the Argentine Pampa in the Colonial Period," *University of California Publications in Geography*, 1927b, 2(10):303–321.

Schmit, Roberto, and Miguel A. Rosal. "Las exportaciones del Litoral argentino al puerto de Buenos Aires entre 1783, 1850," *Revista de Historia Económica*, 1995, 13(3):581–607.
Scobie, James R. *Revolution on the Pampas*. Austin: The University of Texas Press, 1964.
Scrivener, Juan H. *Memorias del Dr. . . . Impresiones de viaje: Londres-Buenos Aires-Potosí*. Transl. and prol. Lola Tosi de Diéguez. Buenos Aires: Imprenta López, 1937.
Semanario de Agricultura, Industria y Comercio. Buenos Aires, 1802–1806.
Senillosa, Felipe. *Memoria sobre los pesos y medidas*. Buenos Aires, 1835.
Senillosa, Felipe, and Emilio Frers. *Informe sobre el engorde de ganado bovino*. Buenos Aires: La Nación, 1887.
Senillosa, Felipe, Ricardo Newton, and José M. Jurado. "Estancia San Juan," *ASRA*, 1878, 12(11):565–570.
Sepp, Antonio, S. J. *Relación de viaje a las misiones jesuíticas*. 3 vol. Ed. Werner Hoffmann. Buenos Aires: Eudeba, 1971.
Shaw, W. A. *The History of Currency*. New York: G. P. Putnam's Sons, 1896.
Slatta, Richard W. "Rural Criminality and Social Conflict in Nineteenth-Century Buenos Aires Province," *Hispanic American Historical Review*, 1980, 60(3):450–472.
Slatta, Richard W. *Gauchos and the Vanishing Frontier*. Lincoln: University of Nebraska Press, 1983.
Slicher van Bath, B. H. *The Agrarian History of Western Europe* A.D. *500–1850*. New York: St. Martin's Press, 1963.
Smith, Adam. *An Inquiry into the Nature and Causes of the Wealth of Nations*. R. H. Campbell, A. S. Skinner, and W. B. Todd (eds.) 2 vols. Indianapolis: Liberty Classics, 1984.
Smith, Daniel Scott. "Underregistration and Bias in Probate Records: An Analysis of Data from Eighteenth Century Hingham, Massachusetts," *William and Mary Quarterly*, 1975, 23:100–110.
Socolow, Susan M. *The Merchants of Buenos Aires 1778–1810*. Cambridge University Press, 1978a.
Socolow, Susan M. "La burguesía comerciante de Buenos Aires en el siglo XVIII," *Desarrollo Económico*, 1978b, 70:205–216.
Stewart, C. B. *Brazil and La Plata. The Personal Record of a Cruise*. New York: G. P. Putnam, 1856.
Stigler, George J. "The Theory of Economic Regulation," *Bell Journal of Economics and Management Science*, 1971 2(1):3–21.
Storni, Carlos Mario. "Notas acerca de la costumbre rural en el derecho agrario," *Revista de Historia del Derecho*, 1986, 14:499–526.
Temple, Edmond. *Travels in Various Parts of Peru including a Year's Residence in Potosi*. 2 vols. Philadelphia: E. L. Carey and A. Hart, 1833.
Thomas, Keith. "Work and Leisure in Pre-Industrial Society," *Past and Present*, 1964, 29:50–62.
Thomas, William L. *Man's Role in Changing the Face of the Earth*. Chicago: Chicago University Press, 1956.
Thompson, E. P. "Time, Work-Discipline and Industrial Capitalism," *Past and Present*, 1967, 38:56–97.
Tjarks, Germán O. *El Consulado de Buenos Aires y sus proyecciones en la historia del Río de la Plata*. 2 vols. Buenos Aires: Universidad de Buenos Aires, Facultad de Filosofía y Letras, 1962.
Tullock, Gordon. "The Welfare Costs of Tariffs, Monopolies and Theft," *Western Economic Journal*, 1967, 5:224–232.
Tullock, Gordon. *Rent-seeking*. Aldershot: Edward Elgar, 1993.

Ulloa, Antonio de. *Relación histórica del viage a la América meridional.* 4 vols. Madrid: Antonio Marín, 1748.

U.S. Congress. "Commerce and Navigation of the U.S." Washington, D.C., 1830–1871.

U.S. Department of Commerce. *Historical Statistics of the United States. Colonial Times to 1970.* 2 vols. Washington, D.C.: Bureau of the Census, 1975.

Universidad de Buenos Aires. Facultad de Agronomía y Veterinaria. *Las plantas forrajeras indígenas y cultivadas de la República Argentina.* Buenos Aires: Peuser, 1923.

Valencia de Placente, Marta E. "La política de tierras públicas después de Caseros, 1852–1871." Ph.D. dissertation. Universidad Nacional de La Plata, 1983.

Van der Wee, Herman, and Eddy van Cauwenberghe (eds.) *Productivity of Land and Agricultural Innovation in the Low Countries (1250–1800).* Leuven: Leuven University Press, 1978.

Van der Woude, A. D., and Anton Schuurman. *Probate Inventories. A New Source for the Historical Study of Wealth, Material Culture and Agricultural Development.* Utrecht, 1980. [Also published in *A.A.G. Bijdragen*, 1980, 23.]

Van Young, Eric. *Hacienda and Market in Eighteenth Century Mexico: The Rural Economy of the Guadalajara Region, 1675–1820.* Berkeley: University of California Press, 1981.

Van Young, Eric. "Mexican Rural History since Chevalier: The Historiography of the Colonial Hacienda," *Latin American Research Review*, 1983, 18(3):5–61.

Vicuña Mackenna, Benjamín. *La Argentina en el año 1855.* Buenos Aires: Revista Americana de Buenos Aires, 1936.

Vidal, Emeric Essex. "Ilustraciones pintorescas de Buenos Aires y Montevideo." In *Colección de viajeros y memorias geográficas.* Transl. Carlos Muzio Sáenz Peña. Intr. Emilio Ravignani. Buenos Aires: Universidad de Buenos Aires, Facultad de Filosofía y Letras, 1923, 77–243.

Vieytes, Juan Hipólito. *Antecedentes económicos de la Revolución de Mayo.* Intr. Félix Weinberg. Buenos Aires: Raigal, 1956.

Vignati, Milcíades Alejo. *Una narración fiel de los peligros y desventuras que sobrellevó Isaac Morris.* Buenos Aires: Coni, 1956.

Wedovoy, Enrique. "La estancia, ¿explotación capitalista o feudal?" *Todo es Historia*, 1994, 27(318):60–78.

Weinberg, Félix. "Estudio preliminar: Juan Hipólito Vieytes, precursor y prócer de Mayo." In Vieytes (1956), 7–133.

Wentzel, Claudia. "El comercio del litoral de los ríos con Buenos Aires: el área del Paraná 1783–1821," *Anuario del IEHS*, 1988, 3:161–210.

Whitaker, Arthur P. "Antonio de Ulloa," *Hispanic American Historical Review*, 1935, 15(2):155–194.

Whitaker, Arthur P. "Antonio de Ulloa, the *Déliverance*, and the Royal Society," *Hispanic American Historical Review*, 1966, 46(4):357–370.

Williamson, Oliver E. *Markets and Hierarchies: Analysis and Antitrust Implications.* New York: The Free Press, 1975.

Young, James A. "The Public Response to the Catastrophic Spread of Russian Thistle (1880) and Halogeton (1945)," *Agricultural History*, 1988, 62(2):122–130.

Zeballos, Estanislao S. *Descripción amena de la República Argentina. Vol. 3: A través de las cabañas.* Buenos Aires: Peuser, 1888.

Zizur, Pablo. "Diario de una expedición a Salinas emprendida por orden del marqués de Loreto, virrey de Buenos-Aires, en 1786 por. . . ." In de Angelis (1910), 5:217–242.

Zorraquín Becú, Ricardo. "El trabajo en el período hispánico," *Revista del Instituto de Historia del Derecho*, 1968, 19:107–200.

Index

353